The Very B[...]
of Creation

Scottish-International Radicalism:
A Biographical Study, 1707–1995

James D. Young

Dedicated to Lorna, Alison, David and Marta

Biographical Note

The author of eight books, including *The Rousing of the Scottish Working Class* (1979), *Making Trouble* (1987), *Socialism Since 1889: A Biographical History* (1988) and *John Maclean* (1992), James D. Young is a veteran radical and advocate of socialism from below. Before he took ill in 1990 and was forced into premature 'retirement', he was a Reader in History at the University of Stirling.

Dr. Young taught Scottish working-class history at Stirling and agitated socialism and the Scottish question for almost a quarter of a century. Although he has lectured in America, Austria, Israel and Ireland and travelled extensively, he has spent most of his life in or around the Falkirk/Grangemouth axis.

The national Chairperson of the John Maclean Society, Young is working on a new book *The World of C. L. R. James: The Unfragmented Vision*. Like the great English socialist Tom Mann, he hopes to grow more dangerous as he grows older. He believes that the Western world is now living through a period of sloth, reaction and counter-revolution; and as someone who stands in 'the tradition of Scottish flyting,' he looks forward to Scottish independence.

A special word of thanks to Alasdair Gray for illustrating the cover and writing the blurb for the back of the cover and to Harry Reid for contributing his Introduction.

Introduction

By Harry Reid, Deputy Editor, *The Herald*

James D. Young is a man apart. He has eschewed the bureaucratic time-serving which characterises so much of Scottish higher education in order to pursue his own academic quest. He is unashamedly a man of the Left, and he remains so, honestly and defiantly, at a time when so many of his erstwhile fellow leftists have shed their beliefs with pitiful if bewildering rapidity.

James Young would probably regard me as being at best a cynical hack, at worst a bourgeois conformist, and I was both flattered and surprised when he asked me to write the introduction to this, his latest book. But he knows that I respect his intellectual integrity and his zealous pursuit of the real history of his country.

Young and I first got to know each other in the very different decade of the 1970s. Since then our paths have crossed from time to time and I have always enjoyed arguing and conversing with him. I have also been able to commission some of his articles and essays for both *The Herald* and the *Scotsman* and I regard this as a privilege.

We first encountered each other because of our mutal regard for the great reforming head teacher R.F. Mackenzie. When I was covering education for the *Scotsman* in the early 1970s Mackenzie was without doubt the outstanding figure around. I am happy to record that Young's assessement of Mackenzie in this book is by far the finest I have ever read.

If Mackenzie has for me pride of place in Young's pantheon of great Scottish radicals that is probably just because I was lucky enough to know him personally. There are other familiar names here – Keir Hardie is perhaps the most famous, though as Young lucidly explains, analysis of his career has too often been perverted by the need of English (and Welsh) historians to filter their judgments through their London and Parliament-dominated world view. There is, alas, no parochialism like English left-wing parochialism (unless it is English right-wing parochialism).

Here also is Lewis Grassic Gibbon, arguably the best Scottish novelist of our century, and as Young forcibly reminds us, a writer of unremitting and extreme radicalism. But for me this book served as an introduction to other much less celebrated Scottish figures such as the poet and essayist James MacFarlan. I hope that many other readers will be as fascinated and moved as I was to read of such men, of their struggles and words and deeds.

James Young is a combative and exciting historian. Reading his work is stimulating in all sorts of ways, but it is especially salutary for three reasons. First, Young understands the importance of literature. He is constantly quoting novelists and poets. In Scotland we have a supremely fecund and controversial literary tradition, but too many of our historians ignore this most rewarding of sources. It is a truism that good writers of fiction often tell the truth about their times in a way that writers of non-fiction simply cannot, but it appears to be a truism often ignored by many Scots historians.

Secondly, Young does not underestimate the sheer forcing significance of personality. His treatment of history in this book is unashamedly personal and biographical, and all the more apposite for that. Furthermore, his biograpical approach makes his history available and readable. Young is, in the best sense, a popular historian.

And thirdly, he is unusual for a British historian in that he is quite prepared to bypass the great institutions such as Parliament and the Empire and thus ignore the 'system' that so often allows history to be written by, for and about the 'winners'. But as we read this book we learn that it is indeed more subtle than that: the race is not to the swift, and if we look at history through less orthodox perspectives, we soon see that conventional notions of 'winning' are trite and false.

I have emphasised that this book is strong meat. Young cannot abide writing that is anodyne. He himself could not write a bromide if he tried. His book will irritate many on the Left – perhaps more on the Left than on the Right. I hope that all Young's intellectual enemies bestir themselves and read it. They might be angered but they will also be enlightened.

James Young has mastered the Scottish technique of flyting. But much more than that: he has exposed much modern Scottish historiography as a genteel sham. The radicals who blaze across his pages are red-blooded and intelligent men, forceful and gutsy, working and pushing and writing for change, real change. They cannot be fitted into any neat, safe theories.

James Young writes about a country in which intellectual and political quarrels used to be bitter. We live in a more bland age, an age in which too much of political and academic life has been taken over by ambitious nonentities and politically correct cretins. Young is breathing fire back into our intellectual life. For him, the interpretation of our past is a matter of bitter partisanship. Yet he himself is not a bitter man. He has an angry pen but a generous spirit, and it is this splendid combination of anger and generosity which makes this book so valuable.

Contents

Preface

Though the Union of Parliaments of 1707 had played a major role in shaping later Scottish consciousness, the really seminal year in the history of modern Scotland was 1688 rather than 1707. Indeed, when they looked back to the past, many of the Scottish radicals depicted in *The Very Bastards of Creation*, and particularly James Thomson Callender and Alexander Robertson or 'Dundonachie', saw the year 1688 as the year of tragedy and setback for Scotland. So, although the Scottish radicalism portrayed in this book is focused on the period from the second half of the eighteenth century onwards, the radicals own reference point was 1688, not 1707. Unfortunately, the modern 'internationalist' Left as a whole remains ignorant of and often indifferent to Scottish history.

At a meeting of the John MacLean Society in Glasgow in November 1993, I was caught up in a political argument with Tommy Sheridan of Scottish Militant Labour and Paul Smith, a pro-English Marxist. Smith's Marxism consists of, in John Carstairs Matheson's immortal phrase, 'internationalism as a sort of international jingoism.' I responded to their anti-Scottish comments by blurting out that 'I am proud to belong to a Scottish radical tradition that is much older than Marxism'. Smith, who was learning some Scottish words, retorted: 'Yes! But it is a *carnaptious* tradition.' It was inevitable that some of my critics would subsequently say - in the *sleekit* tradition of the petty gossips, or 'the bodies' or Greek chorus in George Douglas Brown's anti-Kailyard novel *The House with the Green Shutters* - that I had renounced Marxism.

Though accidentally perceptive, Smith's comment forced me to recognise that Scottish radicalism has been *carnaptious* from the eighteenth century onwards. As I thought about this accusation, it occurred to me that there had been powerful cultural reasons for turning Scottish radicalism and radicals into a *carnaptious* (or quarrelsome) political force. The important thing about this encounter with Sheridan and Smith is that it gave me the energy to look at Scottish history anew in the light of the highly civilised and polite 'middle-class' culture of the Scottish Enlightenment and the 'internationalist' Left.

Despite the ruling classes' recent world-wide counter-revolution, Marxism remains undefeated. Moreover, although this book on the history of the Scots as *The Very Bastards of Creation: Scottish-International*

10

Radicalism: A Biographical History, 1688-1995 - a title inspired by the anti-Scottish English radical, John Wilkes - is pro-Scottish, anti-capitalist and committed to the aspiration of authentic socialist internationalism, it derives its inspiration from the author's own lifelong activity inside the labour movement and inside anti-Stalinist groups. Though *The Very Bastards of Creation* is coloured by Marx's conception of radicalism, it is implicitly hostile to Stalinism and all forms of authoritarian socialism from above.

Unknown to many of the authoritarians of the Left, classical Marxism was inherently libertarian and democratic. Moreover, even before Marx became an advocate of working-class men and women's struggle for democratic socialist (class) struggle from below, he was a radical. However, although he was a radical whose very earliest ideas about radicalism had lodged themselves into the core of classical Marxism, what he said was quite compatible with the cultural history of Scottish radicalism from the eighteenth century onwards. It was in an article written in 1844 that the young Marx insisted that: 'To be radical is to take the matter by the root. And as far as mankind is concerned, the root is man himself.'

In an article in *The Observer* in March 1995 titled 'Doomed by the albatross of Englishness', Melanie Philips asserted that 'the Scottish Enlightenment helped define Scotland.' But, although the Anglo-Scottish ruling class most certainly helped to define their idea of 'Scotland', the eighteenth-century Scotland of the common folk - radical artisans, farm labourers and peasants - existed in opposition to the Anglo-Scots Scottish Enlightenment. In fact, the London-inspired *British* consciousness of the Scottish Enlightenment existed in bitter and hostile opposition to the *carnaptious* radical culture and consciousness of an older Scotland of the common people. From 'the glorious [English] revolution' of 1688 onwards, there were at least two Scotlands.

When I was an eleven-and-twelve-year old school boy in a secondary school in the Scottish town of Grangemouth in 1942 and 1943, I encountered two teachers of history. One was Miss MacPhee, M.A., who tried to force me to read Walter Scott's novel *Old Mortality*, and the other was the wonderful Miss Smith, who taught her pupils that Scotland had been sold out in 1707. A much better and more democratic human being than MacPhee, Smith told generations of schoolboys that a 'parcel of rogues' had signed away Scotland's ancient nationhood as 'the whole of the Scottish population were held back by English soldiers.'

As a twelve-year-old, I did wonder about how the whole of the Scottish population managed to get to Edinburgh in 1707 when they could not afford the journey in the 1940s. Nevertheless, as I grew up and studied Scottish history, I realised that Smith's basic point was valid - the Scots had objected to losing their freedom to a superior English imperialism. Although a better story-teller than a historian, she was also a product of the Scottish radical tradition. As I grew into manhood, she gave me obscure books and encouraged my unworldly ambition to become a historian. Her influence on me was immeasurable, and I did not forget 'wee Miffy', as we called her with great affection. But she always insisted on the importance of asking awkward, difficult, critical and heretical questions.

As a result of Miss Smith's influence and my own discovery of the *Communist Manifesto* in 1948, I have spent my adult life struggling to understand from a genuinely democratic standpoint the history of the relationship between nationalism and a futuristic socialist internationalism. When I met Smith in Lumsley Street, Grangemouth, on my way home from working as a labourer in a local sawmill on a summer's evening in 1947, she advised me to get Lewis Grassic Gibbon's novel, *A Scots Quair*.

Thus 104 years after Karl Marx made his well-known remark about what it meant to be a radical, I discovered and read the *Communist Manifesto* of 1848. By 1948, when I was a seventeen-year-old railway worker, the discovery of the *Manifesto* by Marx and Engels changed my life for ever. The explosive intellectual impact on my already strong Scottish radical consciousness of the ideas of the materialist conception of history and the crucial role of the class struggle in history forced me to see the world in new and unforeseen ways. Before I reached the last page, I knew that I would never be the same again. I wish I could convey the powerful and irresistible appeal of the *Communist Manifesto* of 1848 on a young unskilled Scottish industrial worker a hundred years after its first publication in various languages. But memory has always been deceptive, and historians are aware of the pitfalls of 'inventive memory'. Even now, it is one of the books I would want to have with me if I should end up on a desert island.

Although I did not have the words - or the language - to express my reservations about *the Communist Manifesto's* dismissal of the concepts of national identity and national character, the appeal of the closing words were irresistible.

> The proletarians have nothing to lose but their chains. They have a world to win. Working men of all countries unite.

Indeed, all of my subsequent writings (including my several books on national and international working-class history) have constituted a silent, and hitherto unacknowledged, dialogue with the Marx and Engels who wrote the *Communist Manifesto*.

Before going on to discuss the nature of my reservations over the analysis of the *Communist Manifesto*, I want to stress that, in my opinion, the greatness of Marx resided in his attitude to life itself. When John Swinton (1829-1901), the Scottish-born American radical journalist, interviewed him at Ramsgate, England, in 1880, Marx revealed his closeness to the old Scottish saying 'The Truth against the World.' Towards the end of his interview, Swinton wrote:

> Over the thought of the babblement and rack of the age and the ages, over the talk of the day and the scenes of the evening, arose in my mind one question touching upon the final law of being, for which I would seek an answer from this sage. Going down to the depth of language, and rising to the height of emphasis, during an interspace of silence, I interrogated the revolutionist and philosopher in these fateful words:
> What Is?
> And it seemed as though his mind were inverted for a moment while he looked upon the roaring sea in front and the restless multitude upon the beach. 'What is it?' I had inquired, to which, in deep and solemn tone, he replied 'Struggle!'

And the constancy of struggle - or perhaps even permanent opposition - was central to Marx's conception of 'progress'.

Moreover, as a schoolboy during the Second World War - a schoolboy whose parents were involved in the struggle against fascism - the world of the Scottish Enlightenment as I encountered it through the novels of Walter Scott was alien to my own outlook. But in the air-raid shelters of Grangemouth my father argued for John Maclean and 'the Revolution', while my mother, who distrusted all elites and would-be elites, was already preparing for the punters' opposition when the Revolution came.

It was a far better education than the University education that the father of the famous socialist Victor Serge had called the 'stupid bourgeois instruction of the poor'. Meanwhile I read all the socialist classics that I could get my hands on, though I kept returning to the *Communist Manifesto*. The thing that disturbed me most was the statement that 'modern industrial labour, modern subjugation to capital, the same in England as in France, in America as in Germany, has stripped him [the worker] of every trace of national character.' It was not true in 1848, and it is sadly and tragically less true in the 1990s. In its traditional form, it is perhaps not even valid as an aspiration.

Being cursed with the possession of the ever-questioning and nagging historian's turn of mind, I have spent the past four decades almost unwittingly turning my mind back to my own early experiences in the 1930s and 1940s and the beginnings of my real education at Newbattle Abbey College, Dalkeith, and Ruskin College, Oxford in the early 1950s. At Newbattle, Edwin Muir introduced me to the history of *Another Scotland* that I had not hitherto encountered anywhere else. At Oxford, I was given a copy of the late G.D.H. Cole's and Raymond Postgate's book *The Common People* (1938). And Cole more than anyone else is responsible for sustaining the motivation to research and write *The Very Bastards of Creation*.

Although Cole began with the Scots very traumatic experience of Culloden in 1746, in searching for the origins of Scottish radicalism in our hidden cultural history I have been forced to glance back to the consequences of the Union of Scotland and England in 1707. Despite Marx's denigration of Fletcher of Saltoun, and despite my own endorsement of many of Marx's criticism of that particular Scot, I have been forced to acknowledge Fletcher as a sort of radical who challenged 'the parcel of rogues' in the Scottish nation. Opposing those who sold out Scotland's independence for 'English gold', he displayed some of the virtues of Scottish cultural radicalism. But, although I have also tried to restore Robert Ferguson (1750-1774), the Edinburgh poet, as a Scottish radical, *The Very Bastards of Creation* focuses on the hidden cultural-cum-radical history of Scotland from 1745 onwards.

During the years between 1707 and the battle of Culloden in 1746, Lowland as well as Highland Scots were estranged from the Establishment in London. The Scots silent, sullen resentment and effective disenfranchisenment from British Parliamentary politics, together with the inherited cultural traditions of a primitive egalitarianism, helped to create a mood of disaffection. This mood was, moreover, reinforced at various moments after 1707 by the arrest and transportation of Jacobites to jails in England. The mass transportation of rebellious Scots to jails in London after the Jacobites' defeat at Culloden deepened the existing mood of estrangement and disaffection.

My discovery of John Wilkes's assertion that the Scots were *The Very Bastards of Creation* - bastards who were incapable of becoming radicals because they were 'Jacobites and foreigners' - led me to see those same Jacobites as very real opponents of English imperialism. In doing so, it reinforced my decades-old belief that the very difficult history of the relationship between nationalism and socialist internationalism itself needs to be rewritten.

In his fine introduction to the *Conference Papers* given at Ruskin College, Oxford, in March 1995 on 'Scottish Dimensions', Raphael Samuel argued that: 'British history courses, even when they are called British, remain resolutely Anglocentric, in fact if not in name, and it comes as something of a shock to realise that so popular a book as Cole and Postgate *The Common People, 1746-1938*, a great primer for the labour history of yesteryear and a foundation text for the idea of "history from below" dates the starting point of modern Britain, and the opening year of their own book, from the defeat of the clans at Culloden.' Furthermore, there was no disapproval expressed over the role of 'Butcher' Cumberland's modern English imperialist army in smashing an ancient way of life.

No thoughtful Scottish radical historian could ignore the role of Culloden on later Scottish consciousness. But in an exceptionally interesting footnote to his article on *Scottish Dimensions*, Samuel said:

> It is interesting that G.D.H.Cole was [in 1938] becoming increasingly involved with rehabilitating the reputation of William Cobbett (the critical bibliography of his work, compiled by Maurice Pearl, was undertaken under Cole's aegis); [and] it is possible that for all his left-wing socialist

sympathies, he was also touched by the idea of Tory radicalism.

The argument for 'Butcher' Cumberland's progressive historical role at Culloden in 1746 was presented by Cole and Postgate with crystal clarity - Bonnie Prince Charlie had dared to march into [the new capitalist] England 'with, in the language of Marxian economics, a feudal army.'

English radicals like John Wilkes, William Cobbett, Jack Wade and Richard Carlile will be seen in a less positive light in the pages of *The Very Bastards of Creation* than G.D.H. Cole and E.P. Thompson saw them. If they denigrated and dismissed the Scots radical potential, they did not understand the continuing impact of Culloden on the consciousness of the majority of Scots. In his study of international folk literature titled *The Horn Book* (1970), George Legman wrote:

There operates also in Scotland (as elswhere), a most important sociological fact, which, though examples of it are not difficult to observe, I do not recollect having seen formulated in print. And that is the petrifying but protective influence of great military defeats. As the Scots themselves are the first to recognise, the whole cultural and political life of Scotland is still, basically, attuned to no later period than the mid- or later-nineteenth century, except in the neo-Marxist atmosphere of Glasgow and the industrial area, which has entirely jumped from the nineteenth century into the present, owing to the industrial blight.

Poets, novelists and literary folk have always had sharper insights into national 'peculiarities' than politicians. Therefore this history of *The Very Bastards of Creation* since 1688 has been cast in a biographical form with the focus on writers, poets and radical dreamers; and it has been indirectly influenced by some of Legman's insights.

However, Legman's recognition of the continuing importance of Culloden on Scottish imaginative literature and consciousness after 1746 has been hidden by the unsubstantiated assertions of the Scottish historians Christopher Harvie and Tom Nairn about the unmitigated *Black* and reactionary nature of modern Scotland. Ignoring the formidable importance of 1688 and 1745 in Scottish history, and etching out his own argument - an argument quickly endorsed by the Scottish 'Marxist', Tom Nairn - of the nature of Scotland between 1707 and the present, Harvie wrote:

For the uniqueness of Scotland lies in the power of a *civil society* divorced from political nationalism, and in an intelligentsia which, lacking a political centre, was divided between two loyalties: The Red and the Black. The Red Scots were cosmopolitan, self-avowedly enlightened and, given a chance, authoritarian, expanding into and exploiting bigger and more bountiful fields than their own country could provide. Back home lurked their Black brothers, demotic, parochial and reactionary, but keeping the ladder of social promotion open, resisting the encroachments of the English governing class.

As I have discovered and rediscovered in countless University seminars and in the workers' halls and meeting places, where I feel more at ease, Harvey's suppression and rubbishing of the actual history of radical and socialist Scotland is exceptionally difficult to challenge.

Motivated by a moral commitment to the struggle for radical and socialist goals from 1688 onwards, *The Very Bastards of Creation* seeks to offer an alternative way of seeing the cultural history of Scottish radicalism and socialism between 1688 and 1995. By reconstructing the lives and times of James Thomson Callender (1758-1803), Alexander Rodger (1784-1846), James MacFarlan (1832-1862), Alexander Robertson (1825-1893), John Murdoch (1818-1903), Keir Hardie (1856-1915), John Maclean (1879-1923, Lewis Grassic Gibbon (1901-1935), James Barke (1905-1958), A. S. Neill (1883-1973) and R. F. Mackenzie (1910-1987), an alternative and anti-authoritarian Marxist history of those and many other radicals and socialists will be seen from an *internationalist* perspective. But *this book* has been energised by my own *worries* over the history of the often hidden relationship between nationalism and socialist internationalism inside various labour movements from the 1880s onwards.

The First World War resulted in fascism and the Holocaust; and the German socialists' heroic resistance to fascism has been written out of history. Moreover, since the 1930s the world's peoples have lived through, in Joseph Buttinger's fine phrase, 'the twilight of socialism.' Millions of human beings are now confronted with the choice of 'socialism or barbarism', and the prospects for the Left ought to be very positive. In celebrating the collapse of the fundamentally anti-socialist countries in Russia and Eastern Europe in 1989, historians of the libertarian Left have a duty to challenge the simplistic hagiography of institutionalised 'history' by probing into the less heroic and less inspiring aspects of labour history. Moreover, the rediscovery of the 'nationalism' - or complex dual and triple identities - of socialists like Eleanor Marx - could help to put international socialism back on the agenda.

Before socialism was forced into the twilight in the 1930s, working people in many countries developed dual identities and individual socialists developed multi-identities. Stalinism did enormous intellectual damage to classical socialism; it almost snuffed out the assumption that the way individuals saw themselves was part of their social being. In the 1880s, according to Eduard Bernstein, Eleanor Marx took every opportunity to say with pride: 'I am a Jewess.' 'How often', he wrote, 'have I heard her shout it to the crowd, from the tribune.' She also told Max Beer that 'my happiest moments are when I am in the East End amidst Jewish work-people.'

Furthermore, when James Connolly, the Irish socialist, was speaking at a meeting of the De Leonist Socialist Labour Party in Falkirk at the beginning of this century, he responded to a hostile question from the crowd by admitting that he was a Roman Catholic. Explaining why he could not be an orthodox socialist, Bell recalled: 'How is it possible', I asked,'to reconcile the Catholicism of Rome with the materialist conception of history?' 'Well,' he replied, 'it is like this. In Ireland all the Protestants are Orangemen and howling jingoes. If the children go to Protestant schools they get taught to wave the Union Jack and worship the English king. If they go to the Catholic Church they become rebels. Which would you sooner have?'

Bell was, of course, defending what Eric J. Hobsbawm would subsequently describe as 'anti-fascist nationalism' of the Stalinist variety as 'a new kind of internationalism.'

By 1937 Leon Trotsky, who was to slightly misquote George Bernard Shaw, 'the prince of internationalists', could not avoid recognising the difficult relationship between nationalism and socialist internationalism. As he put it: 'During my youth I rather leaned towards the prognosis that the Jewish question could thus disappear, as it were, automatically. The historical development of the last quarter of a century has not confirmed this view.' Moreover, the American writer Irving Howe (1983) wrote:

Had American socialism not reached such an impasse in the post-war years, I might have continued to think of myself as a cosmopolitan activist of Jewish origin, rather than a Jewish intellectual with cosmopolitan tastes. Had not the post-war years forced upon reflective men and women some major reconsiderations, the feelings of Jewishness that were starting to reappear might have remained dormant.

But because a rotten, immoral world capitalism has shaped the era since 'the Short Twentieth Century', socialists are again confronted with the question of how to respond to nationalism.

At the heart of all my books on historical topics I have tried to grapple with the themes of nationalism and internationalism. Because Scotland has always been a sort of 'Third World country' in the midst of the fabuous wealth the Anglo-Scottish ruling class squeezed out of the British Empire, I have found it much easier to identify with Third World historians, thinkers and writers like C. L. R. James, George Padmore and Edward Said than their metropolitan counterparts. As a Scot and an oppositional socialist internationalist, I can empathise with Said's statement in his book *Culture and Imperialism* that:

> The theme I take up is the uneasy relationship between nationalism and liberation, two ideals or goals for people engaged against imperialism.

Moreover, in rejecting a simplistic nationalism (as distinct from a sympathetic socialist internationalism), I accept Said's argument that 'the "strong" or"perfect" person achieves independence and detachment by working through attachments, not by rejecting them.'

Provoked and stimulated into writing this book by Paul Smith, and inspired by Edward Said to put the history of Scottish radical culture into an internationalist context, I present *The Very Bastards of Creation* as part of one's Scot's critique of Western imperialism inside the Celtic fringe of Great Britain. In doing so, I wish to emphasise my solidarity with the Edward Said who insists that:

> No one today is purely one thing. Labels like Indian, or woman, or Muslim, or American are no

more than starting-points, which if followed into actual experience for only a moment are quickly left behind. Imperialism consolidated the mixture of cultures and identities on a global scale. But its worst and most paradoxical gift was to allow people to believe that they were only, mainly, or exclusively, white, black, or Western, or Oriental.

Far from suffering any anguish about the Scots being made up of 'the refuse of the world', I celebrate the internationalism of this racial mixture. I am proud to be one of the very bastards of creation. Futhermore, I am very conscious of the paradox of the fact that, having spent most of my life as a socialist internationalist denouncing Scots and Scotland, I have increasingly had to defend some of the Scots cultural and radical traditions against a strident ageless, sexless, nationless and immoral international capitalism and imperialism. To counter the anti-humanism of late twentieth-century capitalism, I offer my readers this small book of reflections and history of the radical culture of the Athens of the North.

The rescue and historical excavation of the Scottish radical poets, writers and agitators from 'the enormous condescension of posterity' will not be welcomed by those who are now fostering a worldwide capitalist counter-revolution. However, in new circumstances where nationalism dominates contemporary politics for ill and sometimes good and Branka Magas's book *The Destruction of Yugoslavia* documents the inhumanity of the Serb fascists, it remains essential to make distinctions among different types of nationalism. Detailing some contemporary 'socialist' attitudes to nationalism, Magas complains about 'A repugnance at nationalism that makes no distinction between mobilisation behind an expansionary chauvinist project and mobilisation in defence of national sovereignty - even national existence - under military assault.'

Towards the end of 'the terrible hell of the twentieth century', it has become increasingly difficult for socialists to discuss nationalism in a rational or dispassionate tone. It is even more difficult to get access to a media that is willing to debate the socialist alternative to the barbarism of our times. But humankind is already beginning to stir and international Labour will soon resume its pilgrimage towwards the Promised Land. The author hopes that this book will make a small contribution to the resumption of humankind's unending and undefeated struggle for the better world to come.

Since I developed heart disease and cancer in 1990, I have spent more of my leisure time with poets and literary men like Farquhar McLay, the editor of the best-selling *Workers' City*, Freddie Anderson, the Irish-Scottish poet and novelist, and John Manson, the gifted poet and translator, rather than with academic historians. Anderson and Manson have led me into the obscure byways of Scottish literary history; and they have been a constant source of encouragement and inspiration. They have also taught me the importance of moderate amounts of 'wine and bread' as a pre-condition for being on the side of the exploited and the unprivileged spirituously as well as spiritually, though Manson is sometimes a teetotaler.

Of the radicals portayed in this book, James Barke and R. F. Mackenzie were the only two that I ever met. When I was a full-time student at Newbattle Abbey College, Dalkeith, during the year 1952-53 Willa Muir would not allow either Hugh MacDiarmid or James Barke into the College. But Barke's cousin was a cook at the College; and on a dark Friday night in 1952, he was smuggled into the servants' quarter. He gave his student admirers some fine malt whisky, and he entertained as well as instructed us on Scotland's hidden cultural history.

I also met and became a close friend of R. F. Mackenzie. In 1968 I taught history and English at Braehead Junior Secondary School for a couple of months, while he struggled to survive as the Headmaster against an increasingly hostile Labour Establishment. Open-minded, compassionate and radical, he came to lecture on the awful history of Scottish education to my History students at the University of Stirling in the 1970s and early 1980s. He was a democrat of democrats; and, in using some of his private letters to me with the permission of his wife Diana, in the chapter on A. S. Neill and R. F. Mackenzie, I hope to convey something of the man's rich humanity and simplicity.

In Glasgow Donald Anderson, a fine teacher and historian, has given me rare books and pamphlets on obscure aspects of Scottish history. Encouraging me to be proud of my Celtic origins, he has taken over the role of Hugh MacDiarmid as the guardian of the Scottish national question from the standpoint of socialist internationalism.

Moreover, Sir Ken Alexander encouraged me to complete this book, and he very generously acted as a referee when I applied to the Scottish Arts Council for a research grant. And in London the young historian Jim Clayson has worked on my behalf to search out rare pamplets on eighteenth-century British radicalism. Moreover, the incomparable Peter Fryer has spent many hours in the British Library digging out references that I would not have otherwise been able to obtain without more trips to London. Peter also read the chapters of *The Very Bastards of Creation* and advised me about pruning them of irrelevancies and clumsy phrases. I am proud to have him as a friend. I also owe particular debts of encouragement to Gerry Cairns, Tommy Kayes of Clydeside Press, Dr. Raymond Challinor, Rita Boyd, Anne and Jim Boyd-Thomas, Lorn Macintyre, Ben and Cathie McGinn, Roseanna McKenna, Heather Valencia, Stan Bell, the fine Scottish socialist protester and Christian, Dr. Bob Purdie, John Cooper, John Cooper, Junior, Robert Lynn, Phil McPhee, Hamish Henderson, Brian Quail of Scottish CND, Dr. Arnold and Mary Kloper, Heather Valencia, John Manson, Andre Molyneux, Willie Maley, Bobby Lynn, Paul Buhle, Kent Worcester, Franklin and Penny Rosemont, Ray Burnett, Donal Mooney, editor of the *Irish Post* and Harry Reid, deputy editor of *The Herald*. And a special word of thanks to Alasdair Gray, author of *Lanark* and other fine novels for illustrating the covers of *The Very Bastards of Creation*, and to Harry Reid for contributing his Foreword.

I have been helped by Kent Worcester, Edna Coleman, Richard Greeman, Paul Buhle, Penny and Franklin Rosemont, Phyllis and Julius Jacobson, Martin Glaberman, Jim Murray of the C. L. R. James Institute, New York, and many other American radicals. And at home I have been encouraged by my wife *Lorna*, my daughter *Alison* and my son *David* and his American wife *Marta* Stitenberger-Young. Finally, no man - or woman - is an island and collective mutal aid remains a precondition for civilised life; and it is with pleasure that I acknowledge research grants from the Scottish Arts Council, the Carnegie Trust for the Universities of Scotland and the Barry Amiel and Norman Melburn Trust.

Polmont, Falkirk, Stirlingshire.
August, 1996.

Chapter One

Scottish Nationalism and Plebeian Radicalism 1707-1832

It is easy to make enemies; the difficult thing is to keep them.

William Dean Howells

The Union of 1707, the Jacobites and Scottish Radicals

Scotland lost her independence in 1707. This was the single most important factor in shaping Scottish radicalism. Scotland became, in the fine phrases of the Scottish novelist John Galt, 'a wrong-resenting country' and the Scots a 'history-conscious' people.

The nominal retention of the 'independence' of the Church did not survive for very long; and the 'independence' of the legal system was a farce. At the same time the Scottish universities increasingly became institutions through which systematic attempts were made to get rid of Gaelic and Lallans by imposing the English language. A development initially fostered from within Scotland itself, it had been encouraged by the English ruling class in the wake of the Union of 1707. And, despite the very complicated role of the Scottish Enlightenment intelligentsia in fostering a British consciousness throughout the Athens of the North, the English ruling class repeatedly displayed their colonial attitudes towards the Americans and the Scots.

Jacobitism and Scottish radicalism developed a symbiotic relationship. In 1708 the Jacobite troubles of that year led to the suspension of the Habeas Corpus Act; Fletcher of Saltoun and Lord Belhaven were arrested, taken off and imprisoned in England.[1] As a result of the Jacobite rebellions of 1715 and 1745, the traitorous Jacobites in Scotland were taken to England for trial and execution.[2]

The colonial dimension was real and tangible. In 1711 an English politician by the name of Harley expressed the colonial mentality of the ruling class by asking his fellow members of Parliament: 'Have we not bought the Scots, and may we not claim the right to tax them? [3] For what end, pray, did we give the Equivalent?' Furthermore, the English historian Thomas B. Macaulay wrote:

> The British Legislature violated the Articles of Union, and made a change in the Constitution of the Church of Scotland. Year after year the General Assembly protested against the violation, but in vain; and from the Act of 1712 undoubtedly flowed every Secession and Schism in the Church of Scotland.[4]

Moreover, in circumstances where the Scots were effectively disenfranchised from the decision-making process at Westminster, Morrison Davidson's observation in *Leaves from The Book of Scots* (1914) was salient: 'Until the Reform Bill of 1832, to talk of Franchise Extension in Scotland was a criminal offence of the deepest dye, as many a worthy Scot found to his undoing'.[5]

A Very Scottish Radicalism and English Chauvinism

Unlike the eighteenth-century English radicals, the Scots did not feel anything like the same reverence, respect or awe for the institutions inside the Palace of Westminster or 'the principles of the glorious English revolution' of 1688. (It was significant that R. B. Cunninghame Graham, the Scottish socialist, was the first member of Parliament to be expelled from the House of Commons for using the un-Parliamentary swear word 'damn').[6] There were many specific reasons for this lack of reverence, and some of them were rooted in Scottish history before the Union of Parliaments of 1707. In his authoritative book *English Constitutional History*, the British historian S. B. Chrimes identified the basic political differences between England and Scotland in the sixteenth and seventeenth centuries when he said: 'In Scotland the monarchy had always been decidely weaker than it had been in England; armed resistance to the Crown had been commoner than in England.'[7]

But, although these particular political and cultural sediments of the past helped to fashion Scottish resentments and grievances after 1707, new anti-Scottish forces continued to develop throughout the remainder of the eighteenth century. In his excellent essay on 'A Very

English Socialism', Royden Harrison argued that 'English working-class consciousness was shaped to an unusual degree not just by experience at the point of production, but by the experience of Parliament and the prolonged struggle for Parliamentary reform'.[8] What he did not understand was the very different development of Scottish radicalism - and socialism - from the 1790s.

Moreover, in the twentieth century the British Left have been unusually hostile to the exposition of the view that Scottish radical history was simply different. When popular Scottish radicalism 'exploded' in the 1790s, the well-established English tradition of anti-Scottishness inhibited the development of 'British' radicalism. In his book *Radical Pioneers of the Eighteenth Century* (1886) the Irish historian J. Bowles Daly said: 'The Scotch were considered foreigners and Jacobites, entirely wanting in sympathy with the principles of the Revolution.'[9] The Scots were therefore irrelevant to the English radical project. Although they did not mention it, the Scottish Enlightenment intellectuals' enthusiasm for 'the principles' of 1688 was not shared by many of the 'lower orders'.

Obscured and hidden by the dominant Unionist historiography of the Right and the Left, the Scots were effectively disenfranchised from the Palace of Westminster until well after 1832. However, it was left to the now neglected nineteenth-century Irish historian W. E. H. Lecky to identify the Scots' colonial relationship to 'Great Britain'. As he put it:

> The character of the Scotch members was lowered by the fact that for many years after the Union they alone received regular wages for their attendance in Parliament, their greater poverty exposed them specially to temptation, and one of the worst effects of the Union on *imperial politics* was the great accession it gave, in both Houses, to the corrupt influence of the Crown. It was, indeed, the custom in England to regard the Scotch as the most slavish and venal of politicians, and the reproach was not wiped away till the Reform Bill of 1832 created a real representation. [10]

In contrast to the English experience, eighteenth-century Scottish 'working-class' or plebeian consciousness was largely shaped at the point of production and in the clubs and debating societies. The English and the Scots - or vice versa - did not like each other. As Lecky put it: 'In spite of their admirable education, in spite of their Protestantism, in spite of their growing industry, the aspect of the Scotch population in the latter years of the eighteenth century was still extremely repulsive to an English eye.'[11]

In *The Making of the English Working Class*, E. P. Thompson asserted that English and Scottish 'trade unions were impermanent and immature' until the 1820s.[12] But he, too, ignored the strong evidence of the English radicals' contempt for the Scots. This antagonism was reciprocated; but there was an important difference - the English ruling class had the political power to subdue its neighbour in the North. Moreover, when a new and more 'democratic' plebeian radicalism began to emerge in England from the 1760s onwards, it was deeply antagonistic towards the Scots.

Identifying John Wilkes as a representative figure of 'the forces making for political reform', E. P. Thompson was silent about Wilkes's role in inhibiting a real British radicalism. For, although 'That Devil Wilkes' became and remained one of the 'heroes' of the English Left, he was an out-and-out chauvinist.[13] An advocate of Parliamentary reform and in 1774 a supporter of the Americans' claim to independence, he nevertheless sought to stir up violent passions against the Scots.

At various times a friend of David Hume, James Boswell and Dr. Samuel Johnson, Wilkes was an English chauvinst who hated Scotland and the Scots. On good terms with Scots who personified the Enlightenment, he had been delighted in 1754 when Hume told him in a private letter that: 'Notwithstanding all the Pains, which I have taken in the Study of the English language, I am still jealous of my Pen. As to my tongue, you have seen that I regard it as totally desperate and Irreclaimable'.[14]

Perhaps Wilkes' anti-Scottish prejudices were not helped by the cultural obsequiousness he encountered in Scots like Hume and Boswell.

From 1763 when he first published *The North Briton*, Wilkes perfected what can be best described as racist stereotypes. As J. Bowles Daly explained:

> Wilkes used the plainest words to disclose the most discreditable deeds, and was most vehement in his abuse of Scotland. Playing on the popular

jealousy of foreigners and Scotsmen, he said, "that the River Tweed was the line of demarcation between all that was noble and all that was was base - south of the river was all honour, virtue, and patriotism - north of it was nothing but lying, malice, meanness and slavery. Scotland is a treeless, flowerless land, formed out of the refuse of the universe, and inhabited by the very bastards of creation". [15]

In the January 1763 issue of *The North Briton*, Wilkes published 'The Prophecy of Famine: A Scots Pastoral' by the English poet Charles Churchill. In another issue he published Churchill's epigram:

No flower embalms the air but one white rose
    which
on the tenth of June by instinct blows.[16]

To decode Churchill's anti-Scottish epigram: the white rose was the Stuart flower; the 10 of June was the Pretender's birthday; and it was a stock English joke that the climate of Scotland was so harsh that flowers would hardly ever grow there. Moreover, considering that Wilkes's friends like Hume were anti-Jacobites belonging to the 'higher ranks', it was obvious that he was an opportunist politician of the Left.

"That Devil Wilkes", English Chauvinism, and the Scottish Response

The English were, as my old friend Ralphael Samuel always reminds us, a very special people - free-born with a superior language and more personal and general liberty than people in any other countries.[17] But, although they were reluctant to extend that liberty to the Scots, the Irish, the Americans or other 'inferior' peoples within the Empire, 'That Devil Wilkes' has always been regarded as the major, if transitional, pioneer of 'British' radicalism. As Gwyn Williams explained:

But Englishmen often had a more specific 'warrant'; they were freeborn Englishmen whose right of resistance had been confirmed in 1688. Before the city of London acquired a radical temper and before the John Wilkes imbrogilo, most city riots were obscurely 'traditionalist'; a defence of 'natural' order against the Constitution's myriad enemies (hence possibly the 'No Popery!' of Birmingham in 1791).[18]

But that was the rub - the overwhelmingly majority of Scots were regarded in England as the potentially militant enemies of the Constitution of 1688.

Ignored by the historians of British, English or Scottish radicalism, the most important 'radical' incident of the eightenth century was what happened in 1768. In his excellent old-fashioned book *The Reign of George III, 1760-1815* J. Steven Watson wrote:

> Once Wilkes was in prison his power to arouse excitement as a martyr was much increased. His partisans excited all the anti-minsterial passion of the time. On 10th May 1768 troops round the prison in St. George's Fields were involved in a skirmish with crowds who had come to draw Wilkes in triumph from his cell to Parliament. In this a spectator, a Mr. William Allen, was killed. It was unfortunate that the troops were the Scots Guards - countrymen of Bute... He [Wilkes] proceeded to publish letters on the riots, accusing the Ministry of using Scottish butchers to intimidate free Englishmen. [19]

An indication of the English ruling class's awareness of their colonial relationship with the Scots, the employment of Scottish troops was, though indeed unfortunate, not at all accidental.

The English chauvinism unleashed by this incident was to feed and sustain the half-hidden, inarticulate, sullen and embarassed nationalism of most Scots for a long time afterwards. The English racism encouraged by Wilkes provoked an extraordinary reaction from David Hume and James Boswell. While the better-known *British* Hume of the Scottish Enlightenment, whose generally pro-British outlook was unusually consistent, expressed his almost unbelievable Scottish nationalist sentiments on at least one rare occasion in a very private letter to his Scottish publisher A. Millar. Modern nationalist historians have therefore portrayed Hume as anti-English. On one exceptional occasion, Hume said:

> The rage and prejudice of parties frighten me, above all the rage against the Scots, which is so dishonourable, and indeed, so infamous to the English nation. We hear that it increases every day, without the least appearance of provocation on our part. It has frequently made me resolve never in my life to set foot on English ground. Nothing but a rebellion will open the eyes of that deluded [English] people; though were they alone concerned, I think it is of no matter what becomes of them... Oh!, how I long to see America and the East Indies revolt, totally and finally - the revenue reduced to half - public credit discredited by bankruptcy - the third of London in ruins.[20]

Unfortunately, although Scottish nationalist historiographers, whether ancient or modern, quoted what Hume and Boswell said about the anti-Scottish sentiments expressed by the English in 1762 and in 1768, they did not mention Wilkes or even try to put those incidents into context. In his book *Leaves from The Book of Scots*, the Scottish nationalist Davidson misrepresented Hume by saying that he 'shared to the full the bitter antipathies of his Scottish countrymen'.[21] However, Hume's transitory statement of 1768 was an aberration; and if his nationalism had been so consistent as Davidson said, the whole history of Scottish nationalism and radicalism would have been very different.

Davidson was an industrious and talented partisan, not a trained historian. Instead of making the most of the extreme anti-Scottishness of Wilkes and the reaction it provoked in Boswell's head, nationalist historians have mentioned neither the consistent English chauvinism of Wilkes nor the equally transitory Scottish nationalism of Boswell.

In his conversations with both Wilkes and Dr. Johnson in 1773, the latter told Boswell:

> The Irish mix better with the English than the Scotch do; their language is nearer to English; as proof of which they succeed very well as players, which Scotsmen do not. Then, Sir, they have not

that extreme nationality which we find in the Scotch. I will do you, Boswell, the justice to say, that you are the most *unscottified* of your countrymen. You are almost the only instance of a Scotsman that I have known, who did not at every other sentence bring in some other Scotsman.[22]

But an even more relevant conversation between Wilkes, Johnson and Boswell took place in London in the fateful year of 1776. Despite Wilkes's earlier description of the Scots as 'the bastards of creation', Boswell recalled that:

Upon this [anti-Scottishness] Johnson and Mr. Wilkes could perfectly assimilate; here was a bond of union between them, and I was conscious that both of them were fully satisfied of the strange narrow ignorance of those who imagine that Scotland is a land of famine. But they amused themselves with persevering in the old jokes.[23]

A defender of the Union of 1707 and Britishness, Boswell was a most unlikely Scottish nationalist.

But in the privacy of *Boswell's London Journal*, he (Johnson's later biographer) had, in 1762, reacted to the 'chauvinism of the English by objecting to the behaviour of a Covent Garden audience who greeted the presence of some Highland officers with the cry of "No Scots. Out with them!"' Then he wrote:

My heart warmed to my countrymen, my Scottish blood boiled with indignation. I jumped on the benches, roared out,'Damn you, you rascals!', hissed and was in great rage... I hated the English; I wished from my soul that the Union was broke and that we might give them another battle of Bannockburn.[24]

Ignoring the fact that Boswell did not protest in newspapers or magazines, the professional (Scottish nationalist) historian Harry Hanham from New Zealand misread this comment in *Boswell's London*

Journal when he wrote: 'The significant thing about this sensitivity to suppposed insults to Scotland was that it was marked among those who championed the Union of 1707 as among those who regretted it.'[25] But if Boswell and Hume had not been so inhibited by their already national cultural schizophrenia and had written - or spoken - against the English chauvinist dimension that was crystal-clear in 1762 and 1768, the whole history of Scottish nationalism and radicalism would have developed very differently.

The 'Bastards of Creation' Develop an Embryonic Nationalism-cum-Radicalism

In the 1750s and 1760s Scottish writers failed to answer the English critics of Scotland and the Scots; but in the next two decades at least two broke through the barrier of silence. One was the Edinburgh poet Robert Ferguson (1750-74) and the other was James Thomson Callender (1758-1803). They both consistently, if briefly, defended Scotland's independent identity and culture; and, when Ferguson wrote his thirty-odd poems in Scots between 1772 and 1773, he was lucky to have access to the short-lived Walter Ruddiman's *The Weekly Magazine or Edinburgh Amusement*.

In the concrete circumstances of the life and times of Scotland in the eighteenth century, Scottish nationalism and radicalism had to be both *sleekit* and *carnaptious*. Before the 1790s, only a poet like Robert Ferguson could express his nationalism under his own name. And that was precisely because he was a poet rather than a political pamphleteer. In sharp contrast to the private, probably isolated, anguished and *sleekit* pro-Scottish reaction of Boswell and Hume to the 'Wilkes and Liberty' agitation in 1762 and 1768, most Scots did not have much access to the public prints. Moreover, in conditions where Scotland was deeply and bitterly divided between the exponents and opponents of Unionism, most Scots (with the exception of the small Unversity intelligentsia) used pseudonyms to protect their identities against an exceptionally intolerant and repressive British-Scottish society in which censorship and a vicious legal system discouraged radicalism.[26]

In 1773 Ferguson published his pro-nationalist poem 'The Ghaists' in Ruddiman's *The Weekly Magazine*. Anticipating the obliteration of Scottish nationality under English domination, Ferguson wrote:

Black be the day that e're to
England's ground
Scotland was eikit by the Union's
bond.

In the same poem, he continued thus:

Ah, CALEDON! the land I yence held dear
Sair mane mak I for thy destruction be

while he *thrawnly* or stubbornly, if pessimistically, decided to 'gang his ain gate'

Till Scotland out of reach of England's power

However, he was not just expressing his Scottish nationalism; he was a radical who also identified with the struggles of the poor plebeians:

Yoke hard the poor, and lat the rich chiels be
Pampere'd at ease by ither's industry...[27]

If Hume and Boswell personified the cultural schizophrenia of some of the Scots of the 'higher ranks', the Ferguson who died at a young age was simultaneously radical and nationalist. By the second half of the eighteenth century, poets were regarded as weird, anyway, and so Ferguson had fewer difficulties in publishing under his own name. In his epistle 'To the Principal and Professors of the University of St. Andrews, on their superb treat to Dr. Samuel Johnson,' he expresed his resentment of all the fuss being made of 'Sam the lying loon who had made the anti-Scottish joke about oats in his *Dictionary.*' [28]

In his fascinating and neglected essay on 'Ferguson and Ruddiman's Magazine', John W. Oliver said:

But the most interesting aspect of those Scottish-English discussions in Ruddiman's is on the cultural side. Is Scotland to retain an independent culture of her own, or is she to be merged in the larger entity of "Britain"? Is she, in the meantime, keeping up her reputation as a centre of learning and literature. What is to be the language in which Scottish people write and speak?[29]

Directing attention to the large number of contributors to the *Weekly Magazine* who used pseudonyms, he pointed out that:

> 'Hermes' (how fond those eighteenth century Scots were of classical pseudonyms) complains bitterly of the 'sarcasms thrown out against the **Scots Sawnies** and **Irish Paddies** on account of their language,' and denounces the impoliteness of people who laugh 'at those of another country, because they cannot pronounce the English language in the same way as the inhabitants of London.'[30]

Besides, the anti-Scottish sentiments expressed by Wilkes were still rankling among many Scots and some of them used the *Weekly Magzine* to attribute Scottish economic problems to the unfairness of the Union. In making the point that Ferguson's distrust of alien cultural influences was evidence of a national culture on the defensive, Sydney Goodsir Smith (1952) argued that this defensiveness grew into 'the crippling inferiority complex that has provincialised Scottish life and thought since the Union.'[31] (If so, how did that square with the internationalism and formidable contribution to thought of the Scottish Enlightenment intelligentsia? Addressing this hitherto unasked question later on in this chapter will emphasise the inseparability of nationality, culture and politics.)

It was not, however, the defensiveness of the uncomplicated and radical Scottish nationalism of men like Ruddiman, Ferguson and Callender that provincialised Scotland; it was rather the absence of institutions and agencies independent of 'the principles' of the glorious English revolution of 1688 - universities and publishing houses through which dissident Scots opposed to the Anglo-Scottish identification with 1688 could teach, publish and express themselves without the constant threat of victimisation. Although he did not make anything of it, one of the most interesting features of Oliver's essay was his astute observation that both sides in the often bitter disputes about the consequences of the Union in the early 1770s felt obliged to conceal their identities.

Certainly Lecky was not unaware of Scottish nationalism and radicalism in the 1770s and 1780s culminating in considerable support for the American rebels. Suggesting the existence of links between Scotland's submerged identity and the American War of Independence, he said that such factors 'at the outbreak of the American war may, I think, be inferred from the very significant fact that the Government were unable to obtain addresses in their favour [before 1782] from either Edinburgh or Glasgow', he was providing important insights.[32] Some plebeian Scottish radicals also 'agitated the question' (a favourite phrase) of 'the equalisation of property'.

While there was some truth in T. C. Smout's claim that the 'State' in Scotland 'expected and exacted greater obedience' than in England, his claim that the Scots were 'tame', 'docile' and 'uninflammable' was not supported by the historical experience. Ignoring the history of radical Scotland, he did not even cite the evidence of the Anglo-Scottish ruling class's very repressive authoritarianism in relation to radicals like James Granger.[33]

In 1773 'a great number of sailors defiantly assembled at Greenock and Port Glasgow in a riotous and disorderly manner, preemptorily insisted for an increase of their wages'; and soldiers of the 15th regiment (afterwards The East Yorleshire Regiment or Duke of York's own), who had been called in to 'assist the civil power in putting a stop to such illegal proceedings, were immediately surroundered by a vast number of sailors and most incessantly pelted with stones, bricks, etc'. The sailors were armed; and it took a few days and 'two troops' of extra dragoons to quell 'the uprising'.[34] Furthermore, an 'illegal combination' of weavers in Paisley led the authorities to send three men to prison for one month and four others for four days.[35] At much the same time 'an uprising' of journey weavers in Glasgow had been inspired by American Republicanism, though the Lord-Justice Clerk Thomas Millar did not make his hostile feelings about Republicans in the Colonies public knowledge.

In 1778 and 1779 there were several army mutinies in Scotland In September 1778, there was a mutiny in the Earl of Seaforth's Highland regiment, and in Edinburgh, where three army mutinies occurred, the mutineers were supported by the 'lower orders'.[36] This particular seditious outburst was soon followed by a mutiny of about fifty soldiers in the 42nd and 71st regiments at Leith in April 1779 and in October 1779 by five companies of the West Fencible regiment quartered at Edinburgh Castle.[37] But, although the Scottish press said very little about these mutinies, General J. Adolphus Oughton wrote a confidential letter to Weymouth at the Palace in Westminster:

> I should think it highly advisable to withdraw all the Fencible regiments from *this country*, replacing them with an equal number of English; as I discover too many seeds of discontent, especially among the lower people. Great numbers of dissidenting Ministers, and several of the Established clergy are avowedly Republicans and Americans.[38]

In the very same letter, he suggested that 'the proscriptions' against the Highland Chiefs ought to be abolished and clanship encouraged to stop the drift of people to the 'American colonies'.[39] Historians also ignored the evidence in the *Old Statistical Account* that many Highlanders defied the Anglo-Scottish authorities after 1745 by wearing 'the Highland dress, the bonnet, the philabeg and the tartan hose'.[40] The use of English troops was surely an indication of a colonial dimension.

Moreover, during the bitter strikes of the weavers in Glasgow in 1787, when hundreds of weavers cut the looms of the masters, the troops who were called in shot and killed five weavers. Acting on behalf of their masters in Westminster, the repressive authoritarianism of the members of the Scottish Judiciary was seen when James Granger, one of the leading figures in the agitation, received a sentence to be whipped through the streets of Edinburgh 'to correct those feelings by way of example for the benefit of society'. He was also 'banished from Scotland' for several years.[41]

When he published his anonymous pamphlets the *Deformities of Dr. Samuel Johnson* (1782) and *A Critical Review of the Works of Samuel Johnson* (1783), Callender aimed his arguments at an almost 'underground' nationalist and radical readership.[42] In August 1782 the editor of the pretigious English *Critical Review* speculated about the identity of the anonymous author of the anonymous *Deformities*. With great concern about what had sparked off the deepest [Scottish nationalist] resentment of an obscure writer, he was most upset.[43] The following month the *Gentleman's Magazine* argued that the *Deformities* was a revenge pamphlet inspired by 'an anti-Ossian publication by William ["Nadir"] Shaw in the *Deformities*, who denied the existence of Gaelic poetry'. (Incidentally, Callender's authorship of those nationalist and radical pamphlets was not established until 1940).[44]

Certainly the Revolution in America unleashed pent-up Scottish resentments against the Union of 1707 and the role of English writers like Johnson in ridiculing the Scots. The existence of a formidable undergound literature of folk songs, ballads and broadsheets testified to the extent of a strong anti-imperialist and Scottish nationalist radicalism. At its best, it found expression in the song that 'It was in you that it all began'.[45]

The Platform, A Very Scottish Republican Radicalism, and Glencoe

Unfortunately, some English historians have always played a negative role in our affairs by concealing the very real existence of Scottish radicalism before the French revolution. Arguing in *The Platform: Its Rise and Progress* that the agitation for Parliamentary reform began in England in the 1760s under the leadership of Wilkes, Henry Jephson emphasised the point that 'the Platform' - narrowly defined as 'every political speech at a public meeting excluding those from the pulpit and those in the Courts of Justice' - was called 'into requisition' in Scotland for the first time in 1792 when the Friends of the People met in Edinburgh.[46] This ignored the fact that the Church of Scotland was always more political and much more radical than the Church of England.[47]

As the Anglo-Scottish ruling class understood only too well, radicalism in Scotland existed outside of a Parliamentary framework that was less easy-to-control. Irish and American historians have always grasped this much better than most English historians, whether ancient or modern, though the English Marxist historian A. L. Morton said that: 'In Scotland, whose people were on the whole more educated and who had national grievances of their own, the movement grew more rapidly than in England'.[48]

However, it took the American historian Robert Palmer to portray the complexity of Scottish radicalism. As he put it:

> In Scotland the disaffection was more broadly based... A lingering feeling against England, a sense of exclusion from public life (there were only about 1,300 actual freehold voters in a population

36

of a million), a Presbyterian habit of participation in popular affairs, the repeated splits and disputes among the Presbyterians since the Union, the connection between Church and State, the existence of extreme poverty along with a widespread literacy, the sermons of the itinerant and unauthorised preachers, who were frowned upon by the Presbyterians, and much inclined to anti-aristocratic outbursts, combined to spread discontent, especially as the American and French revolutions, over the period of a generation, began to arouse a new political consciousness. [49]

But the cultural and political traditions of 'A Very English [Radicalism] and Socialism' -traditions steeped in and permeated through and through with Parliamentary politics -have obscured the distinctive features of a Scottish radicalism existing independently of the ambience of Westminster. Instead of the English focus on Parliamentary politics, Scottish cultural alienation and class consciousness were the mainsprings of the dynamic of discontent and disaffection.

It was an interesting fact, too, that the official account of the history of Parliamentary debates and business was published under the title of the Parliamentary *History of England*. But the appendix to *the Second Report from the Committee of Secrecy in 1794-75* was extraordinarily revealing about the extent to which the Scottish radicals challenged the Anglo-Scottish ruling class's interpretation of British history. At a time when there had been even more mutinies in Scottish regiments, particularly in Edinburgh, anonymous printed papers circulating among the soldiers before one of these mutinies refuted what the dominant Scottish Englightenment intelligentsia were saying in their countless volumes on the history of England/Britain.

In 1692 King William III had authorised Campbell of Glenlyon to take action against the MacDonalds because they had been 'too late in swearing an oath of allegiance to William of Orange' and 'the principles' of the glorious English revolution of 1688. [50] Moreover, in the fascinating book on *The Disaster at Darien*, Francis Russell Hart depicted the role of King William III in 1699 in shaping the failure of the Scots' colonial adventure. As he put it: 'The King, however, although keenly desirous to soothe his Scottish subjects, and with his plans of a Union in mind, considered it necessary to express through his Commissioner, the Duke of Queensbury, his regret that for invincible reasons he was unable to assert the company's right to settle in Darien.' [51] By the 1790s, it was the Glencoe incident that was rankling in the heads of radical Scots.

Challenging the dominant interpretation of what had happened at Glencoe, the Edinburgh radicals' anonymous paper told the Highland soldiers:

> The great mass of the people, from amongst whom you enlisted, have been represented as your enemies; believe not the assertion; they have been taught to consider you as foes. Their cause and ours is the same... They [the people] are poor, but they have honest hearts: hearts which sympathise in your cause; they look for the same friendship in you. They rejoice to hear, that you are daily becoming more convinced of the great truth, that the law ought to be the same to the Highlander and the Lowlander, to the rich and the poor... This truth has been carefully concealed from you, but it is no less certain. The will of your Laird cannot without your consent, separate you from your family and friends, although many of you have experience and exertion of such a power, however, unjust, and however contrary to law... This truth has been carefully concealed from you, but it is no less... The cruel massacre of Glencoe *cannot yet be forgotten;* are there not among you, whose forefathers perished there? Their hearts throbbing with kindness and hospitality were pierced with the daggers of their treacherous friends... How will they [your families in the Highlands] look around in vain for your protecting care, when perhaps you are fighting at a distance in a foreign land? Stay, stay on, [in Scotland] and defend your families and your friends! For that purpose alone you were enlisted. There are ready to come forward for you in the vindication of your rights. Thousands join in the same sentiments with you, and ardently wish for your continuance amongst them. The circumstances which might require you to quit your

country have not yet taken place. No invasion has yet happened. You cannot be compelled to go - Leave not your country - Assert your independence - Your countrymen look up to you as their protectors and guardians, and will in their turn lift up their arms to protect and assist you.

Besides, before the United Scotsmen emerged in the late 1790s, the Friends of the People in Lowland Scotland had made big efforts to win the Highlanders.[52]

At the November 1793 meeting of the Friends in Ediburgh, it was decided to recruit support in the Highlands. Therefore they passed a resolution that was never published in the press or referred to by the *sleekit* Anglo-Scot in the late eighteenth or nineteenth century:

That a fund be raised by subscription for defraying the expense of small patriotic publications to be distributed in the Highlands. Every publication shall bear the figure of a Highland man in full dress, with target and broad sword, to attract the attention of the Highlander.[53]

Despite John Prebble's exaggeration of the gulf between Highland and Lowland Scots, it was the early - and indeed the later - Scottish labour movement that sought to unify those two very different ethnic groups. Although Scottish historians including Kenneth J. Logue, author of *Popular Disturbances in Scotland, 1780-1815* (1979) and W. Hamish Fraser, author of *Conflict and Class: Scottish Workers, 1700-1838 (1988)* did not consult any of this material, Logue wrote elsewhere about the mutinies in Scottish regiments during the anti-Militia riots. In his article on 'Eighteenth-Century Popular Protest', he wrote:

John Prebble's book, *Mutiny*, has shown that the eighteenth-century tradition of Scottish, and particularly Highland, military service was not universally or generally accepted at the time... These were mutinies within established regiments of the army and perhaps should not be regarded as part of a more general popular culture. These are, however, examples of popular direct action which do seem to indicate a popular attitude contrary to the generally accepted one.

In the largely Gaelic-speaking city of Perth, where there was mass plebeian support for the Friends of the People, George Penny in *Traditions of Perth* (1830) left a full account of Perthshire radicalism in the 1790s. As he explained:

> Pamphlets, in which Monarchy and Aristocracy were denounced, and the majesty of the people exalted, were circulated with incredible rapidity; and the community became divided into two parties, the Aristocrats and the Democrats. A large hall which stood in the High Street was fitted as a coffee room by the democratic party in Perth. Peter Watson (notorious for Republican principles) was appointed keeper. In this room, the party newspapers and pamphlets were read with extraordinary avidity. Several young merchants attended so closely to read to the mobility, to the neglect of their business, that their affairs went to ruins. A new society was formed, called the United Scotsmen. The members were bound by secret oaths; and its ramifications were extended into the army, as well as among civilians. Their *ostensible object* was Universal Suffrage, and Annual Parliaments, but their *ulterior aim* was purely *Republican*. Vast numbers were sworn in ... Liberty and equality became cant words, that ignorant and deluded people were encouraged in their belief that the equality of property was their grand aim, and that a speedy division was to take place.[54]

Although the major Scottish Enlightenment figures like Hume, Boswell, John Millar, the professor of law at Glasgow, Francis Jeffrey or Henry Cockburn did not ever refer to the Friends of the People's focus on the Highlands and always played down the links between Irish and Scottish nationalism, such links were, though ignored by historians, very prominent and tangible Nevertheless, at the trial of

Thomas Muir of Huntershill in the High Court of Judiciary, Edinburgh, on 30 August 1793, Muir and the Friends were accused of sedition. Focusing on the Address from the Society of United Irishmen in Dublin advocating reform in Scotland as well as Ireland, Braxfield described this seditious paper as 'falsely and assiduously representing the Irish and Scotch nations' as oppressed. In one colourful passage that the officers of the Scottish Judiciary found particularly offensive, the United Irishmen in Dublin said: 'We greatly rejoice that the spirit of freedom moves over the surface of Scotland, that light seems to break from the chaos of her internal government... We rejoice that you do not consider yourselves as merged and melted down into another country, but in that great national question you are still Scotland.'[55]

And in going out of their way to make an identification with the Jacobites of 1745, the legal authorities made it plain that they were not going to, in the Scottish phrase, 'stand any nonsense'.[56]

The trials of Muir, William Skirving, Joseph Gerald, Watt and Downie were 'fixed' with the savage sentences imposed on those Friends of the People being predictable and anticipated; and E. P. Thompson insisted that this was due to the machinations of the Government in Westminster rather than 'the mysteries' of the Scottish Judiciary. Testifying to the colonial dimension of Scottish politics, J. Bowles Daly wrote: 'It was soon apparent that it was as difficult for the Crown lawyers to obtain verdicts in England as it was easy for their brethren to obtain them in Scotland'. The colonial behaviour of the 'State' and the Courts in Scotland was responsible for what Millar, the professor of law and historian, described as the 'fly and cautious temper' of the Scottish people. Of course, what he did not say was that this fly and cautious temper was always transitory.

Moreover, the interaction between the organisations of the Friends of the People and the United Irishmen was very strong. In 1794 the Address from the Four Belfast Societies of United Irishmen to the Scottish Friends of the People praised the universities in Scotland as the 'seminaries who have supplied the world with statesmen, scholars, orators, historians and philosophers'.[57] Then in the 'social thistle and the shamrock', Henry Joy McCracken, leader of the United Irishmen, was the joint author of enthusiastic verses touching on the nationalist Republican radicalism of the Scots and the Irish:

> The Scotch and Irish friendly are,
> Their wishes are the same,

the English nation envy us,
And over us would reign.
Our historians and our poets
They always did maintain,
That the origins of Scottish men and Irish were
the same.[58]

And Muir and the other Friends of the People in Scotland looked to Belfast and the north east of Ireland for guidance, inspiration and solace.[59]

Smout's point about the distinctiveness of the role of the 'State' in Scotland in demanding unquestioning obedience should not be dismissed; it was really very important. [60] Despite the brutal role of Braxfield in crushing the Friends of the People, the Scottish judges were not trusted by the Government and authorities at the Palace of Westminster. Unlike England, many of the 'middle' and even some of the 'higher ranks' in Scotland were not committed to the Crown. Attributing the growth of a Scottish radicalism reputedly 'initiated and encouraged in high places, W. D. Lyell added that: 'A certain element of disloyalty and disaffection in Edinburgh was at this season [in 1793] effectively quelled by a band of youthful advocates, led by a newly fledged barrister named Walter Scott, who cudgelled the malcontents in the Edinburgh Theatre Royal into a chastened and self-sorrowful devotion to the Throne'.[61] As a number of historians have observed, Scott already belonged to the dominant section of the Unionist Anglo-Scottish ruling class. And in using his novels to offer a Unionist interpretation of Scottish history to back up the pro-British writings of Boswell, Hume, Millar and many others, Scott was not too different from the Scottish Enlightenment Whigs. Unlike their English counterparts, however, most of the Scots Sawnies had to be cudgelled into supporting the Throne.

The best-known anecdote about Robert MacQueen or Lord Braxfield is the comment he made to a juror at one of the trials of the People in 1793: 'Come awa' in, Mr. Horner, and help me hang one o' thae damn radicals.' After 1707 the Anglo-Scottish judges did not believe in any nonsense about the rule of law. But, although a proper biography of Braxfield has never been researched or written, he was not the exceptional, eccentric or aberrant Scottish figure of fun of later nineteenth-century Kailyard folklore. In a chapter of a small book on the *Terrors of the Law*, Francis Watt provided a clue to the reasons for

Braxfield's vindictaive response to radicalism in Scotland. As he put it: 'Fifty years earlier, at the commencement of his professional career, he had seen a lad with a few friends land in the Highlands, overthrow Scotland, and all but overthrow the Government. Were Jacobins likely to be less dangerous than Jacobites.'[62]

Furthermore, although 'Dictator' Dundas did not want Braxfield to sit on the bench during the trial of the radicals David Downie and Robert Watt, Braxfield was one of the judges who passed sentence on them under an *English Royal Commission* of 'Oyer and Terminer'. [63] At the instigation of the Government in London, Scottish 'totalitarian' law had been cast aside. If 'totalitarian' or 'Asiatic' legal despotism did not, according to E. P. Thompson, exist in England, the English rulers did not hesitate to impose their 'totalitarian' law on radical Scots in 1793 and in 1820.[64] This was undisputable and concrete evidence of the colonial dimension illuminating Scotland's subordination to the Palace of Westminster; and a general Scottish awareness of this inferior political status contributed to the Scots' well-known 'inferiority complex'.

Furthermore, in circumstances where 'hangings never became the popular institutions that they were in England' because 'the Scots were a humane folk', Watt's fate - Downie had been a spy - was intended to cow and intimidate.[65] The experience of the Jacobite rebellions in 1715 and in 1745 had already contributed to the making of 'the fly and cautious temper' of the Scottish people. And just as the systematic repression in the Highlands after 1745 had been intended to intimidate and cow 'a wrong-resenting country', so had the English ruling class decided to cow potential Scottish radicals by their treatment of Watt. As J. Bowles Daly explained: 'The part of the sentence which related to disembowelling and quartering had been previously remitted; but when the body was taken down from the gallows, it was stretched on a table, and the executioner with two blows of the axe cut off the head, which was received in a basket, and then held up to the multitude, exclaimed aloud, "This is the head of a traitor, and so perish all traitors.' [66] And Watt was, of course, a 'traitor' to 'the glorious English revolution' of 1688, not to the Covenanters or the Jacobites.

As the existing cultural factors responsible for inducing the 'Alias MacAlias' syndrome deepened, Robert Burns, the national bard, was compelled to publish his most radical and revolutionary poetry anonymously. Some of his revolutionary poems were not published in his own lifetime; and 'Scots Wha hae' had to be published anonymously.

Although the poet was, as George Gilfillan asserted in his long biographical introduction to the poetry of Burns, 'gagged and muzzled in politics', he wrote such poems as 'Why Must We Idly Waste Our Prime?' and 'The Tree of Liberty'.[67] However, the most powerful of all his nationalist poems was 'A Parcel of Rogues in a Nation':

> We're bought and sold for English gold
> Such a parcel of rogues in a nation.

John Bull's Chauvinism, and 'The Peculiarities of the Scots'

Moreover, the English chauvinism that was seen during the first part of the eighteeenth century was still further enraged by the French revolution. In his excellent book *The Age of Democratic Revolution*, Eric J. Hobsbawm wrote:

> In Britain 'Jacobinism' would have undoubtedly been a phenomenon of greater political importance, even after the Terror, if it has not clashed with the traditional anti-French bias of popular English nationalism, componded equally of John Bull's beef-fed contempt for the starveling continentals (all the French in the popular cartoons of the period are as thin as matchsticks) and of hostility to what was, after all, England's 'hereditary enemy,' though also Scotland's hereditary ally.[68]

To underline what he was saying, he added a footnote: 'This may not be unconnected with the fact that Scottish Jacobinism was a very much more powerful political force.'[69]

Confronted with a resurgence of plebeian radicalism in 1817, the editor of the *Annual Register* published a survey of Scottish Republicanism between 1790 and 1801. Focusing on the fact that 'the great mass of the people of Scotland are much better educated than the great mass of the people in England', he glanced back to the 1790s:

> During the agitated state of the country soon after
> the beginning of the French revolution, when the
> Scotch convention existed, the most decided

advocates for pure Republicanism were in Scotland; and whoever is acquainted with that country even generally and superficially, must know that, with respect to religion, the Scotch are mostly in extremes... It was in this part of Scotland that the Cameronians and Covenanters chiefly underwent with such heroic fortitude, the persecutions to which they were exposed in the times of Charles II; and there are still to be met with there, men as inquisitive and dauntless searchers after truth as their ancestors were at that period. [70]

But in the Highlands, too, there was mass support for the Republican aims of the Friends of the People and the United Scotsmen.

As early as 1792 the editor of the English radical newspaper *The Patriot* anticipated that 'Scotland would soon take the lead' in the British radicals' agitation for reform.[71] By 1794 the radicals in the English city of Norwich decided upon, as Gwyn Williams put it, 'a heavy publication programme' including J. T. Callender's Scots Republican tract *The Political Progress of Britain*.[72] It was not at all accidental, moreover, that Callender criticised the Darien and Glencoe tragedies, the slave trade, and the bloody massacres committed by British monarchs between 1688 and 1792.

Against the background of this colourful eighteenth-century Scotland - an 'unknown country' for Anglo-Scottish and most English historians - mass plebeian radicalism developed during the first two decades of the nineteenth century. In the absence of a Parliamentary tradition in early nineteenth-century Scotland, the poets and writers produced some of the most telling evidence touching on the Republican dimension of Scottish radicalism. The political aspects of the writings of Callender, Alexander Rodger (1784-1846) and John Galt have been neglected for far too long.

The Scots Jacobins supported the United Irishmen and the Irish rebellion of 1798. In 1799 the *Annual Register* quoted from a current *House of Commons' Committee Report of Secrecy* thus:

Whilst the societies in England were thus endeavouring to form a society of United Englishman, or of United Britons, on the model of

45

the Irish Society, attempts were made in Scotland to form a distinct society of "United Scotsmen" on the same plan. And your committee cannot forbear to remark the industry with which it has been attempted in this instance, as well as in others, to separate Scotland as well as Ireland from England, and to found on the ruins of the established government, three distinct republics of England, Scotland, and Ireland.

The attempts to form a society of United Scotsmen had made little progress till the spring of 1797; but from the month of April until November following (when a discovery was made in the county of Fife, on which George Mealmaker was brought to trial, and convicted of sedition) these attempts appear to have been attended with more success in the neighbourhood of Glasgow, and in the counties of Ayr, Renfrew, Lanark, Dumbarton, Fife and Perth. Glasgow and the county of Ayr, were the places in which this spirit first manifested itself, and from which emissaries were sent into different parts of the country, for the purpose of increasing the numbers of the society, and disseminating what they termed "political knowledge".[73]

The Scottish workers' strikes were also important. Notwithstanding the growth of a substantial minority of plebeian or working-class radicals who were committed to the principles of 1688, many militant Scottish radicals were also sympathetic towards Scottish Republicanism. Unfortunately, by receiving much more publicity in the Scottish press than the Friends of the People or the United Scotsmen, this vociferous minority has been mistaken for the majority of plebeian radicals. Thus the Glasgow Mercury devoted considerable space to a resolution passed by the organised shoemakers of Kilmarnock in 1799:

> Kilmarnock, 19 January, which day and place, the Society of journey shoemakers, consisting of about four hundred members, being convened, when taking into consideration that a report has gone abroad, that a Bill is to be brought into Parliament for repealing the penal statutes made against Popery, at the Glorious Revolution and afterwards ratified and confirmed as one of the essential articles of the Union of the two Kingdoms.[74]

Two of the most important Scottish plebeian radicals in the 1790s were George Mealmaker and Angus Cameron. As major pioneers of the very early labour movement in Scotland, they were particularly important for their role in enrolling the infant plebebian or 'working class' in the struggle behind Scottish radicalism. In circumstances where the United Scotsmen had penetrated Highland regiments, a witness at Mealmaker's trial in 1798 described the secret meetings near Dundee where the United Scotsmen had 'decided to go by themselves' and 'the common people by themselves' instead of 'relying on the gentry'. [75] Analysing what was happening at the same time in Perthshire in his *The History of the Working Classes in Scotland*, Thomas Johnson wrote:

> But up in Perthshire it seemed as if the Revolution had virtually come at last, for 16,000 men and women had risen at the call of Angus Cameron, a wright in the Parish of Weem, and were marching and countermarching, surrounding Castle Menzies, and forcing Sir John of that ilk to repudiate the Militia Act, compelling even his grace the Duke of Atholl to swear he would not operate the act until 'the general sentiments of the country were made known', and despatching a regiment of rebels to Taymouth Castle to clean out the armoury there. But the people were without arms, and when the Government rushed sufficient troops to Perthshire, Cameron's army melted away, and he and Menzies were captured without much difficulty. [76]

The underground United Scotsmen were deeply involved in most of the anti-Militia riots, disturbances and protests in the Highlands and the Lowlands; and in 1797 the authorities in Edinburgh asked Whitehall to withdraw all Scottish troops and replace them with English regiments. In September the *Scots Magazine* reported that: 'In consequence of the late riots for opposing the Militia Act, several regiments have been marched from England. The Shropshire militia, commanded by Lord Clive, have arrived at Dalkeith and Musselburgh. This is the first English regiment that has served in Scotland. Another has arrived in Glasgow.' [77]

Eighteenth-century Scotland was unique. Despite its 'backwardness', there were strong egalitarian and collective features woven into the fabric of Scottish social life. When he published his history of *Celtic Scotland* in 1888, W. F. Skene saw the origins of the agitations of 1788-94 and the socialism of the 1880s in the context of a much older history. As he put it: 'Yet though the conscious socialist movement be but a century old, the labouring folk all down the ages have clung to communist practices and customs, partly the inheritance and instinct from the group and clan life of our forefathers and partly because these customs were the only barrier to poverty; and because without them social life was impossible.'[78]

In his book *Mutal Aid* (1912), Peter Kropotkin observed that in parts of Lowland Scotland this communist aspect of social life was seen 'in certain villages' where it was 'the custom to plough the land for the whole community, without leaving any boundaries, and to allot it after the ploughing was done'.[79] The sense of community was seen in cities like Edinburgh, too, and Victor Kiernan recognised the survival of the collective frame of mind there. The cultural sediments of the Scottish past played a major role in shaping the distinctiveness of radicalism - and even extra-Parliamentary socialism - in the Athens of the North.

Notwithstanding the anti-Scottishness of Wilkes and the English radicals well into the 1780s and 1790s, the more egalitarian culture of the Scots helped to create the atmosphere in which Scottish plebeian radicalism developed very rapidly from the 1770s onwards. Also W. W. Straka, the Canadian historian, argued that the spontaneous protests against the anti-Militia Act facilitated the spread of the United Scotsmen throughout Scotland; but spies soon penetrated the secret 'brotherhood of affection' and reported to the authorities.[80] The system of using English troops in the 1790s, widespread spying and the intimidation of the Whig intellectuals in the Scottish universities were ironically inspired by 'justice-loving' English defenders of 'the English revolution' of 1688. Savage sentences of imprisonment and transportation were intended to stamp out the spirit of revolt and disaffection.

In the very nominally Scottish universities, academics were more interested in fostering Unionism than in acknowledging the advent of the Republican dimension of Scottish plebeian radicalism.[81] Historically speaking, the Scots were a 'history-conscious' people; and, despite Linda Colley's assertion that the Union was *not* 'a piece of cultural and political imperialism foisted on the hapless Scots by their stronger Southern neighbour', many nationalistic Scots would remain very hostile to 'the glorious English revolution' of 1688. [82]

However, the irrefutable evidence for the existence of a Scottish Republican radicalism had to be ignored by T. C. Smout and Linda Colley among many other supporters of the Union. Nevertheless, in his book *The Age of Revolution*, Hobsbawm wrote:

> There were communities such as the Scottish linen-weavers with their Republican and Jacobin puritanism, their Swedenborgian heresies, their Tradesmen Library's Library, savings bank, Mechanics' Institute, Library and Scientific Club, their Drawing Academy, missionary meetings, temperance leagues, and infant schools, and literary magazine (the Dunfermline *Gasometer*) - and of course their Chartism. Class-consciousness, militancy, hatred and contempt for the oppressor, belonged to this life as much as the looms on which men wove.[83]

Recognising the blurring over of trade union and more directly political struggles in Scotland (as distinct from England), Hobsbawm had significantly come out of a European historiographical tradition that was much more sensitive to the impact of the French revolution on plebeian workers' consciousness.

One crucial difference between late eighteenth- and early-nineteenth-century Scotland by comparison with England was the greater degree of industrialisation. Furthermore, industrialisation in Scotland took place inside a country with its own distinctive political and cultural traditions. Unlike many English historians, Franz Mehring, the German Marxist, acknowledged the role of the cultural sediments of the past as well as the influence of French Jacobinism in shaping the distinctive history of German radicalism. In his book *Absolutism and Revolution in Germany, 1525-48*, he argued that 'the great French revolution' had 'restored the vitality of a Germany that had degenerated in the swamp of feudalism'.[84] The same thing had happened in Scotland under the impact of the Revolution in France.

A Conquered Scotland and the Continuity of the English Radicals' Chauvinism

As a consequence of the Union of 1707, Scotland had become a subordinate or oppressed nation; and in a private letter dated 1st January 1794 Charles James Fox, the English Whig, insisted that the sham trials of Muir and Thomas Fyshe Palmer meant that there is 'not a *pretence left* for describing Scotland as *a free country'*. [85] It was not accidental that he made this comment in a private letter rather than in the House of Commons. Furthermore, Braxfield had told Muir at his trial in Edinburgh that the Friends of the People's depiction of Scotland and Ireland as oppressed countries constituted treason.[86] Inheriting and repeating the expression of the chauvinism of Wilkes toward the Scots, there were sharp and recurring nationalist tensions between the Scottish and English radicals before the 'Radical rebellion' of 1820. And Scotland remained an oppressed country until after 1832.

Although the Scottish Whig intellectuals saw themselves as possessing a sharper sense of national identity than their Tory opponents, they had to ignore the powerful features of Republican radicalism in Scotland from the 1770s (including the folk songs recovered by Hamish Henderson). At various trials of Republican radicals in Scottish courts in the 1790s, early 1800s and 1820, the judges made the most minimum references to the Scottish dimension represented by the Friends of the People and the United Scotsmen. Almost entirely expunged from the Scottish Enlightenment intellectuals' writings, poets and writers like Ferguson, Burns, Callender, Rodger and Galt - the conscience of the nation - were much more sensitive to routine English chauvinism than the workaday Scottish radical agitators.

Scottish working people had played a prominent role in strikes from the late eighteenth century. In his authoritative book on *The Rise of the Working Class* internationally, Jurgen Kuczynski suggested that the first women's strike anywhere had probably been that of the women weavers at Pawtucket, Rhode Island in 1824.[87] What was probably the *first* women's strike had occurred in the Scottish town of Paisley as early as 1768. Moreover, there was a full and very detailed account of this novel strike in the *Glasgow Journal*. Though this strike was small and insignificant, it constituted an implicit counterpoint to the stereotyping of the Scots as 'tame', 'docile' and 'uninflammable'. [88]

Moreover, in the eighteenth and early nineteenth centuries, Scottish women 'spoke and did exactly as they chose'. Unlike English women, who took their husbands' opinions in politics and religion, Scots women frequently intervened in political struggles independently of what their menfolk said or did. As R. De Bruce Trotter explained: 'Folk disna lose their name there whun they'r mairry't, and tak shelter in their man's yin. They insist on equal rights there, and the wife's as gude as the man onyday, an whiles a gey deal better'.[89]

From the 1770s Scottish middle-class women had been admitted into the literary and philosophical debating societies in Dundee, Glasgow and Edinburgh. This had been attributed to 'the levelling tendencies' of the age; and it was not stopped until the general witch-hunt against Whigs and 'advanced doctrines' unleashed by the French revolution had gone into decline.[90] By contrast, before and after 1789 plebeian or 'working-class' women were active in a whole range of strikes, political and anti-war struggles, anti-Militia riots and disturbances as independent characters with their own views and opinions. Unlike the English ruling class, the Anglo-Scottish ruling class did not view women's strikes as being innately servile. It was not until 1816 that English working-class women began to accompany 'their husbands and sweethearts' to radical meetings; and another three years would pass before they were allowed to vote at working-class radicals' meetings in the north of England.[91]

Between 1800 and the Radical rebellion of 1820, Scottish workers' strikes were often permeated with political grievances. As Sean Damer puts it:

> These struggles were linked to wider political demands for the abolition of private property and for national independence. It was estimated by the authorities that in Glasgow and the surrounding region there were over 100,000 workers in illegal 'combinations' in 1812.[92]

Besides, in one of his series of books *A Short History of Labour under Capitalism* dealing with the whole history of worldwide labour protests, Jurgen Kuczynski argued that the strike of the Scottish cotten weavers' was 'perhaps the largest strike' in Europe at that time. Summing up, he said: 'Forty thousand weavers were on strike for three weeks. Towards the end, the employers appeared to be yielding, when suddenly the whole strike committee was arrested and the five leaders received prison sentences for the crime of combination. This broke the strike.'[93]

The first decade of the nineteenth century in Scotland witnessed comparative calm and quiescence, although the organisation of United Scotsmen began to revive in 1811. While the continuity of the Scots' working folk's struggles between the crushing of the United Scotsmen and the major weavers' strike of 1812 was not unbroken, the spirit of rebellion and disaffection had not disappeared.[94]

Nor were either the Highlanders or the Lowlanders cowed or beaten into silence or unquestioning submission. In his article on 'Eighteenth-Century Popular Protest', Ken Logue made the important and usually neglected point that in the early nineteenth-century Sir Walter Scott was not 'very keen to collect folk material about popular protest'.[95] Logue could have extended this comment to all the defenders of 1688, 1707 and the *status quo*, whether Scottish Tories or Whigs, almost into perpetuity.

Engaged in the subtle process of falsifying the history of the Highlands, Scott was not interested in preserving memories of resistance to the Clearances or capitalism. But the resistance to a vicious capitalism was not restricted to Scottish radicals. When Malcolm of Poltalloch cleared eighteen families from Arichanan in Argyll between 1805 and 1810, an anonymous poet wrote (in Gaelic) at the time:

> A wicked man is Malcolm
> And I will say it
> When the French come
> Across to rout him
> Who will stand up for Malcolm
> In the rabble round about him?
> Everyone will be wild
> Desiring to strike him
> And I myself will be there
> Urging on the conflict.[96]

Again and again in Scottish history radical and rebellious underground literature and folk material has been expunged from the record.

Those rebellious Scots, who *sleekitly* bequeathed the folk material of resistance to posterity, were usually dismissed by the Tory *and* Whig figures of the Enlightenment like Scott as much as by Lord Cockburn.

However, the Scots, who, in escaping victimisation or 'the terrors of the law' by hiding behind anonymity and identifying with the nursery rhyme that 'he who fights and runs away, lives to fight another day', were not 'tame', 'docile' or 'uninflammable'. [97] Besides, if Scottish radicals have always been *carnaptious*, the radical Scots' collective carnaptiousness was the product of a unique cultural milieu in which traditional outspokenness could be obliterated under the hangman's rope.

In Glasgow in 1812 strikers who begged for 'cheap bread' were actually shot dead by soldiers; some law officers argued that trade unions were illegal under common law; and strikes or combinations were put down with ferocity. Walter Scott looked around Scotland with 'dismay at the power of Scottish trade unionism'. [98] At Deanston there was an attempt to wreck the machines and arms were kept in readiness. [99]

In 1813 there had been a mutiny of the Renfewshire militia. The first major sign of the Scots' nationalism in the nineteenth century was seen when 15,000 working men and women celebrated the Battle of Bannockburn of 1314 at the 'famed spot' under ths shadow of the Scottish flags. [100] When news of Napoleon's escape from Elba reached Glasgow in March 1815, the authorities were worried by the open support that was being displayed towards the Frenchman. [101]

Moreover, in 1815 a retired army officer at Strathaven, organised a meeting of tailors, masons, and weavers' trade union benefit societies. Thousands of 'the democratic' working people in the surroundings towns and villages were, according to the Tory Sheriff-substitute, 'then much elevated by the return of Bonaparte' from Elba to France. Under Hamilton's leadership, it was decided to organise a mass demonstration to 'celebrate the victory gained by the Covenanters over the King's troops at Drumclog, on 13 June 1679'. On 13th June 1815 over ten thousand of 'the democratic people' - men, women and children - marched, in William Aiton's words, 'to the place where the Covenanters defeated Claverhouse, and from thence to a cairn of stones or tumulus, on the farm of Allanton, Ayrshire, about two miles from the field of Drumclog, and where they *imagined* Sir William Wallace had fought his first battle with the English'. [102] Obscured by the absence of a substantial Scottish national and radical historiography, Scots have had a particular difficulty in understanding their own history because Scott, though a Tory, was committed to re-interpreting the history of the

Athens of the North to blend and fit in with the (Scottish) Whig view of the innate progressiveness of 1688 and 1707.[103]

When Aiton, the Scottish Tory, published his own account of the events at Bannockburn in 1814 and at Drumclog in 1815 leading up to the Radical rebellion of 1820 in his neglected book on *The Rencounter at Drumclog* (1821), he explained that his book had been written to refute or 'correct' Scott's account of the history of the Covenanters in his novel *Old Mortality*.[104] Scotland was the only country in Europe where novels interpreting the Scottish past were sources of bitter ideological disputes and quarrels. But the critical and hidden dimension of all of this bitterness over ideas was that (1) many of the Scottish working-class radicals had always been sympathetic towards Sir William Wallace and the Jacobites; and (2) they had fundamental political differences with both Tory and Whig novelists, writers and political figures.

In 1816 there were strikes, riots and political demonstrations throughout Scotland.[105] Notwithstanding the contact with English radicals who wanted political reform of the Parliamentary system, there was a strong nationalist dimension to Scottish radicalism. In Glasgow a meeting of 40,000 working people demanded reform; and in the town of Dunfermline the Provost informed the Home Office at Westminster that several of the working-class radicals who were 'particularly active during the sedious practices of 1793' had been the first to step forward on this occasion.[106] The year 1817 also witnessed the role of revolutionaries in encouraging mass disaffection such as the Rev. Neil Douglas, whose arrest and imprisonment provoked protest in the House of Commons.

Jacobite Relics, the Radicals' Nationalism and the Radical Rebellion of 1820

Setting the scene for the Radical rebellion of 1820, it was obvious that the Scottish radicals had not been cowed by the experience of the 1790s. In a long review of the James Hogg's book *The Jacobite Relics of Scotland* published in the *Edinburgh Review* in 1820, an anonymous reviewer blamed Walter Scott and John Galt as well as Hogg for working-class discontent. The reviewer insisted that:

> Yet we do find a strange sort of spirit lately sprung up - a sort of speculative Jacobitism, not wholly romantic neither, we are afraid, but connected with

the events of the times, and a sort of twin brother
to the newfangled doctrine of legitimacy.[107]

With sadness and dismay the editor of the *Edinburgh Annual Register*,
with which Scott was associated, wrote after the rebellion of 1820 that:
'It was in Scotland, after all, that rebellion stalked with the most open
front.'[108]

Unionist writers had to distort the events of 1820, and Scott and Galt
approved of the role of the Government spies in destroying the radical
Union societies. But most historians have hidden the speculation of
John Stevenson, a participant in the Rising at Strathaven, that the spies
had been successful in thwarting what would otherwise have been a
formidable movement to challenge the *status quo*.

In their book *The Scottish Insurrection of 1820* (1970), P. Berresford
Ellis and Seumas Mac A' Ghobhainn devote considerable space to the
disappearance of the legal records relating to the major radical episode
of early Scottish radicalism. As they explain:

> The original records of the trials, the evidence and
> preparatory statements have completely
> disappeared... An extensive search of the Scottish
> Record Office and other likely places has proved
> negative, showing it extremely likely that the
> original records were destroyed, perhaps by the
> authorities following the startling re-evaluation of
> the use of Government spies, published in 1832,
> when the Government had to give a free pardon
> to all the 1820 Radicals then living.[109]

Ignored by academics, reviewers and historians on this critical point,
Ellis and Mac A' Ghobhainn might have been taken more seriously if
they had placed the disappearance of these papers within the wider
context of the general intolerance of the Anglo-Scottish ruling class in
suppressing a free press, censorship and the exclusion of *carnaptious*
radicals (as distinct from the Whigs) critical of 'the glorious English
revolution' and the Union of 1707 from University teaching posts and
the law courts.[110] To reconstruct the Radical rebellion of 1820 will force
the serious historian to at least look at the evidence in the comments
made by Scott, Galt, Thomas Carlyle, John Gibson Lockhart and other
contemporaries. The writers belonging to or identifying with the Anglo-

Scottish ruling class were just as 'history-conscious' as their 'lower-class' counterparts; and they were determined to eradicate all awareness of the surviving sense of Scottish national identity and separateness amongst the 'lower classes'. Furthermore, in his booklet *A True Narrative of the Radical Rising* (1835), Stevenson was motivated by a passionate attempt to challenge the Scottish Tory and Whig interpretations of what had happened in 1820. He emphasised that there had been widespread support in Scotland for the idea of a rising.[111]

All sorts of small incidents surrounding the main events of 1820 at Strathaven, Bonnymuir and elsewhere, in a context where the names and deeds of Sir William Wallace, the Covenanters and even the Jacobites were being recalled and celebrated, testified to the Scottish nationalism of many of the radicals. Though in itself it was a small, insignificant and usually unnoticed event, the forty armed men who walked into Kirkintilloch in 1820, but 'threw away their pikes and arms when the town did not rally to their call to action' does strengthen Stevenson's view that an uprising had probably been planned by the delegates from Strathaven, Falkirk and elsewhere.[112]

The most significant aspect of the incident at Kirkintilloch in 1820 was that, according to the *Edinburgh Weekly Journal*, 'the men had generally the appearance of *factory men*'.[113] At Strathaven the small group of radicals led by James Willson, a survivor of the struggles of the 1790s, had sent a delegate to the central committee of the Union societies in Glasgow. But, though most of the radicals did not know that the members of the central committee had been caught and imprisoned before spies posted up an almost certainly phoney Proclamation of the establishment of a Provisional Government of the People of Britain and Ireland, Stevenson refuted the argument of Aiton, Peter Mackenzie and others that they had not planned to participate in a general Scottish rebellion.[114]

Before the members of the central committee were arrested, a worker at Carron ironworks, Falkirk, was known to have attended the meeting of the committee on 15th January 1820. In secret communications to the Home Office in Whitehall and the Scottish legal officers in Scotland, the authorities insisted that cannon could not be made at Falkirk without the knowledge of the management. [115] In December 1919, General Bradford informed Lord Sidmouth that there were only a few condemned and large cannon at Falkirk. But on 21st April 1820 the *Dundee Advertiser* carried the following report:

About sixty carronades, and a considerable quantity of ammunition, were lately brought down from Carron, and safely lodged in Leith Fort, beyond the reach of the radicals.

The Sleekitness of Anglo-Scottish Rulers and a Carnaptious Radicalism

There was almost no discussion of the Radical rebellion of 1820 at the time. However, in his two-volume book of *Reminiscences* (1881), Thomas Carlyle recalled the polarisation between the 'lower orders' and the Anglo-Scottish ruling class, particularly in Edinburgh:

> A time of great rages and absurd terrors and expectations: a very fierce Radical and anti-Radical time. Edinburgh agitated all around me by it (not to mention Glasgow in the distance); gentry people full of zeal and foolish terror and fury, and looking disgustingly busy and important; courier hussars would come in from the Glasgow region, covered with mud, breathless from headquarters as you took your walk in Princes Street; and you would hear old powdered gentlemen in silver spectacles talking with low-toned exultant voice about "cordon of troops, Sir, as you went along".[116]

An excellent and poignant account of the mood in Edinburgh, Carlyle's reference was less detailed than that of John Gibson Lockhart. Among the well-fed Yeomen who rode west to put down an anticipated rebellion, Lockhart described his experiences in a letter to his fiancee (Scott's daughter Sophia):

> There seems now to be no doubt that there had been a serious and well-arranged plan on Monday last. On Wednesday evening, the greater part of the roads leading from Glasgow were in the hands of the Radicals, and various places of encampment in the neighbourhood were resorted to by the weavers from the villages. The drum was beat, such was the audacity, within a mile of the Barricks...

The *numerous executions* which must occur in a very few weeks may be expected to produce a salutory effect, but meantime, till they are over, there is no prospect of entire tranquility.

Lockhart also wrote to Sophia Scott informing her that numbers of the weavers of Strathaven and 'some other villages', who marched 'with muskets and pikes, but not being joined as they expected, their men lost heart and went to a neighbouring Justice of the Peace with an offer of surrender'. Looking to the future, he told her: 'I have little doubt the audacity of our northern rebels will, some time or other, lead them to a regular insurrection'.[117]

Moreover, the radicals, according to Stevenson, though caught unawares by what happenened at Strathaven, had anticipated some such event. As he put it:

> The hand-loom weavers of Strathaven had, for a number of years previous to 1820, grappled with the real difficulties of life - a profligate Court, a rapicious Ministry... They knew if they could prove anything like the existence of a conspiracy among the sober and calculating tradesmen in Scotland, that their hands would be strengthened by the suspension of the Habeas Corpus Act; and their capacity as sagicious Statesmen, would be acknowledged by their Royal master, and the worthless minions who fatten and bask in the sunshine of the Throne.

The most important comment on the Scottish nationalism of the radicals of 1820 was touched on in *A True Narrative of the Radical Rising* when Stevenson reported the discussion among the Strathaven radicals when reinforcements did not appear thus:

> John Morrison, who had fought and beat the French often in the Peninsular wars, laughed heartily at the idea of the yeomanry attacking us, he said he would wager his head against a rotten apple, that twenty-five brave fellows like us would rout a regiment of such vermin; he likewise said,

that Wallace and Bruce, had often fought and conquered in the glorious cause of liberty, and that he was proud to see a few Scotsmen leave their homes to tread in the footsteps of such illustrious men, and if we are to perish, let us do it nobly, our names will be recorded among Scotland's patriotic sons.[118]

Testifying to Carlyle's posthumous comments on 1820, there was bitter class hatred between many nationalist working people and the Anglo-Scottish ruling class.

It was, however, significant that none of the non-radicals, whether Tory or Whig, ever discussed the nationalist dimension of the Radical rebellion. Although the Scottish judges at the trials of the captured radicals for High Treason at Stirling, Paisley and Glasgow voiced their outrage over the behaviour of Wilson in carrying a flag bearing the words 'Scotland: Free or a Desert'; they also played down the nationalism of the radicals of 1820.[119] Just as Braxfield had ignored the Scottish nationalist sentiments expressed by Callender in his Scottish Republican booklet on The *Political Progress of Britain*, so did the judges at the trials of 1820.

Despite the falsity of the Proclamation posted up all over Scotland by Government spies, something like 60,000 workers came out on strike in a cry for fundamental social change. In 1817 and in 1820, Sidmouth and the authorities in London worried about using English troops to suppress Scottish radicals. The bitter confrontation between English soldiers and the Scots in towns like Paisley in 1820 and the English radicals denunciation of the Scots as 'a race' vitiated British workers' solidarity. If there was a continuity of regarding the Scots as 'Jacobites and foreigners', many of the Scottish workers were exceptionally militant at the point of production. In his book on the history of the *Lord Advocates of Scotland* (1914), George W. T. Omond wrote thus: 'Political associations sprung up on all sides, and formed the subject of anxious correspondence between the authorities in Edinburgh and the Government in London'. He also insisted that the use of Government spies thwarted what would have been a more broadly based rebellion in 1820. Summing this up, he said:

Events soon clearly showed that a foolish attempt would be made to obtain Reform by force of arms.

Weavers refused to work. Colliers would not enter the pits. The cotton mills were silent. Artisans who began work in the morning were threatened and forced to stop... It is believed that in Glasgow and the neighbourhood fully sixty thousand persons struck work. Bands of desperate men skulked about the country, surrounding country houses at night, and demanding arms. Midnight drilling went on. In some villages blacksmiths' shops were entered and the intruders, forcing the owners to stand aside, set to work to make pikes.

It was evident that there would soon be bloodshed.[120]

Contemporaries like Janet Hamilton with direct knowledge of what happened in Scottish working-class communities in 1820 gave similar accounts. [121]

The culmination of the repressive policy of the Palace of Westminster and the Anglo-Scottish ruling class from 1816-17 onwards, the Radical rebellion was perhaps the major traumatic event in nineteenth-century Scotland. By haunting the class- conscious awareness of the ruling authorities in Whitehall and Edinburgh, it had a lasting impact on the Scots comparable to the Jacobite rebellion of 1745. The Scottish nationalist dimension of the Radical rebellion at the time was only mentioned very infrequently in the courts of Scotland in 1820, and most Scottish writers including the Whig lawyers like Cockburn and Jeffrey refused to face up to it.

Although it was apparently not discussed by the Scottish plebeian radicals between the 1770s and 1820, there was a bitter, unceasing and *sleekit* class conflict going on between the landed aristocracy and the rising bourgeoisie. After the events of 1820, however, the Scottish Whigs took advantage of the new political situation to begin gradually to establish their own hegemony; and there was an increasing coalescence between the literary work and novels of Scott, the Tory, and the Whig intellectuals like Jeffrey and Cockburn in *inventing* a historical interpretation of the Scottish past.[122] It was simultaneously pro-British, compatible with 1688, 1707, and allegiance to the British Throne. At the root of the dilemma of the fragmentation of 'modern Scottish consciousness' as seen in the cultural and political form of 'Dr. Jekyll and Mr. Hyde', 'Alias MacAlias' and the 'Caledonian Antisyzygy', the authentic Scots could not be allowed to produce an honest national historiography about *their* radicalism. [123]

Yet despite the suppression of the real history of Scotland from 1707, quite enough fragmentary and sometimes tangential evidence has survived to illuminate the plebeian and 'working-class' Scots' strong sense of national identity. At *rare* moments of extreme social and political tension, bourgeois Scots like Boswell, Hume and Jeffrey could be touchy when even their distorted consciousness of themselves as Scots came under attack.

Moreover, it was rather ironical that by this time Lord Jeffrey was a close personal friend of Wilkes, and, though he probably did not know much about the earlier quarrels between Boswell and Hume on the one side and Wilkes on the other, he often reflected the Scottish ruling-class's general confusion over their self-images as 'Scots'.[124] Separated from the plebeian Scots who spoke Lallans or Gaelic, Boswell, Hume, Jeffrey and other comparable Enlightenment figures felt insecure about their decisions to cease speaking or writing Lallans or Braid Scots. Inhibited by his identification with King Billy or William of Orange, 1688, 1707 and sharing the same schizophrenic attitude to things Scottish as Boswell, Hume and Jeffrey, Galt ignored the events of 1820 but still tried to defend his *self-image* as a Scot.[125] When he published his novel on the Covenanters considerably later, he would *sleekitly* refer to the Radical rebellion of 1820 not by criticising Sergeant [or Baron] Hullock who had prosecuted the radicals under the imposition of English law but by casting his memory back to the 'Wilkes and Liberty' agitations of the 1760s and 1770s.

In 1772 and in 1776 both Boswell and Hume had both been outraged by Wilkes and other English radicals' denunciation of the Scots, and the memory of those incidents - a memory shared by many Scots - had lingered for a long time afterwards. As late as 1823 Galt recalled the English radicals' campaign against the Scots to emphasise the cultural differences between the two peoples. Moreover, when the anti-Unionist feelings of many Scots were unleashed by the Radical rebellion of 1820, most Anglo-Scots went to great lengths to practise what Lewis Grassic Gibbon would much later call 'the code of repression'. [126] Furthermore, in 1820 as in the eighteenth century, Irish Paddies and Scots Sawnies were still looked down upon by English chauvinists.[127]

Moreover, when Cockburn published his two-volume *Life of Lord Jeffrey* in 1852, he was so reticient about the Radical rebellion that he devoted a mere paragraph to it. And yet it was clear from Cockburn's account that an incident between Hullock and Jeffrey in Stirling - an incident comparable to those incidents of 1772 and 1776 - reflected the latent tensions between the English and the Anglo-Scottish ruling classes.

In the first place, Hullock had been sent, in Cockburn's words, 'to keep us all right in the mysteries of the English treason laws.' Hullock was not aware of who Jeffrey was, nor of his status as a major Scottish intellectual; and, although Cockburn described Hullock as 'a good man', he said that the English lawyer was 'plainly prepossessed with very contemptuous ideas of everything Scotch, especially the lawyers'. While simultaneously acknowledging yet playing down the significance of the tumultuous rammy (or quarrel) in the Stirling courtroom, Cockburn concluded that: 'It is likely that there were faults on both sides. But the fact is, that they got on very ill, and were on the edge of a personal quarrel.'[128]

In his three-volume *Reminiscences of Glasgow* (1856), Peter Mackenzie was obviously unaware of Cockburn's biography of Jeffrey. Insisting that he was revealing to the public for the very first time an account of the bitter quarrel between Hullock and Jeffrey, Mackenzie gave a fuller version of what happened. Recounting the response of the 'old Tory' Ronald MacDonald, the Sheriff of the country of Stirling, who was sitting in on the proceedings, Mackenzie said:

> His Highland blood became aroused on behalf of Jeffrey at one part of Hullock's assault; so he quickly wrote, and threw across the table of the bar to Jeffrey, a note to this effect - "Challenge the———, and I'll be your second, any where out of this country". Jeffrey leaped across the table and grasped the hand of [MacDonald]. The Court in a moment was aware of what was going to take place. A duel, undoubtedly, at the end of an awful trial. But the Lord President interposed, and Hullock was made to apologise.[129]

If the incidents of 1762, 1776 and 1820 had been public knowledge, the nationalistic radical Scots would not have practised the code of repression concerning their frustrated sense of national identity; and the nationalism and radicalism of the authentic Scots would have been much more open, confident, aggressive and articulate. Nevertheless the sense of national grievance engendered by the Union of 1707 was to persist for several decades into the next two centuries, though relations between the two countries and their labour movements improved after 1820 and 1832.

When Galt published his novel *Ringan Gilhaize or The Covenanters* (1823), the Radical rebellion was still rankling in the Scots' consciousness. In what was an oblique or *sleekit* reference to the antagonism that the events of 1820 stirred up in the hearts and minds of even Unionist or Anglo-Scots, he added a poignant and factual postscript to *Ringan Gilhaise* in which he said:

> From the time of *The North Briton* of the unprincipled Wilkes, a notion has been entertained that the moral spine is more flexible in Scotland than in England. The truth however is, that elementary differences exists in the public feelings of the two nations quite as great as in the idioms of their respective dialects. The English are a justice-loving people, according to charter and statute, the Scotch are a wrong-resenting race, according to right and feeling, and the character of liberty among them takes its aspect from that pecularity. [130]

The Whigs' Post-1820 Hegemony and the Scots' Distinctive Radicalism

By forcing the Scottish Whigs to confront the Tory dictatorship and abandon their hitherto qualified radicalism of the mouth, the Radical rebellion became a watershed in the history of the early nineteenth century. Arguing very convincingly in the Preface to the new 1989 edition of his *Scottish Insurrection of 1820* that 'the Bonnymuir rebels' had been led into a trap set by Government spies, Peter Berresford Ellis was belatedly identifying with what Whigs like Cockburn had said at the time. [131] But, although the Whigs' response to the events of 1820 resulted in a partial liberalisation of Scottish life, they, too, were motivated by the desire to prevent a Revolution.

When the Whigs organised their famous Pantheon meeting in April 1820, the first major opposition to the Establishment from the rising bourgeoisie led, in the words of Henry Cockburn, 'to the dawn of a new day on the official seat of Scotch intolerance'. Arguing that the existing cleavage between the upper and middle ranks was 'the great radical evil' threatening Scotland, Francis Jeffrey went on to say that: 'It is to fill up this chasm, to occupy the middle ground, and to show how large a proportion of the people are attached to the constitution, while they lament its abuses, that such meetings as this should be held'. [132] From then on the Scottish plebeian radicals were driven underground without being silenced.

The most obvious sign of the policy of liberalisation was the visit of King George IV to Edinburgh in 1822. As the Whig intellectuals in the universities gradually began to come into their own, the Scottish Tories also encouraged the Whigs' propaganda designed to integrate the plebeian 'lower orders' into the established social order. There was some truth in the statement made in the *Edinburgh Annual Register for 1822* that 'the historic' visit of George IV put 'an end to our Party squabblings and animosities'. [133] By contributing a hundred guineas for the support of the Gaelic schools in the Highlands and by dressing himself in Highland garb, George IV helped Sir Walter Scott to manufacture 'romantic' myths about the Highlands of Scotland. [134]

In the Preface to his new edition of *The Scottish Insurrection of 1820*, Ellis made an important point when he said that his book would provide 'a very necessary corrective to the Scottish historical mythology manufactured by Sir Walter Scott'. [135] Yet despite the growing co-operation between the Whigs and the Tories at a superficial level, ideological tensions broke through the surface when writers like the Tory William Aiton published a book and a pamphlet to refute Scott's interpretation of the events of 1820. [136] Furthermore, the Tories and the Whigs did not - and could not - abandon their Party strife.

Certainly the visit of George VI to Scotland made a big impact on the landed aristocracy and bourgeoisie (as distinct from working folk). Galt, who a was at heart a loyal Tory, would later ridicule the unintelligibility of the Glasgow bourgeoisie for trying to 'speak exquisite English' before the English King. [137] But he also criticised the Republicanism of the radicals of Glasgow. In an ultra-history-conscious Scotland, even John Gibson Lockhart would also criticise the myths that were being manufactured about the Highlands as 'a cruel mockery'. [138]

Notwithstanding the degree of liberalisation that the Establishment in London tried to impose after 1820, bitter class struggles between 'the haves and 'the have-nots' continued to erupt down to 1832. In Paisley in 1821 two cotton spinners, who had fired shorts in the direction of a cotton master, were whipped through the streets before being transported abroad.[139] A great deal of sympathy existed for those two unfortunate men, and as they were flogged by the public hangman troops were used to keep back the crowds of protesters.[140]

When the miners at the Duke of Hamilton's colliery at Redding, Falkirk, tried to organise themselves into a trade union, the delegates were arrested by Sheriff MacDonald, who made clear that trade unions would not be tolerated in Stirlingshire. This happened yet again in March 1828.[141] Then in 1831, when Jeffrey was the Lord Advocate of Scotland, the militant radical newspaper *The Herald to Trades' Advocate* criticised him for not defending 'popular rights'.[142] As the class struggle was intensified, the authorities employed the policy of 'divide and rule' by cynically using the Orange Order.[143]

In circumstances where unprecedented mass meetings of 100,000 and 200,000 men and women of the 'lower orders' were held all over Scotland between 1830 and 1832 to agitate for Parliamentary reform and genuine workers' representation in Parliament, the Whigs worried about using the common people as a battering ram to achieve political power for the rising bourgeoisie. Approving of his fellow Whigs for using the popular forces pushing for reform, Cockburn could not suppress his worries about doing so. Refering to trade unions, he said: 'They are useful at present, because wherever they have been established the peace has been preserved; but they are most dangerous engines'.[144]

On the few occasions when it suited their purpose, Whigs like Cockburn would feign a certain sympathy for an abstract and romantic Scottish nationalism. When he reported on a vast Reform meeting of working people in Edinburgh in 1832, Cockburn claimed to be impressed by the singing of 'Scots wha hae wi' Wallace bled'. Identifying with the plebeian radicals' Scottish nationalism in order to divert and de-radicalise their levelling egalitarianism, he summed up thus: 'This part of the ceremony was sublime and effective; the last song particularly which was joined in by thousands all over the field, with the earnestness and devotion of a sacrament'. [145]

At the end as at the beginning of this essay, the 'wrong-resenting' attitudes of Scotland - and the Scottish nationalism of the 'lower orders' - were, though hidden by the brute force of the Tories and the 'education' of the Whigs, powerful aspects of social and intellectual life. Thus even William Chambers, who was neither a great radical nor a Scottish nationalist, concluded his work *The Book of Scots* (1830) by insisting that the Scottish people were as much *'a subdued* as a *confederated people'*.[146]

Chapter Two

James Thomson Callender (1758-1803): *A Scottish-International Jacobin*

An Fhirinn an aghaidh an t-Saoghail!
(The Truth against the World!)

Scottish saying

One of the more ambiguous legacies of radical democratic history is that of English nationalism - the notion that the English people have been somehow singled out for a special place in history, that the English language is superior to others and that the liberty of the individual is more secure in England than abroad.

Raphael Samuel

Scottish Jacobins and the Biography of James Thomson Callender

One of the major Scottish Jacobins of the late eighteenth century, James Thomson Callender, was born in Glasgow in 1758.[1] The author of the immortal booklet *The Political Progress of Britain*, he was an exceptionallly sharp, and perhaps the first important, critic of modern British imperialism.

Before it was seized by the legal authorities in December 1792, thousands of copies of a very remarkable booklet, *The Political Progress of Britain or an Impartial Account of the Principal Abuses in the Government of this Country from the Revolution of 1688,* were printed, published and sold to Scottish radicals.[2] Although it was written, published and sold during the months of February, March, April and May 1792, before writs were issued for the arrest of the author and printers of this 'wicked and seditious pamphlet', it had been written by Callender.

But, although Callender's booklet has until now always been ignored by Scottish historians, it was the only sustained Scottish nationalist interpretation that was produced in the eighteenth century. Unknown to most Scots, it was well known to American radicals and conservatives alike. Callender had not been included in the multi-volume *Dictionary of Eminent Scotsmen* (1856) by William Chambers or in *The Book of Eminent Scotsmen* (1880) by Joseph Irving; and clearly A. and E. G. Porritt did not have any real biographical informnation about him. Nevertheless in their massive two-volume study of *The Unreformed House of Commons* (1903), the Porritts offered a critical analysis of his booklet, *The Political Progress of Britain*.

Despite brief and often factually inaccurate entries in the British *Dictionary of National Biography* (1886) and the *Dictionary of American National Biography* (1929), Callender's importance in Scottish history has had to be ignored. In *Thomas Jefferson and James Thomson Callender, 1798-1802* (1896), Worthington C. Ford asserted that 'the biographical details of Callender are few'.[3] Reinforcing Ford's point, the entry in the *Dictionary of American Biography* simply observed that Callender, 'the political writer, was born in Scotland in 1758, acquired by some means a fair classical education, and became in 1792 a messenger at arms'. Unknown to British and American historians and literary historians, he had been a student at the University of Edinburgh in 1778. He had, moreover, become a messenger-at-arms in 1787, not 1792.[4] A messenger-at-arms was what is now called a sheriff's officer, though the post enjoyed a higher social status in the eighteenth than in the twentieth century.

At odds with the dominant views represented by most of the intellectuals of the Scottish Enlightenment, Callender was a Jacobite nationalist and a Jacobin internationalist who challenged the legitimacy and efficacy of 1688, 1707 and the British Throne in 1792. He was, however, a product of the Enlightenment; and, far from coming from nowhere or developing in a vaccum, the relatively obscure Callender of 1792 did not lack a substantial biography.

Both as an egalitarian radical and Scottish nationalist, he was, whether in Scotland or America, the most extreme or left-wing of all the Scottish Jacobins of the 1790s. Callender was just as much a product of the Scottish Enlightenment as Adam Smith, Dugald Stewart or John Millar. But because he belonged to the bottom of the 'middle ranks' of eighteeth-century Edinburgh, he did not bequeath to posterity so much biographical information about his life and times in Scotland as did the much better-known Scottish Enlightenment intellectuals. However, the polemical carnaptiousness that he displayed in 1778, when he was a twenty-year old student at the University of Edinburgh, was to become one of the hitherto unacknowledged defining characteristics of Scottish radicalism or extreme leftism as a whole well into the twentieth century.

When he first came into conflict with the Establishment in Scotland in 1778, Callender was a student in Dr. Cullen's medical class. Cullen (1710-90) was a professor of anatomy in the Edinburgh medical school, where he lectured on chemistry, botany and materia medica from 1775; and he was, according to T. C. Smout, 'a popular lecturer'.[5] The outspoken and independent Callender was not impressed by Cullen's ability or integrity.

Unfortunately, Dr. Cullen's class-lists have not survived except for the years 1755-65, 1761 and 1763; and Callender's name did not appear in any of the University of Edinburgh's matriculation albums. However, matriculation was not made compulsory at Edinburgh until 1811, though Callender's education at Edinburgh was known to the exiled Scottish radicals in America.[6]

Though he was a very untypical product of the Scottish Enlightenment, Callender's active political life and practice illuminated some of the hidden recesses of the *'condition of Scotland'* question. Moreover, when he was an English resident in America, William Cobbett, the reactionary Tory and suspected British 'spy', and not yet a radical, published fascinating articles and pamphlets against Callender in the 1790s.

Far from abandoning his radical Scottish nationalism after arriving in America in 1793, Callender would continue to upset Cobbett's English chauvinism. In his pamphlet *A Bone To Gnaw for the Democrats or Observations on A Pamphlet entitled The Political Progress of Britain*, Cobbett unwittingly paid tribute to Callender's importance as a major radical thinker and writer comparable to Thomas Paine when he asserted that: 'The Political Progress is in Politics; what mad Tom's *Age of Reason* is in religion, and they have both met with encouragement from some people here, for nearly the same motive'.[7] Furthermore, as Callender's most bitter and unrelenting enemy in America, he focused on the Scot's *Jacobitism* to discredit him with the Americans:

> Is it anything to us whether he prefers [Prince] Charley to [King] George, or George to Charley, any more than whether he used to eat his burgoo [oatmeal porridge] with his fingers or with a horn spoon? What are his debts and misery to us? Just

as if we cared whether his posteriors were covered with a pair of breeches or a kilt, or whether he was literally Sans culotte? In Great Britain...his barking might answer some purpose; there he was near the object of his fury; but here he is like a cur howling at the moon.[8]

But because Callender's life and times in Scotland and America throw so much powerful new light on nationalist opposition to the dominant ideology of the Scottish Enlightenment, the general milieu in which emerged both many Friends of the People and the United Scotsmen will need to be reconstructed.

The Enlightenment, the Class Struggle and the Genesis of Marxism.

Despite the apparent backwardness of eighteenth-century Scotland and the slower current of economic change by comparison with what was happening in England, Scotland played a much greater role in the genesis of classical Marxism than England. The eighteenth-century Scottish intellectuals were the precursors of nineteenth-century bourgeois ideology. They were not, however, the precursors of an independent Scottish Marxism. The Scots' role in the genesis of Marxism was inseparable from their major role in formulating British *laissez-faire* liberalism.

The Scottish Enlightenment intelligentsia made a huge contribution to the development of *laissez-faire* economics, the materialist conception of history, 'Marxist sociology', medicine, and much else. As J. F. C. Harrison explained:

> The intellectual renaissance in Scotland after 1745 produced a notable school of moral philosophers and political economists who were concerned to establish "an empirical basis for the study of man and society". In their discussions of human nature, social forces and institutions, economic processes and government all included in the omnibus category, moral philosophy - there emerged the beginnings of modern sociology and the social sciences.[9]

However, the almost immeasurable achievements of the proponents of the dominant ideology of the Scottish Enlightenment - an ideology challenged by Callender, the Friends of the People and the United Scotsmen - were shaped by the unique circumstances in which the Anglo-Scottish ruling class found themselves after 1745.

Despite the *Arguments Within English Marxism* between E. P. Thompson and Perry Anderson and others, they have, in defending 'the glorious English revolution' of 1688, lost sight of 'The Peculiarities of the Scots'.[10] Although English Marxist historians Thompson, Royden Harrison, Eric J. Hobsbawm and others have focused on the Scots enormous contribution to the development of modern British capitalism, they have had to ignore the negative anti-democratic features of the Enlightenment Scots in order to argue for the prominence of a 'democratic educational system' and so-called 'democratic intellect'. They have also failed to take sufficient account of the unique material milieu of eighteenth- and early nineteenth-century Scotland.

Nevertheless the crucially important Scottish Enlightenment played a major role in the genesis of some aspects of classical Marxism. For a small, poor and underpopulated country, the Scots achievements were outstanding. As John Merrington said:

> For the proponents of the new and revolutionary "conjectural" history of civil society - Adam Smith, Dugald Stewart, Adam Ferguson, John Millar - the origins of the division of labour and the market in the commercial stage of capitalist civilisation were to be sought in the separation of town and country. (The Highland-Lowland division in Scotland provided first-hand evidence).[11]

In circumstances where there have been very few Scottish Marxist scholars, the English Marxist historians have been more interested in the impact of the ideas of the Scottish Enlightenment on modern Britain than on the unique features of the history of Celtic Scotland.

In his path-breaking article on 'Capitalism and Agriculture: The Scottish Reformers of the Eighteenth Century', Eric Hobsbawm argued that the real significance of Adam Smith's seminal book *The Wealth of Nations* was that it became 'a handbook of [Scottish] development economics'. Moreover, the Scots became 'the pioneers of political economy, historical sociology and Scottish literature which virtually invented the "historical novel"'.[12] The Scottish contribution to the development of modern historiography was also formidable. But in challenging the dominant Scottish Enlightenment interpretation of Scottish history between 1688 and 1792, Callender's Scottish nationalist history of Britain was an implicit embarassment to the Whigs and later on the Stalinist historians of the Athens of the North.

Focusing on the really anti-Scottish Scottish Enlightenment intellectuals' development of their intense capitalist con- sciousness, Hobsbawm added that:

> In fact, they probably represent the first example, and one of the rare examples, of a bourgeoisie which was able to envisage its aims and historical function in these precise terms. It would even appear that the terms "feudal system" and "feudalism", as a description of a whole socio-economic legal and political order, were formulated by Scottish intellectuals in the course of their discussions.[13]

Unfortunately, none of the English Marxist or socialist historians has raised the question of if, when or where the class struggle so central to a Marxist interpretation of history fitted into the Scottish Enlightenment thinkers' conception of their own (as distinct from British) history.

In the extensive Scottish Enlightenment historiography, Callender was the only one who came near to recognising a class struggle in Scottish and British history after 1688. It was also significant that he wrote what was perhaps the most blistering critique of British imperialism in the whole of the eighteenth- or indeed nineteenth-centuries. While the dominant Scottish Enlightenment intellectuals like Millar criticised slavery, the slave trade, and the slavery of the colliers in the Lowlands, they stopped short of denouncing the murder of millions of Africans and Asians.

When he pinpointed what had happened at Glencoe, Callender placed the role of King William of Orange in murdering members of the MacDonald clan within the context of an evolving British imperialism. By French standards, the Scots intellectuals, including the Whigs, were less sympathetic towards the plebeian poor or emerging 'working class'. In his book *A Survey of Marxism*, A. James Gregor argued that a class struggle between the bourgeoisie and an embryonic 'working class' was already visible in eighteenth-century Europe. As he put it: 'Writers such as Quesnay, Voltaire, Rousseau, Helvetius, Mably, Raynal, Necker and Turgot among others, employed the class struggle as an explanatory device to render intelligible the political history of the period'. Furthermore, many French Enlightenment intellectuals were already in the 1770s predicting that 'the increasing misery of the working class would drive them to revolution'.[14]

But, although he died before open class struggles in Scotland became a critical problem for the Anglo-Scottish ruling class after 1789, Adam Smith was afraid of the latent class struggles that he saw around him. In a lecture on jurisprudence at the University of Glasgow during the session 1763-64, he asserted that 'Till there be property there can be no government, the very end of which is to secure wealth, and to defend the rich against the poor'.[15] When *The Wealth of Nations* was published in 1776, Smith offered a much fuller version of the role of the State in Scottish society:

> For one very rich man, there must be at least five hundred poor, and the affluence of the few supposes the indigence of the many. The affluence of the rich excites the indignation of the poor, who are often driven by want, and prompted by envy, to invade his possessions. It is only under the shelter of a civil magistrate that the owner of that property which is acquired by the labour of several years, or perhaps of many successive generations, can sleep a single night in security.[16]

Before he died in 1790, Scotland would begin to be torn asunder by bitter class struggles.

However, in some ways the most critical class struggle in Scotland in the 1790s was the struggle between the landed aristocracy and 'the men of trade'. The novel *Cyril Thornton* by the Scottish writer Thomas Hamilton - a writer who influenced Marx's ideas on the class struggle in nineteenth-century America - was described by Lewis S. Feuer as a talented portrayal of 'Scottish University life'.[17] Though the book was first published in 1829, Hamilton glanced back in *Cyril Thornton* to the University Callender attended in 1778:

There does, or perhaps rather there did, exist in Scotland a strong undisguised dislike between the landed and the mercantile interest. The former, of course, consider their trading rivals as being of an inferior caste... The latter feeling, if not the former, is not unreturned by the men of the trade, who profess themselves equal in all respects to their acred antagonists, and are little disposed to conciliate them by any supererogatory demonstration of respect. [18]

And since Callender obviously belonged to the ambiguous 'middle rank', he was destined to feel uncomfortable and ill at ease at the University of Edinburgh.

In Glasgow, too, there was a class struggle between the landed aristocracy and the mercantile interest before the outbreak of the French revolution. In his book *Glasgow* (1888), Andrew MacGeorge depicted the Glasgow of the 1770s and 1780s:

They [the Tobacco Lords] had a privileged walk at the Cross, which they trod arrayed in long scarlet cloaks and busy wigs; and such was the state of society then, that when any of the respectable master tradesmen of the city had occasion to speak to them, he required to walk on the other city of the street until he was fortunate enough to catch his eye, as it would have been a presumption to have made up to him. It was dangerous, indeed for a plebeian to quarrel with any of these magnates. From 1781, however, the growth and increased wealth created new conditions in which 'the middle class became more independent'.[19]

But the massive Tory witch-hunt of the 1790s crushed the confidence of the rising bourgeoisie.

In his important book *Popular Disturbances in Scotland, 1780-1815,* Kenneth Logue quoted an extract from a letter that Lord Dundonald had sent to the Lord Advocate in 1792: 'I do not my Lord heighten the picture of many of this Class of men, They are Enemies of subordination. So prevalent is the levelling spirit that few of the labourers or Tradesmen will diff [sic!] their Scots Bonnet or shew any Mark of Respect to those of the Higher Class. A spirit like this is not soon altered'.[20] By interpreting this letter solely as evidence of a class struggle between Dundonald's landed aristocracy and 'the workers', Logue was helping to obscure what Dundonal saw as the real conflict - the struggle between 'the Higher Class' of landed aristocrats and 'the men of the trade' or merchants.

It was the landed aristocracy who constituted 'the Higher Class'; and they were men like the feudal-minded Robert McQueen or Lord Braxfield, who dominated the Scottish Judiciary. When Dundonald published his *Description of the Estate of Culross* (1793), he was really attacking the Scottish Enlightenment Whig intellectuals (as distinct from the plebeian radicals) for contributing to 'the misguided frenzy of opinion' by 'making a bustle about the Slave Trade, Freedom, and the emancipation of the Negroes'. [21]

Class Struggles, The Retardation of Human Awareness, and a Tory 'Totalitarianism'

The struggle between the landed aristocracy and 'the men of the trade' was a critical factor in eighteenth-century Scottish history; and what made Callender such an important figure was that, in common with plebeian radicals like George Mealmaker and Angus Cameron, he tried to push the radical side of the bourgeois-democratic revolution to extreme egalitarian and Republican limits. [22]

However, it was the almost one-sided struggle between the landed aristocracy and the rising bourgeoisie which shaped future Scottish history after the outbreak of the French revolution. The Scots did not have their own Parliament in Edinburgh and, in contrast to the situation in London, the Judiciary in Edinburgh and Glasgow ruled the country by imposing 'the terrors of the law'. In the *Autobiography of a Scotch Gentleman* (1865), John H. Gray said:

> The members of the Bar in my day [i.e., the late eighteenth century] belonged to the families of the landed gentry, and many of them were eldest sons, and heirs to large fortunes... The Bar held in Scotland a very much higher social position than it held in England.[23]

The leading members of the feudal-minded aristocracy, though somewhat cynically loyal to the liberty established in England in 1688, were indifferent to 'the rule of law' in Scotland.

Through their dominance of the Judiciary, the landed aristocracy constituted the main arm of the State; and from 1789 they used their enormous power to tame the Whig intellectuals in the Scottish universities. As the guardians of 1688 and 1707, the Tory feudal landed aristocrats in the Judiciary interfered with the Whig intellectuals who were teaching free trade and the principles of liberal economics. As Dugald Stewart explained:

> The doctrine of Free Trade was itself presented as of a revolutionary tendency; and some who had formerly prided themselves on their zeal for the propagation of his [Adam Smith's] liberal system, began to call in question the expediency of subjecting to the disputations of philosophers the arena of State policy, and the unfathomable wisdom of the feudal ages.[24]

When they criticised the Stalinist version of the allegedly innate progressiveness of the process of industrialisation, Lewis Coser and Irving Howe wrote:

> From [the] process of social struggle rather than as an automatic corollary of industrialisation, the *great democratic triumphs* which we associate with the [late eighteenth and nineteenth centuries] were won. They came not simply because England was being industrialised; they came because the industrialisation was accompanied by a rich social history in which a vast growth of human awareness took place.[25]

Despite the importance of the Scottish Whig intellectuals' contribution to political economy, the materialist conception of history, 'Marxist sociology', etc., they contributed little to any awareness of the pre-conditions for human liberation. Contrary to Hobsbawm's inferences, the Scottish Whig intellectuals were no revolutionaries. Nonetheless the Scottish plebeian radicals like Callender were far in advance of their

English counterparts in developing a thorough and far-reaching critique of British imperialism.

Initially sympatheticic to the French revolution, Adam Ferguson, Dugald Stewart and John Millar caved in under crude and direct pressure from the Tories.[26] Professors like John Robinson at the University of Edinburgh and Henry Dundas, the Tory political manager, attacked the basic philosophy of the Whigs by arguing that circulating libraries were 'Nurseries of Sedition and Impiety'.[27] The Whigs believed in their ability to influence the 'lower orders' by means of circulating libraries, and, though resenting the 'brute force' on which the power of the dominant Tory faction rested, Stewart and the other Whigs were crushed and silenced. [28]

In 1793 the Senate of the University of Edinburgh sent a message of loyalty to King George III. Besides praising the English constitution established by 'the glorious revolution' of 1688, the Senate promised to labour 'with increased assiduity' to instil into their students 'just sentiments with respect to the nature of society'.[29] The bitter conflict in the University between the Tories and Whigs culminated in a 'species of proscription' being imposed on the discussion of 'political questions'.[30]

In 1794 Lord Craig and Lord Abercromby wrote private letters to Dugald Stewart in which they accused him of egging on the 'lower orders' by publishing his essay on 'the Use and Abuse of the General Principles of Politics'. In his reply to Craig, Stewart retracted a whole number of his public utterances. He also praised 'the peculiar excellencies of the *English* constitution of 1688' and expressed disapproval of 'sudden changes in established institutions'.[31] 'The Peculiarities of the Scots' in the eighteenth century were partly shaped by the Whig intellectuals' surrender to the Tories in the universities and the judiciary, the circumstances which forced John Millar to publish his pamphlets under a pseudonym marked the beginning of 'Alias MacAlias', the 'Caledonian Antisyzygy' and 'Dr. Jekyll and Mr. Hyde'.[32]

Unfortunately, the peculiarities of 'the ascendant class' in Scotland were hidden behind a new sleekitness and the Whigs could not display, in the words of John Stuart Mill, 'their [natural] feeling of class superiority'. In 1791 Stewart had gone to Paris 'where he harangued the mob in the streets *pour la libertee*'. [33] But within two years he had backed away from supporting the Revolution in France. So did Ferguson. It was, however, the sociological function of the historiography of the British Communist Party - and the New Left - to ignore Callender,

Mealmaker and Cameron and to portray Whigs like Millar as the pioneers of the early Scottish labour movement.

Concocting a very influential and enduring 'Marxist' interpretation of the Scottish Enlightenment, the Communist Party historians have helped to obscure the real history of plebeian radicalism. It was an interpretation born out of the Stalinists' preoccupations with the 'Popular Front' and the co-operation of all social classes in the 1930s and immediately after the Second World War; in accepting its main premises even historians like Thompson and Hobsbawm portayed the Scottish Whigs as revolutionaries.[34]

By insisting that Millar, a professor of law at the University of Glasgow, was a member of the Friends of the People in the 1790s, Roy Pascal and Ronald Meek actually helped to prevent the rediscovery of Callender. Indeed Meek asserted that: 'He [Millar] was a rather unorthodox left-wing Whig with Republican sympathies, who in every political crisis ranged himself on the side of the angels'.[35] A moment's reflection, or consideration of the Whig intellectuals' staunch support for 'the glorious revolution' of 1688, would have inhibited any description of Millar as a Republican.

Although he published the anonymous *Letters of Crito on the Causes, Objects and Consequences of the Present War* (1796) , Millar, though certainly the most left-wing of the Whig intellectuals, was no revolutionary, Republican or critic of the evolving capitalism. In spite of his very real differences with Tories like Braxfield, he shared the attitudes of the Scottish Whigs about the importance of developing capitalist 'common sense' and the use of circulating libraries and education to inculcate the principles of thrift, industry and obedience in the 'lower orders'.[36] To Smith, Hume, Lord Kames, Ferguson, Stewart and Millar any notion of 'Scottish democracy' or a 'democratic intellect' would have been anathema. Many years before the French revolution Hume had summed up the collective viewpoint of the Scottish Whigs:

> Nothing appears more suprising to those, who consider human affairs with a philosophical eye, than the easiness with which the many are governed by the few; and the implicit submission, with which men resign their own sentiments and passions to those of their rulers. When we enquire by what means this wonder is effected, we shall find, that, as FORCE is always on the side of the

governed, the governors have nothing to support them but opinion. It is therefore on opinion only that government is founded; and this maxim extends to the most despotic and most military governments, as well as to the most free and most popular. [37]

An opponent of democracy, who would not have rejected any idea of totalitarianism, Hume did not live long enough to see a form of 'totalitarianism' imposed on Scotland in the 1790s.[38]

Side by side with their assault on the dominant feudal cast of mind of Scottish society with its lingering egalitarianism, the great Scottish Enlightenment intelligentsia, whether Whig or Tory, tried to de-radicalise the plebeian radicals' agitation for massive reform and a redistribution of income. Since they tried to eradicate any class struggle between the rich and the poor, they could not even acknowledge Callender's contrary interpretation of Scottish history. The recent scholarship of Michael Ignatieff, Norbert Waszek and other non-Marxist historians has refuted the myth that Whigs like Millar were the precursors of the early Scottish labour movement. As Ignatieff argued: 'Dugald Stewart, the teacher of James Mill and the *Edinburgh Review* generation, was perhaps the most forward in looking to the diffusion of the true principles of political economy as a means of pacifying and calming the turbulence of the masses'.[39]

In the anonymous letters of Crito, Millar explained why he had regarded the French revolution as a progressive historical development comparable to the English revolution of 1688: 'The French revolution, which took place in 1789, was not hostile to Kingly government. It went no further than to establish a limited constitutional monarchy.'[40] Distancing himself from the real Friends of the People like Thomas Muir of Huntershill and Callender without mentioning them by name, Millar explained that he had turned against the Revolution in France as soon as the Jacobins began to 'equalise the different ranks, to expel or extinguish the superior class of inhabitants, and to annihilate every monument or vestige of the ancient distinctions'.[41] Unlike Callender, Millar had no historical awareness of the primitive communism surviving in Scotland and depicted by informed writers and historians like Peter Kropotkin.[42]

Unlike Callender, Millar criticised the slavery of 'the Negroes' and the Scottish colliers in his book *Observations on the Distinctions of Ranks in Society* (1806) without criticising the role of British imperialism in Africa, Asia or Scotland. Before any other scholar or historian, George Lichtheim (1969) emphasised the role of the Scottish Enlightenment intellectuals in developing 'a naive doctrine of social harmony arising spontaneously through the liberation of private initiative'.[43]

More recently, Ignatieff has refuted all the romantic and un-historic nonsense about Millar and the other Scottish Whigs (as distinct from the Friends of the People and the United Scotsmen) being either 'unorthodox left-wing Whigs', 'Republicans' or political activists who were on the side of the plebeian radical 'angels'. Reconstructing the role of the dominant Scottish Enlightenment intelligentsia, Norbert Waszek wrote:

> Social inequality, as Smith and Ferguson insist, is fostered by the division of labour. The wealth that results from the division of labour is unevenly distributed... Although this may sound like an anticipation of Marx's theory of exploitation, the Scots were no revolutionaries, but considered the problems as resolvable within the existing social structure.[44]

But these problems could only be resolved through the Whigs' control of the educational system from top to the bottom.

After the Tory witch-hunt in the universities and the use of the judiciary to crush the plebeian radicals, the Whig intellectuals, including the extreme left-wing Millar, did not deviate from their project of resolving social problems and class conflict within the established social order. As Ignatieff explained:

> Yet Millar could not be called a Jacobin. Medick does pay attention to his repeated disavowal of forcible "levelling", but he misses his emphatic endorsement of "our mixed constitution", his rejection of Cartwright's manhood suffrage in the lectures and his condemnation of Paine's atheism. Indeed, he conceived of the enfranchisement of artisans as a "solid refutation of popular doctrines then afloat", as a strategy of conciliation to "rally

the great body of the [British] nation around the constitution.[45]

However, Callender was an extreme Jacobin leveller and Scottish nationalist. But, unlike Callender, none of the Scottish Whig intellectuals were interested in Scotland's distinctive history or national oppression. Refuting all the accumulated and almost immovable historiography of the Comunnist Party of Great Britain, Ignatieff has removed the walls of the perceptional prison blinding us to the reality of a Scottish national plebeian radicalism during the first phase of the Industrial Revolution in Scotland. Summing up what Millar was about, Ignatieff wrote: 'Millar's was not a social vision of reform, an artisanal Republic, but a narrowly political reformism, aiming at maintaining the constitutional balance between the executive and legislative achievement of 1688'. [46] Yet there was no doubt that Millar and Callender associated with each other before the latter was forced to escape from Scotland.

Callender, Enlightenment Edinburgh and the Origins of his Disaffection

The disputes that Callender's had been involved in at the University of Edinburgh in 1778 and the High Court in 1792, when he was falsely accused of blaming Lord Gardenstone for the authorship of The Political Progress of Britain, were to plague him for the duration of his short exile in America between 1793 and 1803. When his dispute with Dr. Cullen was being used against him in America, he wrote in an undated letter of 1801:

> Perhaps it was Mr. Wagner, who, had at an early period, made himself very busy with my name. He circulated a report that I had behaved villainously in Scotland. Mr. F. Mulenberg, sent for me, and told me the particulars and gave Wagner as his author. I had luckily preserved some Scots letters, which explained the manner in which I parted with Gardenstone, the matter referred to. I did not, until some time after, know the original author of the story. It was one John Millar, whose lady, a daughter of Dr. Cullen, took this dirty method of

81

revenging an attack which I had, fifteen years before, made upon the quack synopsis of her father, when I was attending a medical class. The bad health of my family prevented me, at the time, from waiting upon Wagner, to whom I am personally a stranger; and Millar, who is long ago stiff, was always exceedingly smooth to my face.[47]

If Callender was hypersensitive about his 'plebeian' background, he made and kept powerful connections in Edinburgh and Glasgow.

Always a controversial figure within the militant and carnaptious Scottish nationalist and radical tradition, Callender was already in 1782 a gifted pamphleteer. An intuitive leveller, he did not share James Boswell's elitist and Unionist admiration for Dr. Samuel Johnson. It was the latter who told Boswell: 'You are to consider that it is our duty to maintain the subordination of civil society; and where there is a gross or shameful deviation from rank, it should be punished so as to deter others from the same perversion'.[48] But Callender was not cowed or intimidated by the great English writer; and one of the most interesting features of Callender's anonymous pamphlet *The Deformities of Dr. Samuel Johnson* was his admission that he did not belong to the polite middle-class culture *of belles-letters*. As he put it:

> It will be demanded why a private individual, without interest or connections, presumes to interfere in the quarrels of the learned? But when the most shameless of mankind is hired to abuse the characters of his countrymen, to blast the reputations of the living and the dead; when such a tool is employed for such purpose, that those who are insulted cannot with propriety stoop to a reply - Then the highest degree of goodness may degenerate into the lowest degree of weakness, silence becomes approbation, and tenderness and delicacy deserve different names.

Motivated by Scottish nationalism, an embryonic plebeian radicalism and Johnson's ignorance of Gaelic poetry, Callender criticised the Englishman's 'dishonesty, pride, vulgarity [and] prejudice' against the Scots. Then he attacked Johnson for being the patron of this poor scribbler William Shaw and concluded that: 'From this single circumstance, Dr. Johnson stands convicted of an illiberal intention to deceive'.[49] An interesting aspect of the angry reaction in the *Critical Review* was the assertion that 'the pamphlet... is apparently written by some angry Caledonian, who, warmed with the deepest resentment for some real or supposed injury, gives vent to his indignation, and treats every part of Dr. Johnson's character with the utmost asperity'.[50]

In the second anonymous pamphlet, *A Critical Review of the Works of Dr. Samuel Johnson*, published in 1783, Callender exhibited tremendous confidence when he wrote: 'The author of the present trifle was last year induced to publish a few remarks on the writings of Dr. Samuel Johnson. Like the former essay, these pages will endeavour to ascertain the genuine importance of Dr. Johnson's literary character'.[51] For it was not the polite world of middle-class culture that caused offense and outrage in 1782 and 1783, but the intervention of a Scottish nationalist plebeian writer who challenged aspects of English cultural imperialism. And the genuine outrage felt by Callender's contemporaries led writers like Ford and G. J. Kolb and J. E. Congleton (1971) to depict him as 'a Scots master of scurrility and a vicious scandalmonger on both sides of the Atlantic'.[52] To see Callender in a wider historical perspective, however, it should not be forgotten that (1) Jefferson described him as 'a man of genius', and (2) English plebeian radicals like Thomas Paine were similiarly attacked by the polite literary journals and magazines.

Callender began to work as a sub-clerk in the Sasine Office, Edinburgh, in 1782, the year when he published his first (anonymous) pamphlet on *The Deformities of Dr. Samuel Johnson*. When he was appointed a messenger-at-arms on 29 March 1789, he was already a well-established clerk with a reputation in Edinburgh as a writer and poet. Outspoken, carnaptious and disaffected from the established social order, he was friendly with Gardenstone, Lord Kames, Lady Henderson and other members of the 'higher ranks'.[53]

In most of the surviving private letters to his 'superiors', including Andrew Stuart, the Keeper of the Sasine Register and later on the American 'Jacobin' Thomas Jefferson, Callender displayed the contradictory qualities of obsequiousness *and* outspokenness. He was a most unusual man, and he would display the typical characteristics of successive Scottish radicals.

As a clerk in the Sasine Office in 1789, Callender witnessed the corrupt practices of some of his fellow clerks and sub-clerks. The letters designed to expose corruption were just as interesting for what they revealed about his complex character. When he wrote to Stuart on 5 December 1789, he said: 'I venture to plead for some indulgence as having literally, though unintentionally, risked my life to serve you'. After detailing the extensive corruption in preparing and keeping the Register of Sasine, he informed Stuart that: 'It was originally intended to print this letter and sell it for a shilling a copy in the Parliament House. The obvious consequence of this measure must be the annihilation of the General Register. The conduct would at once have been unjust and unfair'. [54] Although Stuart's replies to Callender have not survived, he did not suffer for his outspokenness.

On 19 December 1789, in the year of the French revolution, he again wrote to Stuart to complain about an official in the Sasine Office:

> There is not an assistant clerk about the Sasine office who has not heard him [Steele] solimnly [sic!] vow my destruction. If I had followed the dictates of resentment I had easily got him secured. For his own clerk would attest to his ringing pistols in his pocket to the office. But I considered that you would soon be in town, and that it was better to keep out of the way. And let the quarrel expire in silence. [55]

An interesting feature of those letters to Stuart was Callender's occasional spelling mistakes and the odd ugly phrase.

Despite being noticed by A. and E. G. Porritt just after the beginning of this century, Callender has attracted surpringly little or no attention from historians (except a few American literary historians). In his book *Artisans and Sans-Culottes*, the Welsh historian Gwyn Williams (1968) made a brief reference to Callender's 'Scottish Republican tract'. [56] Then in 1975, Andrew Hook, a Scottish literary historian, asserted that:

> A man named James Thomas [sic!] Callender was suspected, but he denied all connection with the work and tried to incriminate Lord Gardenstone, then the one judge in the Court of Sessions sympathetic to the reform movement. At this point, James Anderson identified Callender as the author of the articles. [57]

The truth was that Gardenstone, who had been friendly with him from 1787, accused and identified Callender as the author of 'the wicked and seditious' booklet.[58]

But in private Robert Dundas, the Tory 'Dictator' of Scotland, informed the Home Office in London that Callender had 'absconded' on the morning of 2nd January 1793. He also insisted that, in spite of Gardenstone's denial, 'I have still my own suspicions he is the man'.[59] Even more interestingly, in his 'precognition' or preliminary examination by the legal authorities in Edinburgh, Gardenstone said that he had become friendly with Callender in 1787 and had 'conceived a favourable opinion of his *genius* after perusal of some poetry composed by him'.[60] But, although none of the poems has been handed down to posterity, Callender did bequeath to his fellow Scots his very important *The Political Progress of Britain*.

It was clear from the *Minute Book of the High Court of Judiciary* that Braxfield was indifferent to the Scottish nationalism expressed in Callender's booklet. In his own handwriting, however, Braxfield singled out the denunciation of British imperialism abroad and a handwritten note by Callender at the bottom of page 23 of 'the said wicked and seditious pamphlet', where he had written: 'What our most excellent Constitution may be in theory I neither know nor care. In practice, it is altogether a conspiracy of the Rich against the Poor.'[61]

On 28 January 1793, Walter Berry, bookseller, South Bridge Street, Edinburgh, James Robertson, bookseller and printer in the Housewynd of Edinburgh and James Thomson Callender were cited by Robert MacQueen or Braxfield for 'the crimes of writing, printing, publishing and circulating a seditious pamphlet'. Then Robertson was sentenced to six months in jail; Berry was sentenced to three months in jail; and Callender was sentenced to 'fugitation and outlawry'.[62] (Although he had been made a fugitive from the law, he was welcomed in America as a hero). But, although *The Political Progress of Britain* was frequently quoted at the later trial of Thomas Muir of Huntershill, Scottish and British historians have shown surprisingly little interest in the Scottish-International Jacobin who had been far to the left of Muir or Millar.

The Plebeian Radicals' Hidden Scottish Nationalism and Critique of Imperialism

Those English historians the Porritts did not know any more about Callender than did the American editor who published the correspondence between Thomas Jefferson and Callender. As the Porritts put it:

> Unscrupulous as Mr. Worthington C. Ford's sketch of Callender shows him to have been, Callender was not without insight and discernment, and his characterisation of 1792 was an apt and truthful picture of Scotch representation [in Parliament] from the Union of 1707 until 1832.[63]

When they depicted the relatively historical egalitarian Scottish background which engendered *The Political Progress of Britain*, A. and E. G. Porrit, wrote:

> Before Scotland came into the Union, its Parliament had established an excellent system of poor relief. It had provided an effective remedy against the evils of arbitary or illegal imprisonment. It has established a complete and universal system of public instruction; introduced a humane but effective system of criminal law; awarded to all prisoners the right of being defended by counsel; provided for the protection of the poor in litigation against the rich.[64]

Almost a century before the Porritts' book on *The Unreformed House of Commons* was published, Jefferson wrote a private letter to the American politician Monroe to inform him that: 'I knew him first as the author of *The Political Progress of Britain*, a work I had read with great satisfaction, and as a fugitive from persecution for this very work. I gave to him from time to time such aids as I could afford, merely as a man of genius suffering under persecution'.[65] And whatever his precise faults were, Callender was made to suffer for his critique of the foreign policy and imperialism of Britain between 1688 and his death in 1803.

The very hostile attitudes of conservative Americans, and of pro-English chauvinsts in America like William Cobbett, resulted in Callender's importance in Scottish history being expunged from the historiography of modern Britain. When he was remembered at all, he was always portrayed in a negative way. But in spite of the grudging and unsympathetic vignette of Callender in *The Unreformed House of Commons*, the Porritts admitted to his grasp of politics. As they put it:

> Callender, who had lived in Edinburgh, and may not inaptly be termed a Radical - for, apart from his political bent as a Parliamentary reformer, he had some of the qualities which made many eighteenth-century Radicals distrusted - evidently understood the Scotch electoral system and its workings...Callender's first published his pamphlet in 1792. Soon afterwards he was compelled to leave Edinburgh for the United States, to escape prosecution for the opinions to which he had given expression. There, of all the foreigners who were connected with American journalism at the beginning of the nineteenth century, Callender was 'easily first in the worst qualities of mind and character'.[66]

Unfortunately, the Porritts did not analysis the contents of Callender's important booklet or his critique of the evil consequences of 1688 and 1707 for subsequent Scottish history.

The Political Progress of Britain was a remarkable and well-documented analysis of British history between 1692 and 1792 interspersed with frequent glances back to 1688, and with occasional backward-looking glances to much earlier periods. Drawing on existing British historiography, political commentary and literature, this eighty-page booklet of some 40,000 words was both nationalist and internationalist. Criticising British imperialism everywhere, Callender wrote: 'In the wars of 1689 and 1702, this country was neither more nor less a hobby horse for the Emperor and the Dutch. The Rebellion in 1715 was excited by the despotic insolence of the Whigs'.[67]

In his brief introduction to a booklet designed to 'prove the ruinous consequences of the popular System of War and Conquest', Callender was quite modest when he said:

> The style of this work is concise and plain; and it is hoped that it will be found sufficiently respectful to all parties. The question to be decided is, are we to proceed with the war system? Are we, in the

progress of the nineteenth century, to embrace five thousand fresh taxes, to squander a second five hundred millions Sterling, and to extirpate twenty million people?[68]

Denouncing British imperialism root-and-branch, Callender anticipated John Galt's refutation of propaganda about English liberty and 'the free-born Englishman'. But he went much further than Galt would ever do by focusing on the 'dialectic' of English liberty at home and imperialism abroad. As he put it:

> At home Englishmen admire liberty; but abroad, they have always been harsh masters. Edward the First conquered Wales and Scotland, and at the distance of five hundred years, his name is yet remembered in both countries with extreme horror. His actions are shaded by a degree of infamy uncommon even in the ruffian catalogue of English Kings.[69]

In a direct reference to King William of Orange, he said: 'I pass over the tragedies of Glencoe and Darien, for, on such a character, they reflect no particular reproach'.[70]

In a comment that would set at least part of the Scottish radicals' agenda for a long time afterwards, Callender wrote:

> There is a cant expression in this country, that our Government is deservedly the wonder and envy of the world. With better reason it may be said, that Parliament is a mere outwork of the Court, a phalanx of mercenaries embattled against the reason, the happiness, and the liberty of mankind. The game laws, the dog act, the shop tax, the window tax, the attorney tax, and a thousand others, give us a right to wish that their authors had been hanged.[71]

An interesting feature of his pamphlet is the admission that he had known and had disagreed with Adam Smith's interpretation of British history while admiring the latter's dislike of war.[72]

In the long opening paragraph of *The Political Progress of Britain*, Callender wrote:

> Within the last hundred years of our history, Britain has been five times at war with France, and six times at war with Spain. During the same period, she has engaged in two rebellions at home, besides an endless catalogue of massacres in Asia and Africa. In Europe, the common price which we advance for a war, has extended from one to three hundred thousand lives, and from sixty to a hundred and fifty millions Sterling. From Africa, we import annually between thirty and forty thousand slaves, which rises in the course of a century to at least three millions of murthers [murders]. In Bengal only, we destroyed or expelled within the short period of six years, no less than five millions of an industrious and harmless people; and as we have been sovereigns in that country for thirty-five years, it may be reasonably computed, that we have strewed the plains of Indostan, with fifteen or twenty million of carcases.[73]

No one attempted to refute his facts or his interpretation of the role of British/English imperialism in Asia, Africa, Scotland, Wales or Ireland; and his stress on the difference between 'English liberty' and Scottish oppression was highlighted by the fact that the Scottish radicals did not have the freedom to express their own views in pamphlets or speech.

But his most salient points and powerful arguments for breaking-up the Union of 1707 were expressed in the opening first chapter. With fierce clarity and passion, he asserted that:

> The people of Scotland are, on all occasions, foolish enough to interest themselves in the good or bad fortune of an English Minister; though it does not not appear that we have more influence with such a Minister, than with the Cabinet of Japan. To England we were for many centuries a hostile, and we still are considered by them as a foreign, and

in effect a conquered nation. It is true, that we elect very nearly a twelfth part of the British House of Commons; but our representatives have no title to vote, or act in a separate body. Every statute proceeds upon the majority of the voices of the whole compound Assembly: What, therefore, can forty.-five persons accomplish, when opposed to five hundred and thirteen? They feel the total insignificance of their situation, and behave accordingly. An equal number of elbow chairs, placed once for all on the Ministerial benches, would be less expensive to Government, and just as manageable. I call these, and every Ministerial tool of the same kind, expensive, because those who range themselves under the banners of opposition, can only be considered, as having rated their voices too high for a purchaser in the Parliamentary auction. [74]

Scottish nationalist, Jacobin leveller, internationalist and already a supporter of the 'upstart' American Republicans, Callender was forced to leave Edinburgh and made his way 'with some difficulty' to Philadelphia with his wife and children.

The America Years: The Conflict between Callender and William Cobbett

In 1792 Cobbett settled in America, where he published pro-British pamphlets under the pseudonym of 'Peter Porcupine'. Before returning to England in 1800 to become a Tory journalist, he was very assiduous in his attacks on the radicals. From his conversion to *a very English* radicalism in 1804 until his death in 1835, he was regarded as a man of the Left. But, although the third edition of the *Oxford Companion to English Literature* (1946) descibes him as 'arrogant and quarrelsome', historians have ignored his persistent English chauvinism and imperialist attitudes.[75]

When he settled in America a year before Callender, Cobbett was assured of greater material and moral support than Callender could have expected. From the perspective of the class struggle, late-eighteenth-century America was not too different from the Scotland he had fled from. Offering a social picture of America at that time, the American historian W. E. Woodward wrote:

> The country had become an oligarchy, with wealth and land as the determining factors of leadership. Only a small faction of the male population could qualify as voters. The men elected to all important offices were either men of wealth or they possessed a far-reaching influence among the wealthy. The poor - the farm hands, the mechanics of the towns and cities, the clerks in the shops - none of these had anything to say about the problems of the nation, the state, or the city. Trade unions were forbidden by law, and there was no regulation of working hours or living conditions.[76]

The Revolution had been transformed by a Counter-Revolution; and it was not the American Revolution but the Counter-Revolution that gradually began to 'devour the children' of the international Revolution such as Callender.

When the anti-slavery clause was struck out of the American Declaration of Independence in 1776, it was a portent of what was yet to come.[77] Unlike Callender and Paine, Thomas Jefferson was not hostile to the institution of 'Negro slavery'. To Paine's mind whites and 'Negroes' were equals; and Paine's biographer Moncure D. Conway speculated about how 'Paine got along with his friend Jefferson, who, at the time of the French revolution, had a slave in his house at Challiot'.[78]

Like Cobbett, Callender was also quarrelsome and highly principled. Unlike Cobbett, Callender was forced to earn a living in a very hostile milieu. It was not, however, Callender's quarrelsome nature that drew so much hatred towards him; it was rather his extreme radical ideas. Despite what Jefferson's conservative critics said about his alleged 'Jacobinism', he was really a cautious politician. For example, when the American Congress debated in March 1790 a petition from the Anti-Slavery Society, signed by Benjamin Franklin, Jefferson, in Conway's phrase, 'had no word to say for it'. Summing up the consequence of this debate in Congress, Conway said:

Thenceforth slavery had become a suppressed subject, and the slave trade, whenever broached in Congress, had maintained its immunity. In 1803, even under Jefferson's administration, the Negroes fleeing from oppression in Domingo were forbidden asylum in America, because it was feared they would incite servile insurrections'.[79]

Identified with the struggles of the losers of history, Callender was destined for a tragic end.

From his arrival in America in 1793, Callender earned his living by reporting the proceedings of Congress for the *Philadelphia Gazette*. By 1795 bitter political disputes in Congress between the conservative Federalists and some 'extreme Republicans' led to him being edged out of his job as a reporter. Although he had many enemies among the pro-British Federalists, it was Cobbett, the English chauvinst, who set out to hound and harry the Scottish Republican Jacobin.[80]

In 1795 Callender published the first of several American editions of *The Political Progress of Britain*. It was quickly 'answered' by the famous pamphlet *A Bone to Gnaw* (1795) by 'Porcupine' or Cobbett. Worried by the circulation of Callender's pamphlet in and through the English radical groups, Cobbett made sure that a third English edition of his pamphlet was issued later on in 1795.[81] Considering the brilliance and sophistication of Callender's historical and political analysis of Cobbett's British/English imperialism and the stridency of the response, the mystery of Callender's extirpation from Anglo-American historiography remains almost inexplicable.

Motivated by the negotiations over Jay's Treaty between the British and the Americans, Cobbett's pamphlet was exceptionally important because of the threat posed to British/English imperialism. [82] Unlike Scotland, where uncomfortable arguments could be met by charging radicals with sedition and treason, the powerful conservatives forces in America could not ignore the criticisms of the *Brits* by men like Callender. Acknowledging the importance of the negotiations over Jay's Treaty, Cobbett's biographer G. Spater said: 'The ostensible reason for Cobbett's essay was the publication in Philadelphia of *The Political Progress of Britain*, the work of James Callender, an earnest [radical] democrat who had recently fled to America from England [sic!]'. [83]

In her book *Cobbett in America*, M. E. Clark also describes Callender as 'another Englishman'.[84] Quoting Cobbett's own words that *A Bone to Gnaw* was 'a little rambling tract which never would have been written but with a design of decrying the republication of a most detestable British publication', Clark was much more generous in her assessment of Cobbett than in her treatment of Callender and his works. But she did admit that in a pamphlet issued by *The Philadelphia Jockey-Club* in the summer of 1795, Cobbett had been accused of displaying 'the avowed character of a British agent'.[85] In England and America, unlike Scotland, Callender's arguments and critique of imperialism had to be answered with counter-arguments.

In *A Bone to Gnaw*, Cobbett identified Callender as a part of an international Jacobin conspiracy against the established social order. Denouncing the radical programme represented by the Jacobins in America, he referred to the mania reformatio... if this malady is not stopped at once, by the help of a hempen neck-lace, or some remedy equally efficacious, it never fails to break out into Atheism, Robbery, Unitarianism, Swindling, Jacobinism, Massacres, Civic Feasts and Insurrections. Now, it appears to me, that our unfortunate Author, must be affected with this dreadful malady...[86]

Attempting to blacken Callender's name and character, Cobbett used a rhetoric lacking the relative grace of Callender's writing by asserting that:

> Let this be a warning to you, all you understrappers of Democratic Clubs; leave off your bawling and your toasting, go home and sell your sugar and your snuff, and leave the care of "Posterity" to other heads; for when the hour of discomfort arrives, your Jack Straws and your C. Foxes will leave you in the lurch.[87]

But, although 'Porcupine' was attacking Jacobin levelling in general, he set out to make life difficult for the radical Scot. To make his own motives clear, he wrote: 'Ah! Mr. Author of *The Political Progess*; you think I have forgotten you, I did not like you, bring my pamphlet ready fabricated, from Scotland'.[88]

However, Callender should not be seen as a deviant or isolated Scottish radical in exile, though he was already to the Left of the other exiled Scottish radicals in America. He still represented a significant current of radical opinion, and his opinions close to Paine's. Although Paine did not return to America until 1802, he had had his *Open Letter to George Washington* published in Philadelphia in 1796. Full of foreboding and disappointment about the course of the American revolution, he said:

> Monopolies of every kind marked your administration in the moment of its commencement. The lands obtained by the Revolution were lavished upon partisans; the interest of the disbanded soldier was sold to the speculator, injustice was acted under the pretence of faith; and the chief of the army became the patron of the fraud.[89]

Too radical in a Scotland that had been almost 'totalitarian', Callender was too radical for the exiled Scottish radicals in America. Unlike them, he was a poor man who had difficulty earning a crust.

Embittered by the progressive Americans' failure to secure him a job as a schoolmaster or a postmaster, Callender wrote to James Madison in May 1796:

> It is very long since I envied the independence of a journeyman carpenter. But I am now in my thirty-ninth year, with a wife and four young children; and it is too late to think of anything of the sort by at least a dozen years.[90]

Depicting the exiled British radicals in America, Gwyn Williams said:

> They were active in the liberty settlements, British-Republican Sparta in New York state, Welsh Beula, the new Scotland that the son of John Millar tried to create. They were so concentrated in key areas that one Federalist asserted that Jefferson's [Presidental] victory and the "revolution" of 1800 was their doing. [91]

The new Scotland that Millar's son was trying to reproduce in America was light-years away from Callender's Jacobin vision of the existing world turned upside down.

94

Nor could Callender have fitted into the communities of most of the exiled Scottish and Irish radicals. Alienated from them by his egalitarian politics, he was still further separated from them by his awful poverty. The gulf between Millar and Callender can be detected in the letter that Archibald Rowan, the exiled United Irishman, sent to his wife in Ireland from Wilmington, on the Delaware, in 1796:

> Mr. Millar, the son of Professor Millar of Glasgow, who was introduced to me in Scotland by Thomas Muir, is concerned with a Scottish company, who have made a large purchase of lands here, and would be glad to induce persons who were known, to be among the first settlers.[92]

Millar died in America a few months later; but Cobbett was still making life exceptionally difficult for Callender.

Earning an inadequate living by school-teaching and journalism after his dismissal from the *Philadelphia Gazette*, Callender was employed by Matthew Carey to prepare and write manuscript entries for *Guthrie's Geographical Grammar*.[93] Journalist and pamphleteer, Callender had a passion for historical research and writing. During the few years between 1796 and Jefferson's election to the Presidency in 1800, he was financed by Jefferson. From 1796, when he published his *American Historical Register or Historical Memoirs of the United States for the year 1796*, Jefferson funded his publications to a limited extent.[94]

Making enemies by publishing another *American Historical Register* for the year 1798, Callender attracted even more enemies from the conservatives' ranks, including Cobbett. This was when his real personal troubles began; and his *Register* was denounced as 'the veriest catchpenny that ever was published, the mere tittle-tattle of Jacobinism'.[95] Cobbett began to help the continuing campaign to victimise and persecute him; and in 1797 Callender and Paine were listed as the legatees of Porcupine's Will. Indeed, in the *Political Censor* for April 1797, Cobbett wrote:

> My friend J. T. Callender, the runaway from Scotland,... as a particular mark of attention, I will and bequeath him twenty feet of pine plank, which I request my executors to see made into a pillory,

to be kept for his particular use till a gibbett can be prepared.

(Equally hostile to Paine, he wrote: 'Tom Paine...I bequeath a strong hempen collar, as the only legacy I can think of that is worthy of him').[96]
Though *carnaptious* or quarrelsome and prickly, Callender was no worse than Cobbett. Besides, when he was still on friendly terms with Jefferson in October 1798, he wrote thus:

> I am sure you will be shocked to hear the treatment I have met with even from men, whom I really consider good men. For instance, Mr. Giles, in Congress, made a splendid reference to the esteem in which Muir and Palmer were held in America; vid., debate on Democratic Societies. I was their intimate friend, and quite as deep in the unlucky business as they were.[97]

The exceptionally bitter class struggles of the 1790s would soon result in the Alien and Sedition Acts.

The Alien and Sedition Acts and the Demise of Callender

The anti-Jacobin Acts of 1798 were designed to get at the French, Irish and Scottish Jacobins in America, and especially the Republican and 'intemperate' Jacobin newspapers engaged in the sustained criticisms of the Federalists. The Acts were used to punish the critics of President Adams, while the Federalists' unending attack on Vice-President Jefferson were ignored. [98] Since Callender was a particular target for the Federalists, Cobbett joined in the witch-hunt against him.

The American historian John Spencer Bassett has argued that the Alien and Sedition Acts developed out of 'a momentary hysteria, not incomparable to that which produced the Salem persecutions for witchcraft'. [99] In the view of the Welsh historian Gwyn Williams, the Acts of 1798 were directed against the Jacobin artisans as much as against the Irish:

> Most were artisans... Federalists hated them, and the Alien and Sedition Acts were directed as much against them as as against the Irish. Cobbett in

Philadelphia, then a scurrilous Tory was apoplectic about them, accusing Daniel Isaac Eaton of taking a squaw - a "yellow-hided frow" - and gloating over Citizen Richard Lee's imprisonment. [100]

When he published the second part of his *A Bone to Gnaw* (1797), Cobbettt contributed to the witch-hunt against Callender by emphasising his hostility to British/English imperialism. Accusing Callender of advocating Revolution everywhere and of predicting the decline of Britain as a world power, Cobbett asked his American readers to 'suppose Bradford, the Wat Tyler of the West, were to go over to London, and write a *Political Progress of America*, foretelling the dissolution of the Union, would he not deserve a horse-whip in place of encouragement?' [101] Contributing an article to the *Gazette* in November 1797, he described his Scottish opponent as a 'little reptile, who from outward appearances, seems to have been born for a chimney-sweep'. But what really got under his skin was Callender's 'most audacious libels on the British Ministry and every branch of the Royal Familiy.' [102]

Then, in the second part of *A Bone to Gnaw* (1797), Cobbett could not conceal his hatred for the Scot's nationalist radicalism:

> ...the reader has seen to what advantage they turned the apostate paw of a mountaineer from Scotland, and he cannot but have observed what a considerable part these persecuted emigrants have borne in all the violent abuse that has poured out against the Federal government for two years past. [103]

This was a reference to the United Irishmen - and for the remainder of his life, Cobbett would continue to express his hatred of the Scots and the Irish. In an article in the *Philadelphia Gazette* in September 1798, he again gloated over the tragic fate of the Scottish radical:

> ..he [Callender]...took shelter under the disgraceful roof of the abandoned hireling editor of the *Aurora*: while in his employment, he buried a poor, abused, broken-hearted wife, who left behind her a family of ragged, half-starved children, to be sent to the

poor-house...the wretch has a most thief-like look;
he is ragged, dirty, has a downcast with his eyes,
leans his head towards one side, as if his neck had
a stretch, and goes along with evident signs of
anger against his flees and lice.[104]

But, although most American historians past and present have
approved of Cobbett's nasty rhetoric against the Republican Callender,
Worthington C. Ford complained because Cobbett (1796) described
an American thus: 'That lump of walking tallow, streaked with lamp-
black, that calls itself Samuel F. Bradford, has the impudence to say
that my wardrobe consisted of my old regimentals'. [105]

Despite the hostile and one-sided remarks made about Callender by
Jefferson's many biographers, he was seen in 1800 as the victim of the
continuing witch-hunt against all radicals. Jefferson had financed his
book *The Prospect Before Us* (1800). By attacking the conservative
Alexander Hamilton, one of the founding fathers of the Revolution,
for engaging in 'improper pecuniary speculation', he helped to get
Jefferson elected as the President in 1801.[106] He was tried under the
Alien and Sedition Acts for publishing *The Prospect Before Us*, and was
jailed as a result of a rigged trial. He became 'a popular martyr' - the
voice of the poor and the disaffected.[107]

Overlooking the very real factors responsible for Callender's
embitterment, most American historians have dismissed him without
offering a *social picture* of American capitalism at that time. As one of
the few historians who considered Callender's trial at Richmond in
1800 at all objectively, John Spencer Bassett said: 'Judge Chase ruled
so partially that the lawyers for the defence, one of whom was the
young William Wirt, gave up their case, protesting that their client could
not get justice.' When he became President, Jefferson declared the Alien
and Sedition Acts null and void, issued Callender a pardon and
remission of the fine of $200.[108] Foreshadowing what was yet to come,
Jefferson had written a private letter to the radical Scot in which he
said: 'A period is now approaching during which I shall discontinue
writing letters as much as possible, knowing that every snare will be
used to get hold of what may be perverted in the eyes of the public'.[109]

Even so, Callender was always a *carnaptious* Scottish radical - the
first of a long line of similar characters. Clearly, there were grievances
and faults on both sides. Offering the usual anti-Callender comments,
Jefferson's biographer Merrill D. Peterson wrote: 'Expecting to be

rewarded for his past services - crowned for martyrdom - he [Callender] at once cast covetous eyes on the Richmond Post Office'. But Jefferson appointed 'a gentleman of respectable standing in society'; and Callender joined forces with the President's enemies to expose Jefferson's social hypocrisy and role in fathering children by his Black 'slave mistress Sally'.[110] As a unique figure within American radicalism, Callender gained the distinction of attacking and savaging three American Presidents.[111]

Conclusion

Expressing himself honestly and openly, Callender did not exhibit the Scottish Whigs' *radicalism of the mouth*. In Scotland and America, he used his writings to articulate the new and unprecedented intervention of the common people in politics. However, Cobbett's denunciatory rhetoric should not be allowed to conceal the fact that Callender had belonged to the bottom rung of the 'middle ranks'. He came from a 'superior' social background to Cobbett's army background; and he had not been a 'rough' imperialist-minded English soldier with a talent for writing.

But, although Callender had mixed socially with Lady Henderson, Lord Kames - a man he described as 'a shallow character' - Lord Gardenstone and other Scottish aristocrats, he played on his self-styled 'plebeian' behaviour to justify his rough literary style and hostility to the tradition of polite literature.[112] When he wrote to Jefferson in April 1801, he said:

> I am not, to be sure, very expert in making a bow, or at supporting the sycophancy of conversation. I speak as well as I write what I think; for God, when he made me, made that a part of my constitution. But Mr. Jefferson should recollect that it is not by beaux, and dancing masters, and by editors, who look extremely well in a muslin gown and petticoat, that the battles of freedom are to be fought and won.[113]

As the voice of 'the voiceless' in Scotland and America, there was an element of 'inevitability' about Callender's ultimate fate. Despite the Federalists' denigration of Jefferson as 'a Jacobin and atheist', he was no revolutionary.[114] By 1801, the American counter-revolution was triumphant. As Paine's biographer Conway explained:

> Tammy, having begun with the populace, had by this time got up somewhat in society. As a rule the "gentry" were Federalists, though they kept a mob in their back yard to fly at the democrats on occasion. But with Jefferson in the Presidential chair, and Clinton, Vice-President, Tammany was in power.[115]

Callender's fate was sealed.

In the September 1803 issue of *The Gentleman's Magazine*, the editor gave vent to his pent-up hatred of the Scottish-International Jacobin by reporting the alleged suicide of 'Iscariot Hackney'.[116] From an authentically radical perspective, Callender's friends could have responded by pointing out that he was at the beginning of a long line of *carnaptious* Scottish radicals and socialists who stood in the dissident tradition of 'The Truth against the World'.

By the spring of 1803, Callender had felt a bitter hatred for Jeffereson for over two years. However, in discussing this, Dumas Malone wrote:

> His [Callender's] fury was diminished or dissipated in the spring of 1803... The death was officially designated accidental, proceeding from intoxication, but *The Examiner* regarded it as suicidal, claiming that this unfortunate man had descended to the lowest depths of misery, having been fleeced by his partner.[117]

By asserting against all the evidence that after 1707 all 'the stay-at-home' Scottish intellectuals were Black reactionaries and all 'the outward-bound' ones were invariably progressive Reds, Christopher Harvie and Tom Nairn have been compelled to ignore Callender and many others.[118]

Anticipating the uncompromising Scottish radicalism of Alexander Rodger (1784-1846), James MacFarlan (1832-62), Alexander Robertson (1825-93), John Murdoch (1818-1903), John Maclean (1879-1923) and R. F. Mackenzie (1910-87) among others, Callender was simultaneously 'a stay-at-home' Red and a Red 'outward-bound' Scot who deserves his place in the Pantheon of Scottish-International radicalism.

Alexander Rodger (1784-1846) and James MacFarlan (1832-62): *The Voices of a Subdued People*

> The belief is widespread that poetry is not about
> the expression of opinion, not about 'politics', not
> about employment, not about what people actually
> do with their time between waking up and falling
> asleep each day; not about what they eat, not about
> how much the food costs.
>
> *Tom Leonard*, Radical Renfrew *(1990)*

The Extirpation of the Memory of James Thomson Callender

Alexander (Sandy) Rodger (1784-1846) was born at East Calder,
Midlothian, nineteen years before the death of James Thomson
Callender (1758-1803). By contrast, James MacFarlan (1832-62) was
born in Glasgow twenty-nine years after Callender's death in America
and forty years after the publication of his Scottish nationalist booklet
The Political Progress of Britain (1792). As they grew up in very different
Scotlands separated by the first Reform Act of 1832, Rodger and
MacFarlan did not inherit very much of the specific political culture of
Callender's generation of radical Scots.

To put this important point another way, the most notable
characteristic of Scottish radicalism between 1707 and the virtual
collapse of Chartism in 1848 was the repeated breaks in the continuity
of the Scots' consciousness of their own distinctive national history.
For most nationalistic Scots from the eighteenth century onwards, 1688
was a more seminal year than 1707 had been. Moreover, by the time

that a new Scottish radical movemenent developed from 1815 onwards, consciousness of Callender's role as a Scottish historian and Jacobin practitioner in the Athens of the North had been extirpated.

However, although the generations to which Rodger and MacFarlan belonged were not aware of Callender's life and work, they were informed about the patriotism of Robert the Bruce, a de-nationalised and de-radicalised William Wallace and Thomas Muir of Huntershill. Against the grain of the dominant Presbyterian Church and the Anglo-Scottish educational and legal systems, a national working-class culture developed and survived. Nursing Scottish *national* as well as *class* grievances, the new working-class radicals like Rodger and MacFarlan had inherited a limited consciousness of Scotland's historic and complicated oppression.

Scottish Poets' Opposition to the De-Nationalisation of the Scots

When the industrialisation of Scotland got under way in the late eighteenth century, two very different and antagonistic Scotlands were crystallising - the world of the Anglo-Scottish Enlightenment and the more democratic world of the early working-class radicals. Far from the Scottish Enlightenment constructing or defining 'Scotland', it really defined the fundamental Britishness of the anti-Scottish Anglo-Scottish ruling class.

Moreover, when Rodger was expressing his political sympathy with the struggles of the Blacks in Haiti and South America, Hume expressed the racist ideas that Marx and Engels imbibed later on. As early as 1753 Hume had written: 'I am apt to suspect the Negroes, and in general all the other species of men (for there are four to five different kinds) to be naturally inferior to whites'. As Peter Fryer has shown in his essay 'Their Feet of Clay: the un-Marxist side of Engels and Marx', the pioneers of 'scientific socialism' were racists of the nineteenth- (as distinct from the twentieth-) century variety in relation to the Gaels and other so-called 'un-historic peoples'.[1]

It was moreover very surprising that, unlike Marx and Engels later on, the Scottish plebeian or working-class radicals like Rodger and MacFarlan did not imbibe or subscribe to the British/English or racist ideas of the dominant side of the Enlightenment. For Anglo-Scottish thinkers like Adam Smith, Hume, John Millar and Stewart, the 'Negroes', the Gaelic Highlanders and the Irish belonged to an 'naturally inferior' species of humanity. In his multi-volume *History of England* (1778), Hume argued that:

> As the rudeness and ignorance of the Irish were extreme, they were sunk below the reach of that curiosity and love of novelty by which every other people in Europe had been seized at the beginning of that century... The old opposition of manners, laws, and interests was now inflamed by religious antipathy, and the subduing and civilising of that country seemed to become every day more difficult and impractical.[2]

From the standpoint of Hume and most of the other thinkers of the Scottish Enlightenment, Ireland was, in Richard Ned Lebon's phrase, 'Black Ireland'. What annoyed Scots like Hume was that English writers like Cobbett and Wilkes would persist in equating the 'superior' Scots Sawnies with 'the Irish Paddies.'[3]

But the most important hidden aspect of British history between the birth of Rodger in 1784 and the death of MacFarlan in 1862 was that Marx and Engels would imbibe the racist ideology of Hume and Scott, in Marxist terminology, as a 'necessary false consciousness', and not the anti-imperialist radicalism of Rodger and the Scottish labour movement. Far from being of mere academic interest, the impact of the pro-Highland Clearance ideas of Engels on the later Scottish socialist movement (including the Gaelic-speaking De Leonist John Carstairs Matheson) was actively pernicious and reactionary. Thus in a letter that he sent to the German socialist Eduard Bernstein in 1882, Engels prophetically anticipated Stalinist attitudes in the Scottish labour movement when he wrote about the Balkan Slavs:

> And even if these chaps were as admirable as the Scots' Highlanders celebrated by Walter Scott - another bunch of terrible cattle-thieves - the most we can do is to condemn the ways in which society today treats them. If we were in power we also would have to deal with the banditry of these fellows, which is part of their heritage.[4]

Hobsbawm was careful to omit the sentence where Engels insisted that 'if we were in power', 'we would do the same except only more humanely'. Besides, if Rodger and his generation of Scottish radicals did not inherit the anti-imperialist culture of Callender, he was nevertheless much more anti-imperialist than Marx and Engels were to be from the 1840s onwards. To appreciate the extent of the born-again anti-imperialism of the Scottish labour movement in the early nineteenth century, it will be necessary to glance at the life and times of Rodger.

Sketching the early biography of Rodger, George Eyre-Todd kept the immortal memory of the man he characterised as 'the "Radical Poet"' from being extirpated or obliterated. In his substantial book on *The Glasgow Poets* (1906), Eyre-Todd wrote thus:

> His mother was weak in health, and for the first seven years of his life he was cared for by two maiden sisters named Lonie. His father, meanwhile, having given up the farm of Haggs, near Dalmahoy, of which he had been tenant, had become an innkeeper in Mid-Calder, and there the future poet was put to school. Five years later the family removed to Edinburgh, and the boy was sent to learn the trade of silversmith with a Mr. Mathie. This apprenticeship, however, was cut short by twelve months by the financial collapse of his father, who fled to Hamburg. The lad was then brought to Glasgow by his mother's friends, who had become strongly attached to him, and who apprenticed him to a weaver named Dunn, at the Drygate Toll, near the Cathedral.

Like other radicals before him, Rodger was, in 1803, 'seized with the prevailing fever of patriotism'. He joined the Glasgow Highland Volunteers and he remained in that regiment until 1812.[5]

In 1806, when he was twenty-two years of age, Rodger had married Agnes Turner. To support 'a quickly growing family' in the village of Bridgeton, to the east of the city of Glasgow, where he worked as a weaver, he added to his income by teaching music. As a witness to the brutal process of industrialisation, he became interested in radical politics. In 1816, when a mass meeting of disaffected Scottish workers met in 1816 to demand Parliamentary reform, he wrote 'A Word of Advice' or 'Sooty Rabble':

> But be they poor, or be they rich,
> Their chartered rights ye daurna touch,
> Their sacredness has aye been such,
> And shall be still
> That whaur's the base unhallowed wretch
> Daur do them ill?
> Ye'll cry for equal rights to all,
> Without regard to great or small,
> For Annual Parliaments ye'll bawl;
> But what are ye?
> A blank - a mere political Non-entity.[6]

Light years away from a truly enlightened Scotland, Alexander Wilson, the radical poet in Paisley had, in 1793, already been 'ordered to destroy all copies of "The Shark", two of which he had *publicly* to *burn* on the steps of the Tolbooth at ll a.m. on 6th February.'[7] Moreover, when Rodger was arrested and jailed in 1820, he was guilty of the wicked 'crime' of circulating his radical poems. But they were not only radical; they were also nationalistic and anti-imperialist.

When Rodger read a report in the *Glasgow Chronicle*, in 1816, that the patriot Bolivar had freed seventy thousand slaves in Venezuela, he wrote what was probably his first poem. Occupying a thought-world that was spiritually and political alien to the class and *racist* attitudes of the last phase of the Scottish Enlightenment, his poem 'Bolivar' was important for a whole host of reasons.

Although he did not know anything at all about Callender, the Rodger who was radicalised by his own experiences and times was already aware of the Friends of the People, Muir of Huntershill, and the new anti-imperialism of the Scottish radical movement. In 'Bolivar' he celebrated the

> Spirit of immortal Wallace,
> Bruce, Tell, Doria, Washington,
> And ye noble six of Calais
> Sterling patriots every one!

Identifying with the radicalism of the recent Scottish past, he wrote of:

106

Hampdem, Sidney, Marg'rot, Gerald,
Palmer, Kosciusko, Muir!
Names which tyrants can't endure[8]

Expressing an inherited Scottish nationalism and anti-British imperialism, in his poem 'My Country' he empathised with the Hatians:

But the ill-fated Negro, from home rudely torn,
And o'er the Atlantic a poor captive borne;
How frantic the grief of the untutored mind,
While sharp galling fetters his manly limbs bind.

However, Rodger died in 1846; and before MacFarlan began to publish his first work in the 1850s, consciousness of the continuity of the people's radicalism was broken up again and again. Yet despite the breaks in the continuity of the class-consciousness of the evolving Scottish working class between 1816, when Rodger began to write poetry and journalistic pieces, and 1854, when MacFarlan published *Poems* in London, 'the pedlar poet' was also very sensitive to the wrongs committed against working folk.

In 1819 Rodger had joined the editorial staff of the Scottish radical newspaper *The Spirit of Union*; and a few months later (in 1820) he was jailed on the 'evidence' (*sic!*) provided by his 'own songs'. The title of this important pioneering newspaper was inspired by the radicals' determination to achieve the Union of the various Universal Suffrage Societies of Scotland. Contributing his poems to such distinguished English radical newspapers as the *Black Dwarf*, he did not come into greater prominence in England until the year following the Scottish 'Radical rebellion' of 1820.[9] Though he wrote several important poems between 1816 and 1820, he was already displaying the uncompromising, intransigent radicalism that had characterised the life of Callender. He was, of course, already foreshadowing the same extreme extra-Parliamentary radicalism of Alexander Robertson (1825-1893) and John Maclean (1879-1923).

In his important and fascinating *Autobiography of a Working Man* (1848), Alexander Somerville, son of a landless agricultural labourer from the village of Birnyknows, Lammermoor, seventy miles from Glasgow, depicted in some detail the antagonism created between the farmers' and the farm labourers' children by the events of 1820. In a vivid description owing much to inherited folklore, he described the events leading to the imprisonment of Rodger just after the spies' Proclamation was posted up in various parts of Scotland:

> The great body of radicals were composed of honest working people; but there were attached to them a few persons of wealth and high social station, while all below the working classes, that is to say the idle, and dissolute, and the rambling makers of speeches, who went from town to town exciting the industrious people to rise against the landlords and effect a radical transformation, or revolution, by force of guns, pistols, and pikes, were as a matter of course called, and were proud to be called radicals. Those last succeeded in getting many of the more honest men and youths to join them ... and [they] were abandoned by those leaders and instigators who had given information to the authorities where and when the radicals were to be met with, and who then slunk away to live on the rewards paid to them.[10]

No less interesting than the 'enlightened' Anglo-Scottish bourgeoisie's use of spies in the labour movement was their unenlightened suppression of radical poems, literature and newspapers. In so far as there was a Scottish Enlightenment dedicated to a 'democratic intellect' and the general diffusion of knowledge, it resided in the early labour movement.

The Anglo-Scottish bourgeoisie detested *The Spirit of the Union*. To grasp why they felt such hatred for the Scottish radicals, it will be enough to quote from Thomas Johnson's *The History of the Working Classes in Scotland*:

> Cobbett's pamphlets, *Wooler's Gazette*, and *The Black Dwarf* had a widespread circulation, and in October, 1819, a rebel sheet, *The Spirit of the Union*, appeared in Glasgow. Only eleven issues were allowed to appear before Gilbert Macleod, the editor, was arrested and the paper suppressed. It was a live, rebel sheet, and in its pages we get a glimpse of the real red-hot agitation which was

being carried on. At that time, too, according to Johnston, 'Neilson musicians' were arrested for playing 'Scots Whae Hae' by the immortal national bard Robert Burns.[11]

In 1819 just before Rodger began to write for the Scottish radical newspaper *The Spirit of the Union*, English radical journalists like Jack Wade, Richard Carlile and William Cobbett were so hostile and condescending towards their Scottish counterparts, and particularly towards their annoying 'metaphysics', that they refused to recognise any of their other cultural 'peculiarities'.[12] And yet Scotland was no more 'a free country' during the first four decades of the nineteenth century than it had been in the 1790s.

Unlike the English ruling class, the Anglo-Scottish ruling class did not believe in democracy, free speech, a free press, the freedom of assembly, or the rule of law. An aspect of the dictatorship in Scotland in circumstances where there was no real centre of political power was untypically highlighted by Lord Hamilton in the House of Commons in 1817:

> The system acted on there [Scotland] was that of employing spies and tampering with witnesses. If any of those spies denounced an individual, that individual was instantly arrested - and carried off to gaol - to a secret gaol; even magistrates were prevented from having access to him.[13]

To underline the major peculiarity of the colonial dimension of a Scotland administered and ruled from afar (in the Palace of Westminster or Whitehall), the authorities in London with the automatic approval of the Anglo-Scottish Establishment decided at the beginning of 1820 to made the selling or distribution of the radical newspapers the *Black Dwarf* and *The Spirit of Union* a 'treasonable offence.'[14]

English Imperialism in Scotland and the English Radicals

But, although Carlile criticised Cobbett for his fondness for the monarchy, they both expressed their shared English chauvinism towards the Irish and the Scots. The English radical newspapers' anti-Scottish prejudices were notorious; and in 1817 the newspaper *The*

Gorgon complained about the soldiers in Scottish regiments in Manchester who were 'getting drunk, drawing their bayonets, insulting the inhabitants and committing a variety of excesses'.[15] But *The Gorgon* and Carlile's *The Republican* remained silent when English soldiers behaved in a similar way towards Scottish working men and women in Paisley and Glasgow in 1819.

Indeed, the editor of *The Gorgon* insisted on lumping Scotland, Wales, and Ireland under the rubic of England before going on to assert that:

> To an Englishman every place and every person in England [meaning Britain] ought to be alike; and all local [i.e., Scottish, Irish and Welsh] distinctions and attachments - remains of a barbarous age - ought to be obliterated as useless and pernicious.[16]

Moreover, in a leaflet *A New Year's Address to the Reformers of Great Britain* [1820], Carlile discussed the Government's use of troops thus:

> Their object is, as far as possible, to keep alive provincial prejudices, by removing the soldiers from their native provinces, and interchanging them; so that Scotland is generally filled with Irish and English troops; England with those of Scotland and Ireland; and Ireland with those of England and Scotland.

Ridiculing those Scottish and Irish radicals who were struggling to preserve their own national cultures and sense of national identity, Carlile accused them of keeping alive 'provincial prejudices' in the face of the beast of English imperialism.[17]

The tragedy confronting Scottish radicals like Rodger was the absence of a free press, Parliamentary representation, the rule of law and a democratic ethos. When he depicted the general situation in Scotland between 1795 and 1820, Cockburn said:

> Nor was the absence of a free press compensated by the freedom of public speech. Public political meetings could not arise for the elements did not exist... Nothing was viewed with such horror as

any political congregation not friendly to the existing power. No one could have taken part in the business without making up his mind to be a doomed man.[18]

(However, in contrast to the rising bourgeoisie of Whigs represented by Cockburn, the Scottish radicals like Rodger could not be silenced). Cockburn was really describing the small group of Whig University teachers and lawyers rather than the evolving labour movement. Viewing Scottish history from the narrow, class standpoint of the Anglo-Scottish bourgeoisie of which he was a part, he had to remain blind to the extent of working folk's aggressive nationalism and radicalism.

Despite the countless romantic myths and propaganda concocted by some Scots and not a few English Marxists about the Scots' unique [British] role in developing a 'democratic intellect', the countervailing power of the semi-colonial status of Scottish society was seen in the private correspondence of Scott, John Gibson Lockhart, Dugald Stewart and others. As early as 1812 Scott had expressed his 'dismay' over the growing power of Scottish trade unions; and in 1817 the *Edinburgh Annual Register* with which he was associated attributed 'the proscription' of so-called radical 'views' in the Scottish universities to the fact that 'talent' was 'naturally democratic'.[19] But at the same time as Scott and the other Tories helped to crush 'democratic' talent in the universities, he increasingly assisted the Scottish Whigs to rewrite Scottish history to fit in with 'the principles' of the 'glorious English revolution' of 1688.

Rodger and MacFarlan were two of the most oustanding voices of Scottish radicalism, poetry and literature between 1819 and 1862. As a poet, writer, agitator and radical weaver, who first inherited and then reflected the folklore, folk literature and songs of the Scottish past, Rodger came to prominence during the Radical rebellion of 1820. He was a much more complicated Radical than the mythical figure portrayed in the German Stalinists' volume of *Essays in Honour of William Gallacher* (1966).[20] He was, moreover, an important voice of the new Scottish working class, and, together with MacFarlan, who was also recognised during his lifetime as an important poet, Rodger came to maturity during a moment of extreme and sharp class struggles between the workers and their bosses.

In the excellent introduction to his book *Radical Renfrew: Poetry from the French Revolution to the First World War*, Tom Leonard has analysed the complicated reasons explaining why Renfrewshire poets and writers of the same stature as Rodger and MacFarlan have been excluded from the 'canon' of Literature. In an insightful paragraph touching on the new Anglo-Scottish middle class's abhorence for working folk's Scots or Lallans, Leonard wrote:

> The proletariat of the West of Scotland, Protestant or Catholic, freethinking or of any other religion, of immigrant stock or not - all could be seen as forming linguistically *a colony within a colony*... The contempt that was heaped on the speakers of the new urban diction was based on class, and sometimes religious, prejudice as much as a desire for a return to the mythical 'purer' diction of a pure race of pre-proletarian Scottish folk.[21]

The Anglo-Scottish ruling class that developed with the new industrial society was culturally unique. In his essay *On Liberty* the outstanding Scottish intellectual John Stuart Mill insisted that 'a large proportion of the morality' of 'an ascendant class' emanated from 'its class interests and its class feelings of superiority'. However, the most striking feature of the Anglo-Scottish ruling class during the nineteenth century was its lack of collective self-confidence.

Though it was very authoritarian and repressive in relation to the irrepressible radicalism and militancy of working people, the Anglo-Scottish ruling-class did not behave like other 'ascendant classes'. In his much-quoted book *Scottish Men of Letters in the Eighteenth Century,* Henry G. Graham had reported a conversation between James Boswell and Dr. Samuel Johnson in the 1770s thus: 'Mr. Johnson', said I, 'I do indeed come from Scotland, but I cannot help it.' 'That, Sir, I find is what a very great many of your countrymen cannot help.' At which retort the apologetic Scotsman owns he was 'a good deal stunned.'[22]

By the end of the century, Francis Jeffrey was typifying the cultural schizophrenia of the Anglo-Scottish ruling class as well as their separation from their own 'lower orders' by getting rid of his 'broad Scots' at Oxford.

> When he went to the University of Oxford in the 1790s, Jeffrey was determined to 'purify' himself of 'the national inconvenience' of the Scots'

language. Personifying the cultural uniqueness and spiritual separation of the Anglo-Scottish ruling class from the 'lower orders', he tried to justify himself by saying: 'My opinions, ideas, prejudices, and systems are all Scotch. The only part of a Scotsman I mean to abandon, is the language; and the language is all I expect to learn in England.'[23]

Rodger, The Radical Rebellion and King George IV

By the early nineteenth century, the Anglo-Scottish writers and poets who reflected the thought-world of a unique ascendant class agonised over the nature of their national identity. Thus in his autobiographical volumes on *The Literary Life*, John Galt could theorise about the differences between the Scots and the English without examining the social conditions or distinctive way-of-life of the new and emerging Scottish working class.

Attempting to construct the consciousness of a new sense of Scottishness irrelevant to the real Scotland of an evolving industrial society, Galt - and many others, like Sir Walter Scott - would speculate about 'the English' not being 'very correct theoretical metaphysicans' and rationalise his own politics by declaring that 'I was surely born a Radical and owe my Tory predilections entirely to a prankful elf'.[24] Occupying a very different thought-world to Rodger or MacFarlan, Henry Cockburn could not acknowledge that the Anglo-Scottish ruling class's own conflict over the use of the English language had created a strange cultural schizophrenia within their own consciousness of being Scots.[25]

The Radical rebellion was a seminal event in Rodger's biography. In a poem written about 'The Rising', he said:

> The laws were suspended - the prisons were
>   glutted, -
> Indictments preferred, and Juries enclosed;
> But mark! In her own wicked efforts outwitted -
> Corruption at once is defeated - exposed!
> For truth must prevail over falsehood and error,
> - In spite of the Devil, Corruption and Spies;
> - Who down to their dens shall be driven in terror
> - While man to his scale in creation will rise.

In his edition of *Poems and Songs: Humorous, Serious and Satirical* by Alexander Rodger, Robert Ford (1897) resurrected the radical who 'played a hand in the game of revolutionary politics so splendidly that he was a "kenspeckle" figure in the streets of the ever-Radical western metropolis seventy years ago'. Besides, he 'enjoyed a fame alike for politics and lyrical letters which, even in our own time, was as wide as the limits of his native land'. Sketching in Rodger's fate after 'the Treasonable Address' had been posted up, Ford wrote:

> The spirit of the indignant poet rose, superior to the petty malice of the small-souled officials; and he solaced himself and tantalised them by singing at the top of his lungs his own political compositions. These, highly spiced as they were by the awful Radicalism of the time, gave his jailors "fits", and their repressive measures became more drastic. But the Radical bard was irrepressible, and the singing did not cease - yea, he embalmed their very cruelties in new and equally pungent measures which rang in their ears every hour of the day and the night.[26]

At once sharply nationalistic as well as revolutionary, the Scots' radicalism did not make any enduring impact on the imperialistic chauvinism of the English radicals. Even so, a year after the Radical rebellion of 1820 Richard Carlile published a slender twenty-four-page book of Rodger's *Scotch Poetry*. In a preface to the poems 'Advice to the Priest-Ridden', 'The Dairo Anthem, 'Friendly Advice to John Bull', 'Savings Banks', 'National Amusements', 'The Heaven-Born Minister', 'The Twa Weavers' and 'Priestcraft Exposed', Carlile introduced Rodger to an English radical readership. In this forgotten preface, Carlile wrote thus:

> The manuscripts of the following sheets were sent to London in the latter part of the year 1819, after every effort to get them printed at Glasgow had failed. The Publisher put them to the press immediately on their receipt, and the first sheet was worked off; but his peculiar situation at that moment, combined with the pressure of business,

prevented their being then finished, and a succession of obstacles has delayed them to the present moment. The Publisher regrets the delay on his own accompt as well as that of the Author, who is a poor man, and had reasonably anticipated some alleviation of his distresses from the friends of freedom, by his zeal and the exertion of his abilities in the good cause.

The Publisher, anxious to remedy the evil of the delay to the Author, as far as is now possible, pledges himself to give up all profit that might arise, and content himself with paying the stationer and the printer. Should this meet the Author's eye, or the eye of any of his friends, any information of the Author's present residence and situation will be thankfully received by the Publisher.[27]

It was an interesting commentary on those later British labour historians, who wrote romantic accounts of the 'unity' of the British radical movement in the nineteenth century, that when *Stray Leaves* was published in 1842 Rodger was still not aware that Carlile had published his *Scotch Poetry* in 1821. In 1821 Rodger became an inspector of cloths at Barrowfields Printworks; and, remaining in that post for the next eleven years, he did not abandon his role as a radical agitator.

In 1822, when Walter Scott publshed his Anglo-Scottish Unionist poem 'Carle, Now the King's Come' to welcome the visit of King George IV to Scotland, Rodger persuaded the *London Examiner* newspaper to publish his anonymous response titled 'Sawney, Now the King's Come.' In an attempt to de-radicalise and de-nationalise the disaffected and nationalistic 'sotty rabble' after the massive repression of the Radical rebellion of 1820, Scott was stage-managing George IV's coronation visit to Edinburgh. The first Prince of the House of Hanover to set foot in Scotland since 'Butcher' Cumberland's brutality at Culloden in 1746, Scott was very upset by Rodger's Scottish Republican poem. As Ford wrote in his introduction to Rodger's *Poems and Songs*:

> [When] His Majesty was enriching his Scottish subjects with the first glint of his royal person, the *London Examiner* made its first appearance in Auld Reekie, containing the satirical lyric, "Sawney,

Now the King's Come", which caused scarcely less sensation. It certainly greatly annoyed the sensitive loyalty of Waverley, and speculation ran wild as to the identity of the author, until, by and by, Rodger chose to reveal himself.[28]

In one poignant verse of 'Sawney, Now the King's Come', Rodger wrote:

Mak' your tribe in good black claith.
Extol, till they run short of breath,
The "Great Defender of the Faith",
Sawney, now the king's come.

Unknown to most present-day Scots, who have been denied access to their own heritage of Scottish poetry and radicalism, the few literary specialists interested in Rodger have not noticed that English chauvinists (including the English radicals) were still at this time speaking of 'Scots Sawnies and Irish Paddies' in the same breath. When it becomes obvious that Rodger was challenging the English denigration of the Scottish workers as 'Scots Sawnies', the following two verses have an even stronger resonance:

Tell him he is great and good,
And come o' Scottish royal blood, -
To your hunkers - lick his fud, -
Sawney, now the king's come
Tell him he can do nae wrang,
That's he's mighty, heigh, and strang,
That you and yours to him belang,
Sawney, now the king's come.

To justify their own almost 'totalitarian' repression of the spontaneous radicalism of the 'lower orders' in Scotland, the Anglo-Scottish ruling class could not admit to the centrality of the Scots effective disenfranchisement from Parliamentary representation at Westminster in shaping the greater militancy of Scottish working-class men and women by comparison with their English counterparts. Although the Scottish Whig John Stuart Mill could write very abstractly about 'the feelings of superiority' of 'an ascendant class', the Scottish thinkers and intellectuals who remained at home, whether Whigs or Tories, did not feel the same 'superiority' as their English, French or German ruling-class counterparts.

A victim of reactionaries like Sheriff Allison, he always struggled to earn a crust for himself and family. His second volume of poetry to be published, though the first that he knew anything about was *Peter Cornclips, a Tale of Real Life, and Other Poems and Songs*, in 1827. But, although he would always remain poor at the same time as he enriched his readers, he was to be much more fortunate than James MacFarlan.

In 1838, when Sheriff Archibald Allison had glanced back to his own role in casting aside any idea of 'the rule of law' in the treatment of militant trade unions, the Anglo-Scottish ruling class once again felt the need to justify their own authoritarianism and extreme repression. Attempting to justify himself before the Select Committee on Combinations of Workmen, he said:

> I should not think there is less intelligence; perhaps in some cases there is superior intelligence; although I am satisfied that the common opinion in reference to the extent of moral and religious feeling among the working class is unhappily exaggerated, at least in the great towns. But I think the great circumstance of difference is that the Scotch have not been habituated to the enjoyment of wealth, and to the long enjoyment of liberal institututions which the English have. I think that in fifty or a hundred years, when wealth is more generally diffused, and the enjoyments and artificial wants of society consequent upon wealth have taken roots in the lower classes of society, we may then be prepared for liberal institutions, such as those connected with combinations [trade unions], which possibly may be perfectly innocuous in London; but I am clear that we have not arrived at that state yet.[29]

Justifying their own illegal and 'totalitarian' behaviour towards the Scottish workers down to the mid-nineteenth century, Henry Cockburn argued that: 'Scotland has very few individuals with heavy purses and dogged obstinacy to stand up, as in England, for their rights.'[30]

Just as the most extreme of the English radicals, like Bamford, Blake, Carlile, Cobbett, Paine and Shelley, had been outspoken in their denunciation of all the violations of 'the rule of law' in England, so they were always less outspoken in their criticism of British/English imperialism abroad than were their Scottish counterparts.[31] At the same time, Scottish reactionaries like Sir Walter Scott were more aware than their English counterparts of the impact of the process of industrialisation on working-class consciousness.

Out of their close observation of the brutal process of industrialisation in Scotland, Scott and Thomas Carlyle made important intellectual contributions to the subsequent genesis of Marxism. In a private letter of 1820, Scott wrote:

> Things are pretty quiet in the West but the poison remains to foment and bubble when fitting oportunity offers. The unhappy dislocation which has taken place betwixt the employer and those who are in his employment has been attenuated with very fatal consequences. Much of this is owing *to the steam engine.*[32]

Scotland was already a highly industrialised society, and Carlyle's observations of this process would influence the later thought-world of Marx and Engels.

Walter Scott and Thomas Carlyle Anticipate The Communist Manifesto

In an essay that he contributed to the *Edinburgh Review* on the new 'Signs of the Times' in Scotland as early as 1829, Carlyle had anticipated some of the analysis of the *Communist Manifesto* of 1848 when he said:.

> What changes, too, this addition of power is introducing into the Social System; how wealth has more and more increased, and at the same time gathered itself more and more into masses strangely altering the old relations, and increasing the distance between the rich and the poor, will be a question for political economists, and a much

more complex and important one than any they
have yet engaged with.[33]

Touching on some of the same social problems in his radical poetry as
Carlyle was pinpointing in his political essays, Rodger would
increasingly represent the evolving politics of the new class-divided
industrial society that he had been born into.

The Scotts and the Carlyles never met or talked to radicals like Rodger
or the poet and radical writer from the Borders, John Younger. Typifying
the new thought-world of the Anglo-Scots, Carlyle added the comment
in 1829 that: 'There is a deep-lying struggle in the whole fabric of society,
a boundless grinding collision of the New with the Old. The French
Revolution, as is now visible enough, was not the parent of this
movement, but its offspring.' [34]

But because Carlyle, Cockburn, Scott, John Gibson Lockhart and
other Anglo-Scottish writers and literary figures refused to acknowledge
the personalities and politics of working people or put the poets and
writers like Rodger into their literature, poetry or journalism, the
ordinary Scots' sense of their nationality was despised and demonised.

Unlike Rodger, the adult life of MacFarlan, 'the poor pedlar poet',
highlighted a period like the late twentieth century when the Scottish
labour movement was vulnerable to the winds of a powerful and
aggressive anti-humanist capitalism. But he was a complicated poet
and man: a genius who could not and would not compromise with the
social injustice that he saw all around him.[35] Upsetting easy
generalisations about the near disappearance of Scottish radicalism
and socialism during the mid-Victorian era, it was nevertheless true
that MacFarlan had struggled to earn a crust as a radical poet and writer
during a time of comparative de-radicalisation, that is, when there was
no strong or supportive working-class network of newspapers,
magazines, clubs or other alternative institutions.

But, although both Rodger and MacFarlan forced themselves upon
the consciousness of important English radicals and literary men during
their active lives as poets and writers, they have been expunged from
all the books on *Scottish history*. [36] Moreover, inside a Scottish
educational system that was increasingly de-nationalised from the early
nineteenth century onwards, the precious poetry and literature of the
working people of the Athens of the North could not be incorporated
into the 'canon' of institutionalised 'literature'.[37] It was, moreover,

incompatible with the ongoing process of English cultural imperialism frowned upon, though seen as inevitable, by men like Henry Cockburn.

Since the Scots language was increasingly seen as irrelevant to the process of British industrialisation and imperialism, Scots like Rodger and MacFarlan simply could not have the same recognition or immortality bestowed upon them as happened to comparable English figures like Samuel Bamford (1788-1872), William Blake (1757-1827), Richard Carlile (1790-1843), William Cobbett (1763-1835), Thomas Paine (1737-1809), or Percy Bysshe Shelley (1792-1822).[38] Testifying to the existence of a radical Scottish literature existing outside the ambience of the 'canon' of English literature, James Thomson Callender, Rodger and MacFarlan were the voices of *the other revolutionary Scotland*, the Scotland of *national* working-class radical dissent.[39]

Ignorant of and indifferent to the existence of the important Scottish radical witnesses like Rodger and MacFarlan, Marxists such as Tom Nairn, who have not understood that there is a continuity of radicalism in Scotland which is much older and more critical and searching than Marxism, are really blind to the existence of the alternative counter-culture represented by writers like 'Hawkie' and James Kelso Hunter.[40] In any case, the Anglo-Scottish ruling class was unimaginably philistine and socially insensitive. In touching on this problem in a rather one-sided way, Tom Nairn wrote: 'So what was there, instead of the missing Zolas and George Eliots, those absent Thomas Manns and Vergas? What there was increasingly from the 1820s onwards, until it became a vast tide washing into the present day, was the Scots "Kailyard" tradition.'[41]

What the conformist 'Left' like Nairn and Christopher Harvie have not understood is that, in contrast to the Scottish Chartist Alan Pinkerton, the famous enemy of radicals and trade unionists in America, there have always been, in their idiom, the very 'Red stay-at-home' Scottish intellectuals like Rodger, MacFarlan, John Murdoch and Alexander Robertson.[42] Unknown to most Scots, a man like Hawkie could be just as radical as the much better-known Bamford.[43] But, although history has always been written by the winners and English and American radicals and leftists have also been hidden from history, in contrast to someone like Bamford the Scots like Rodger and MacFarlan were made even more *infra dig* by their sharp insistence on sometimes using Lallans or the Scots language in their inherently radical poetry. The 'Pecularities of the Scots' and their collective radicalism (as distinct from E. P. Thompson's 'The Pecularities of the English') have yet to be recognised by the practitioners of Scottish and in particular radical and Marxist historiography [44]

The warm admiration that Karl Marx and Frederick Engels were to express in later years for Scottish Enlightenment thinkers like Adam Smith and the novelist Walter Scott has inhibted English Marxist historians like Royden Harrison from looking at Scottish history at all critically. In recent years it has been left to the Scottish nationalist scholar Andrew Noble to explain the ideological symbiosis (in the sense of 'necessary false consciousness') between the Whig intellectuals' history of Scotland and the Tory novelist Scott's re-writing of Scottish history. As Noble puts it:

> The great fictional exemplar of the Whig interpretation of history, Walter Scott wanted to verify the theories of David Hume and Adam Smith which predicted that a new economic order entailed a new harmonious psychological social order. That is to say, that a commercial and "improving" society is inherently more stable and less violent than a more traditional one. Thus while the bloody nature of the Highlands had to be exaggerated, the actual fact of the enormous and accelerated change in the Scottish urban and rural life had to be disguised. Scott thus seized upon a simplistic and overtly optimistic vision of historical development which he embodied in the controlled environment of historical novels where they could be safely cleansed of the grim sort of realities with which a contemporary like Stendhal dealt.[45]

Nevertheless the task of explaining why English Marxists like Harrison are so hostile to criticisms of the Scottish Enlightenment intellectuals and Scott resides within the hidden history of Marxism itself.

In response to my own pioneering criticisms of the Scottish Enlightenment thinkers including Scott, Harrison said: 'It is necessary to expose romantic myths concerning the revolutionary record of the wee men with bunnets and nae teeth. But you don't need to kick all the shit out of them at once.' Uncertain of the ground he was treading, he asked with a plaintive poignancy: 'If Noble is correct, why did Karl Marx have such a high regard for him?' [46]

121

A key to understanding the admiration that Marx and Engels felt for Scott was the Anglo-Scot's denigration of the Scottish Gaels and so-called 'historyless' or 'non-historical peoples'. Accepting Hegel's idea that 'these residual fragments of peoples' (including 'the Gaels' between 1640 and 1745) always become fanatical standard-beaers of counter-revolution', Engels and Marx empathised with Scott's *sanitised* history of eighteenth - and nineteenth- century Scotland.

Although he continued to be active in revolutionary politics, Rodger remained a working man and, in his leisure time, a teacher of music. A champion of Irish freedom, he was just as a true an internationalist as Callender had been before him. Summing up the highlights in his life up to the birth of MacFarlan in the seminal year of 1832, Ford said: 'Rodger's life, as we are beginning to realise, was marked by considerable variety. Already he has been a silversmith, a weaver, a poet, a teacher of music, a political martyr, a cloth-inspector, and a Champion of the Rights of the People'. [47] Anticipating the relative political quiescence of the 1850s, Rodger's name became increasingly associated with 'Whistle-binkie' and other more respectable volumes close to the Kailyard tradition in literature.

The Scotland in which Rodger came to political consciousness was a very heartless evolving industrial society in which life was 'nasty,brutish and short' for most working-class men and women. But out of the misery created by industrialisation, the Scottish workers created their own people's culture in the most unfavourable conditions. Furthermore, if 'every brick of the [British] Industrial Revolution was', in the idiom of Eric Williams, 'covered in the blood of a Negro slave', Glasgow was at the very heart of the triangular trade.[48] In a pioneering newspaper article entitled 'Hurricane whips up our murky past', Stuart Cosgrove wrote:

> In these Jamaican hills much of Glasgow's wealth was founded. In these villages Scots stole sugar at gunpoint using the cruellest and most inhuman methods of enslavement, and in these woodlands psychopathic Scottish foremen dressed up their slaves in red tartan shirts so that they could shoot them as they tried to escape.[49]

Moreover, John Campbell, who transferred from tobacco to sugar in the late eighteenth century, engaged Raeburn to paint and hang his portrait. Although the judgment that it was one of 'Raeburn's best portraits' could be questioned, it illuminated the connections between Scottish capitalism and slavery in America, the West of Scotland and the West Indies.[50] The 'dialectic' at the core of the development between slavery, Scottish capitalism and the British Empire was to play a major part in inspiring the anti-imperialism originally inspired by James Thomson Callender's powerful booklet *The Political Progress of Britain*.

The Real Scottish Radical Literary Tradition Versus Sir Walter Scott

Yet despite the limited and sometimes grudging recognition bestowed upon Rodger and MacFarlan by influential English radicals and literary figures, the spokesmen of the Scottish bourgeoisie were always reluctant to acknowledge their formidable contribution to imaginative literature.[51] Thus in the introduction to *The Modern Scottish Minstrel or the Songs of Scotland of the past half century* (1856), the anonymous editor wrote about Rodger's poetry: 'Many of his poems, though abounding in humour, are disfigured by *coarse* political allusions.' Moreover, in the obituary of MacFarlan in the Scottish radical and working-class newspaper the *Glasgow Sentinal*, the editor wrote: 'In his dull life amid our city vennals he still preserved the wayward experiences of his early and vagrant journeyings; but any references to his love for nature was to be gathered from his writings than from his reserved conversation.'[52] Faced with - and almost overwhelmed by - a very dull bourgeoisie that English poets and writers like Bamford, Blake, Carlile, Cobbett, Paine and Shelley could not have imagined in their wildest nightmares, the Scots' poets Rodger and MacFarlan produced their poetry and radical journalistic articles and essays in the most unpropitious of circumstances. [53]

In his neglected and well-written *Autobiography* Younger criticised novelists like Scott for their ignorance of the day-to-day lives of 'the souters, tailors, weavers, shopkeepers and labourers about St. Boswells and other villages'. Indeed, he accused Scott and his ilk of 'sitting in their open coaches' and 'taking notes of the rural pleasures and beauties of the harvest fields.'[54] From Rodger's entry into working-class politics in 1819, the Scottish radicals would increasingly develop their own distinctive politics. Moreover, by 1841 the Scottish newspaper the *Chartist Circular* not only criticised Scott's biographical *Life of Napoleon*; it also appealed to Chartists not to read the falsified history in the novels of Scott, the Rev. Henry Duncan and Elizabeth Hamilton.[55]

The Scotland portrayed by Rodger did not bear any relationship to the *social picture* of the 'Scotland' chronicled by Linda Colley in her pro-Unionist book *Britons: The Forging of the Nation 1707-1838*. In the 1830s Rodger belonged to a group of writers who met at Liberty Hall, in the Trongate. James Kilpatrick, the historian of literary Glasgow in the nineteenth century, described him at this time as 'a kindred spirit, who knew the depth of the Sun Tavern punch-bowl, but was a fellow of infinite good humour with a fine ear for the jingle of rhyme'. But Rodger did not abandon his revolutionary nationalist working-class politics during a decade when the Scots' sense of national identity was threatened by the intensifying process of anglicisation.

Yet despite the attempts after 1820 to integrate the Scots into Great Britain, the mood of most ordinary working people remained dour, sullen and rebellious. To 'establish' her argument for the Scots' alleged integration into the United Kingdom, Colley has to ignore all the counter-evidence by writers like William Chambers and even the English radical Jack Wade.

In *The Book of Scots* (1830), Chambers depicted a Scotland light years away from Colley's propaganda masquerading as history. As he put it:

> To this day they [the Scots] feel as if they were a distinct people, and reigners to the supreme Government. They seldom nor ever speak of our King, our Parliament, our troops, our navy, our Government. They in general never mention them in the third person; and this is because they imagine they could not do otherwise with propriety, although by the Articles of the Union, they would be fully entitled to use these phrases; and it is to this scarcely defined feeling that they are as much a subdued as a confederated people.[56]

Much to the annoyance of Rodger, the English people were continuing to denigrate 'the Scots Sawnies and the Irish Paddies'. And in 1835 Jack Wade, author of *The Black Book or Corruption Unmasked*, wrote thus:

> Scotland has benefited by the Union: her soil has been fertilised by our capital, and her greedy sons

have enriched themselves by sinecures and pensions, the produce of English taxes; but what has England gained from the connexion? The generous and intellectual character of the Saxon race has not been improved by the amalgamation with Scotch metaphysics, thrift, and servililty. Again, what benefits have we derived from the conquest of Ireland? Her uncultivated wastes, too, will be made fruitful by English money, unless the connexion be prematurely severed: but what boon in return can she confer on England? Her miserable children have poured out their blood in our wars of despotism; our rich aristocracy have been made richer by the rental of her soil; and the aggregate power of the Empire has been augmented: but we seek in vain for the benefits communicated to the mass of the English population.[57]

Like John Wilkes and William Cobbett before him, Wade did not believe in the unity of the British labour movement. In the 1830s, too, Cobbett made similar remarks to those of Wade and he, too, detested 'Scotch metaphysics'.[58]

Furthermore, when T. C. Smout insists that the English radicals like Cobbett 'would have raised an eyebrow to hear latter-day Scottish historians boasting of the "democratic intellect" of the North', the historical evidence is on his side rather than Colley's. But in his serious underestimation of the scope, extent and depth of Scottish radicalism, Smout stands in the same company as Rosalind Mitchison, R. H. Campbell and the other Anglo-Scottish Establishment historians.

In defending my interpretation of Scottish labour history against Smout and Mitchison, the distinguished English historian John Rule has argued that 'there is some justice in the claim that with the activities of the Glasgow spinners and weavers, Edinburgh artisans and papermakers and Lanarkshire colliers to the fore, by 1831 the "Scottish working class was already the most militant, class conscious and politically aware working class in Europe."'[59] Moreover, the Scottish radical newspapers that Rodger worked for in the 1830s and 1840s testified to the existence of a mass working-class counter-culture.

In the introductory section on 'the author's life' in Stray Leaves, John M'Kechnie wrote: 'In 1832, one of his friends, who had begun business as a pawnbroker, induced him to leave Monteith's works, and take the management of his business. But such employment was ill-suited to the feelings of such an individual as Alexander Rodger; and at the expiration of nine or ten months, he gave up that engagement.' He then worked for a year as a reporter of local news for the *Glasgow Chronicle;* and in 1834 he joined the editorial staff of the John Tait's left-wing radical newspaper *The Liberator.* As M'Kecknie explained:

> Here, while Tait lived, the Poet was quite at home.
> He was in the midst of kindred spirits - able,
> intelligent, and, withal, democratic; and he felt
> himself in a new element. He continued to be
> connected with this paper, till, from the death of
> Mr. Tait, and the subsequent embarassments of
> the concern, it ceased to exist.[60]

Suffering unemployment yet again, he joined the editorial staff of the *Scotch Reformers' Gazette* in 1837 and remained there until his death.

He became a Scottish Chartist and a working-class radical who was not satisfied by what the First Reform Act had offered working folk The 1830s were productive years for the Radical poet; and in 1838 his *Poems and Songs: Humorous and Satirical* contained such new poems as 'The Bill, The Whole Bill, And Nothing But The Bill' with his usual anti-imperialist and simultaneously pro-Irish and pro-Scottish radical sentiments:

> Peace, peace! Johnny Bull, but what the deuce are
>   you growling at?
> Can't you keep gnawing your bone and be still?
> *Sandy* [or Sawney] and *Paddy,* too, what are you
>   howling at?
> Have you not all of you now got your will?
> Did you not lately most loudly vociferate -
> Loudly at Boreas on cold wintry hill -
> Threatening your old whippers-in at so stiff a rate
> That they were fain just to give you your "Bill?"

The same volume carrying his poem 'The Emerald Isle', and the poet expressed the wish that :

Like thine own Patron Saint, may a Patriot arise
soon,
To banish the vile yellow snake from thy soil,
From clouds of black locusts to clear thy horizon,
Which eat up the fruits of the thy children's toil;
May freedom descending in all her mild glory,
Her bright angel wings spread benignantly o'er
there,
And give thee new splendour - sweet Emerald
Isle.[61]

By the 1830s the ucompromising radical poet and journalist derived strength from the small literary group that he met with in Liberty Hall, though the others were not radicals.[62] In 1836 his friends and admirers invited him to a public dinner and presentation in the Tontine Hotel; and in his *Old Reminiscences and Remarkable Characters of Glasgow*, Peter Mackenzie paid a warm tribute to his versalility.[63]

When he was summing up Rodger's contribution to Scottish songs, Ford said: 'The songs will keep Sandy's name in evidence throughout another century at least - no matter how rapidly the new "Kailyarders" may multiply and luxuriate - and no writing of mine or any other man's will keep that living when these fail to do so.' Unfortunately, in spite of the publication of George Douglas Brown's novel *The House with the Green Shutters* (1901), the Kailyarders were to become even more succcesful than he could have anticipated; but as the twenty-first century comes towards us Scots will surely reach out for books about their real radical culture.

Moreover, in 1836 the editor of *The Weavers' Journal* appealed to those Scots who 'possess the Republicanism of Buchanan, or the patriotism of Wallace.'[64] But, although the Chartist movement was founded in England rather than Scotland in 1838, J. Morrison Davidson insisted that by 1840 'In Scotland almost alone, at this season of disaster, were there any reassuring signs of Chartist vitality.' Also he described the role of the Lowland agitators in carrying the demand for the People's Charter into the Scottish Highlands and stressed that 'the Highlands presented no barrier which their irrepressible energy could not surmount'.[65]

Continuing to expose the insidious influence of Walter Scott's un-historic romantic propaganda about the Scottish Highlands, the *Chartist Circular* in 1840 reported on the activities of Highland landlords in 'burning' peasants out of their 'cottages'.[66] Testifying to the persistent colonial dimension in the British administration of Scotland, Irish troops were, in 1842, brought over from Belfast to restore 'order' in the Lanarkshire coalfields, Rodger would continue to speak for a culturally, though not politically subdued, Scottish working class.[67]

Although the English authorites did not treat their own Chartists with too much tolerance, they did not brush aside the 'rule of law' as their Scottish counterparts did. Scottish dictatorship was at its worse in the city of Dundee; and in 1844 John Duncan 'endeavoured to impress his hearers with the belief that the magistrates and the police would wish to pick a quarrel with them for the purpose of getting them in their grasp and they would destroy them.' A Queen's proclamation to read the Riot Act in Dundee was already drawn up at Windsor Castle on 13th August ; and on 23rd August 1845, Lord Provost Duncan read the Riot Act and twelve of the local Chartist leaders were arrested. The Chartist movement in Dundee was broken, John Duncan was declared 'insane' (as Alexander Robertson and John Maclean would be later on) and died in a lunatic asylum a victim of 'the constant terrors of the law'. [68]

Far from moving to the Right as the Stalinist historian Dave Leslie has asserted, Rodger did not lose his revolutionary voice. An anti-imperialist and a champion of workers' rights, the editor of the *Chartist Circular*, in 1841, recommended Rodger's poetry. In an editorial devoted to 'the Radical poet', the editor said:

> Is our old friend Alexander Rodger, still wagging his poetical pow...among the amateurs of his musical genius? He is, and is likely to do so for many years... May God prosper and preserve him; and may he continue a talented humorous man, a scientific vocalist, a Radical Reformer... We hope he will favour the world with a new edition of his newest and wittiest unpublished productions.[69]
> And in 1842 he did.

On 25 January 1843, he was entertained at a 'splendid banquet', in the Trades' Hall; and he had worked on the *Scotch Reformers' Gazette* between 1837 and his death. In a tribute to him in that radical newspaper in 1846, the editor wrote:

We found him to be pre-eminently an honest man, with a warm, and we believe, a spotless heart. He discharged his duties in his own social circle, whether as a husband, a father, or a friend, in an exemplary manner; and, whatever may have been his failings, if he had any, they always leaned "to virtue's side". His health had been in a feeble state for some time past; and although he wrote comparatively little during the last twenty-four months, the soul of the Poet never forsook him.[70]

And if he was sometimes too fond of a 'heavy dram', he was always the radical, anti-John Bull voice of a 'subdued [Scottish] people'.

To appreciate the full extent of the anti-imperialism of Scottish and Irish radicals, the attitudes of Rodger towards the Irish question should be contrasted with that of even the most left-wing of the English Chartists. Moreover, Julius Braunthal, the historian of the International, wrote about the English Chartists' hostility to the agitation for Irish independence. As he put it: 'At a subsequent meeting [of the First International], a letter from the Chartist veteran, George Julian Harney, who had emigrated to Boston, was read out, in which he protested againt the attitude of the International to the Irish question: "Ireland", he wrote "is an integral part of the British Empire". [71]

As MacFarlan grew up in the 1840s, there was a strong and radical Scottish labour movement. According to the English historian Royden Harrison, Scotland between the second half of the eighteenth century and the 1840s developed a 'democratic intellect' in the universities of the Athens of the North. As he put it: 'Scotland made a uniquely important contribution to the development of a provincial culture... The Universities of Glasgow and Edinburgh were, in contrast to Oxford and Cambridge, open and democratic, austere and practical.'[72]

Though undoubtedly open, austere and practical in a much narrower sense than the English bourgeoisie in Oxford or Cambridge, the Scottish universities were not democratic. And in so far as there was any 'democratic intellect' in Scotland it had been created by the Scottish radicals, not by the Enlightenment intellectuals.

Arguing that there were really 'three cultures' in Britain during those decades, Harrison holds that the classical, aristocratic and literary culture with its ideals of 'the Gentleman' was centred in Oxford and Cambridge. Furthermore, the provincial bourgeois culture of the British ruling class with its scientific, practical and useful ideals of 'the Professional Man' had been developed and perfected by the Scottish Enlightenment. But in so far as the 'third culture' that he has sketched in - of the 'painful process' of redrawing the map of learning in ways appropriate to the needs of participatory Democracy existed in Scotland - it belonged to the world of the Scottish radicals like Rodger.

James MacFarlan: A Scottish-Irish Outsider and a Philistine Bourgeoisie

When MacFarlan began to write, Rodger had been dead for a few years. Moreover, the predominantly Presbyterian Scottish working class had been relatively de-radicalised following the virtue collapse of Chartism in 1848; and as Irish immigrants increasingly poured into industrial Scotland after the Irish famine of 1848 a strong Orange minority of Scottish workers weakened organised Labour by waging sectarian warfare against the Irish in Scotland. Although none of those who wrote MacFarlan's obituaries in 1862 acknowledged the ferocity of anti-Irishness in Scottish working-class communities, he had undoudoubtedly suffered from religious prejudice and the Calvinists' cultural philistinism. Certainly, a strong section of the Scottish working class became hostile to the Irish workers in their midst, though the labour movement in the Athens of the North did not abandon the anti-imperialism of men like James Thomson Callender and Alexander Rodger.

With the death of Rodger and industrialisation gaining pace, the revival of trade unions in the 1850s reflected, in the words of the Scottish historian W. H. Marwick, 'the change in the balance of economic power' in favour of the bourgeoisie.[73] The Scottish labour movement was de-radicalised, suppressed and disoriented in the 1850s and early 1860s; and MacFarlan did not have the same access to a supportive radical culture or radical newspapers as Rodger had enjoyed. It was a period of hiatus for radicals and the Scottish labour movement, and because he did not inherit much of the radical culture of Rodger's generation, MacFarlan had to become a new voice of the Scottish working class in the difficult circumstances of the 1850s.

While paying a grudging tribute to his genius as a poet, most Scots who have written about MacFarlan, the man, have always been very hostile and unsympathetic. By the time he came on the Scottish scene as a poet and writer, the Liberty Hall gathering place for poets and writers at 188 Trongate no longer existed; and in his fine book on the *Literary Landmarks of Glasgow,* James Kirkpatrick did not even mention MacFarlan. In a recent article on MacFarlan in the book *A Glasgow Collection,* Hamish Whyte argues that:

> Other [more conventional] contemporaries of comparable talent and circumstances, such as Alexander Smith, James Thomson, David Gray and Robert Buchanan achieved some measure of fame and, if not fortune, comfort. Why not MacFarlan? The short answer is his lack of stability. He was shiftless, a wanderer by nature. He was his own worst enemy.

Citing a comment in an obituary from the *Fifeshire Journal* that 'When at his best, MacFarlan was, from the Christian point of view, a dangerous enemy', Whyte used the evidence from 1862 rather uncritically. As an atheist of Catholic and Irish origin, he must have been particularly uncongenial to the Anglo-Scottish bourgeoisie of Glasgow and the West of Scotland. The son of the hated Irish immigrants who were not yet properly integrated into the culture of, in E. P. Thompson's phrase, 'time, work-discipline and [Scottish] industrial capitalism', MacFarlan was also a defender of the sacred Rights of Labour.[74] Focusing on his 'later untoward character' and 'destitution' in his *Dictionary of Eminent Scotsmen,* Joseph Irving ignored his Irish ancestry, the women in his life, and his expression of Scottish working-class grievances.[75]

It was very interesting that few of the obituary writers, including the editor of the Scottish working-class newspaper the *Glasgow Sentinel,* mentioned that MacFarlan's father had been an Irish immigrant. (Incidentally, no one bothered to mention his mother's nationality). Although Alexander Campbell, the editor of the *Glasgow Sentinel,* did not mention his national origins, he hinted at the role of his Irish ancestry in aliening him from the philistine bourgeois Glaswegians with money and influence:

> The songs which would not sustain him in life are an heritage which shall not let his memory die. He has written verses few in number, it may be, but worthy enough to find a place in our literature... With some half-dozen, say, he leaves to other

generations the richest record of our own place and progress which we have it in our power to hand down... MacFarlan had not the gift of drawing around him such friends as adored poet Hugh MacDonald, but no one who has learned anything of him but must feel a pitiful interest in all that belongs to him. We know the coldness with which our townsmen regard the want of succeess; but in the case of MacFarlan this *mercenary spirit* receives its rebuke from the fact that Mr. Charles Dickens acknowledged by a kindly interest the talent of the poet, and gave a place in *All the Year Round* to contributions which were munificently paid for.[76]

But not even the sympathetic Campbell appreciated McFarlan's contribution to Scottish journalism and radical literature.

MacFarlan's father was an Irish pedlar from Augher, Tyrone, and the poet was born in Kirk Street, Calton, Glasgow on 9th April 1832. At the school he attended in Glasgow for two years he was described as 'one of those boys a teacher has a pride in - always obedient, assiduous, and attentive'. His father was 'something of a rhymer'; and his mother 'used to chant a store of old ballads which were an inspiration in themselves'. In one of the least hostile accounts of his early life, George Eyre-Tood wrote:

But about the age of ten he began to accompany his father over the country, and among the towns and villages of the West of Scotland. By this means he may, it is true, have acquired impressions of nature which were to be of service later in his verse. But it is certain he also acquired habits of vagrancy which were to prove fatal to his character and career. An accident presently opened to his sight the magic world of poetry. He picked up on a Lanarkshire road an odd volume of Byron which some rambler had dropped... From his allusions in his poem "Bookworld" it is evident that he found his way at once to the greatest masters of the world's song, and he himself says that by the time he was twenty there was scarcely a standard work in the language which he had not read.[77]

In 1854 Robert Hardwicke published a small volume titled *Poems*. It was favourably noticed by some of the literary reviews in London; and later he attracted the attention of both Dickens and Thacheray. Edinburgh was no longer so important as a powerhouse of publishing; and MacFaralan had been forced to make a personal visit to publishers in London. In 1856 a publsher in Glasgow issued his *City Songs*; and in 1856 David Bogue published his *Lyrics of Life*; and, when he was suffering from terrible poverty in 1862 he published his small sixteen-page pamphlet of essays titled *The Attic Study: Brief Notes on Nature, Men and Books*. It was not until 1882 that a Glasgow publisher Robert Forrester issued a substantial volume entitled *The Poetical Works of James MacFarlan* with A Memoir by Colin Rae-Brown.

In 1856 he married 'a very respectable' girl, a steam-loom weaver from Belfast. No one ever bothered to mention her name, but George Eyre-Todd said:

> She did her best in the miserable Drygate attic, which was the poet's home, to eke out a livelihood by dressmaking. But what with the constant births and deaths of children, and the chronic inclination of her husband to go 'on the ran-dan', she must have led a sorry life.[78]

So did countless other working-class women in Glasgow and elsewhere without being noticed by comfortably- off writers.

In a brief 'Sketch of the Author's Life' introducing MacFarlan's *Lyrics of Life*, A.A. wrote about the origins of MacFarlan's endemic ill-health:

> Exposed to the extremes of heat and cold, wandering in remote districts in all kinds of weather, lying in damp beds and rising to undried cloths, which sadden and depress the wearer, it is no marvel we see the young man labouring in consumption, and the old twitched with aches and asthma... Till arriving at his twentieth year, MacFarlan continued his severe trade, having

indeed never learned another, circumstances preventing his settlement at any regular calling.[79]

Unable to forgive him for having failed to develop a 'regular calling', the great and good of the new Glasgow would soon clarify their collective attitide to scribblers and poets.

Despite the initial success of his first book, MacFarlan did not have much luck in selling the two hundred copies that he had brought with him from London. Before acquiring a job as a librarian in the Glasgow Athenaeum at £20 a year, MacFarlan suffered a number of bad experiences. As A. A. explained: 'In this institution he had to attend from nine in the morning till half past ten, and sometimes late at night, always on foot, subjected to the caprices of the enlightened frequenters of the establishment. He gave up that job; and in 1857 he began to contribute occasional pieces to the new Glasgow newspaper *The Bulletin*.

The Challenge to Kailyard Literature and the Anglo-Scottish Bourgeoisie

Attempting to assist the Scottish working class to develop their own class identity as Scots and workers, MacFarlan's poetry challenged the dominant Kailyard literature being fostered by the Anglo-Scottish ruling class. Despite his shortcomings as a man, he carved out a name for himself as the voice of a subdued Scottish working class. When he tried to sell copies of his *City Songs* in Edinburgh in 1857, he was not successful. As A. A. put it:

> Here [in Glasgow] MacFarlan met with the most decided discouragement, and in the hour of the direst distress, when the last article had been sold to pay his lodgings, and remaining for two days without food, he wrote to an eminent man of letters, and friend of the people, not for direct pecuniary aid, but the influence of the self-raised man to procure him some slight employment. No answer was ever returned, and the Poet went back to Glasgow in that state, when, to use his own words, 'suicide becomes almost a necessity, and death a relief.' In his native city he met with little

more success, and on one occasion, when calling on a minister of the gospel, who had also aspired to authorship, the good evangelist, instead of purchasing a copy of the poet's works, shut the door insolently in his face! [80]

Notwithstanding his gifts and literary talent, MacFarlan did not, in 1855, meet with any sympathy or support. As George Eyre-Todd noted: 'He returned to Glasgow to suffer further rebuffs, one man bidding him to *burn his books*, as he pushed him from his office'.[81] Cropping up again and again, the 'democratic intellect' existed alongside awful intolerance among the Anglo-Scottish bourgeoisie. Despite MacFarlan's love of Robert Burns and poor working people, he had had no reason to recognise any 'democratic intellect' in Edinburgh or Glasgow. His critics were not even softened by the fact that he did not use Lallans, except very occasionally.

In 1855-56 he was appointed by Colin Rae-Brown as a police-court reporter on the *Daily Bulletin*. Many of his unpublished poems and articles were published in a wide range of newspapers; and before he was dismissed by the *Daily Bulletin* for not submitting his copy on time, the editor published his reports and novelettes. He wrote a brief autobiography for Colin Rae-Brown; and in discussing MacFarlan's experiences after 1856-7 Rae-Brown wrote:

> One bright passage at least would have appeared in the poet's autobiography - had it been brought down to a later date - descriptive of the hearty welcome and liberal recompense vouchsafed by Charles Dickens when he accepted, time after time, MacFarlan's very distinguished poetical contributions to *Household Words*.[82]

Then he contributed essays to the *Glasgow Weekly Journal*; and his scattered writings and poems remain to be gathered together and published.

In his poem 'A Voice from the City', Macfarlan must have spoken for many Scots and Irish workers who had been dispossessed from their land:

Oh! I long to see the fields again, to hear the sky-
lark sing, To look upon the hedgerows and the
fruit-trees blossoming; To hear the sweet and silver
sound of streamlets as they run; Where they creep
beneath the willows, or leap out to feel the sun.

In his poem 'The Land of Burns' he expressed the irrepressible
radicalism of the Scots thus:

O, large the heart and proud the soul
Of him who gave those fields to fame:
Whose being never brooked control
Of lordly mien or titled name!

Although most of his poetry was much less political than Rodger's
had been, Campbell used his obituary in the *Glasgow Sentinel* to assert
that:

It can be no condescension to honour the genius
which Dickens recognised, although the novelist's
friend was never clothed in purple nor fine linen;
and notwithstanding the questionable standard of
respectability set up by our respectable bagmen,
we cannot doubt MacFarlan's merits will receive
such recognition as may bring timely succour to
the kindly woman he called his wife.[83]

Yet despite the bleakness of his life and the Presbyterian bourgeois
censoriousness of most of those who have written about him, MacFarlan
made some friends.

The good Scots' bourgeoisie, who were 'interested' in imaginative
literature, were less generous or socially sensitive than the civilised
Dickens and his ilk. On the basis of a short interview with him, Charles
Roger wrote:

He was a poet born, yet rags, meanness, leasing,
and drink were in a manner native to him... Low
society he loved, and his best verses were written
amidst the fumes of tobacco and drink. His muse
was always ready, and on the margins of old

newspapers, amidst the distractions of a taproom, he would inscribe admirable verses. With equal promptitude he could invent a tale of distress, or feign a family bereavement, to obtain sixpence.[84]

(He published a poem supporting 'Garibaldi' and as an opponent of the slavery of the Blacks in America he wrote a poem on 'William Lloyd Garrison' and the Abolitionists, though no copy seems to have survived). And it did not occur to the sanctimonious and censorious Roger that MacFarlan's dodges for obtaining money had been induced by awful poverty and deprivation in the land of the so-called democracy and the 'democratic intellect'.

James M. Slimmon, the now forgotten Kirkintilloch poet, identified MacFarlan as a great poet. Summing up his contribution to imaginative literature, Slimmon wrote:

> If ever a human being breathed in whom the divine fire burned with unquenchable flame, that man was the ragged, unkempt, mean-looking tramp, who from dingy garrets and common lodging-houses in the slums of Glasgow sent forth to the world such beautiful lyrics as 'The Poet', 'The Ruined City', and that superb piece of marching music, 'The Lords of Labour'.[85]

Struggling against poverty and constant ill-health during the last few years of his life, MacFarlan continued to produce poems and essays. In 1859, when Samuel Lover returned from Glasgow and went to the Garrick Club, in London, with a copy of 'The Lords of Labour', he was well received. As soon as he had finished reciting it, Thackeray sprang to his feet and said: 'Not Burns himself could have taken the wind out of that man's sails'.[86] The critics were usually much less generous, and in his obituary William Hodgson wrote:'What wonder that there is ever in his writings a protest against this oppression, or that occasionally, as in the "Bard of Overtile," there comes forth this faith in the unknown rewards of the poor?

The Bard of Overtile was poor -
His Home a garret high,
Yet nearer than the bawling world
To God, and sun, and sky.[87]

Even in death, MacFarlane could still upset the assumptions of the arrogant mid-Victorian Anglo-Scottish bourgeoisie.

In the first two verses of 'The Lords of Labour', MacFarlan expressed his irrepressible Scottish radicalism:

They come! they come in a glorious march!
You can hear their steam-steeds neigh,
As they dash through Skill's triumphal arch,
Or plunge 'mid the dancing spray.
Their bale-fires blaze in the mighty forge,
Their life-pulse throbs in the mill,
Their lightings silver the gaping gorge,
And their thunder shake the hill
Ho! these are the Titans of toil and trade,
The heroes who yield no sabre;
But mightier conquests repeath the blade
That is borne by the Lords of Labour
Brave hearts, like jewels, light the sod -
Through the midst of commerce shine -
And souls flash out, like stars of God
From the midnight of the mine.
No Palace is theirs, no castle great,
No princely, pillared hall;
But they can laugh at the roofs of state,
'Neath the heaven which is over all.

Reflecting the way of life of the new Scottish proletariat during its painful transition to heavy industries unknown to Rodger's generation of radicals, MacFarlan, like Burns, had a sharp eye for human foibles.

A few months before his death, he wrote and published his collection of essays titled *The Attic Study*. It was an utter failure commercially and it did not bring any income to the unfortunate author of the brief essays on 'Participation,' 'Nature and Art,' 'The Past,' 'Opinion,' 'Conventionalities,' 'Masks,' 'Selfishness,' 'Genius,' 'Science,' and 'Poetry'. In his essay on 'Genius', he wrote:

138

Genius is the star of God's Legion of Honour. Each one of the proud fraternity wears the order unmistakably on his breast. Counterfeit badges may, and have been formed, but the rich weird light sparkles only in the real... The great epic, fine picture, or noble statue existed first as floating ideas in the minds of the artist, but the great Creative Faculty alone is able to form the planet out of atoms.[88]

On poetry, he said: 'There can never be a clear analysis of Poetry. It is a thing at all times to be felt than defined.'

In his essay on 'Opinion', he said: 'Laws are opinions enforced, but as a country advances in growth the girdle will snap and fall off, when a wider must be provided. What is true of nations is also true of individual man, and the wisest have been the most progressive'. Discussing 'Conventionalities', he wrote:

I have somewhere found it asked 'what man is bold enough to break through his conventional glass-house, and come out and live naturally?' Scarcely any man will do it from his fear of some other man. The invisible genius of Fashion, seated in Paris or London, directs us how we shall eat and drink, and what we shall wear, and lays down her code for the whole course of our conduct. To rebel against this or munmur at it renders you an outsider, a *marked man*, an oddity and a *malcontent*.[89]

Using his experiences and knowledge of the Courts in Glasgow, he came closest to a Marxist understanding of consciousness and 'false consciousness' in his essay titled 'Masks'. In adittion to expressing his sympathy for the working-class victims of a brutal industrial society, MacFarlan did not conceal his radicalism. In one sentence he wrote: 'The great man appears only to the world attired in the fine costume of his office; he speaks only in accordance with the popular place assigned him'. Again he would have agreed with Peter Kropotkin's assertion about the need for the 'justice our minds seek' rather than mere 'judicial justice'. He wrote about judges thus:

The judicial character, too, is almost inseparable in our minds from wig and gown, and the most solemn gravity. A joke from the Bench strikes most people as an amazing condescension, while to some it appears as unnatural. The man is entirely kept from view with all his affectations and humours; and our sense grasps only an antiquated red garment and some curled white hairs.[90]

MacFarlan died in indescribable poverty, and he was buried in 'the Cheapside Cemetery' on 10th November 1862. On 22 November the *Glasgow Gazette* reported that 'we are happy to learn that a few gentlemen, who were kind to the poet during his last days, have associated themselves into a small committee, for the purpose of raising a fund for the relief of his humble and desolate home.'[91] And the Scottish Labour newspaper *The Glasgow Sentinel* also appealed to the organised workers for help for his wife and child.

With the death of 'the pedlar poet,' a chapter of the history of the de-radicalisation of the Scottish working class was coming to an end. In his life, poetry and literature, MacFarlan testified that even in the worst of times from a radical/socialist perspective the voice of radical poets cannot be silenced.

Conclusion

Though keeping alive the Scots anti-imperialist counter-culture and radicalism, MacFarlan did not live long enough to see the Scottish labour movement's support for President Lincoln and the struggle for the emancipation of 'the Negroes' during the American civil war. In the city of Edinburgh, where Robert Knox was giving the racist lectures that went into his book *Races of Men* (1862), the Trades Council, trade unions and radical groups were organising pro-Lincoln meetings.[92] Similar meetings were held all over Scotland.

When the Scottish workers were radicalised from the early 1860s onwards, the labour movement moved to the left of its English counterpart. In my article on 'The American Civil War and the Growth of Scottish Republicanism', I have documented the revival of Republicanism in Scotland and the impact of that war on some of the Irish immigrants in Edinburgh.[93] It was a pity that this revival did not come soon enough to ensure a wide readership and 'bread and wine' for the heroic 'pedlar poet'. And, because history is written by the winners, he was kept out of books on the history of modern Scotland.

Alexander Robertson (1825-1893) and John Murdoch (1818-1903): *Highland Land and Labour Agitators and the Wider World*

George the Third's horror of Scotch metaphysics is shared by not a few in the present day, while the benefits of Physical discovery are proportionally extolled.

Alexander Robertson,
The Philosophy of the Unconditioned *(1866).*

The Anglo-Scottish Ruling Class and the Land Question

The two distinctly or peculiarly Scottish radicals, Alexander Robertson (1825-1893) and John Murdoch (1818-1903) were products of a Presbyterian Highland milieu: thrawn, intransigent, thoroughly *internationalist* in their outlook and hostile to the unprincipled money-grubbbing of the Anglo-Scottish ruling class.[1] Although they were born into a society without a real national historiography of its own or an awareness of earlier Scottish radicals like James Thomson Callender or Alexander Rodger, they inherited - and ultimately contributed to - a folk culture that was opposed to the anglicised culture, politics and historiography of the dominant Anglo-Scots in the universities and institutions of civil society.[2]

Moreover, the formidable contributions of Robertson and Murdoch to Scottish politics, literature and historiography were equally destined, in the fullness of time, to be marginalised by the Anglo-Scottish ruling class. As Scottish Highlanders, who were interested in the land question as the key to the emancipation of Labour, they were too intelligent and too principled to ignore the detrimental impact of Victorian capitalism on the lives of the vast majority of their fellow Scots. By challenging the unfair distribution of political power and the pattern of land ownership in the Highlands, they got caught up in the wider political struggles of their times.[3]

However, in challenging the inherited and still evolving Anglo-Scottish historiography that had originally come out of the Union of 1707, Robertson and Murdoch imbibed and developed the dissident culture and radical traditions of a much older Scotland. But because radicals have always been made by the circumstances of their own times, they had to undergo important personal and social experiences before they would eventually challenge the whole power structure of the Anglo-Scottish ruling class.[4]

The Early Lives of Alexander Robertson and John Murdoch

Unlike Murdoch, Robertson did not develop the detachment to write an autobiography. But, although he bequeathed less knowledge of his biography to posterity than Murdoch did, he was better known in the Scotland of the 1850s and 1860s than the more obscure Murdoch. Robertson however made a big imprint on the Scotland of his time; and he carved his name on the tree of knowledge by writing some memorable books and pamphlets.

Robertson was born in Dunkeld, Perthshire, on 25 January 1825 into a respectable middle-class family;[5] and he died in Glasgow on 29 October 1893.[6] In the slight biographical sketch of Alexander Robertson, popularly known as 'Dundonachie' or chief of the Robertson clan, Henry Dryerre interspersed some of the basic facts of his subject's biography with his own Anglo-Scottish Establishment-minded prejudices. As Dryerre put it:

> His father, Alexander also, and native of the same place, carried on an extensive business as a joiner and contractor for over 50 years, doing the joiner work of a large number of gentlemen's houses all over the countryside, dying in 1857 highly esteemed by the whole district.

Educated partly in the Royal Grammar School at Dunkeld and at Dumfries Academy, where his uncle was the rector, there was nothing in his background to suggest that Robertson would become a major radical thinker, writer and very Scottish Land and Labour agitator.[7] If his formal education did not contribute anything to his sense of Scottish identity, he was brought up in a Gaelic-oriented community where traditional egalitarian traits had not been stamped out. In the course of time, he became an expert on Gaelic folk literature and song.[8]

Certainly, Robertson was given a very good basic Presbyterian education in Dunkeld and Dumfries. He served and completed his time as an apprentice accountant in the Dunkeld branch of the Commercial Bank. In 1845 he was appointed as the Commercial Bank's accountant at Cromarty in the north of Scotland: the successor to the distinguished geologist - and outstanding radical also in the Free Church - Hugh Miller.

Unfortunately, the paucity of biographical information about Robertson's early life in the various obituary notices in the Scottish newspapers was not rectified by Dryerre's biographical sketch. In a few pages breathing hostility toward 'Dundonachie' from beginning to end, Dryerre wrote:

> It is a coincidence, to say the least, that the young and ambitious Dunkeld accountant suddenly developed a fierce enthusiasm for geology, and was to be seen smashing away at the rocks in the district on every possible occasion. If neither fame nor fortune resulted therefrom, no harm was done - unless it happened to be a disagreement which is said to have arisen between our friend and the bank agent, and which led to the former tendering his resignation and coming to Perth, where he started as coal and potato merchant.

(The Scottish radical trait of *carnaptiousness* was already evident, though it would get him into much bigger trouble later on.) However, though equally hostile towards 'Dundonachie', the anonymous obituary-writer in the 'advanced' or left-wing *North British Daily Mail* insisted that 'between the two [Robertson and Miller] there sprung up an intimate acquaintance, which had a profound effect on the succeeding life of Robertson.'[9]

The most interesting aspect of Dryerre's biography of 'Dundonachie' was his denunciation of the Highland agitator as a *carnaptious* [Scottish] radical. By then, although no one ever acknowledged it, radicals in Scotland from the standpoint of those who voiced opinions contrary to those of the Anglo-Scottish ruling class were always dismissed as *carnaptious and lunatic*.[10]

In 1852 Robertson moved to Strathford and, according to Dryerre, 'finally removed to his native place [Dunkeld], where he set up at Birnham as coal, lime, and wood merchant and, gaining the patronage of the Duke of Atholl, who was his best customer for several years, established a splendid business for himself - one result of which was the erection of the villa up Strathbraab from which he derived his popular cognomen, and probably another, that he assumed the headship of Clan Robertson. But 'Dundonachie' or the 'Chief' of the Robertson clan was described by Dryerre as a man whose '"his spirit was one of those which would

> Eat into itself for lack
> Of somebody to hew or hack

and, before the destruction of toll-bars and the abolition of pontages (or charges for crossing bridges) became the absorbing business of his life, it is something of the nature of a surprise to find him preparing to wage "grim-visaged war in such a totally different a sphere of activity as "metaphysics"'[11] With the effortless Oxbridge ease of the Anglo-Scot, Dryerre made this assertion without explaining why it was so surprising that Robertson should have written about philosophy. Clearly, Scottish radicals were never intended to be more intelligent than their rulers.

When I was doing full-time research in 1968 for my doctoral thesis on Scottish radical and working-class movements during the second half of the nineteenth century, I came across the extensive newspaper reports of Robertson's political activities in 1868 before I searched for biographical information about him. But, although there is no evidence that Robertson and Murdoch met before the 1880s, they had, in their very different ways, made a major contribution to the development of the Scottish labour movement in the 1860s and 1870s.

At the same time as I encountered Robertson in Scottish newspapers, so I somewhat amazingly discovered Murdoch's handwritten and still unpublished multi-volume autobiography in the Mitchell Library,

Glasgow. In 1925 the handwritten 'Autobiography of John Murdoch' was desposited in the Mitchell Library by Professor Magnus Maclean. It was not entered in the manuscript catalogue, and Scottish historians had been hitherto unaware of its existence. In 1968 I located it in Glasgow after I had found a scrap of screwed-up paper in the manuscript catalogue referring to a pamphlet by John Murdoch in the small safe.

John Murdoch, who was to play a key role in the Highland land agitations in the 1870s and 1880s, was born on 15 January 1818 at Lynemore, Nairnshire. When he died on 29 January 1903, he was ultimately destined to force his name and deeds into Scottish history. He lived to be 86, and his life was filled with many-sided activity, whose significance has not received the attention it deserves. Moreover, there are aspects of his life and work which have a special significance for Scottish as well as labour historians.[12] To play down the real importance of radicalism from below in Scottish history, in his book *A Century of the Scottish People, 1830-1950*, T. C. Smout had to ignore Robertson and Murdoch.[13]

His father was John Murdoch, and his mother was Mary Macpherson, the daughter of a sea captain: both families had roots which stretched far back into Scottish history. In 1827 the family moved to the island of Islay, and John Murdoch lived there till 1838. His 'agricultural education' was inaugurated on 'the little farm which had been selected and conferred on my father'.[14] Moreover, he imbibed the rich folklore, customs and culture of the Highlanders among whom he lived and grew to manhood.[15]

Islay in the 1820s and 1830s was geographically remote and culturally alien to the industrial society, with its rigid social stratification and class conflict, which had emerged in the Scottish Lowlands and the north of England. Murdoch's life in Islay was happy, exciting and satisfying: the social structure and the wholeness of a common culture, shared to some extent by all 'classes' from the Highland aristocrats down to the small farmers, had a profound influence on his subsequent social and political thought.[16] His experiences there were, in due course, to turn him into a left-wing radical; and his hatred of the squalor and ugliness of industrialism inhibited him from making common cause with the industrial workers before the early 1880s. By contrast, Robertson identified with the industrial workers from his first interventions in Scottish politics during the general election of 1868.[17]

In 1838 Murdoch went to 'serve in the shop of Mr. William Boyd, a grocer in the High Street, Paisely'. Mr. Boyd was 'an earnest and prominent Radical'. But within six weeks of his arrival in Paisely 'there was a letter from my father stating that he had been favoured with an appointment for me in the Excise'. Murdoch reluctantly decided to accept a job in the Excise service; and he began and completed his training in Edinburgh under 'an English gentleman who had strong Highland sentiments from his serving some time when a young man in Islay'. Then he worked as an Excise officer in Kilsyth, where coal mining was in its infancy, and in Middletown. He was already very critical of the drink trade (his only real criticism of Islay was that the island's prosperity depended on whisky); but he was not above taking an occasional glass of whisky himself.[18]

In 1841 he was promoted to 'a Ride' in Shuttlesworth, Lancashire. He was appalled by the 'comparative savages' he saw in the factories, mills and places he visited. Here he came into contact with 'the Mormons, the followers of Robert Owen, the Chartists and the Anti-Corn Law League agitators'. He also 'met with the lowest class of Englishman, and I cannot help repeating that they were a disgusting lot'. Nor was their character improved, in his opinion, by their surroundings. The Tom and Jerry shop 'was often no more than a kitchen with a scullery on the one side, and some sort of sleeping place on the other. In the kitchen, the water was boiled, the malt in a wash tub in the middle of the floor... In this atmosphere...the young "Lankie", as the Lancashireman was often called, was brought up; and one can imagine the kind of education which girls received in such schools, the discourse over the pots of beer in keeping with the rest'. From then on he was a life-long advocate of temperance.[19]

Murdoch's experiences in Lancashire in the 1840s had a lasting influence on his thought and radicalism. By 1843 the 'very backward state of the land' with the 'periodical depressions of trade' stimulated him towards formulating the ideas which were to influence his thought and agitations for many years to come. He began to write about 'the desirability of bringing the land and labour questions together'; and his first article on the land question appeared in the *Bolton Free Press* about 1843. He encountered 'some of the Chartists', but his 'impression of them was not very good. I might have heard Feargus O'Connor, but did not. I am sorry I did not, for I sympathised with him when he was assailed on all sides for his attempt to plant land colonies on the land in England. I never met Ernest Jones, nor Bronterre O'Brien, but I took in their teaching in regard to the land and see no ground today to reject it'.[20]

In 1843 Murdoch's father was killed in a shooting accident, and 'the factor' took advantage of the situation to evict his mother and her children from the farm. Murdoch was apparently not embittered by this experience; and he was always a more aloof and less emotional man than 'Dundonachie'. A short time later he was to return to 'a Ride' in Islay, and he was soon involved with a group of fellow radicals in discussing 'science, poetry, theology, and politics'. [21] Before long, however, he was destined for service in Dublin, Shetland and Inverness. While engaged in Dublin as a customs and excise officer, he was active in an agitation to improve his fellow workers pay and conitions. In Dublin, too, he contributed articles on a wide variety of topics to such newspapers as *The Nation*. He was a practical land improver as well as a political agitator. His employers disliked him: he was always too much his own man in spite of his temperamental cautiousness.

While he was a thorough internationalist, he was already identifying with Scottish and Irish nationalism behind the scenes. At this time, too, while attempting to stimulate Scottish national sentiment, he wrote for Irish nationalist newspapers. Unlike Robertson, who would become by 1868 a fighter indifferent to his personal fate, Murdoch was more of a survivor. By tactfully encouraging radicalism and anti-Unionist Scottish and Irish nationalism while still in the pay of the British government as a civil servant, he represented the more 'respectable' strain of Scottish radicalism which had begun with Thomas Muir of Huntershill. There was the obvious continuity of the *carnaptious* extra-Parliamentary, 'direct action' tradition and the suspicion of constitutional Parliamentary politics, though Robertson used the courts more than any other Scottish radical before or since.

Murdoch's Obscurity and Robertson's Prominence in the 1850s and 1860s

Unlike Robertson, Murdoch did not play any direct role in Scottish radical politics before he founded *The Highlander* newspaper in Inverness in 1873. When he was transferred to Ireland in 1855, the Irish were assigned, in the phrase of James Hunter, 'a pretty lowly place in that pseudo-scientific scheme of things which so appealed to Victorians and which viewed Anglo-Saxon Protestants as the most perfect product of human evolution'. [22] Identifying Ireland and the Scottish Highlands as two components of a single Celtic civilisation, Murdoch increasingly deepened his interest in and support for Irish and Scottish nationalism as the most important forces of radicalism.[23]

Although he tried unsuccessfully to get articles criticising the Scottish landed aristocracy published in Scotland, Murdoch did not have any influence on the politics of the Athens of the North in the 1850s or 1860s.[24] But, although the years between the collapse of Chartism and the rebirth of the Scottish labour movement around 1865 constituted a bleak phase in the history of radicalism, 'Dundonachie' developed a critique of the Anglo-Scottish ruling class and industrial capitalism. It was also something of a paradox that Murdoch rather than Robertson would ultimately gain a place in Scottish labour historiography, since 'Dundonachie' had more to say about and in defence of working folk over a longer period of time than Murdoch ever did. It was also somewhat surprising that W. H. Marwick did not mention Robertson in his book *A Short History of Labour in Scotland* (1967), though he gave Murdoch a place of honour in the story of Scottish radicalism. [25]

By the beginning of his intervention in Scottish politics, 'Dundonachie' struggled to put into a historical context the social and political problems facing the rural and industrial working class. His first extant publication was a twenty-six-page pamphlet *Extermination of the Scottish Peasantry: Being a Reply To A letter from the Most Noble the Marquess of Breadalbane* (1853). Written under the pseudonym R. Alister, it opened with a rebuttal of his Lordship's denial that 'extensive Clearances have been made upon his Highland Properties'. In the light of the dominant Anglo-Scottish historiography's refusal to acknowledge the hard evidence of 'Dundonachie's' observations about what was happening in the Highlands, his testimony will be quoted:

> The Sutherland and Gordon clearings are known to the world, and yet the fact of Highland depopulation is said to be inconsistent with truth... Now on Lochtayside, and especially at Acharn, I certainly understood that some thirty or forty tenants looked at Whit Sunday next as the time when their doom would be fixed.[26]

In his first book, *The Barriers to the National Prosperity of Scotland* (1856), published under the pseudonym of 'R. Alister', Robertson expressed his antipathy for the socialist ideas of the time. Nor did he ever depart from this coolness towards atheistic socialism, though his own Scottish radicalism was always egalitarian and democratic. In 1856 he put his argument thus:

> No; we are not socialists, nor ever will be, although we think nevertheless that the working classes are as entitled to enact such laws as would rob the upper classes, as the upper classes are to pass laws for their own benefit to the loss of other classes.
>
> And yet he took socialism so seriously that he described Fourierism as 'the best of the 'socialist systems.'[27]

Raising the questions of patronage, the Game Laws, the awful conditions endured by ploughmen and the bothy system, he observed that 'If any stranger were to overhear a conversation regarding ploughmen in Scotland, by some large farmers, they would be justified in concluding that the ploughman occupied some such position on a large farm as the horse does'. Compaining, too, about the lack of an authentic Scottish national historiography, he said: 'The Sutherland clearances are a standing disgrace to Britain, and they have been exhibited in their true light by foreign historians.'[28]

While some of Robertson's Anglo-Scottish contemporaries who cynically attributed the birth in 1868 of his 'direct action' radicalism to his failure to be appointed a professor of philosophy, the passionate nationalism scattered throughout *The Barriers to the National Prosperity of Scotland* tells another story. Locating the origins of the barriers to the nation's well-being in the development of 'entail and primogeniture' in 'the glorious [English] revolution' of 1688 rather than in the Union of 1707, he argued that the result of the patronage 'concentrated in the hands of the feudal aristocracy' had 'created an incalcuable amount of sycophancy and servility among all classes in Scotland'. And it was this particular social and intellectual atmosphere in Scotland which forced even a man like Robertson to write at first under the pseudonym of 'R. Alister'.[29]

If his Presbyterian religion inhibited him from being a conventional socialist, he was most certainly a radical democrat. As he put it:

> What a change has taken place in the Highlands of Scotland in regard to mannners since the

democratic clan system was broken up. Not many years ago, there was liberty for everyone to act as he chose; equality, for all classes were on a level; and fraternity, for the chief was bound to shake hands and associate with every member of his family or clan. Now the case is so different that every one seems anxious to outstrip his neighbour in sycophancy.[30]

But in the deeper sense of being a radical like the Marx of 1844 - that is, as a critic who went to the root of everything - Robertson was a socialist.

Moreover, in expressing the same theme that he would return to in one of his last publications - the pamphlet entitled *Hanged for the Game Laws* (1884) - he argued that: 'Land being a gift to all, it follows that all have equal rights thereto originally, and whatever interferes with this law is contrary to nature and justice.' In a devastating critique of the Anglo-Scottish ruling class, he wrote:

Nowhere probably in history is mention made of a class of men who have deprived greater advantage from the industrial efforts of the people, and yet have trampled upon, banished, and abused them, more than the Scottish lairds have done for the past eighty years... Poets feel a pleasure in contemplating the pure patriachal or perhaps Celtic system before it was poisoned with Saxon feudalism, as it has been for a hundred years; that is, before the Highland gentry were smitten with the Saxon love of gold.[31]

In 1864 and in 1866 Longmans, Green, the prestigious London publishers, put out two of Robertson's quite technical books on philosophy entitled *The Laws of Thought* and *The Philosophy of the Unconditioned* Both books were well received by the newspapers and magazines. In a review of the second edition of *The Laws of Thought* in *The Spectator*, an anonymous reviewer said: 'The language of the work possesses remarkable clearness, and no inconsiderable grace, and it discloses an intimate acquaintance with Ciceronian and other sources of modern philosophy not often studied nowadays'.[32] By what turned out to be an irony of history, in 1865 Robertson dedicated the second edition of this book to 'his friend Sheriff Barclay'. Within less than three years, Barclay would side with the Duke of Atholl against 'Dundonachie' and the rebellious Robertsons.

As a result of the success of his first book on the subject, he tried to become a professor of philosophy. As Henry Dryerre put it: 'Encouraged thereby, his next step was to apply for the Chair of Moral Philosophy which happened to be vacant in the University of Glasgow; and that the Highland metaphyscian did not lack faith in his own abilities is evident from the terms of his application'.[33] But he did not get the appointment at Glasgow, though Dryerre attributed his increasing involvment in radical politics to a 'grudge' he developed against the Duke of Atholl.

In 1867 Longmans, Green published Robertson's substantial pamphlet on behalf of the Highland Economic Society of Glasgow. Criticising the activities of the large number of Highland and Celtic societies and groups in the Lowland cities, he wrote: 'Had there been a tithe of the enthusiasm extended upon the SOCIAL ASPECT of the Highlands that has been, in a measure, thrown away upon the Ossianic controversy, our country would be in a very different position from what it is at the moment.'[34] In that pamphlet he also criticised wicked deeds of 'the noble family of Sutherland' and the 'threatened evictions of Skibo'. With views like those, he was certainly naive to think that he could become a professor in any Scottish university.[35]

By contrast, Murdoch was much more interested in Celtic literature than Robertson. It was a frequent theme of his writings in the 1850s and 1860s. And in 1873 a large and elaborate book of *Illustrations from Ossian's Poems* by Paolo Priolo was published in Inverness; and the *Arguments were Collated* by John Murdoch, the editor of *The Highlander*.[36]

Robertson was simply incapable of being dull as a writer or as a radical agitator. In *The Philosophy of the Unconditioned*, he wrote: 'Now is the time for Professor Masson to deal a blow for his Scottish lion; and even his friend Professor Blackie, by a few of his fiery philippics, might do something to rouse our patriotism... Like the poet's tree of Clan Alpine, the ruder the storm, the firmer it will take root.'[37]

His two books on philosophy were written to justify religion against the free thinkers Charles Bradlaugh and George Jacob Holyoake with whom he debated in the Hall of Science in Glasgow and London.[38]

It was in 1867 that Robertson set out on a path that led him into permanent opposition to the Anglo-Scottish ruling class. Although he detested 'Dundonachie', Henry Dryeer provided one of the best accounts of the origins of the Dunkeld bridge affair:

> To get at the beginning of the agitation one has to go back to 1803, when great Duke John (who died in January 1828) obtained an Act of Parliament empowering him to build the bridge at a cost of £18,000, which sum was to be repaid him by means of the tolls and pontages... As the years pass the conviction grows in the public mind that the debt on the bridge is wiped out... But the pot boiled over towards the end of 1867, when the Duke refused to receive a deputation from the Free Church with the object of getting permission for the members to pass and repass over the bridge [at Dunkeld] on Sundays free.[39]

At a public indignation meeting, Robertson was elected as the Convencr. After carefully acquiring and studying all the accounts, he reported that all the debt owing to the Duke of Atholl had been paid to him by 1853.

In 1868 the Chief of 'Dundonachie' used the British general election that had taken place six months previously to push the Bridge agitation to the forefront of Scottish consciousness. Supported by the whole of the Scottish labour movement, with which he became increasingly identified, he came into conflict with Sheriff Barclay. The *Glasgow Sentinel*, newspaper of the Scottish labour movement, supported Robertson's leadership of the mass movement against the Duke of Atholl. In the next few months Robertson's employment of 'direct action' tactics of attacking the bridge and allegedly the toll-keepers made a big impact on working-class opinion; and Alexander Campbell's editorship of the *Glasgow Sentinel* meant that a long and influential editorial entitled 'How Highlanders Abolish Tollls: The Revolt of a Clan' could help to keep the agitation alive'.[40]

Troops were called in, and Sheriff Barclay arrested 'Dundonachie'. Not yet back in Scotland, Murdoch was collecting taxes at a time when Highlanders, in common with the whole Celtic race, 'had', in the words of the *Glasgow Sentinel*, 'a decided aversion to tolls and taxes'. As the editor of the *Glasgow Sentinel* continued:

The same impatience which prompted the Gaul to set the gauger at defiance, made him conceive an unconquerable aversion to tolls where regular roads were introduced into the Highlands, and that aversion is still as strong as ever, as evinced by recent events at Dunkeld, where a state of affairs prevailed which bordered on revolution or rebellion.[41]

Like Murdoch, Robertson frequently appeared in public in full Highland regalia. Besides, they were both Scottish nationalists as well as extreme radicals. In 1868 Robertson was very active politically; and he was already working with the radicals in the Scottish National Reform League, and particularly with those in Glasgow. When he spoke at a mass meeting of thousands of working people and farm workers in Perth in 1868 'The Chief himself was in fine fettle and finished his oration with a couple of stanzas of "Scots Wha Hae."'[42]

In his brief history of his clan, David Robertson (1894) did not make a single reference to Alexander Robertson. However, he did say that: 'It is stated that after 1745 a number of Robertsons were obliged to conceal their identity, by changing their surname to the generally English name of Robinson'.[43]

But ancestors of 'Dundonachie' had not been among them. However, unlike James Thomson Callender, Robertson did not express a preference for Bonnie Prince Charlie over the Hanoverian kings, though he shared some of Callender's Republican traits. But just as he called for sharper focus on the 'social aspect' of the Highlands instead of Walter Scott-like romanticism, he would increasingly stand out against the Anglo-Scottish ruling class that had been personified by Scott, Lockhart and Thomas Carlyle.

'Dundonachie', Murdoch and the Scottish Labour Movement

Before Murdoch began to issue *The Highlander* in Inverness in 1873, Robertson was both closer to the Scottish labour movement and the best-known land and labour agitator in Scotland. After the general election of 1868, he kept up a formidable agitation against the Duke of Atholl. But he came into great national prominence towards the end of 1869 when he criticised Sheriff Hugh Barclay in two petitions sent to the House of Commons.

By then the Anglo-Scottish ruling class were out to get 'Dundonachie'; and the petitions were used by the Judiciary to charge him with 'murmuring' a Judge under 'an Act passed in the Seventh Parliament of King James the Fifth of Chapter 104 in the manner mentioned in the libel.' [44] The main evidence cited against Robertson was the statements in the petitions where he wrote:

> On 18 July 1868 Sheriff Barclay, forgetting his status as a Magistrate, and, acting as a criminal detective officer, personally dogged me, and made inquiries about what time I would leave a hotel I was calling at Dunkeld. He watched me passing the pontage gate, and, while I was standing beside it, he assaulted me, and, addressing foolish challenges to me, did all he could to get me involved in a squabble.
>
> Accusing his old 'friend' Sheriff Barclay of assisting the Duke of Atholl to uphold a fraud', he was sentenced to imprisonment in the prison at Perth for one calendar month, and 'further fine' of £50. [45]

When he came out of jail a month later, the people of Dunkeld and Perth gathered a large sum of money for him. But, although he was seen as a popular hero, he was destined to spent the rest of his life in an uneven battle against the Establishment.

Though he continued to defend the principles of the Presbyterian religion against 'the London radicals', he nevertheless helped the radicals' political campaigns on behalf of the working class, with which he increasingly identified. In 1874 Robertson wrote to the Secretary of the Labour Representation League in London:

> I daresay you will recollect my mentioning to you that I have for a considerable time entertained the idea that the City of Perth if appealed to might be very likely to return a Working Man's Candidate to Parliament. So much is this the case that I have spoken to a number of my friends about appearing as a candidate myself at the expected dissolution. Before however announcing myself I write to ask

you if the coast is clear and to say that if you have
any other party in view I will say nothing more on
the subject.

In an interesting postscript to the Radicals in London, he said:

You may make what use you like of this note. I am
now issuing an Appeal to the People of Scotland
on the question of the Dunkeld Bridge grievance -
the Edinburgh folk are promising to come to the
rescue and it is expected that the provincials will
follow suit.[46]

John Murdoch, Scottish Liberal-Labourism and Socialism

In his introduction to *For the People's Cause: From the Writings of John
Murdoch*, James Hunter said:

'The masses are beginning to learn that they
possess enormous power and that power is
valueless unless it is concentrated', John Murdoch
wrote during the 1870s when advocating the
establishment of more effective trade unions. It was
essential, he asserted in the course of the same
decade, that Scotland was not permitted 'to sink
into an English province' and was provided instead
with its own national Parliament." 'No doubt there
are emasculated Scotsmen', Murdoch continued,
who would reject the enfranchisement of their own
nation just because the Irish demand it for theirs,
but the thing is getting into the atmosphere, and
even they will inhale it by and bye.[47]

But, although there is no concrete evidence that they ever met or
referred to one another in their writings except briefly in Glasgow in
1885, when they met Michael Davitt, Murdoch and Robertson
contributed more than a mite to the development of the radical Scottish
nationalism of the labour movement in the Athens of the North.

Murdoch's publication *The Highlander* was published in Inverness
between 1873 and 1882. It was a very Scottish radical paper in which

Murdoch 'advocated the cause of the people, and particularly the right of the Gaelic people to their native soil'.[48] Through *The Highlander* and Murdoch's personal intervention in disputes between crofters and landlords the way was prepared for the rise of the Crofters' Party and the successful speaking tours of Henry George and Michael Davitt in the 1880s.[49]

The American Land League was founded in 1879; Irish-Americans 'flocked to join it and to contribute money'; and Patrick Ford 'pledged his paper to the cause'.[50] At the same time Murdoch toured America, and Ford introduced him to Dr. William Carroll, who with 'three other gentlemen' gave him 'two thousand dollars' to save *The Highlander* from collapsing. Ford was the link connecting Murdoch with Michael Davitt and Henry George.

In the 1870s Murdoch agitated through the columns of *The Highlander* for the setting up of a Royal Commission on the Highlands. In 1883 he gave valuable evidence before the Napier Commision on the Highlands, chaired by Lord Napier. In 1884 Davitt toured the Scottish coalfields advocating the nationalisation of the land and minerals. John Murdoch simultaneously made *his* first efforts to win support for land reform among the coal miners and other industrial workers. By this time he was living in Glasgow; and, unlike Robertson - who had allied with organised Labour long beforehand - he began moving to the Left.

Before Murdoch began to agitate in industrial Scotland in the 1880s, the Scottish labour movement had been enchanted by 'American democracy.'[51] By tracing poverty, unemployment, poor wages and ill-health back to the structural factors within capitalism, Henry George, Murdoch and many others helped to destroy this enchantment. The accusation that poverty was created by capitalism struck at the cultural, psychological and spiritual roots of the hegemony existing in Scottish society, and James Leatham, a leading young socialist in Aberdeen, subsequently recalled this forgotten aspect of the combination of George's and Mudoch's propaganda: 'Like Henry George at a later date and from a different opening, Marx taught *la Misere (sic!)* - the identification of misery, or as George called it, the increase of want side by side with the increase of wealth.'[52]

Once Murdoch and the Scottish Land Restoration League had been formed in 1884, the image of America as 'a land of golden opportunity' for working people was increasingly blurred; the class struggle within America was discovered or rediscovered; and a discovery of widespreead poverty among ordinary people in all capitalist countries led a new generation of working-class Scots to look to American labour organisation for ideas, inspiration and moral support.

At the forefront of this agitation, Murdoch worked easily and naturally with the growing left-wing socialist tendencies in the labour movement. He worked with Bruce Glaiser, who told a mass meeting of Lanarkshire miners that the extension of the vote would not touch the problems confronting working people. As he put it:

> In America, France and other countries those measures so loudly called for have already been obtained, and the working classes in those countries were as badly off as were the masses in Great Britain. The reason why people were compelled to waste their lives day after day without sufficient reward was because labour was day by day systematically robbed.[53]

Murdoch was one of many radicals who agitated 'the [Scottish] land and labour question', particularly among the coal miners; and his speeches were frequently quoted in *The North British Daily Mail* - a newspaper that the Scottish novelist James Barke would use in his best novel, *The Land of the Leal* (1939).

Murdoch was more important than anyone else for bringing the ideas of Henry George into the Scottish labour movement. But, although Murdoch joined the Scottish Labour Party in 1888 and worked with socialists, he could not accept the ideas of Marxian socialism any more than Robertson could abandon his earlier theoretical objections to socialist doctrine.

In Edinburgh, Andreas Scheu, an Austrian emigre, con- centrated on influencing the supporters of George and Murdoch. In a letter to Miss Jean Reeves, a leading member of the Edinburgh branch of the Scottish Land Restoration League, he said:

> Not that I believe you to be a socialist; but I am aware that you are supporting a movement which goes very far in the direction of socialism. Two years ago I heard Mr. Henry George admit that himself by saying he knew full well that the nationalisation of the land would not solve the

social question; but he was convinced that it was a
sure step toward bringing that solution about.[54]

A profound fear of social revolution was deeply rooted in the consciousness of the Anglo-Scottish ruling class, and in 1887 a member of the Glasgow branch of the Scottish Land and Labour League (affiliated to the William Morris Socialist League in London) described the response of one influential Liberal academic to the socialists' threat to social stability:

> I have just come in from the [Glasgow] Philosophical [Society] where I heard Smart deliver a lecture on Factory, Industry and Socialism. Marx almost from beginning to end - vigorous and outspoken - conclusion of the whole matter something like this: 'If we who call ourselves the upper classes do not take Carlyle's advice and become real Captains of Industry and organisers of the people working not for gain but for the good of all, so as to open up to every man the opportunities for the higher life of culture at present the possession of a few - if we do not do this within a very few years, then we shall have to prevent Revolution by leading it.[55]

Nonetheless the Scottish Liberal Association repeatedly rejected the demands of the radicals and the socialists for land nationalisation and a legal eight hour day, and the Liberal-Unionists like Lord Melgund, who had just left the Liberal Party, criticised the agitations for the disestablishment of the Church of Scotland and for Irish Home Rule. In his election address to the people of Selkirk and Peebles, Megund denounced 'the Irish-American agitators' who were working with Murdoch, Keir Hardie and the socialists.[56]

Moreover Scottish Liberal-Unionism, in contrast to its English variety, was a conservative rather than a radical social force, and the Scottish Liberal-Unionists were frightened by the land agitations in the Highlands, where the Whig elements were being challenged by the Crofters' Party. By then Murdoch, who had obtained financial help from Dr. William Carroll of Philadelphia, was a very prominent agitator among industrial workers in Lowland Scotland.[57]

Murdoch was working with George and Michael Davitt to win support for the agitation for the nationalisation of mineral royalties to provide State insurance for the miners. Working with left-wing socialists like the important William Small, Murdoch helped to form the Scottish Anti-Royalty and Labour League.[58] And at this stage Andrew Carnegie, who had robbed his own workers in America, developed a sentimental concern for the Scots.

Through Davitt, George and Murdoch, William Small tried to enlist the support of John Weir, the miners' leader in Fife. Estranged from orthodox Liberalism, Weir and the Fife miners formed a radical organisation called the People's League. A radical organisation by the standards of 'canny Fife', the Fife People's League - a group financed by Andrew Carnegie - supported nationalisation of the land and the abolition of the monarchy and the House of Lords. But in 1887 Carnegie warned the Dunfermline Radical Association not to confuse Republicanism with revolutionary socialism.[59]

In a whole host of ways, the American connections were of crucial importance in alienating Scottish working people from the sloth of orthodox Liberalism. Moreover, under the sympathetic influence of the Roman Catholic clergy in the West of Scotland coalfields, the miners supported the radical demands of men like Small and Murdoch.[60]

Questioned in Aberdeen about the famous Homstead strike in Anerica and the importance of the Knights of Labour, on whom the Sons of Labour had modelled themselves, he said:

> Say rather, we had. It was one of those emphermeral organisations that go up like a rocket and come down like a stick. It was founded on false principles, viz., that they should combine unskilled labour with skilled.[61]

From then on Carnegie backed away from the developing radicalism of the Scottish working class.

After that American strike, the Glasgow Trades Council denounced Carnegie as 'a new Judas Iscariot', though they thanked him for 'calling world attention to the plight of labour'. But, although Robertson was working with more disparate groups of unorganised radicals in Glasgow in the 1880s, where he worked for a spell as a clerk with the Water Corporation, he too visited other radicals in America, collected money for his pamphlets, and distanced himself from the Anglo-Scottish bourgeoisie's Kailyard images of 'canny', 'peaceful' and slumbering Scotland.

The Two Agitations of Murdoch and Robertson Coalesce

Murdoch's agitation and that of Robertson converged in the 1880s. But not in a straightforward way. Robertson also joined Keir Hardie's Scottish Labour Party. But, unlike Murdoch, he did not play a prominent role in it; and this helps to explain why he was kept out of the books on Scottish labour history. Angry and frustrated by the obvious injustice of his imprisonment and subsequent impoverishment after 1870, he kept up sufficient pressure in the Scottish and English courts to force the abolition of polls and pontage under the 1878 Roads and Bridges Act. But he continued to expose the illegal behaviour of the Anglo-Scottish courts, and was increasingly portrayed in newspapers like the so-called Liberal-Radical newspaper the *North British Daily Mail* as 'eccentric', 'impossible' and *carnaptious*. So he did not attract so much press attention as Murdoch did.

By 1880 Robertson was poor, though he worked in the Highland societies of Glasgow and Edinburgh to defend the remnants of Gaelic civilisation in the Highlands. In 1881 he went to the USA, where he spent several months delivering lectures on 'Scottish song, life, and character'. In America, where he earned big lecture fees, he was in great demand.[62] 'Dundonachie' moved in more cultural and intellectual circles than Murdoch did on his trips to America, and the attempts of the Anglo-Scottish ruling class to dismiss him as 'a lunatic' did not succeed.

In the precognitions or pre-trial papers concerning Robertson's trial in the High Court, Edinburgh, in February 1891, there were indications that he had been jailed again in 1884. However, a thorough search of the legal papers in the Scottish Record Office has not uncovered any evidence of his trial, the reasons for it, or how long he spent in jail. But 'Dundonachie' published a small pamphlet at his own expense entitled *Hanged for the Game Laws*; dated 31 March 1884, it created quite a stir. In the opening paragraph, addressed to the Right Honourable the Earl of Rosebery, he said:

This morning there was gloom and sadness to be witnessed on many countenances in this city [Edinburgh], when the hoisting of the black flag on a battlement of the Calton Hill Prison announced that two fellow mortals had just been launched into eternity. The crime which they have just expiated with their lives was committed in December last, on one of your Lordship's estates, and the victims were two men employed on the property from which you derive your title. The coal miners, Innes and Vickers, whose bodies are still warm while I write this letter, were found on the morning of 13 March of that month roaming on a field near Rosebery, and as they carried guns it was presumed that they were in pursuit of wild animals, and for this real or imaginary offence, they were about to be arrested, when they fired upon your Lordship's employees fatally wounding two of them, while the third man ran the risk of sharing the fate of his companions. Had the two men been taken, they would have got sentences up to six months' hard labour, for being suspected of a crime which had not been committed.[63]

The oral evidence of the late Bob Selkirk, a veteran Scottish socialist, who died in 1974, emphasised that the primitive egalitarian social values of Highlanders who ended up in the coalfields of Lowland Scotland did not die out as they were turned into industrial workers.[64] In the pamphlet *Our Deer Forests* (1867) Robertson had already defended poaching and poachers since game and 'birds of the air' belonged to everyone rather than a small elite of landed aristocrats.[65] In a letter that he sent me in 1974, Selkirk said:

Poaching was not regarded as a crime. When a child I often heard remarks which seemed to imply that a man who was hanged for shooting a gamekeeper was a hero. I think his name was McVickers *(sic!)* and the gamekeeper was shot somewhere in the Rosewell area of Midlothian. Poaching was widespread, the idea which dominated the thinking was that 'the Laird has no right to the game' and 'we are are not going to starve.'[66]

Unusual among Scottish radicals in 1884, Robertson was more advanced than any of the left-wing socialists in defending workers' *moral* right to poach. Moreover, he was the only one who spoke up for Innes and Vickers by protesting against their hanging.

By contrast with the *sleekit* Scottish radicals like Henry Cockburn, Francis Jeffrey and, in Robertson's own time, Dr. Charles Cameron, Member of Parliament and editor of the *North British Daily Mail*, who, while encouraging men like Robertson and Murdoch to 'agitate the land question', informed the legal authorities on them behind their backs.[67] In combination with the contradictory public and private statements written by Cameron, Selkirk's oral evidence touches on the importance of what E. P. Thompson called 'the unwritten tradition' of workers' resistance to capitalism.

Absorbed in legal battles against the Establishment going back to what he always regarded as his false imprisonment in 1870, Robertson was less active in the formal Scottish labour movement than Murdoch. But in the 1880s he continued to publish a spate of pamphlets for which there was a big demand among ordinary folk, including members of the middle class whose Scottishness had remained important to them.

Better known and more reported in the Scottish newspaper press than Murdoch, 'Dundonachie' was interested in George's ideas about 'the single tax'. Though he had not read Marx's analysis of the Highland Clearances in *Capital*, Robertson was placing himself in the Marxist tradition of analysis of the 'original economic sin' of capitalism when he published his pamphlet *How They Got The Land: Or The Origin, Nature, and Incidence of the Land Tax* (1892). But he was more radical in Marx's original definition of what it meant to be radical than were Murdoch, Keir Hardie or many of the Marxian socialists of the late nineteenth century except William Small. But both Murdoch and Robertson moved to the Left as they grew older and wiser, though their common motivation could be seen in their experiences rather than in their age or maturity.

To the very end of his life, 'Dundonachie' continued to think, agitate and write. Criticising the Duke of Atholl's family and other members of the Anglo-Scottish aristocracy, he kept up his legal battles to clear his name in the interest of the TRUTH about his imprisonment in 1870 as he had continued to regard it.

Robertson emerged during the 1880s as an expert on Scottish law. Having been jailed as we have seen in 1870 for 'murmuring a Scottish judge' under a medieval law, he became a man who unceasingly inspired ballads and pamphlet literature about his dissident role as chief of the Robertson clan. [68]

Unable to make any progress against an exceptionally repressive and reactionary Scottish judiciary, he went to Edinburgh to draw attention to his grievances. Waiting for and knocking the hat off the head of the Right Honourable John Inglis, the Lord Justice General, he was apprehended and locked up in the Edinburgh Royal Infirmary Asylum. The precognitions for late 1890 and early 1891 testified to the wide support he enjoyed across a wide spectrum of support, particularly in Glasgow. No longer rooted in his beloved Perthshire, he was still regarded in Lowland Scotland as a *carnaptious* radical and champion of the common people.

The newspaper *The Scotsman* insisted that Robertson had bombarded the Court of Session for 'some years pass' and had taken a dislike to the Lord President. A witness for the State, Dr. George Robert Wilson found that the prisoner was 'suffering from a delusional state.' He thought he had 'personal enemies in Lord Inglis and Queen Victoria due to their interference against him.' Other doctors said similar things; but Wilson asserted that, although he was 'a (clear) case of monomania in relation to the charge of assault and his agitations against the landed aristocracy, he was sane upon other points'. [69] In any event, *The Scotsman* reported the verdict of the Court in 1891 that Robertson was to be confined to the Royal Infirmary Asylum, Edinburgh, for assaulting Inglis and kept there during her Majesty's pleasure.[70] But in the *Minute Book of the High Court* dated 21 February 1891, it was decided that 'Dundocnachie' was to be kept in strict custody 'until her Majesty's pleasure be known'. Despite Lord Inglis's extreme 'conservative instincts', Robertson was freed from the Insane Aslyum a few weeks later without any announcment in the press.[71]

Far from being tamed or silenced, he kept up his various agitations on behalf on 'land and labour' until his death in 1893.

Grudgingly summing up 'Dundonachie's' career, Henry Dryerre said: 'Finally he removed to Glasgow, where he finished his checkered course in the Western Infirmary on 24 October 1893.' [72] No one bothered to say whether he had married or not; and the male members of his family were at Dunkeld Cathedral on 30 October when his remains were interred by a Presbyterian clergyman. [73]

By the early 1890s Murdoch lived for a spell in the city of Radical culture - Glasgow. Helping Robertson and other radicals to weld Scots from the different regions of the country into a national power by raising the Scottish national question, Robertson and Murdoch unleashed the forces helping to weld together a new national-cum-class identity against the definitions of the Anglo-Scottish ruling class. But Murdoch, though not a Marxist, moved further to the Left. In Glasgow he joined the Independent Labour Party and became chairman of its Govan branch. In old age he completed his still unpublished Autobiography and until his death in February 1903 provided a link between the older and newer generations of Scottish radicals and socialists.

Conclusion

When he tried to create an agenda for a new Scottish national historiography in the 1930s and 1940s, Hugh MacDiarmid did not know of the existence of James Thomson Callender or Alexander Robertson. In his book *The Company I'Ve Kept: Essays in Autobiography* (1966), he said:

> I bracket with Maclean's name the names of John Murdoch (the crofters' leader - Maclean's agrarian counterpart), Thomas Muir and John Swinton (who aided the Negroes in South Carolina before the Civil War, became a friend of Walt Whitman, and knew Karl Marx), as examples of Scots who are relatively far too little known and yet, in our opinion, of far more consequence than most of those who figure prominently in our history books and contemporary life.[74]

In present-day Britain some radical figures just cannot be incorporated into the official historiography, and Robertson was to remain even more of an outcast than Murdoch.

When they died in 1893 and 1903 respectively, Robertson and Murdoch did not attract any obituary notices in Labour or socialist newspapers or annual volumes like *Labour Annual* and its successor the *Reformers' Year Book*. But, although there were more obituary tributes in the bourgeois press to Robertson than to Murdoch, later twentieth-century labour historians have been more interested in the latter than in the former.

When I began to do full-time research into Scottish labour history over a quarter of a century ago, it was not yet clear that the Labour historiography of the late twentieth century would favour John Murdoch rather than Alexander Robertson. Although at various moments in their lives, both men supported constitutional and extra-Parliamentary agitation against an oppressive social system, Scottish leftist historians like David Lowe, William Stewart and later on W. H. Marwick, could not find space for Robertson, the 'direct action' or revolutionary practitioner, in their books on working-class history.

Ignoring Robertson and sanctifying Murdoch, Low set the agenda for later Scottish historians in his book *Souvenirs of Scottish Labour* (1919).[75] Despite the fact that Robertson was better known to newspaper readers in the 1880s than Murdoch, it was the former Customs and Excise officer who gained most attention from historians of the Left. Then, when Stewart in his biography of James Keir Hardie (1921) chronicled Murdoch's role in chairing the foundation conference of the Scottish Labour Party conference on 19 May 1888 with verve and colour, Murdoch's place in the Pantheon of 'Labour mighty dead' was guaranteed. As Stewart put it: 'Mr. John Murdoch, a man well known in connection with the Highland Crofters' agitation, sturdy in frame as in opinions, presided, and Hardie explained the object for which the meeting had been called, viz, the formation of a bona fide Labour Party for Scotland'.[76]

But, after their brief appearance in the books by Lowe and Stewart in 1919 and 1921, Robertson and Murdoch were kept out of books on Scottish history. In 1968 the bureaucratic chief librarian at the Mitchell Library, Glasgow, was ostentatiously indifferent to my discovery of Murdoch's *Autobiography*. Moreover by the 1970s, when the historian James Hunter began to work on Murdoch's Autobiography and write academic articles about the Crofters' leader, he could barely bring himself to acknowledge my discovery of Murdoch's five-volume work. It was not until 1986 that Hunter's book *For the People's Cause* was published in Edinburgh by the conservative Her Majesty's Stationery Office. History has always been written by the winners.

However, if the winners have always written the dominant history, it was clear from the basic facts of Robertson's biography that he would never be incorporated into the Establishment history concocted by the Anglo-Scottish ruling class. But, although I was initially startled and surprised by the Scottish Tory Establishments's attempt in 1968 to co-opt Murdoch into the new Anglo-Scottish history, it was clear to me that they would continue to ignore Robertson.

Though both Robertson and Murdoch were distinctly Scottish in their radicalism, 'Dundonachie' was always more *carnaptious than* the important radical who had been an Excise officer for a large part of his adult life. But from the days of James Thomson Callender in the Ediburgh of the 1780s and 1790s, there had always been two clearly defined radicalisms in modern Scotland. Just as Thomas Muir of Huntershill looked to Members of Parliament in the British House of Commons to rectify the people's grievances and burdens, and Callender depended on the extra-Parliamentary muscle of the artisans and other pre-industrial workers, so Robertson was the Callender of his time and Murdoch the Muir of his. This distinction between the two types of radicalism was again obvious by the time that Keir Hardie and John Maclean came on the Scottish scene.

Despite my own introductory articles on Robertson in the *New Edinburgh Review* the *New Edinburgh Review Anthology*, the references to him in *The Rousing of the Scottish Working Class*, (1979) and a recent article in *Cencrastus*, it is now evident that a man who was repeatedly jailed for his democratic opposition to the Anglo-Scottish ruling class will not be incorporated into the new official history of Scotland.[77]

He belonged to the same company of outcasts and oddities as Callender, Alexander Rodger, James MacFarlan, John Maclean and R. F. Mackenzie.

In an obituary notice in the advanced or left-wing Liberal newspaper the *North British Daily Mail*, an anonymous writer emphasised that 'the last twenty years of his life were spent in America, in London, Edinburgh, and Glasgow, where he earned his livelihood chiefly by his pen'. Then, in summing up his assessment of Robertson's life, he concluded thus:

> Unfortunately, he put himself under the power of the law, and was punished by imprisonment, his offence being "murmuring a judge". As the Act under which he was convicted had not been enforced for 300 years before, he considered his treatment by the authorities unjust, and he has made many unsuccessful attempts to prove this in a Court of law. Constant brooding over his wrongs had somewhat impaired his intellect, and the last few years of his life have been spent in a vain endeavour to arouse public sympathy in his cause,

and in the hope that he would ultimately get his conviction cancelled.[78]

However, anyone who reads his pamphlet *Hanged for the Games Laws* will have to conclude that his years of experience under the constant 'terrors of the law' had not impaired his intellect; and even Henry Dryerre was forced to admit that he was a popular lecturer in America at various times during the last two decades before his death.

Despite the growing strength of the Labour movement in Scotland and John Murdoch's active membership of the Independent Labour Party in Glasgow in the 1890s, his death did not attract much attention. Indeed, most of the Scottish newspapers ignored his death when he passed away at his residence in Saltcoats in January 1903. One of the few newspapers to notice his death was the *Glasgow Weekly Mail;* and in two slender paragraphs, it was reported by the newspaper's correspondent in *Inverness* that the famous land reformer had been 'almost totally blind from cataract'.[79]

Unlike the English socialists, who could always identify with John Wilkes, William Cobbett, Richard Carlile and Jack Wade, by the late nineteenth century the Scots simply did not know anything about James Thomson Callender, Alexander Rodger or James Farlan. Furthermore, Keir Hardie and John Maclean did not know anything about Alexander Robertson, though Hardie knew Murdoch, and none of them seemed to know anything about the Radicals of 1820.

Keir Hardie (1856-1915) and John Maclean (1879-1923): *Nationalists and Socialist Internationalists*

Ramsay MacDonald, as the English knew well,
they could not breed the like of Ramsay in England:
though Ake Ogilvie said they smothered them at
birth. But that was just one of his tink-like says,
the English aye needed the Scots at their head,
right holy and smart at the same bit time
Lewis Grassic Gibbon, Cloud
Howe *(1933).*

The Messianic figure of John Maclean was
reincarnated in two biographies in 1972 rather than
understood.
Christopher Harvie,
Scotland and Nationalism *(1977).*

The 'Peculiarities' of Scottish Radicalism and Socialism

One of the oddities of modern Scottish history is that novelists like
Robert Louis Stevenson (1850-94) and Lewis Grassic Gibbbon (1901-
1935) have offered better insights into the radical history of the Scots
than most of the professional historians. Yet, despite the Scottish
workers' utter absence from the House of Commons before 1906, the
prediction of Hardie's biographer, William Stewart (1921), 'that the
passing of the years will establish Keir Hardie as one of the *permanently*

historic figures in that great age-long progressive movement' will be increasingly questioned by a much more cynical and sceptical late twentieth century.[1]

The Scottish people were effectively disenfranchised from Westminster politics until well after 1832. Furthermore, from the 1830s to the 1870s, there was not one Scottish M.P. who was sympathetic to Chartism or organised Labour. By contrast, there were several such English M.P.s in the House of Commons. And the Scots did not produce a single radical lawyer comparable to the Victorian W. P. Roberts.[2]

In 1874 the first two working-class or Lib-Lab M.P.s or Liberal Labour M.P.s (including Alexander MacDonald, the Scottish miners' leader), were elected to the House of Commons to represent English constituencies. In 1892 the first Independent Labour M.P.s, and in 1900 the first socialist or Labour M.P.s, were similarly elected by English constituencies, while Scottish Labour remained disenfranchised. At the beginning of the present century, no one could have predicted that later twentieth-century Labour historiograpy would focus so much on Keir Hardie and James Ramsay MacDonald.

MacDonald, the Scottish miners' leader, was a Lib-Lab member of Parliament for an English constituency. When he stood for election to Parliament in the earlier general election of 1868 he could not persuade voters in Kilmarnock to elect him. The same fate awaited Hardie when he stood for election to Parliament in the Mid-Lanark constituency in 1888; and the Scottish socialist, who was both Red and pro-Scottish before he was elected for the English constituency of West Ham in 1892, lost some of his radical bearings without ceasing to be an outspoken opponent of British/English imperialism.

Certainly, Grassic Gibbon's irreverence towards Ramsay MacDonald showed much more insight than the powerful and overwhelmingly Parliamentary slant in the writings of Eric J. Hobsbawm, Tom Nairn, Chrisotpher Harvie and Kenneth O. Morgan. Ignorant of the real history of Scotland, Nairn, Harvie and Morgan did not understand that Scottish radical movements had been much more anti-imperialist and to the Left of their English counterparts from the days of James Thomson Callender in Edinburgh onwards. As I argued in my essay on 'The Rise of Scottish Socialism', the persistent myth that 'Scotland has always been a radical country' did not acknowledge the crucial distinction between the Scottish working class as a whole and the Scots own radical and labour movements until the advent of the Red Clydeside.[3]

James Keir Hardie (1856-1915) and John Maclean (1879-1923) never met or correponded with each other. By the time Maclean was propelled to the forefront of international Labour as an anti-war agitator during the First World War, Hardie was dead. However, in articles written in 1910 and 1921, when he glanced back to Hardie's role in British politics in 1906 and in 'the now dead Second International', Maclean criticised him for being too moderate.[4]

In the light of the inherent pro-Parliamentary bias of British Labour and socialist historiography, it is astonishing that no one has discussed the fact that Keir Hardie never represented a Scottish constituency in the House of Commons. Unlike the English working class, whose consciousness was, according to Royden Harrison, shaped 'by the experience of Parliament and the prolonged struggle for Parliamentary reform', the Scots did not elect their first two Lib-Lab members of Parliament until 1906.[5] Besides, although the Scottish socialist R. B. Cunninghame Graham (1852-1936) was the first M.P. expelled from the House of Commons for swearing, he sat in Parliament for North Lanarkshie between 1886-92 as a Liberal rather than as a socialist. Indeed, the first Scottish socialist M.P.s were not returned to Parliament until the general election of 1918.

When I first read Kenneth O. Morgan's biography of *Keir Hardie: Radical and Socialist* in 1975, I was not surprised by his preference for Keir Hardie (1856-1915) rather than the infamous Clydeside socialist, John Maclean (1879-1923). What did surprise me, however, was his unsubstantiated assertion about Maclean's 'Glasgow parochialism'. Against the whole grain of the overwhelmingly historical evidence, he insisted that:

> He [Hardie] lived in Ayrshire; he and his family had recently moved into "Lochnorris", they had built in Old Cumnock, with money loaned to them by Adam Birkmyre, a Glasgow businessman who later emigrated to South Africa. Hardie's visits to the constituency of West Ham, then, could only be intermittent. But it was clear that his horizons was extending far beyond his native Scotland; his instincts were naturally outward-looking, in contrast to John Maclean and the later generations of Glasgow socialists after 1917 who conceived their socialism firmly within a Celtic context.[6]

171

A close reading of Morgan's *Labourist* biography revealed that the essence of the 'Glasgow parochialism' (*sic!*) of Maclean and his generation of Scottish radicals resided in their anti-imperialist rejection of John Bull's Empire and Parliamentary socialism. Defining, reflecting and refining the dominant traditions of 'Great British' and Anglo-Scottish historiography, Kenneth O. Morgan, Tom Nairn, Christopher Harvie, Eric J. Hobsbawm and many others have repeatedly expressed their preference for the tame, respectable and constitutional Parliamentary socialism of Keir Hardie and J. Ramsay MacDonald rather than the direct-action extra-Parliamentary socialism of John Maclean.[7] Even when they were engaged in a bitter polemical exchange in the pages of the London-based *New Left Review* in the 1970s over the growing Scottish agitation for Home Rule for Scotland, both Eric J. Hobsbawm and Tom Nairn ignored John Maclean's contribution to socialist politics.[8]

But, although they came from very different and antagonistic Marxist generations and traditions, Nairn and Hobsbawm had much in common. In *The Break-Up of Britain* and in Hobsbawm's rejoinder in the *New Left Review* they ignored John MacLean or wrote him out of 'British' working-class history. Identifying with 'the brilliant political inheritance nutured by Keir Hardie and Ramsay MacDonald', Nairn had even less reason than Christopher Harvie to resurrect the history of Maclean's life in Scottish radical politics. Indeed, in his own silent attachment to 'Parliamentary socialism' via Westminster, Harvey tried to write the famous Clydeside socialist out of history

Moreover, in his book *Industry and Empire: An Economic History of Britain since 1750* (1968), Hobsbawm also, though less surprisingly, ignored Maclean. In a penultimate chapter titled 'The Other Britain,' he wrote:

> Keir Hardie became the leader of British socialism (and his [*sic!*] Independent Party had its firmest base on the Clyde), James Ramsay MacDonald became the first Labour Prime Minster of his country, and Clydeside became, during the First World War the synonym for revolutionary agitation and helped to give the post-1918 Labour Party a slant to the left and the Communist Party a solid core of leaders.

Employing the typical 'economistic' Marxism of the Stalinists, Hobsbawm went on to relate the emergence - really the re-emergence - of Lallans and 'Scottish nationalist culture' *(sic!)* to 'the collapse of Scots industry between the wars.' Clearly, from Hobsbawm's historical perspective no Scottish radical who rejected the efficacy of Parliamentary institutions at Westminster, London, for turning the world upside down could be important or relevant to the anti-imperialist struggle of authentic socialism from below.[9]

Origins of Scottish Socialism and Keir Hardie

Despite the very large number of biographies or biographical studies of James Keir Hardie and his incalculable role in creating the Scottish Labour Party in 1888, he moved towards socialism in a cautious and belated way. However, when he began to come to political consciousness in the 1870s, he already belonged to a working-class culture opposed to the Scottish Enlightenment and was struggling to define a new sense of radical Scottishness. At first, it was rather hostile towards Irish immigrants; and Hardie himself was something of a racist.

Rebels and radicals are always made, not born. Idealistic and courageous, Hardie was no more born a socialist 'saint' than John Galt or anyone else had been born a radical or anything else. He was, however, very ambitious from an early age; and his socialism was influenced by the fact that he was deeply hurt by what he thought society had done to him.

In his important and pioneering book *J. Keir Hardie: A Biography*, William Stewart depicted Hardie's birth on 15 August 1856 at Legbrannock, Holytown in Lanarkshire 'amongst the miners'. Ignoring Hardie's illegitimacy, he wrote: 'His father David Hardie, was not, however, a miner, nor of miner stock. He was a ship carpenter by trade, drawn into this district by the attractions of Mary Keir, a domestic servant, who became his wife and the ultra-independent mother of the future labour agitator.'[10]

However, his origins were much less simple than that. Emphasing the role of Hardie's own autobiographical writings about the monotony, awfulness and complexity of his life in Glasgow and later on as 'a trapper boy' in the pits, Fred Reid argued that: 'It may be at least as important, if we are to understand the complex labour politician, to pay more attention to his recollections of sunnier and happier moments'.[11] Even so, Hardie's illegitimacy was a major factor in his subjective emotional life. As Reid explained:

> In the years following his death, one of his political opponents in the socialist movement in Lanarkshire was to find in Lanarkshire a boyhood friend of Hardie's who recalled that Hardie believed his real father to have been a doctor from Airdrie, who bribed the miner, William Aitken, to leave the district so that his name could be used in an action of paternity which Mary Keir brought in the Sheriff Court. Hardie, this witness declared, was a 'damn sight prouder to think himself the son o' a doctor than the dacent man wha gae him and his mother a name and brocht him up.' [12]

Certainly, he had no small conceit of himself, and his illegitimacy helped to energise his ambitions. Nevertheless he made positive use of his energy to advance the cause of Scottish radicalism.

When he was appointed as a full-time Miners' Agent in Lanarkshire in 1879, he had to move a resolution of welcome to Alexander MacDonald, the veteran Scottish miners' leader and M.P. At a significant meeting in Larkhall, when in comparing MacDonald's work for the miners to that of [Martin] Luther in the rise of Protestantism, he had to be protected from assault.

In such essays as 'Changing Images of American Democracy and the Scottish Labour Movement, 1866-1900' (1973) and 'The Rise of Scottish Socialism' (1975), I have chronicled and analysed the ideas and *personalities* responsible for forging Highlanders and Lowlanders, women and men, industrial workers, farm workers and sections of the dispossessed and middle class into a re-made Scottish working class with a new national-cum-class identity.[13] Hardie, though not the most precocious or radical, was at the centre of this new development. With a formidable presence and nous, he was a man who could not be easily ignored.

Yet, despite Marx's comment about 'rural idiocy', Scottish socialism began in the coalfields, not the cities. Nevertheless socialists in the towns and cities were important, and they have attracted more recognition and comment than their brothers and sisters in the coalfields and rural communities.

The descendants of John Galt's 'wrong-resenting' Scots began to rediscover their own cultural heritage in the 1880s. However, before Hardie became a socialist, Marxists like John Leslie (1856-1921) and William J. Nairn (1856-1902) 'agitated the question' of socialism in the cities of Edinburgh and Glasgow against considerable hostility from the bourgeoisie and large sections of the Scottish working class. To convey something of the bitter *opposition* to socialist ideas, it will be useful to quote from what the left-wing liberal journalist James Cameron wrote in his obituary (1902) of Nairn:

> Twenty years ago in Glasgow, when the gospel of socialism was reviled and literally spat upon by those who regarded it as the vapourings of dreamers and madmen, Nairn never wavered nor hesitated, but held right on with his face dogged to the foe with voice and pen, right manfully did he proclaim his message. He was as rugged in mind as he was uncouth in his personal appearance, but the sharp tongue with the clear strong brain behind it, the battered hat - it was his ruggedness that disclosed the sturdy independent character of the man.[14]

At one of the first major socialist meetings in Glasgow in December 1883, 3,000 men and women crowded into the St. Andrew's Hall to hear William Morris. Analysing the composition of the audience at this meeting, J. Bruce Glasier recalled that: 'There were, of course, among his listeners a considerable number of university and art school students, artists, and literary people, but by far the greater number were artisans of the thoughtful and better-read type, who in those days formed [in Glasgow] a large proportion of the working class.'[15] In his colourful account of the new forces in Glasgow just before socialism's first public baptism, Glaiser wrote:

> Perhaps in no other city in the [United] Kingdom could audiences of a higher level of intelligence be obtained than those which assembled on Sunday evenings in Glasgow at that period to listen to lectures of the variety of Professor Tyndall. Alfred Russell Wallace, Ford Madox Brown, John Stuart

Blackie. For while the Sabbatarian ban, then still stringent in Scotland, kept away the more timid of the intellectual elite, it ensured, on the other hand, that the audiences which attended the Sunday Society lectures were for the greater part composed of men and women whose minds had been roused from orthodox sloth and were prepared to take unconventional paths.

The land question was the most important political question in Scottish socialism in the 1880s. It dominated the thinking of such early Scottish socialist pioneers as Keir Hardie and shaped the early socialism of the Athens of the North. The development and intervention of the Scottish Land Restoration League in the general election of 1885 marked the beginning of what G. D. G. Cole called 'the pioneer battles for independent labour representation'.[16] The organised workers in the Scottish labour movement (as distinct from the unorganised working class) was to the Left of its English counterpart. By the 1880s, however, Fred Reid has insisted that 'the discontent of the working class' was 'the main basis for the divergence between Scottish and English politics.'[17]

A whole number of American ideas and influences contributed enormously to the growth of Scottish socialism during the decade of the 1880s. The new social forces were personified by Henry George, the American advocate of land reform and a land tax, the American workers' organisation the Knights of Labor and, less directly or wittingly, Andrew Carnegie. Playing a major role in shaping the emergence of Scottish socialism, Keir Hardie was pro-Scottish and anti-imperialist. When he glanced back to this fertile period of Scottish nationalism and radicalism-cum-socialism, he recalled that: 'Some years later, Henry George came to Scotland and I read *Progress and Poverty*, which unlocked many of the industrial and economic difficulties which beset the mind of the worker trying to take an intelligent interest in his own affairs and led me, much to George's horror in later life, into communism.'[18] Hardie's self-image of that of an extreme leftist. Though his pride in it [his leftism] was usually ignored and underestimated by many of Hardie's biographers, he was very proud of his Scottish identity. In his early articles in *The Miner*, he wrote in Lallans from a strong Scottish viewpoint. In 1888 he wrote:

'I am also strongly in favour of Home Rule for Scotland, being convinced that until we have a Parliament of our own, we cannot obtain the many and great reforms on which I believe the people of Scotland have set their hearts.'[19]

Joining the Scottish Labour Party (SLP) in 1888, Scottish radicals like John Murdoch and Alexander Robertson helped Hardie to keep the agitation for Home Rule in the forefront of their general agitations. When the SLP affiliated to the Second International and sent Hardie and John Ogilvy as their delegates to its first meeting in Paris in 1889, the two Scots protested when they were described as 'English' delegates. Furthermore, when the Scots affiliated to the Second International, a comparable Labour Party did not yet exist in England.

The nationalism and anti-Englishness of the Scottish radicals and socialists were sharpened by the aggressive nationalism of the English Left at that time. In his book *A Short History of Socialism*, George Lichtheim put the nationalism of the Scottish Left into context when he wrote:

> At the same time Toryism was reconstituted on a new social and ideological basis: no longer merely the bulwark of the landed gentry and the Church, but increasingly the Party of the Empire and the fountainhead of the English (as distinct from British) nationalism. The nationalism, that is to say, of the dominant majority within a multinational society; for the Scots, Welsh and Irish all had their own forms of national sentiment: not to mention India, the White-settler 'Dominions', and the African colonies - all garrisoned by British-officered armies and navies who looked to the Conservative Party to uphold their status.[20]

Stiffened by the Scots tradition of metaphysics and Marxism, the nationalism of the Scottish labour movement was sharpened by the imperialism of the English workers' movement.

Many Scottish socialists belonging to the thirty-nine varieties of socialist groups and organisations were sensitive to their nation's subordinate role within the United Kingdom and hostile to the arrogant English nationalism of John Bull's Social Democratic Federation and Socialist League. When a Socialist League was set up in London at the end of 1884 a bitter row broke out between the English and the Scottish socialists over the questions of policy and autonomy. The League's metropolitan leadership was very annoyed because the Scots had set up their own organisation and issued their own membership cards without discussing this with William Morris or anyone else in London. This conflict led James Mavor, the Scottish secretary, to inform his counterpart in London of the Scots stance in a country with its own distinctive problems and cultural traditions:

> We formed ourselves into a branch of the Scottish Land and Labour League [the Scottish section of the Socialist League]. In these circumstances our executive do not see any necessity for seeking any authorisation from your executive.[21]

Moreover, the Scottish socialists in the League objected to some of the statements in the London Manifesto. A. K. Donald, secretary of the Edinburgh branch, complained that the denunciation of religion would 'create unnecessary bitterness against us in religious Scotland'.[22] However, as the Scots were prepared to suffer 'family and social ostracism' by trying to make socialist ideas popular, they were simply asking for recognition of their distinctive traditions and national attitudes.[23]

The agitation against British imperialism and the struggle for Home Rule for Scotland permeated the labour movement from bottom to top; and the Aberdeen Trades Council had been in the forefront of the agitation for Scottish national autonomy before the SLP was formed in 1888.[24] Even as late as 1892, when H. H. Champion stood as a socialist candidate in one of the Aberdeen constituencies during the general election, he kept the agitation for 'Scotch Home Rule' before his potential working-class electors.[25]

However, if the Scots predilection for metaphysics was denounced by English radicals in the eighteenth and early nineteenth centuries, it was romanticised in the twentieth century. When he glanced back to the Scots superiority in socialist theory in the 1880s, T. A. Jackson wrote: 'I fancy - though this is only a guess - that an early drilling in the Shorter Catechism had something to do with giving our Scottish comrades their respect for logic.' The English socialist Frank Budgen, who knew Willie Nairn, also acknowledged the superiority of the Scottish socialists who had received the flimsest of formal education in State schools: 'It was not easy for an Englishman brought up in an Anglican village school to move easily among Marxist categories. The Scots with their Calvinist upbringing seemed to find the going much easier.' [26]

Far from weakening their hatred of capitalism, the Scottish socialists like Nairn remained, as William Morris and others acknowledged, tough and untamed. As David Lowe wrote: 'After Agnes Henry lectured to the Glasgow Social Democrats she was of the opinion that the anarchists were as doves compared to them.' [27] But, although the strong Republican dimension of Scottish socialism has been expunged from the history books, it lived and thrived. Stretching back to the eighteenth century, it merged with the socialism and radicalism of the new labour movement. In his account of the life of R. B. Cunninghame Graham, A. F. Tschiffely recalled that:

> One of the most daring things Don Roberto [Cunninghame Graham] did was on the occasion of Queen Victoria's visit to Glasgow. On learning when the Royal train was due to arrive at St. Enoch Station, he promptly called for a mass meeting of the miners, to be held in St. Enoch Square, with the result that when the Queen arrived, countless ill-clad and grimy men were crowded together in front of the station, listening to Don Roberto, who made a fiery speech in their defence.[28]

Originally chosen by the Mid-Lanark Liberal Association as the Lib-Lab candidate before the death of the sitting M.P. precipitated the famous by-election, Hardie was preoccupied by the fact that the Scottish coal miners did not have one M.P. in the House of Commons. Ousted by the Liberal Constituency to make way for an English barrister, he could not persuade many workers to vote for him as an indepedent Labour candidate. Out of this experience, he helped to form the SLP.

During the Mid-Lanark by-election, Ramsay MacDonald wrote to Hardie thus:

> There is no miner - and no other one for that matter - who is a Scotsman and not ashamed of it, who will vote against you in favour of an obscure English barrister, absolutely ignorant of Scotland and Scottish affairs and who only wants to get to Parliament in order that he may have the tail of M.P. to his name in the law courts.[29]

The SLP helped to make Hardie famous; and, although he lost something of his radical edge after 1892, he did not abandon his pro-Scottish opposition to British imperialism. When he produced his autobiography *Further Reminiscenes* (1912), H. M. Hyndman felt compelled to pay a grudging tribute to the pioneers of Scottish socialism when he said:

> Scotland was the country in which the independent labour movement began... it seemed probable that Scotland, by far the best educated portion of the United Kingdom, would come to the front and take the lead in the political arena on behalf of the disinherited class. That I know was the hope and ambition then, not only of Graham and Hardie and Burgess, but of many who have since fallen into the muddy ways of capitalist Liberalism.[30]

What he left out of his account of the Scottish labour movement was that the twin factors of nationalism and extreme left-wing radicalism had motivated the foundation of the Scottish Trades Union Congress (STUC) in 1896.[31]

From the 1870s the Scots and the Irish took it for granted that their distinctive affairs were being neglected by the British Trades Union Congress; and they had always believed that they were more radical than English trade unionists. Summing this up, a delegate told the conference that:

They had many trades in Scotland carried on under conditions not known in England, and they had many questions coming up which would not be of any interest to Englishmen or even Irishmen. There was no reason why they in Scotland should not strike a line for themselves. They had dragged the English behind them for a long time, and he did not see why they should do so any longer.[32]

Furthermore, despite his election as a Labour M.P. for the West Ham constituency in 1893, Hardie played an important role in founding the Independent Labour Party in 1893 and in helping to sustain it thereafter.

The decade of the 1890s was just as interesting, exciting and promising from a socialist perspective as the previous decade. Yet the imperialist attitude of the dominant English socialism of all groups and tendencies - it was really John Bull's socialism - has also coloured and dominated British labour history, especially since the end of the Second World War.

In his book *Industry and Empire*, Eric J. Hobsbawm did not just ignore John Maclean. He also wrote James Connolly out of Irish labour history. Touching on the Irish contribution to what he revealingly calls 'British' socialism, Hobsbawm wrote:

They provided the British working class with a cutting edge of radicals and revolutionaries, with a body of men and women uncommitted by either tradition or economic success to society as it existed around them. It was no accident that an Irishman, Feargus O'Connor, was the nearest thing to a national leader of Chartism, and another, Bronterre O'Brien, its chief ideologist, that an Irishman wrote 'The Red Flag', the anthem of the British labour movement and the best British working-class novel, *The Ragged-Trousered Philanthropists*.

But he was careful not to mention Jim Connell, the Irishman's name.[33]

Reflecting the Communist Party of Great Britain's deep attachment to British Parliamentary institutions, Hobsbawm felt a revulsion for the two great socialists from the Celtic fringe, John Maclean and James Connolly.

Moreover, Jim Connell, who wrote 'The Red Flag', was not a Brit. Unknown to Hobsbawm, in 1898 Hardie's ILP published his anti-imperialist pamphlet *Brothers At Last: A Centenary Appeal to Celt and Saxon*. Celebrating the anti-English/British imperialism of the United Irishmen of 1798, Connell proposed that:

> 'The ILP place on its programme National Independence for Ireland. Let National Independence be clearly defined as meaning not the unintelligible Home Rule of political time-servers, but absolute National Separation.'[34]

Written out of British labour history by the dominant historiographers, there were always Scots and Irish socialists who challenged John Bull's conception of the English-oriented Parliamentary socialism.

Moreover, when the Edinburgh-born Irish immigrant James Connolly and friend of Hardie belonged to the Social Democratic Federation (SDF) of William Nairn and James Leslie in the 1890s, he, too, supported Scottish Home Rule.[35] Hidden from history by the dominant Stalinist historiography, the bitter dispute between the right-wing followers of Hyndman and the left-wing De Leonist Scots led by Connolly and Connell touched on the 'impossibilist' Scots nationalism. Although the two Scottish-Irishmen - Connolly and Leslie - and the Scottish Gael John Carstairs Matheson did not advocate Scottish independence, other Scottish Marxists did.

At the annual conference in 1901 William Gee, the full-time Scottish organiser of the SDF, supported the De Leonist 'impossibilists' criticisms of Hyndman's jingoism. Though he did not join the De Leon-inspired Socialist Labour Party founded by Connolly, Matheson and other Scots, Gee remained aggressively Scottish. At the SDF conference in 1901, before the De Leonists broke away, he told the delegates that 'in spite of the canting, hypocritical gang of Presbyterians in the Land of Cakes, yet in the near future Scotland is destined to take a more prominent place under the Red Flag than England was'.[36]

By the beginning of the twentieth century, De Leonism in Britain, in Matheson's fine phrase, turned 'internationalism into a form of international jingoism'. The Scottish national question was increasingly marginalised by an 'internationalist' Left, though Scottish socialists like

Hardie, Matheson and others remained strong critics of British imperialism. Hardie was particularly critical of British imperialism in India. But, before his death in 1915, he realised that his real life existed outside of Scotland. Unlike Maclean, who probably joined the SDF in 1901, Hardie was already ceasing to be an effective radical. As Fred Reid has argued from 1894:

> Most of his political life, however, was spent on the platform, in committee rooms, living overnight in hotels and travelling by day on railway trains. These were not the places to make intimate contacts with the unemployed, the casual dockers and the sweated women. They were encountered only as audiences, as objects of pity.[37]

(Incidentally, Hardie shared with most of the other Scottish radicals and socialists of the period down to the outbreak of the First World War the characteristic of being *carnaptious*). This had been seen, for example, in his speech in the House of Commons attacking King Edward VIII).

But many of the Scottish socialists who remained in Scotland were better immunised against the virus of John Bull's ever so 'civilised' English socialism than was Hardie. One was John Carstairs Matheson, and the other was John Maclean. The two major - indeed, the only two significant - Scottish socialist thinkers before the First World War, though both were committed to class-struggle socialism from below, disagreed passionately about the Scottish national question.[38]

John Maclean, 'the Queer Folk of the Shaws' and the Scottish National Question

Born on 14 August 1879 in King Street, Pollockshaws, where according to eighteenth century legend 'the Queer folk of the Shaws' lived, John Maclean would soon be regarded as the strangest of them. From a much more sympathetic standpoint than was usual in more academic articles or books on him, Guy Aldred wrote in 1932:

> We know not what spells the three Fairy Godmothers were weaving at the moment of his birth. But, to judge from the character and

conclusion of his career, they certainly bestowed upon him anxious interest in human welfare, simplicity, uncompromising dourness, and years but a little beyond the normal dying-age of the rebel sans-culotte... It is supposed that, on that August day in 1879, the three Fates left Pollockshaws in state and never returned again, as though Pollockshaws had contributed all it could be expected to contribute to the glory of man, this side of the Social Revolution.[39]

In the light of the corrupt role played by Stalinism in the world labour movement between the mid-1920s and 1989, the reference to 'the three Fairy Godmothers' was particularly appropriate. Just as there was a strong spiritual dimension to Aldred's anarchism, so the same was true of Maclean's Marxism.

Maclean's father Daniel was a potter by trade. Born on the Isle of Mull in 1845, he ended up in the Lowlands. In 1876 he went to work in Pollockshaws as a potter; and he died there in 1888 from a 'potter's chest' when John was only eight years old. Maclean's mother, Anne McPhee, was a weaver when she met Daniel Maclean. Where and when they met remains unknown, but they were married at Nitshill in 1867. It was an interesting fact that both Anne and Daniel were victims of the infamous Highland Clearances. As Maclean's daughter Nan Milton emphasised in her excellent biography *John Maclean* (1973), the 'stories' of his parents' fate in being cleared 'sank deeply into the boy's mind, and when, years later, he read *Capital*, he was able to appreciate to the full Marx's harrowing description of the notorious Sutherland Clearances'.[40]

When Daniel died in 1888, Anne McPhee began to work again at her old trade of weaving. An exceptionally cheerful woman, she was very ambitious for her youngest son; there was an elder brother - Daniel. In his biography *John Maclean: Fighter for Freedom*, Tom Bell wrote:

John Maclean in later years informed his companion James D. MacDougall, 'that it was the knowledge of the sacrifice made, and self-denial endured, by his mother and sister to enable him to be educated, that made him resolve to use his education in the service of the workers.'[41]

Even after his marriage to Agnes Wood in 1909, Maclean's mother remained a central character in his life. Accepting her son's rejection of the life she had prepared for him as a Presbyterian minister of religion without rancour or disappointment, Anne would soon embrace his advocacy of revolutionary socialism. In his booklet *Comrade John Maclean*, *M.A.* (1944), Tom Anderson said:

> His mother, whom I had the pleasure of meeting, was a woman with a great personality. As I see her now I see John Maclean - the same face, the same merry twinkle in the eye, the same quick impulse, the same in height and build... We had our tea with her, and the scones and cakes on the table were the work of her hands. We talked of socialism, of the 'Coming Day'; for your must know we lived for socialism then, and we were not afraid. Comrade John said, 'Mother, when the '"Day" comes, there will be no rich and no poor.' If any of us had been asked at that time to give our life for the 'Cause' we would willingly have done so, and none more so than John Maclean.[42]

In another fine biography of John Maclean (1973), John Broom admitted that little had been known about Daniel Maclean. As he put it:

> They had seven children (three died in infancy) of whom John was the sixth. John described his mother as being stout and large-boned with a rosy face, high cheek bones and twinkling blue eyes. Not much is know of Daniel Maclean, but it is said he was fond of discussion and argument, and had classes of young men in his house to teach them to read. [43]

As a boy, Maclean had a tough life. But his mother was ambitious for him in the way of all good Scottish radicals' mothers; and she was determined that he would get a University education. In his perceptive account of Maclean's early life, Aldred recognised that the already famous Clydeside socialist was radicalised by the holocaust of the First World War. As he wrote:

> His experience of poverty and struggle converted John Maclean to socialism. In 1901 he joined the Social Democratic Federation. From this time onwards he devoted himself to the propagation of socialism. To our mind, his socialism remained immature until the Great War tested its vigour. Only then did it discover its radical integrity.[44]

But, although Aldred's comments and distinctions were sound at their core, he did not understand Maclean's inherited anti-imperialism, sense of Scottish national identity, and passion for radical education for working class men and women. Unaware of Maclean's role as an educator of the working class in State primary schools, his work with Matheson in the Scottish Socialist Teachers' Society and his campaigns in the wider labour movement against corporal punishment, Aldred did not recognise his hostility towards all ruling classes, but particularly the Anglo-Scottish ruling class.[45]

When he undertook socialist propaganda in Hawick in 1907 Maclean had met Agnes Wood; and they were married on 30 December 1909. Quiet and shy, Agnes displayed her own unrecognised greatness during her husband's unceasing anti-war agitation during the First World War. Although Agnes Maclean's loyalty to her *carnaptious* radical husband was tested to the limit during that war, she and their two daughters did not repudiate their controversial father in 'the land of Cakes and the Kailyard'.

At various moments in Scottish history different generations of the Anglo-Scottish Establishment have depicted Callender, Rodger, Macfarlan, Murdoch, Robertson and Hardie as *carnaptious* and queer. In distinctive books and articles at different times, they have all been portrayed as carnaptious, eccentric and idiosyncratic. After struggling to understand the history of Scottish radicalism during the past forty-odd years of my own life, it was not until November 1993 that it dawned on me that those great dissidents had come out of an extra-Parliamentary, 'direct action' and (by the standards of the Anglo-Scottish 'middle rank' and middle class) radical plebeian and workers' culture that did not expect any concessions from Westminster.

Though the Scots radical culture did not enjoy an unbroken continuity, it always re-emerged with its dominant *carnaptious* characteristics during moments of sharp political struggle. In the specific sense of belonging to a peculiarly Scottish radical culture, Hardie - before he got caught up in Westminster politics - and Maclean were 'idiosyncrastic'. In his capacity as a socialist agitator in 1907, Maclean displayed 'eccentric' behaviour when he marched unemployed workers through the Glasgow Stock Exchange. Abolishing and campaigning against corporal punishment in the primary schools where he taught, he was always at war with his employers, the School Boards. Before he was dismissed from his post as a teacher in 1915, his year-old conflict with the reactionary Headmaster, Mr. Fulton, led him to send a letter to the Clerk of the Govan School Board:

> My refusal to be bullied by Mr. Fulton was seized upon to single me out. I tell the Govan School Board that I shall never again be bullied by anyone. The next time anyone tries, down he goes. If the Board does not afford its protection, then I fall back on primitive justice.[46]

It was the Scots radical culture that was 'eccentric' and *carnaptious*, not individuals like John Maclean.

As an important member of the Social Democratic Federation, who joined Socialist Labour Party (SLP) on its foundation in 1903, Matheson became the leading De Leonist thinker in Scotland. Though he was a supporter of Home Rule for Scotland in the 1890s, he came more and more under the influence of James Connolly before the Scottish-Irishman went to America to work for Daniel De Leon and his American Socialist Labor Party.

Contrary to an almost ineradicable myth that De Leon was responsible for Matheson's anti-Scottish attitudes and abstract 'internationalism', the American had grasped that the Union of Scotland and England in 1707 had been a milestone in the development of English imperialism inside the Celtic fringe. In his neglected article on 'The American Flag', De Leon acknowledged the distictive peculiarities of different nations and their cultures in the making of diverse working classes. Arguing that in contrast to the Union Jack with its 'Three Crosses quartered' to symbolise 'the practically forceful annexation of Scotland and Ireland to England', the American War of Independence had conferred 'upon the Stars and Stripes the lofty distinction of being the first on earth to urge the brotherhood of nations'.[47]

Far from the American De Leon being responsible for Matheson's increasing hostility to Scottish national autonomy, the real culprit was the Anglo-Scottish University of Edinburgh, where he was taught British/English history.[48] Unlike most of the other Celts who denounced the English chauvinism and pro-imperialism of Hyndman and the SDF's London leadership, William Gee and Jim Connell, author of 'The Red Flag', remained critics of British/English imperialism in Scotland, Ireland and abroad without becoming De Leonists.

Active in the anti-imperialist agitation in Glasgow against the Boer War, Maclean joined and took an active part in the SDF until the outbreak of 'the Great War'. As a comparatively young socialist, he probably did not know anything about the disputes between Connolly, Matheson, Gee or the other 'impossiblists' - a name given to the extreme Left in Scotland by Hyndman and his friends - in the SDF in the early 1900s.

At the University of Glasgow, the young Maclean got average marks or grades in every subject he studied for his Master of Arts (M.A.) degree - with one exception - economics. In economics his marks were exceptionally high. Similarly, at the University of Edinburgh, Matheson, the Falkirk-born Gaelic-speaking Scot, got average marks in everything he studied except British history. As an outstanding student of British history, who never got less than 85 per cent, he was taught - and accepted and propagated the idea - that Scotland had ceased to exist as a nation in 1707.

Ignored by labour and other historians, Maclean and Matheson did not know anything at all about the basic facts of modern Scottish history. But when they became De Leonists, Matheson and Connolly advocated Irish independence at the same time as they opposed the agitation for Scottish self-government. Furthermore, as the most prominent member of the SDF in Edinburgh, Leslie abandoned his earlier advocacy of Irish and Scottish self-government to promote workers' internationalism.

Though he was a courageous, idealistic and scholarly socialist, Matheson's Anglo-Scottish ideas about Scotland were, in spite of his own good intentions to the contrary, pernicious and detrimental to the self-autonomy and do-it-yourself approach of the struggle for socialism from below. From the perspective of the late twentieth century, it was Maclean's and Scotland's good fortune that he did not study history at a nominally Scottish university. He was a proud man, who, struggling to defend his sense of national identity as a Scot, knew nothing about the radical culture he had inherited. Just as Alexander Rodger did not know about James Thomson Callender, or Alexander Robertson about Rodger, so Maclean did not know anything at all about his illustrious Scottish radical forebears from the eighteenth century onwards.

However, thanks to an accident of birth, Maclean did know something about the Highland Clearances and wrote about them from time to time. Unlike Marx, Engels and Matheson, he did not regard the Clearances as a 'progressive' historical development; and, unlike the latter, as an educator of the working class he always supported the agitations for Scottish Home Rule. And, despite his more complex character and increasing absorption into Parliamentary 'democracy', so did Keir Hardie.

But because he did not study British history at a Scottish university, Maclean was much more sensitive to the Scottish national question than Matheson. In 1910, defending the continuing evictions in the Highlands as a *progressive* development, Matheson and the SLP criticised *Forward*, the Scottish socialist newspaper, and the Independent Labour Party for supporting the crofters, who were resisting evictions at the hands of the Highland landowners, and thus associating 'socialism in Scotland with a backward agrarian movement'. [49] By contrast, Maclean supported the crofters. [50]

The only controversial Scottish question that Matheson and Maclean agreed on before the First War World was their shared hostility in 1914 to the celebration of the Battle of Bannockburn of 1314, though the famous Clydeside Red changed his mind about this after the war. Moreover, although he joined the SDF after Connolly, Gee and Connell had left it, again and again he raised Scottish questions inside the British labour movement.

Like Matheson, who was hostile to Scottish nationalism, Maclean simply did not know much about Scottish history. Thus when he discussed the Scots Radical rebellion of 1820, he was not aware of its inherent Scottishness. Writing in *Justice*, organ of the SDF, he referred to Baird, Hardie and Wilson by asserting that:

> Through the sacrifice of these brave men, and
> many others after them, we have the privilege to
> vote and send men of our class to Parliament. [51]

At the same time he supported the agitation for a Scottish Parliament. Arguing against Matheson and the De Leonists in Scotland, he said:

> It must be borne in mind that, whatever policy we in Scotland choose to adopt, there is a remote - a distinctly remote - chance of a revival of the Scots Parliament, and, therefore, we ought to be ready to make of it a democratic machine, and to use it for all it may produce.[52]

Out of his frustration over the English socialists' domination of the SDF and the British Socialist Party, in 1913 he launched a new monthly paper titled *The Vanguard*, with a strong Scottish radical and Marxist orientation. In the July 1913 issue, J. W. Keith wrote:

> Remember this, we Scots are not sheep. Our forefathers, yours and mine, fell on scores of battlefields in Europe fighting in the mean quarrels of small States, or for the wee German 'lairdie.' We, their descendants, will have other ways to fight for the land they, like us, loved and lost. Though I am a socialist and an Internationalist, yet my heart warms to the tartan, and I am proud to have the honour to call on all the Scots who read *The Vanguard* to 'Bide and fecht' with your voice, your vote, and your industrial action to make bonnie Scotland the land of the Scots indeed, and to abolish these twin curses of all lands, Landlordism and capitalism.[53]

Although Scottish nationalism was not Maclean's major preoccupation before the First World War, he knew how important the Scottish national question was. In December 1911, after the British Socialist Party had been formed, he wanted the Scottish District Council to be replaced by a Scottish National Council. He objected to the Scottish socialists' subordination to England; and he wrote in Justice: 'It is bad enough for Parliament to alot only a day and a half to Scotland; it is worse still to have a British Socialist Executive without a representative from Scotland.'[54]

Inheriting the long tradition of 'Scotch metaphysics', the most outstanding feature of Scottish socialism between 1900 and 1914 was its passionate advocacy of the need for a counter-culture and an alternative way of seeing the world. Oppositional, anti-imperialist and contemptuous of the world view being promulgated by the Anglo-Scottish ruling class, the 'bastards of creation' committed their resources to libertarian education. When they published their book on *Creative Revolution* (1921) under a dominant English Bolshevism that was hostile to Scottish nationalism, Eden and Cedar Paul had glanced back to identify the uniqueness of Clydeside socialism within the so-called United Kingdom:

> The first attempt at Independent Working-Class Education in Britain had no such [French] origin. W. Nairn of the SDF organised Marxist classes on the Clyde as long ago as the 'nineties. Nairn died young, and the work was carried on more systematically by George Yates and Jim Connell, who led the left wing of the Scottish SDF against Hyndman and Quelch.[55]

Unknown to Kenneth O. Morgan and Eric J. Hobsbawm, the Pauls' self-styled 'Leninism' had not inhibited them from recognising Connell and Maclean as more important international socialists than Keir Hardie. Much later an English historian glanced back to this period to ask: 'Is there at the present time any town in the country that could fill two theatres every Sunday night for socialist education and politics as happened in Glasgow before the First World War?'[56]

The most powerful feature of Scottish socialism between 1900 and the First World War was that it had not been drawn into - or tamed by - the institutions of *a very English system* of Parliamentary 'democracy'. Despite the weaknesses of Scottish nationalism and the currents of socialism in the Athens of the North, the undercurrent of opinion in favour of Home Rule burst through the polite and respectable proceedings from time to time. Emphasising the undeniable strength of Liberalism in Scotland at this time, and ignoring the fact that the Scottish labour movement was both more anti-imperialist and more radical than its English counterpart, T. C. Smout adopts a very condescending attitude towards Hardie and Maclean. In his book *A Century of the Scottish People, 1830-1950*, he concludes that as a result of the anti-Irishness of Hardie and Bruce Glasier 'many Scottish Independent Labour Party leaders, like Hardie, Glaiser and Ramsay MaDonald found their political careers flourished better in England and Wales than in their native land.' And, attributing the anti-Irish prejudices of Glaiser and Hardie to the inherited culture of the Covenanters, he argues that 'the Covenanting tradition had its disadvantages in uniting the workers of the world.' But the clever and condescending rhetoric Smout employs does not conceal the fact that the Scots socialists at home and abroad did not identify with John Bull's socialism.[57]

Long before the advent of the basically anti-Parliamentary Red Clydeside, many Scots wanted to see, in Maclean's phrase, 'the revival of the *Scots Parliament'*. The issue of Scottish Home Rule was, in various guises, debated fifteen times in the House of Commons between 1889 and 1914, and Keir Hardie could not have escaped his consciousness of being a Scot, anyway. In his book *The Growth of Nationalism in Scotland*, Keith Webb analysed this trend.

In 1913 a Home Rule Bill passed a second reading. In every case after 1893 when Home Rule was debated a majority of the Scottish Members voting were in favour. In the 1913 debate on the second reading there were forty-five Scottish members for the bill and only eight against.[58]

Maclean and the First World War

Despite the systematic denigration of Scotland and the Scots by the English cultural imperialists in the Scottish universities, whether Anglo-Scots or English, no one can deny that the Athens of the North was renowned for its cultural and political radicalism. When he paid tribute to the Glaswegians' role in putting socialist ideas on the map all over the world, Edward Roux, the famous South African socialist, argued that: 'The socialists' chief centres of activity seemed to be Chicago and Glasgow.' And from both of those radical cities 'came streams of journals and pamphlets'.[59] With the outbreak of the war, Maclean and the Left came into their own.

The Keir Hardie who denounced the Boer War also opposed the First World War. Before he died in 1915, he wrote and agitated against the twin evils of British imperialism and militarism. From Hardie's viewpoint the war was 'a crime and Britain's part in it wicked and foolish.'[60] He was depressed and disillusioned by the European workers' support for the war; and, when he died, a myth developed that he had died of a broken heart. By contrast, the war transformed Maclean into an international symbol of anti-miltarism and the struggle for socialism from below.

As Maclean, James D. MacDougall, James Maxton and countless rank-and-file socialists opposed the '"Great" War' from 4 August 1914 onwards, the Red Clyde became an ineradicable part of the social reality of many Glaswegians. At the heart of this radicalisation of countless working-class men and women on Red Clydeside was the indomitable and incorruptible figure of Maclean. Despite the myths and counter-myths as early as 1914, no one challenged the argument that the Scots were to the Left of their English counterparts. In his article on 'After Empire' (1977), the English historian Victor Kiernan wrote:

> Scotland, or at least Clydeside in its great days, stood apart; it was preserved by the Scots intellectual (including theological) tradition, more widely shared than any systematic thinking in England. But the Red Clyde of 1915-1920 found itself isolated (the other militant area was South Wales), and thereafter Scottish labour was to relapse, along with Scottish education, towards the English average.[61]

Imprisoned again and again, Maclean never faltered in proclaiming his socialist message. He displayed the meaning of socialist principle, vision, and anti-militarism by his personal example. He took the 'socialist precepts' in *The Socialist Sunday School Hymn Book* very seriously indeed. Writing in the American *Labor Year Book* at the end of 1916, Alexander Trachtenberg said:

> The most active opposition to conscription and the Munitions Act came from the Clyde district, where John Maclean, the leader of the Clyde movement, had for years imbubed his followers with a strong socialist spirit of revolt. This aggressive spirit found expression in a number of extended strikes which were put down with exceptional brutality by the British government. Maclean was arrested and condemned to a long stay in prison.[62]

Released under the pressure of mass agitation by the British labour movement in 1917, he would soon support the Bolshevik revolution.

Before the Easter Rising in Dublin, James Connolly reported in his illegal anti-war newspaper the *Workers' Republic* on Maclean's anti-war activities of 1915.[63] In reporting the trial and imprisonment of James D. MacDougall, James Maxton and Jack Smith in May 1916, the socialist newspaper the *New York Call* revealed that MacDougall and Smith had been caught with copies of Connolly's *Workers' Republic* in their possession.

Confirming much of what the *Workers' Republic* reported about State repression on Clydeside and the use of violence against striking workers and conscientious objectors, the *New York Call* gave vivid details of the repression the 'free', 'democratic' British press could not mention. In addition to giving prominence to British repression in Ireland after the Easter Rising in Dublin, the American socialists did not hesitate to report what the British press dared not acknowledge during the 'glorious war' to defend British 'democracy'.

With a simple matter-of-factness, the *New York Call* carried such stories in March 1915 and April 1916 as '14,000 Out in Clyde Strike, Berlin Hears' and 'Clyde Arms Strike Spreads.' [64] Then in December 1916 the same newspaper published an article titled '50 Exiles of British Isles form "Four Winds" Fellowship.' Gathering fifty persecuted British socialists who had been brutally mistreated for refusing to join the British army, Jim Larkin organised a Fellowship in New York. When he described the treatment of socialist conscientious objectors in Glasgow, one Clydesider said: 'I can tell you of men strung up by the heels for refusing to put on the khaki'. Commenting on the experience of another Clydeside exile, the *New York Call* said: 'A man from the Clyde gave a hint of the Clyde workers' struggles when the Red Flag sung by the workers at a meeting addressed by Arthur Henderson, government "labor man", was the signal for the loosing of all the fury of the police upon them'.[65]

Moreover, in an early issue of the American edition of the *Irish Worker* published by Jim Larkin in Chicago in March 1917, the activities of the Glasgow Catholic Socialist Society in agitating for Maclean's release from prison were given prominent coverage. In one of the few surviving issues of Larkin's probably short- lived *Irish Worker* in exile, it was reported that: 'Harry Hopkins roused our meeting to some tune on Sunday. His withering, scalding of the labor leaders of today (and the little budding traitors of tomorrow) seemed quite up our street. A word of praise for John Maclean brought forth a great wave of applause, which could it have penetrated prison walls would have done John's *radical* heart good'.[66] A week later, Larkin was campaigning in America for the liberation of 'his old friend', John Maclean'. [67]

In February 1918, when hundreds of engineers met Sir Auckland Geddes to discuss manpower, a resolution was carried calling for an immediate armistice.[68] And in the Scottish coalfields the Miners' Union conducted a ballot on peace negotiations, and 18,767 voted for immediate peace and only 8,249 voted for the continuance of the war. Then, when 10,000 working folk took part in a march from George Square to Glasgow Green to protest against the imprisonment of Maclean, the newspaper *Forward* hailed this demonstration as 'a great victory on the Home Front'.[69]

The Scots became increasingly conscious of the mass support they now enjoyed compared with the English Left; and the Scottish socialists and nationalists, who were grouped around Ruaraidh Erskine of Marr's quarterly magazine *The Scottish Review*, started to agitate for national independence. Inspired by the example of the Russian revolution, the Scottish labour movement supported the cottars' land raids in Sutherland and Skye as the application of 'Bolshevik tactics' in the Highlands.[70] Then in late November a giant workers' demonstration hailed the German revolution as the beginning of international socialism, and this new radical mood found a number of expressions.[71] Seven Labour or socialist M.P.s were elected to the House of Commons; and by contrast with the general election of 1910, when all Labour and socialist Parliamentary candidates polled no more than 33,000 votes, the Left in Scotland could now claim a third of the votes cast - 319,572. As Erskine of Marr, the second son of the fifth Lord Erskine, identified himself with the land raids organised by the Highland Land League at the same time as *Forward* and many socialists were doing likewise, there was a fusion of old-fashioned Scottish radicalism with modern socialism and nationalism.

In 1916 and 1917 the Scottish Trades Union Congress had articulated the general working-class agitation for Home Rule; and by 1918 they were going beyond the moderate proposals of the bourgeois Liberals by demanding separate Scottish representation at the Paris Peace Conference.[72] The Labour Party in Scotland reverted to its older name of the Scottish Labour Party. The active co-operation of the Highland Land League and the Scottish Labour Party [was] 'a significant sign of the times'; and in a joint appeal to the people they emphasised 'the

195

necessity' for a Scots Parliament and the encouragement of Gaelic culture.[73]

By 1918 Maclean was well-known to readers of socialist newspapers throughout Russia, Europe, Canada and Austrialia. Furthermore, the constant reports in the American socialist press about the treatment of socialists and conscientious objectors raise the question of Maclean's ill-treatment in Scottish jails. Although there is no evidence of drugging in his so-called 'medical file' in the Scottish Record Office - except for one statement by James D. MacDougall recorded by the special branch - the evidence touching on his ill-treatment is overwhelming and saddening.

In America, Larkin predicted that the Irish working class would resist 'the draft'.[74] In what was probably his first public identification with the agitation of the Irish in Scotland for complete independence, John Wheatley, together with Neil Maclean and Agnes Dollan, opposed the introduction of conscrption.[75] Though Maclean did not come out of prison again until December 1918, the Irish newspaper *The Voice of Labour* reported on the growing militancy of the Irish and Scottish workers.

On 23 April, 1918 a one day general strike against conscription was organised by the Irish Trades Union Congress.[76] A turning-point in the radicalisation of Irish working people, it was 'effected with impressive unanimity over the greater part of Ireland - all but the Orange and "loyalist" quarter in Ulster - and that memorable illustration of workers' power, that day when Ireland did nothing and did it with a vengeance, had a profound effect'. Then on 1 June, 1918 *The Voice of Labour* carried an opening article by the Hon. R. Erskine of Marr entitled 'The Anglo-Scottish Menace and the Celtic Entente'. It was now clear that the radicalisation of Ireland was accompanied by growing ethnic conflict in Ulster.[77]

Scottish and Irish Republicanism: An Idea Whose Time Had Come

At first sight, Harvie's comment about Maclean being reincarnated in the 1970s rather than understood did not make sense except as an expression of the prejudices of Brtitish Parliamentary democracy and the major London publishing houses. It was, on reflection, consistent with Kenneth O. Morgan's contrast of Keir Hardie's 'outward looking' horizons by comparison with Maclean's inward-looking 'Celtic communism.'

In a profound sense that I did not grasp until quite recently, the comments by Morgan and Harvie were dictated by the previous British Labour historiography. More than in the history of other countries, including England, much of the history of the Scots radical culture from the eighteenth century onwards was restricted to folk songs and folk culture. By contrast, any Scottish radical like James Keir Hardie, who fitted into the British framework of London publishing and Parliamentary democracy, was destined to enjoy 'immortality' inside the Brits' official culture.

Although Hardie was an uncompromisingly pro-Scottish and anti-English/British imperialist for most of his life, he was *posthumously* co-opted by the British Parliamentarians after his death in 1915. However, this complex process of co-option began before his death; and it was reflected in the large number of biographies written about him. This process began in 1909 when Frank Smith published *From Pit to Parliament: The Man and the Movement* (1909) followed by the same author's *From Pit to Parliament: Keir Hardie's Life Story* (1915), John Bruce Glasier's *James Keir Hardie: A Memorial* (1915), and *Memoir of James Keir Hardie, M.P., and Tributes to His Work* by Robert Smillie, J. Ramsay MacDonald, M.P., and Mary MacArthur (1915).

In the 1920s there were four biographies published on Hardie: they were William Stewart, *J. Keir Hardie: A Biography* (1921), Francis Johnson, *Keir Hardie's Socialism (1922), David Lowe, From Pit to Parliament: The Story of James Keir Hardie* (1923) and William Stewart, *The Making of Agitator* (1929). In the 1930s there were two biographies by Henry Hamilton Fife titled *Keir Hardie* (1935) and John Emmet Hughes, *Keir Hardie: Some Memories* (1939). Furthermore, during the complicated decade of the 1940s, G. D. H. Cole published *James Keir Hardie* (1941); and in the 1950s John Emmet Hughes published *Keir Hardie* (1950) and John Cockburn published *The Hungry Heart: A Romantic Biography* (1956).

Hyman Shapiro published *Keir Hardie and the Labour Party* (1971), Iain Mclean, *Keir Hardie* (1975), Kenneth O. Morgan, *Keir Hardie: Radical and Socialist* (1975) and Fred Reid, *Keir Hardie: The Making of a Socialist* (1978). Reflecting the marked decline of Labourism in English working-class constituencies, there was no biography on Hardie during the the whole of the decade of the 1980s except for a play titled *Keir Hardie: The Man They Could Not Buy* (1984); and whether anticipating British

Labour obituaries or not, *Keir Hardie* (1992) by Tony Benn's wife, Caroline.

Against this enormous historiography on Hardie, there have been only four substantial biographies of John Maclean. However, the Clydeside socialist, who gave critical support to the Russian revolution and all agitations for working-class rights and socialism from below, was recognised as an out-and-out internationalist with wide horizons by Lenin, Trotsky, Eugene Victor Debs, the American socialist, Claude McKay, the West Indian socialist and father of the Harlem renaissance, and a host of other major figures in international socialism. But, although he stood for Parliament in 1918 and later, he promised the Clydeside workers that he would never sit in John Bull's Parliament.

When the Communist Party of Great Britain published Leon Trotsky's book *Where Is Britain Going?* in 1926, Trotsky had already written about Scotland and John Maclean's anti-war agitations on Clydeside from the very beginning of the First World War. In one of his most significant passages in *Where Is Britain Going?*, he wrote:

> The most radical elements of the contemporary British labour movement are mostly of the Scotch and Irish race. The union in Ireland of social with national oppression, in face of the sharp conflict of an agrarian and capitalist country, gives the conditions for sharper breaks in consciousness. Scotland set out upon the road of capitalism later than England; the sharper break in the life of the masses of the people causes a sharper break in political reaction.

But impersonal social or historical forces have always found expression in and through exceptional individuals; and Maclean personified the Red Clyde between 1914 and his death in 1923.

Maclean was already a major socialist internationalist in 1919, and his brutal treatment in Scottish prisons did not blunt his irrepressible radicalism or humour. When Crystal Eastman, the sister of Max Eastman, the distinguished American and editor of *The Liberator* magazine came to Glasgow in 1919 to report on the Red Clydeside, she met Maclean. Eastman was a feminist, who wrote a very sympathetic profile of him, for American socialists. Praising Maclean and the working-class men and women of the Clydeside for keeping the city of Glasgow 'an anti-war city throughout the five years' of war, she then described him as 'a mild-mannerred, smiling conspirator, with a round-eyed, apple-cheeked face, and white hair.' Quoting some of his dialogue, she wrote:

> 'Be cheerie, comrades', he says, 'you never can win
> a revolution without being cheerie.' Maclean
> believes in revolution now.'[78]

The argument about the Scottish national question within the British labour movement began in 1919. Just as Trotsky, the Eastmans and other European and American socialists were aware of the radical Scots being well to the Left of the English during and after the war, so were the early English 'communists'. At the birth of the Third International in 1919, Augustin Hamon, a French socialist, challenged the orthodox Leninist interpretation of British labour history during 'the "Great" War'. In a book titled *Le Mouvement Ourvrier en Grande-Bretagne*, he argued that the Scots 'were more supple-minded" and 'displayed more intellectual vivacity than the English workers.' By saying so, he upset the English communists Eden and Cedar Paul by attributing to 'racial differences' the much greater 'intensity of the class struggle in Scotland by comparison with England.'[79] Opposing Maclean and the substantial Republican movement for a Scottish Socialist Republic as a diversion from the unified British class struggle throughout the 'United Kingdom', Eden and Cedar Paul attributed the working-class radicalism on Clydeside to 'the characteristics of local conditions' rather than a different 'national temperament'. Arguing against Hamon, they refused to concede the possibility that the Red Clydeside might have been a combination of local circumstances and national temperament.[80]

Yet, in contrast to Scottish socialists such as Robert Smillie who agitated for the revival of the Gaelic language during the war years, Maclean's Scottish Labour College was criticised by *The Scottish Review* for 'the absence of any definite place for the study of Scottish history from the national and democratic point of view.'[81] But, though Maclean was slower than Maxton, Smillie and other socialists to come out in favour of Scottish independence, he was assured of mass support by his uncompromising support of the Bolshevik revolution.[82] (However, Maclean's idea of socialism was light-years away from the later Stalinist 'communists', who tried to impose a dictatorship over the working class. When he was released from prison in December 1917 on 'ticket of leave', he told a mass meeting that when we 'come to power we will do away with all courts, judges, lawyers, and everything connected with the police system of capitalism.')[83]

In recovering the lost historical fact that Maclean began to co-operate with Erskine of Marr in early 1919, Harry Hanham did not realise that Cathal O'Shannon helped to bring the ideas of the two men to public attention through the pages of *The Voice of Labour*.[84] When James D. MacDougall published his article on 'Marxism in Scotland' in May 1918, he did not even mention the Irish question.[85] Despite the fact that *The Voice of Labour* appealed to the Irish community to vote for Maclean when he stood as the official Labour candidate in the Gorbals, Glasgow, in 1918, he alienated many of the Irish at his eve-of-the poll meeting.[86]

But, although Maclean's conversion to the policy of Sinn Fein did not develop before 1919, it is possible to pinpoint certain landmarks which influenced his attitude to rebel Ireland and radical Scotland. One was the 'Republican Demonstration' in the St. Andrew's Hall, Glasgow, on 16 February under the auspices of the Scottish committee of Sinn Fein. In reporting this meeting attended by over 5,000 men and women, *The Voice of Labour* said:

> The publication of the Democratic Platform in the *Forward* has removed many misconceptions about the social aims of the Irish people. Further intercourse between Ireland and Scotland, between the forces of Labour in particular, and concerted action for common ends, will help the workers of both countries - and the Belfast worker is the natural link.[87]

From 1 May, 1919, Maclean was committed to the Irish cause as a part of the worldwide anti-imperialist struggle. When he, John Wheatley, and Countess Markievicz spoke at the Glasgow May Day in the presence of 100,000 workers, Irish tricolours were openly carried among the crowd and the Soldiers' Song was sung along with the Red Flag.[88] Jailed in 1915, 1916, 1918 and again for a year in 1921, Maclean nevertheless played a major role in shaping the Scots own radical socialism. A Scottish nationalist by 1919, he had no illusions about either Parliamentary socialism or the Parliamentary 'democracy' of Westminster.

In 1924 William Bolitho, an English journalist, wrote *The Cancer of Empire*. In his brilliant sketch of the new radical culture, he tried to identify its distinctive features: 'Shadowy yet in details, but already crystallised by two phrases as fatal as the motto of the first French Republic, Liberty, Equality, Fraternity, a new socialism, different from, but no less fierce and sincere than the communism of Lenin, evolved on the Clyde. It is a Western socialism, an unfatalistic socialism, apt for Western peoples, which the stockyards of Chicago, the thrifty faubourgs of Paris, the conservatives miners of the Ruhr, may one day hear and understand.'[89]

But the Irish were just as disaffected as the Scots. When Maclean went to Dublin in July 1919 as a guest of honour of the Irish labour movement, he met prominent socialists, left-wing nationalists, poets and literary men. *The Voice of Labour* trumpeted the fact that they had had 'the rare pleasure' of entertaining the legendary Maclean. In providing a report of Maclean's first visit to Dublin, O'Shannon said:

> A reception was held in Liberty Cafe, Eden Quay,
> on Monday 21 July, when he had the opportunity
> of exchanging views with the representative people
> of various schools of thought in Irish Ireland.[90]

Maclean's meeting with Irish nationalists had a big impact on him; and, already disgusted with the official leaders of what was to be launched as the Communist Party of Great Britain a year before that new 'Bolshevik' Party's foundation in 1920, he became a Scottish Republican.[91]

Responding to the Scots heightened sense of national awareness, the suppression of their culture, and the fragile beginnings of a Scottish historiography that was hostile to the Anglo-Scottish one developed by the Scottish Enlightenment, Maclean began to advocate a Scottish Socialist Republic before he organised the Scottish Workers' Republican Party.[92]

When the Scots National League organised a public meeting in Arbroath in September, 1920, to celebrate the sex-centenary of the Arbroath Declaration of Scottish Independence of 1320, Maclean took the chair. But though John McArthur apologised for the absence of Marr, who was ill, and Maclean and Sandy Ross advocated an independent, democratic Republic, the two latter speakers did not join the League.[93] What appealed to Maclean was the League's support for the Irish struggle and their interpretation of Scottish history. This was made clear in the League's magazine *Liberty*: 'Introducing Mr. John MacArthur, he [Maclean] said that Mr. MacArthur was trying in his pages to teach them true Scots history instead of the false and perverted variety taught in the school-books.' [94]

In an article in Maclean's resurrected *The Vanguard* entitled 'The Irish Tragedy', he told his readers about his motive for sharing a platform with John MacArthur, the editor of *Liberty,* in quite unambiguous language: 'Why did I visit Arbroath on Saturday ll September, but to protest the hollow mockery of the centenary celebration of the Scottish Parliament's declaration of independence to Pope John XXII, whilst Scots boys dressed in the garb of the English government were then and now daring the Irish to set up a free and independent Irish Parliament elected by the overwhelming vote of the Irish people.' [95] However, if he was influenced by the nationalists' fundamentalist interpretation of Scottish history, Marr's assertion that 'the community' would be 'the ruling power' in a future Scotland conflicted with his more radical idea of a Scottish Socialist Republic as a really democratic society. [96]

Maclean distanced himself from the Scots National League when Marr, in 1920, began to adopt the fascist philosophy of 'blood and soil'. Meanwhile a growing number of Scottish socialists believed that the Scots had moved far to the left of their English counterparts; and the agitation for a Scottish Parliament was put at the top of their agenda. [97] When the Scottish ILP met at their annual conference in 1921 they again demanded the setting up of a Scottish Parliament. At the annual conference of the Scottish Trades Union Congress, the Left defended their attitude to the national question by arguing that they were well to the Left of the English. A delegate from the Scottish Dock Labourers said: 'There would have been no Triple Alliance failure North of the Tweed if the Scottish workers had been free to decide for themselves.' He also made the common complaint that the Scots could not move far without the consent of the 'great' people in London. [98]

Ignored and hidden by Establishment historians including Stalinist ones, the Scottish national question engendered deep splits in the labour movement. In the newspaper *The Communist*, an opponent of Maclean and Home Rule wrote:

> I am afraid I cannot attach great importance to the decision of the Scottish Trades Union Congress to

affiliate to the British section of the Red
International. It is good in its way, but it was passed
by a Congress that 'after an animated debate'
decided to support Home Rule for Scotland... Are
the Clyde men going to stick to their determination
not to accept a wage cut, or are they too busy with
Home Rule for Scotland?

To underline his John Bull hostility to the Scots agitation for Home
Rule, the writer signed himself 'John Ball.'[99] In contrast to Maclean's
support for Scottish independence, John S. Clarke and the Communist
Party of Great Britain attacked the Scottish Left for fostering 'nationalist
sentiments' and 'dangerous delusions'. The Scottish socialists defence
of the Gaelic language was also denounced as an attempt to destroy
the perspective of international socialism.[100]

The year 1922 was a turning-point in modern Scottish labour history.
Out of the seventy-four Scottish constituencies contested by the Left
in the general election of that year, thirty mostly left-wing Labour M.P.s
were elected to the House of Commons on a very radical programme.
At first the Scottish socialists were optimistic. By 1923 James Maxton
told a meeting of the Scottish Socialist Teachers' Society in Glasgow of
the frustrations felt by the radical Scots at Westminster:

It was a humiliating experience to sit in the British
House of Commons, one of a majority returned to
the House of Commons to push on a policy of
fundamental social change for the benefit of the
Scottish people, and to find the Scottish majority
steadily voted down by the votes of the English
members pledged to a policy of social stagnation.
It was now over two hundred years since the Union
of Parliaments, and although one was perpetually
told of the blessings conferred on Scotland by the
Union, it was difficult to find any blessings except
the somewhat doubtful one of fighting England's
wars.[101]

But Ramsay MacDonald had not been smothered at birth; and as well
fawning on the Monarchy, he helped to integrate the Scottish Labour
M.P.s into the social fabric of the established social order.

Maxton raised the Scottish question in Parliament and told an audience of working-class Glaswegians that:

> He would ask no greater job in life than to make English-ridden, capitalist-ridden, land-owner-ridden Scotland into the free Scottish Socialist Commonwealth, and in doing that he thought it would be rendering a very great service to the people of England, Wales and Europe, and to the cause of Internationalism generally.[102]

The Scottish labour movement was de-radicalised by mass unemployment and disillusioned dreams of the better world to come. Summing up the role of a sleekit Parliamentary Establishment in absorbing the radical Scots at Westminster, C. M. Grieve (Hugh MacDiarmid) wrote: 'The majority of the Scottish Labour members returned to the House of Commons went there as "internationalists." A short experience of Westminster transformed them completely.'[103] And Scotland is still paying a heavy price for that ignoble transformation, though the case for democratic socialist-humanism at home and abroad will become increasingly obvious as we move towards the twenty-first century.

Conclusion

During the holocaust of the First World War, two socialisms emerged. The socialism represented by thinkers and activists like Maclean and Rosa Luxemburg put people and an international working-class conscious of the need for democratic socialism before an abstract world culture. Unlike Maclean and Luxemburg a new breed of socialists like the Scottish poet Hugh MacDiarmid began to put consciousness and 'culture' before people.

Maclean's socialist-humanism was evident from the beginning; and the 'Great War' strengthened his earlier attitudes. No one in Scotland or anywhere else developed such a strong 'democratic intellect' independently of established educational institutions as Maclean did. But, although he was a Marxist and a humanist who loved books and man's spirituality, he always put people before books or culture.

When in Pollockshaws in 1905 he fought the petty capitalist elements, who were more interested in spending money on supporting the prestigous Campbell Library than investing in measures to promote good health, Maclean wrote:

> I ask the people to think. Are libraries or books the first thing required? Certainly not. Pure, unadulerated milk, free from disease germs, ought to claim the first attention of the 'Shaws folk.'[104]

By the early 1930s, when Lewis Grassic Gibbon was writing his triology of novels titled *A Scots Quair*, Maclean's surviving idea of democratic culture was struggling to exist against a powerful bureaucratic Stalinist machine in Scotland, in the now dead Rosa Luxemburg's Germany and elsewhere in a world threatened by Stalinism and Hitlerite fascism.

Ignored and neglected by most labour historians, the Celts' distinctive humanist-socialism was thoroughly internationalist in orientation and stance. In Glasgow, Dublin and London, there were socialists like Maclean, Jim Larkin and Sylvia Pankhurst who were criticial of Lenin and the Third International founded in 1919. When he returned from America in 1923, Larkin, who in common with Maclean in Glasgow and Sylvia Pankhurst in London helped to organise the Irish Workers' League, Larkin forged an alliance with Maclean. Libertarian and left-wing groups throughout the world were already very critical of the Third International's interference in the socialist politics of other countries; and they soon founded a Berlin-based Fourth International.

Maclean founded the Scottish Workers' Republican Party. However unlike Hardie, whose life culminated in increasing isolation from his own class - the last few years of Maclean's life were spent among the poorest of the poor. The growing anti-imperialism and pro-Irish sentiments of many Scottish workers were portrayed in a first-hand account of Scottish life in the American sociologlist Whitling Williams's book *Fed Up and Full Up: What's On the Workers' Mind in Crowded Britain* (1921); and, although Maclean kept up his friendship with such English socialists as the legendary Tom Mann, he shared Claude McKay's critique of the imperialist attitudes of the English 'communists'.[105]

It was signficant, too, that Larkin, Maclean and the nationalistic Scottish and Irish workers, did not just struggle for self-government for their own countries against John Bull. They also took the unpopular path of opposing the racism of English seamen. In 1923 Irish workers stood in solidarity with the Black seamen against Havelock Wilson's *Brit* National Union of Seamen in Liverpool . As *The Voice of Labour* explained:

> Everything looked good until, lo! a crew of whites,
>   Britishers
> Sons of the Sea,
> Glorious and free,
> took the place of the despised 'nigger' at the reduced rate
> 'Superior' race, eh? Which?[106]

Moreover, at a moment when most of the English communists in the Third International were refusing to denounce British imperialism, Maclean agitated in the streets of Scotland for racial equality and old-fashioned radical egalitarianism. When he stood for election to Parliament in 1922, he defended the colonial revolution, the Black wage-slaves in South Africa, and 'Gandhi and thousands of other splendid champions of Indian independence' [107] When he spoke to the Second Congress of the Third International in Moscow in 1920, Tom Quelch caused Lenin deep disappointment. As Ralph Fox explained: 'This question [of the English communists' softness in the face of imperialism] was discussed on a report made by Lenin, and one of the English delegates, Tom Quelch, the son of the revolutionary socialist who spoke up so boldly against imperialism at Stuttgart, declared that any British worker who attempted to defend the colonial revolution would be considered a traitor by his fellows.'[108]

Whatever the outcome of the struggle for socialist internationalism will be in the twenty-first century, the Quelchs will be forgotten and the Macleans, Larkins and Tom Manns will be rediscovered by a new generation searching and struggling for social justice. Although many thousands of people attended Maclean's funeral after his death in Glasgow on 30 November 1923, a ruling-class counter-revolution comparable to Margaret Thatcher's counter-revolution of the 1980s marginalised his memory.

Yet, despite the oppressive weight of John Bull's socialism on the Scots, Scotland remained distinctive in several important ways. The attempt to create a 'colour bar' in hotels, restaurants and dance halls in Edinburgh and Glasgow failed in the 1920s. Unlike London, where the ILP acquiesced in the 'colour bar', in Edinburgh the ILP's demonstrations and pickets inhibited this pernicious development.[109]

Consequently, a Black Briton wrote to Dr. Harold Moody, founder of the League of Coloured People, in the late 1920s:

> I came here with my family to undertake post-graduate study in London. Alhough I tried for a whole day I could not discover any place where I could obtain lodgings of any sort. I therefore had to take a night train to Scotland where I received my medical education and where I knew I would be treated with more courtesy.[110]

But, although Maclean's character would be increasingly denigrated by Anglo-Scottish Tories, Labourites and Stalinists alike, his memory would live on to haunt the imagination of those who strove to re-connect themselves to the broken continuity of Scottish radical culture. In an interview in the magazine *Scottish International* (1970), Sorley Maclean, the Gaelic poet, summed up the enduring significance of the Clydeside socialist:

> He was a terrific man, you know, I remember when I was a student in Edinburgh, I was going to Glasgow to see some of my relations, and what looked like a prosperous Glasgow business-man came into the compartment and started talking, and he said, he asked me what my name was, and I told him. Ah, he said, you have the same name as the man we all thought was going to be the King of Scotland. He was a neighbour of his... He was not related to me, he was of Mull extraction. The impact... Whatever the Communists have done since is not the fault of poor John Maclean.[111]

Chapter Six

Lewis Grassic Gibbon (1901-1935) and James Barke (1905-1958): *Scotland, Marxism, and Internationalism*

The test of a first-rate intelligence is the ability to keep two contradictory ideas in the mind at the same time and still retain the ability to function.
F. Scott Fitzgerald

You painted our Scottish scene and told its story,
Deep-rooted, loving, hating, the drudgery of its toil,
No erudite, fantastic tale of glory,
Knowing its real history-makers, those who toil.
Soft, lilting cadences of Mearns folk,
Kinraddie's quens, and childis, coarse, crude and kind,
No Chauvinist platitudes when your pen spoke,
This land of ours has still its soul to find.
Mary Brooksbank

Lewis Grassic Gibbon and James Barke: Biographies of Two Carnaptious Radicals

Leslie Mitchell (1901-1935), who wrote under the pseudonym Lewis Grassic Gibbon, and James Barke (1905-1958), who always wrote under his own name, were both men of the people. As left-wing novelists and socialist agitators, they made a slow and cumulative impact on Scottish imaginative literature. Yet, despite the extensive and intensive industrialisation of the Lowlands of Scotland, they both came from very rural backgrounds.

However, Mitchell was by far the better writer of the two - a man of many-sided talents as a writer. Better known to the world from the 1930s onwards as Lewis Grassic Gibbon, he was the son of poor farming folk. In the volume of essays and short stories entitled *Scottish Scene* that he shared with Hugh MacDiarmid (1934), he wrote:

> I like to remember that I am of peasant rearing and peasant stock. Good manners prevail on me not to insist on the fact over-much, not to boast in the company of those who come from manses and slums and castles and villas, the folk of the proletariat, the bigger and lesser bourgeoisies. But I am again and again, as I hear them talk of their origins and beginnings and begetters, conscious of an overweening pride that mine was thus and so, that the land was so closely and intimately mine (my mother used to hap me in a plaid at harvest time and leave me in the lee of a stook while she harvested).[1]

Loving and hating the land simultaneously, the historian of Scottish radical history *par excellence* would have had no difficulty in seeing himself as belonging to the same radical cultural tradition as James Thomson Callender, Alexander Rodger, James MacFarlan, Alexander Robertson, John Murdoch, Keir Hardie and John Maclean.

At Arbuthnott School, Gibbon emerged as a brilliant student of history and english. Encouraged by his headmaster Alexander Gray, he soon went to Mackie Academy, Stonehaven. The First World War was already underway, and Gibbon and the Rector of the Academy did not get on very well. Gibbon soon walked out without completing his education, and, defying his father's exhortation to get 'a fee' as a farm labourer, Gibbon started work as a cub reporter on the *Aberdeen Journal*.

In *Scottish Scene*, Gibbon recalled how he and George MacDonald had 'attended the foundation meeting' of the Aberdeen Soviet inspired by the Bolshevik revolution and were soon 'elected to the Soviet Council, forgetting we were press-men'.[2] Certainly, Gibbon attracted trouble: it was not wise to salute every Red flag that one saw or to smoke Russian cigarettes as an expression of solidarity with the

Bolsheviks. He was often impulsive; and his quick impulses came out of his compassionate radical heart-and-head.

At the beginning of 1919 he went to work as a reporter for the *Scottish Farmer* in Glasgow. He witnessed the class struggle in Glasgow at first hand, joined an anarcho-communist Group, and landed himself in serious difficulty by falsifying his expense' claims by the then large sum of £60 presumably - if we are to believe the, autobiographical clues in his novels - to start a socialist newspaper. Before he returned home in disgrace as 'the speak of the place', he fortunately botched an attempt at suicide. On 31 August 1919 he became a soldier, and remained in the army for the next four years. In 1923 he entered the Royal Air Force as a clerk and completed his six years' engagement on 31 August 1929.[3]

From the Establishment's viewpoint, Gibbon was always 'a trouble-maker.' He simply not could ignore social injustice. Douglas F. Young, a Gibbon scholar, has recorded that Alexander Gray was, in 1928 or 1929, 'approached by the police in Stonehaven who enquired about Leslie's communist sympathies. There had been trouble in a camp [at Upavon] on Salisbury Plain, rumblings of revolt, and the police wanted to know if Leslie could have been behind it. Mr. Gray thought he probably was.' But for the remainder of his short life, Gibbon was free to make his outstanding contribution to Scottish - and international - literature and socialist struggle. For, although his triology of novels *A Scots Quair* was his outstanding contribution to universal literature, he wrote book reviews, articles and letters to publishers in which he tried to foster the writing careers of men like James Barke.

Like the other Scottish radicals portrayed in this book, Gibbon was not just on the extreme Left. So were James Barke and Hugh MacDiarmid during the most creative part of their lives in 'the devil's decade' of the 1930s. Gibbon was also pro-Scottish, anti-Establishment, critical of a major part of the labour movement and, above all, *carnaptious*. But of all the major Scottish radicals portrayed here, there was something almost mysterious about the intensity of his radicalism - the passionate sympathy with the poor throughout thousands of years of history; the belief in a libertarian international socialism from below (as distinct from Stalinism from above); and the rare commitment to books and culture.

The key to the enigma of Gibbon's personality was hinted at in the book by Peter Whitfield, *Grassic Gibbon and His World* (1994). Revealing for the first time that Gibbon's two elder brothers were really his half-brothers, he said:

> She [Lilias Gibbon] was one of a dozen children,
> and as for so many poor country girls, the only
> work open to her was to leave home and enter
> domestic service. In her nineteenth year, she was
> living at Belhelvie, near the coast, and it was there
> that her first child, George Donald Gibbon, was
> born in January 1893. He was registered as
> illegitimate... Where Lilias and her child lived for
> the next four years is unknown, but by November
> 1897 she was back in Leochel Cushie, where her
> second son, John Grassick Hall Gibbon, was born.
> He too was illegitimate, but in January 1898 Lilias
> entered a paternity suit naming the father as
> Alexander Hall, a farm servant in Banchory.[4]

Later on Gibbon's wife, Rebecca (or Ray) Middleton rather unconvincingly insisted that Gibbon had not been aware that his two brothers were illegitimate.

Lilias Gibbon was always known for her sharp intelligence and independence of mind. She married James Mitchell, a small crofter, on New Year's Eve 1898; and from an early age the rebellious traits of the young Mitchell or Gibbon would cause his parents distress. But he was lucky: Robert Middleton, later portrayed in *Grey Granite* as Long Rob of the Mill, took a liking to Gibbon when he was still a boy. His headmaster Alexander Gray, who saw his intellectual potential at an early age, remained devoted to him during - and indeed well beyond - his short life. Encouraged too by his future father-in-law 'Long Rob', he married Ray Middleton at Fulham Registry Office, London, on 15 August 1925.[5]

At his best James Barke was also a very *carnaptious*, sometimes 'eccentric', and extra-Parliamentary Scottish radical, agitator and writer. Nevertheless his radicalism was never so intense as Gibbon's; and as a novelist he reported rather than created his characters. Before returning to this point later on, it is worth pointing out that he invites comparison with the American novelist Howard Fast.

The son of farm labouring folk, Barke was born in Torwoodlea, Selkirk, in 1905 before his parents moved to Tulliallan in 1907. The future radical lived there until 1918 when the Tulliallan estate near Kincardie on the river Forth was broken up and his family moved to Glasgow.

Barke's Socialist Kailyard and Gibbon's Alienation from Bourgeois Scotland

In his autobiography *The Green Hills Far Away* (1940), Barke said: 'And it is of those Tulliallan years that I write.'[6] Unlike Gibbon, he did not experience trauma, poverty or hurt at the hands of the society he grew up in, although he was probably belted by a teacher. Moreover, he did not at any time *feel* Gibbon's utter contempt for bourgeois Scotland. In his sentimental autobiography, in which he expressed a sort of Stalinist Popular Front nostalgia for Scotland before the Great War, the tone of hard-line 'Marxist-Leninist' orthodoxy that coloured his article in the *Left Review* in 1936 had gone by 1940.

As a sentimental socialist and most unlikely Marxist, Barke did not possess the same sharp intellect or sustained anti-capitalist attitudes as Gibbon. Rather surprisingly he wrote:

> It [Tulliallan] was much like any other Scottish vilage - a pretty fair amalgam of Kinraddie or Barbie; Ecclefechan or Auchtermuchty. Take the village bodies as you found them: they were as douce and decent as any to be found in broad and bonnie Scotland.[7]

(Shades of a new socialist Kailyard that would colour his novels on Burns after the Second World War). Barke's autobiography can be searched from beginning to end to find psychological clues for the origins of the socialism that energised his novels in the 1930s. They are not there, except perhaps the trauma of ending up as an engineering worker, and then manager, in a large Glasgow shipyard. One of the most interesting things in his preamble is the comment about the Clydeside Scot being 'afflicted with many of the sores and running wounds of modern industrialism'. Furthermore, in the light of the sustained comment by a small army of Stalinist scholars about Gibbon's failure to understand the Scottish industrial proletariat, it was interesting that Barke described the 'Clydeside Scot, because of the peculiar significance of his historical conditions, [as] the most glorious Scot of them all'.[8]

Before he retired in 1933 as the manager of a ship-building firm in Glasgow in 1933 to devote himself to full-time writing, Barke had worked in the Glasgow shipyards. He did not portray the working class any better than Gibbon had done; but by contrast with the author of *A Scots Quair*, Barke attracted favourable attention from the Communist Party of Great Britain (CPGB). Towards the end of his autobiography, he said:

> Nor was I to know of the prejudice and silly snobbery of the Old School tie. We were such honest barbarians at Tulliallan we didn't know there were scholars who wore ties. No: Glasgow with its future Engineering, Drawing, Trigonometry, Latin, Shorthand, Book-keeping, Business Methods...remained in the middle distance of my immediate perspective as a vast smoking hell seething with damned and tortured souls.[9]

However, he did not like the 'Anglicised Scots' of the ruling class and shared Gibbon's strong antipathy towards fascism.

But, although he would become a writer, he did not apologise for the 'democratic intellect' possessed by many radical Scots as a part of their hard-fought struggle for a national identity and historiography against the counter-activities of the Anglo-Scottish ruling class. As Sydney Goodsir Smith explained in his tribute to Barke in the *Saltire Review*, 'he was essentially a tradesman and his trade was writing'. Summing up this ineradicable trait in Barke's democratic personality, Smith said:

> But he was not concerned with your work or your reputation when he met you; he regarded you first and foremost and all the way as a man, a chap - not as a poet or a musician or a bus-driver. He shared this open-minded attitude with his great idol Burns, and maybe it was this sense of emotional kinship that set off his hero-worship.[10]

Burns, the national bard, would play a major role in his life after the Second World War.

Meanwhile, after being close to the Independent Labour Party in the early 1930s, Barke seems to have joined the CPGB in 1936. At the beginning as at end of his life as an unaffiliated socialist, he was frequently criticised as a *sentimental* socialist and novelist. He was very upset when forests were cut down near Tullillan during the First World War as part of the war effort. In *The Green Hills Far Away*, he complained bitterly:

> A tough he-man critic in the Glasgow *Socialist Star* reviewing *The World World His Pillow* wrote: "... think of it - depopulating the forests of wood. Trees - mushrooms and cowwebs - fungus in a beer cellar - shed a tear for them and you have a soul! You get the drift unmistakably even if the meaning eludes you."[11]

Being much less macho, later generations of socialists would be very grateful to James Barke for his prefigurative ecological consciousness.

But, although it has become fashionable to make dismissive remarks about some of the novels of Gibbon and Barke being 'feats of memory', they both did considerable research into Scottish radical history. Few except radical historians could appreciate Barke's research into the radical *North British Daily Mail* or Gibbon's research into the Covenanters. Though neither writer said so, they faced the same major problem as their predecessors - the absence of a national historiography of Scottish radicalism including socialism. Barke's novels before the Second World War were *The World His Pillow* (1933), *The Wild Macraes* (1934), *The End of the High Bridge* (1935), *Major Operation* (1936) and *The Land of the Leal* (1939). For all its faults as a novel, this last and best novel of that period offers a rich panoramic view of Scottish history from the agricultural and industrial revolutions onwards. Certainly, it was, like *A Scots Quair*, an expression of accumulated Scottish folk culture, and it was influenced by his parents experiences' in Galloway.[12]

By conventional academic standards, Barke was a more consistent Marxist than Gibbon. Unlike Barke, however, Gibbon was a genius: intense, introverted, at times incisive, analytical, unconventional and often very emotional about oppression and injustice. Emotionally and intellectually on the extreme Left, he understood and hated the social injustice engendered by modern society. Nevertheless he was a sharper and much deeper thinker than Barke; and, unlike the CPGB's much acclaimed 'Marxist-Leninism' of Barke from 1936, in his novels, too, Gibbon was much less sentimental and more analytical than Barke.

On 12 December 1932 Barke wrote a long letter to Gibbon in which he praised the genius that shone through *Sunset Song*.[13] Through Hugh

MacDiarmid, both Gibbon and Barke were active in the CPGB's attempt to form an association of revolutionary writers. And, together with Willa and Edwin Muir, Barke attended Gibbon's cremation at Golders Green on 11 February 1935.

When he was writing for the Scottish nationalist magazine *The Free Man* before his death in 1935, Gibbon reviewed Barke's first novel *The World His Pillow* (1933). Sharing Barke's antipathy for the horrible life of the workers in the city of Glasgow without dismissing its potentialities as a cauldron of potential social revolution, he wrote:

> He has all the Scots virtues and most of the faults;
> he is apt and acute and passionate, and an excellent
> hand with a claymore. And he preaches and proses
> and halts through long stretches to tell the bored
> reader, over and over again, just how his hero felt
> and considered and was spiritually uplifted and
> spiritually tormented (generally tormented by Life
> and Fate and Fortune) and the vagaries of Mr
> Bernard Shaw... As it is, it surely gives promise of
> good things to come, unless Mr Barke, like his hero,
> has fled to a Balcreggan from the terrors of
> Glasgow. In dealing with life in that deplorable
> city, the vomit of a cataleptic commercialism, Mr
> Barke is at his best, however he may long to
> describe the banks and braes and couthy knowes,
> and kye in sunset clover and the beauty of a
> pibroch.

Inevitably Barke's autobiographical hero Duncan failed to cope convincingly with the dialectic in his encounters between the industrial capitalism of Glasgewian society and the struggles of its potential gravediggers.[14]

When he reviewed Barke's next novel *The Wild Macraes* in *The Free Man* (1934) less than a year later, Gibbon stressed that his novel was about the modern Highlands. In another enthusiastic review, he wrote:

> Where are the claymores of '45? Or the wealthy
> returned emigrant? Or the sweet-voiced, gentle
> priest? And where - oh, where? - is Nurse Elspeth,
> the faithful, fatuous, flat-footed Elspeth who

throughout the last three hundred Highland novels
has reared the young laird in godly ways until he
attains to manhood... His crofters and fishers and
village folk are faithfully living and life-size; the
Wild MacRaes themselves - four sons of a game-
keeper - are heroic figures of myth, and not the
less real for that. They centre and epitomise the
struggle of the classes that is waged just as bitterly
in the remote glen as in the nearby factory; for a
time, sheep-stealing, land-raiding, they almost
dominate the lanscape. Their countryside,
oppressed under the demands and restrictions of
clownish lairds, alien and Scots, seems on the verge
of rising to their leadership in a miniature peasant
rebellion.[15]

Struggling to compensate in his novels for the comparative absence of
a Scottish national historiography to accommodate the Highlands
Clearances, early radicalism and later socialism, Barke took a wrong
political turning. Joining the CPGB *after* Gibbon's death, he was to
become by 1936 the Party's ideological policeman in Scotland.

Moreover, during the years after the end of the Second World War,
Stalinist scholars in some of the universities in the former 'communist'
countries of Eastern Europe devoted great attention to Gibbon at the
expense of Barke. By concealing Gibbon's anti-Stalinist, and indeed
anarchist and Trotskyist, sympathies, they tried to co-opt him as one
of *their* novelists. Moreover, although Barke belonged to the CPGB
from the late 1930s until he dropped out of it without fuss or ceremony
in 1949, he did not experience the same rejection by the Left at the
height of his creative power as Gibbon did. And if that was good for
his political morale, it was bad for his creative art.

Stalinist 'Communism' and Gibbon's Libertarian Socialism

In 1956, when the miners' leader Lawrence Daly resigned from the
CPGB in protest against the use of Russian troops against the Hungarian
revolution, Mick McGahey, a leading member of the CPGB, denounced
him as 'a bastard.' Then, during a strike of Scottish coalminers in the
1960s, when the two men were fighting the National Coal Board, a
journalist from the *Daily Express* reminded McGahey that he had once

called Daly 'a bastard'. 'Yes! I did', said McGahey. 'But he is one of *our* bastards'. Yet, despite the British, German, Czechosovak and Hungarian Stalinists' wide array of articles on Gibbon, he was never one of the CPGB's 'bastards'.

Notwithstanding his unfashionable belief in the diffusionist theory of history, Gibbon was a communist and an anarchist. In a letter to George MacDonald dated 20 January 1924, he said: 'Funny, you know, but I believe it lives in me yet - faith in the ultimate coming of Communism; faith in the belief that I'll yet write something worth while; faith that love is a shining glory greater than mere physical desire.'[16] But it is the comments in Gibbon's private letters rather than his books which have allowed the CPGB to claim him as one of *their* 'bastards'.

Writing to the Scottish nationalist and novelist Neill Gunn at the beginning of November 1934, Gibbon said: 'By the way, I am not an official communist. They refuse to allow me into the Party.' Over a month later he wrote to his former headmaster and friend: 'I'd love a heart-to-heart talk on communism - but for the fact that communist papers frequently attack me as a disruptive anarchist! A beard and bombs would appear to be in order'.[17] And Gibbon was indeed closer to anarchistic communism and 'Trotskyism' than the Stalinists have ever acknowledged.

At the heart of Gibbon's novels *Stained Radiance, The Thirteenth Disciple* and the trilogy *Sunset Song, Cloud Howe* and *Grey Granite*, entitled *A Scots Quair*, was his preoccupation with the role of *the* classical Socialist Party in the struggle for world communism. In *Stained Radiance* the name of his fictional Party was the Anarcho-Communist Party. Touching on the themes of socialist attitudes towards the martyrdom of Labour, culture and 'the Party,' and the importance of sharpening democratic consciousness, he was quite familar with socialist history and theory.

Extirpating consciousness of pre-Stalinist socialism from the late 1920s onwards, the CPGB placed an enormous emphasis on the communists' role in creating a 'vanguard' Party of 'a new type'. The classical Marxist approach to the role of the Party was summed up by Karl Marx and Frederick Engels, who, as early as 1846, argued that a mass transformation of working-class consciousness was an indispensable pre-condition for socialism, when they wrote:

> But for the production on a mass scale of this
> communist consciousness, and for the success of

the cause itself, the alteration of men on a mass
scale is necessary, an alteration which can only take
place in a practical movement, a revolution; this
revolution is necessary, therefore, not only because
the ruling class cannot be overthrow in any other
way, but also because the class overthrowing it can
only in a revolution succeed in ridding itself of all
the muck of the ages and become fitted to found
society anew.[18]

Although those words were written in 1846, Marx and Engels never
departed from them. Years later, Marx reiterated his view that working
people had to transform themselves: 'You must go through fifteenth,
twenty, fifty years of war and civil war, not only to alter existing
conditions but to alter yourselves and make yourselves fit to take over
political power.' [19]

However, it was Karl Kautsky who revised this classical socialist idea
of the role of consciousness in the socialists' struggles. Influencing Lenin
himself, he argued that 'modern socialist consciousness can arise only
on the basis of profound scientific knowledge.' When he developed
his argument, Kautsky said:

The vehicles of science are not the proletariat, but
the bourgeois-intelligentsia: it was out of the heads
of this stratum that modern socialism originated,
and it was they who communicated it to the more
intellectual-developed proletarians who, in their
turn, introduce it into the proletarian class struggle
when conditions allow that to be done. Thus
socialist consciousness is something introduced
into the proletarian class struggle *from without*, and
not something that arises within it spontaneously.
Accordingly, the old [Austrian] Hainfeld program
quite rightly stated that the task of social
democracy is to imbue the proletariat with the
consciousness of its position and the consciousness
of its tasks. There would be no need for this if
consciousness emerged from the class struggle.[20]

Repudiating Marx's emphasis on the need for a mass *socialist consciousness* developing in 'a practical [workers'] movement leading to the alteration of men on a mass scale', Kautsky's stress on the decisive role of 'the vanguard Party' already appealed to Lenin and the Bolsheviks before 1914.

The questions about *where* socialist consciousness had come from originally was to assume a major practical importance after the Bolshevik revolution. In contrast to Kautsky, who revised classical Marxism, his great contemporary Antonio Labriola asserted that socialism had been 'born in the soul of the oppressed' European workers.[21]

It was not until the mid-1920s that the older ideas of Kautsky on the role of 'the vanguard Party' and the newer ideas of Romain Rolland about socialist attitudes towards culture and art would coalesce to provide Stalinism with a 'socialist' mask. Despite his fundamental commitment to libertarian socialists ideas, Trotsky told the thirteenth congress of the Communist Party of the Soviet Union:

> In the last instance the Party is always right, because it is the only historic instrument which the working class possesses for the solution of its fundamental tasks... One can only be right with the Party because history has not created any other way for the realisation of one's rightness. The English have a saying: 'My country right or wrong.' With much greater justification we can say: 'My Party right or wrong...'[22]

From the beginning of his life as a writer, Gibbon did not agree with those whom Lewis Coser and Irving Howe called, 'the authoritarians of the "Left"'. It was clear from Gibbon's novel *The Thirteenth Disciple* that he was very aware of the support given by H. M. Hyndman and *Justice*, organ of the Social Democratic Federation, to the capitalists' First World War. As a result of reading *Justice* in 1914, Malcolm Maudslay, the hero of Gibbon's novel 'imagined himself a National Socialist, as patriotic as anybody.'[23] However, when Maudslay joined the Left Communist Group of Glasgow soon after the end of the war, he became an internationalist.

Working-class members were not prominent in the Left Communist Group of Glasgow. In an oblique reference to them, the reader is informed that Malcolm's girl friend 'danced with partners who discoursed industrial unionism and passive resistance.'[24] The autobiographical Maudslay was based on Gibbon or Mitchell himself; and he is secretary of the Group. The chairman is an unnamed 'engineer from the shipyards'; and the anonymous treasurer is 'an evicted schoolmaster, an enthusiastic and ambitious and robust young conscientious objector'. But the most intriguing and obscure character of all is 'the white-bearded Anton Meierkhold, then a Professor of Russian literature and now an exile in Siberia from the Soviets'.[25] Enthusiastic as he always was about the Bolshevik revolution, Gibbon was never at any stage of his short life uncritical of Soviet Russia.

The Left, broadly and generously defined, just did not know how to respond to Gibbon's books. Although most of the literary critics wrote favourable reviews of his novel *Spartacus*, J. F. Horrabin, one of the most cultured and independent-minded of the English socialists of his generation, contributed a hostile review to *Plebs*, organ of the National Council of Labour Colleges, in which he concluded:

> Never for a moment do *Spartacus* or any of the characters look or behave or talk like flesh-and-blood human beings. The book reminded me more than anything of a *Hollywood Sign of the Cross*.

And he concluded by saying that *Spartacus* 'ends with a tableau which Mr Cecil B. de Mille would doubtless love to fix for [his] screen'.[26]

But, although *Plebs* was much more interested in literature and cultural questions than were *Labour Monthly* and the Scottish socialist newspaper *Forward*, it ignored all of Barke's novels. (So did *Forward* ignore Barke's first three novels). Similarly, ignoring the three novels that made up *A Scots Quair*, *Plebs* restricted itself to reviewing *Sparatacus* and *The Thirteenth Disciple*. Certainly, the latter novel was given a sympathetic write-up by 'G. M.' Touching on the beginning of Maudslay's life as one born into the traditional life of a little farm, who starts life as a rebel, and ends up in Glasgow as a socialist, 'G.M' was impressed by J. Leslie Mitchell's exposure of 'the shams and hypocrisies of modern civilisation'.

In his penultimate paragraph, 'G. M.' suggested the existence of a link between Gibbon and Oswald Mosley. As he put it:

> In the end, Malcolm forms a new society or new party of intellectuals, and thus anticipated, and,

for all we know, may have inspired Comrade Mosley. 'The committee members, however, found it hard enough to slough off years of cynicism and irreverent wit. The repartee was extraordinarily good...' After that one almost suspects that the author must have been at one of those Easton Lodge week-ends that have been darkly hinted about recently.

(At a time when Mosley was already supporting fascism and Gibbon was probably the British writer most critical of European fascism, the English Left was not very perspicacious.) Even so, the *Plebs'* reviewer concluded that *'The Thirteenth Disciple* may not, on the whole be an optimistic novel, but it is stimulating, and to socialists especially is crowded with interest.'[27]

The Thirteenth Disciple, Guy Aldred and Trotskyism

Though Gibbon did not have real knowledge of such theoretical controversies, in his novel *The Thirteenth Disciple* his 'Left Communist Group of Glasgow' was much closer to Marx and Labriola than to Kautsky or Lenin in its understanding of the socialists' role in the class struggle. In a fine, stimulating and as yet unpublished essay on 'Grassic Gibbon's Glasgow', my friend John Manson has argued:

> There were several models for the name. As early as 1912, a Communist Propaganda Group had been formed in Glasgow by Guy Aldred. Aldred's biographer writes: 'During Guy's years in jail the members of his Group merged informally with anarchists.' Glasgow anarchists had arranged Aldred's meeting on 3 February 1919, and the title of their Group had now become Glasgow Communist Group, the nearest match to Gibbon's fictional group (though this may be coincidence). Guy Aldred is the only revolutionary figure (in Scotland) to whom Gibbon refers by name, and one of the epigrams to *The Thirteenth Discipline* is a pro-anarchist quotation from Anatole France.[28]

Clearly, Gibbon was not one of the Stalinists' 'bastards'.

In *The Thirteenth Disciple,* there was little evidence of working-class socialists in the Left Communist Group of Glasgow. Nevertheless John Manson's speculation about the influence of the English anarchist Guy Aldred on Gibbon is very suggestive and leads the historian into the byways of Scottish socialist history. For at a moment when Gibbon was contributing articles and book reviews to *The Free Man,* Aldred contributed an article entitled 'Wanted - A Workers Scottish Republic' in which he said:

> I would have the workers seize Scotland instead
> of marching to London. I would *industrialise* the
> Highlands, for freedom comes through industry
> and machinery, not through *rural* backwardness.
> I would not wait on England to solve our economic
> problems, but, taking full advantage of the
> existence of a border, I would raise the Red Banner
> in Scotland and establish directly and immediately
> a Workers' Scottish Republic. I prefer a Workers'
> Scottish Republic to a Scottish Workers' Republic.
> I would expect a Workers' English Republic to
> follow at once.[29]

At the heart of Gibbon's socialism was his belief in a mixture of diffusionist, Marxist, anarchist and even 'Trotskyist' ideas. And his interest in those seemingly disparate ideas is of particular importance in the the light of Aldred's critical support for the Bolsheviks' industrialisation in spite of his later criticism of the Stalinist New Economic Policy.

When Emma Goldman published articles in 'the capitalist press' in 1922 on her experiences in Soviet Russia at a time when anarchists and independent socialists were very sympathetic to the Soviet experiment, she alienated most people on the Left. In 1925 Aldred published an article on '"Red" Emma and the Money Power Dictators' in which he accused her of being 'a revolutionary scab.' In 1929 Aldred devoted the whole of the March issue of his newspaper *The Commune* to the theme of 'Trotsky Again in Exile: His Message.' In one paragraph he said:

Trotsky declares that his expulsion from Russia has cast a far too enormous shadow. Maybe. But it has brought home to everyone an understanding of the reality of the Russian situation. It is the culmination of the policy, with which Trotsky himself was too long associated, of martyring the real communists in Russia, of counter-revolution, and terming the process revolutionary discipline.[30]

As early as 1929 Aldred hinted that he was willing to work with Trotsky and the Left Opposition in building a new International of anti-Stalinists, anarchists and other independent socialists. Acknowledging what he saw as some of the negative features of Trotskyism, including their attitude of the revolt of Red sailors at Kronstadt in 1921, he wrote in his newspaper *The Council* in June 1932:

We are told, by men who never were and never will be a force, mere parrots of mediocrity triumphant, that Trotsky is a spent force. Maybe. We do not know. We cannot say. But genius in exile has more fire by which to warm our being than mediocrity in place. And we prefer the more useful association with Trotsky to the puerile dictatorship of Stalin.[31]

Throughout 1932 *The Council*, published sympathetic reviews of Trotsky's *History of the Russian Revolution*, and articles on 'Trotsky's Military Genius' and 'Towards Trotskyism'.

Then, when Trotsky lectured to socialist students in Copenhagen at the beginning of 1933, Aldred welcomed 'his return to active revolutionary activity in Europe'. In a front-page article entitled 'Trotsky's Return?', he concluded: 'But Stalinist objections and the royal denunciation will make little difference to the interest in Trotsky's lectures and outlook. Trotskyism looks to the future, and to the workers' struggle, for its vindication.'[32] And as late as 1937 Aldred financed the trip of Vera Bush, an American representative of the Left Opposition in New York, to speak in Glasgow and other Scottish cities and towns.

Against an exceptionally powerful international Stalinist political machine, anarchists and Trotskyists co-operated in the combined struggle of the late 1920s and 1930s in a number of different countries.

But, although we do not know whether Gibbon and Aldred ever met, Gibbon sided with Trotsky against Stalin. He was always on the extreme Left.

Gibbon's interest in and sympathy for Leon Trotsky had developed during the Bolshevik revolution. But he refused to repudiate 'the Old Man', as Trotsky was known, when it required courage to stand out against the well-financed CPGB. In a letter to the headmaster Alexander Gray and his wife, dated 13 July 1929, Gibbon wrote:

> What do you think of those snivelling Labourists? Safety first! Keep out Leon Trotsky - a dangerous revolutionist, and whatever would the *Morning Post* say? Keep down the school-leaving age - the dear industrialists will still require cheap labour. Persecute the unemployed like criminals: good for them - Swine! [33]

Struggling to explain the significance of the betrayal of the 1926 general strike and the psychological roots of James Ramsay MacDonald's betrayal of the militant working class in 1931, the Stalinists did not know how to handle Gibbon. By the early 1930s, when Aldred was especially unpopular inside the CPGB, Gibbon saw the anarcho-communists in a very favourable light.

Lewis Grassic Gibbon's Stalinist and other Critics

In many ways Gibbon was, though most certainly a man of the extreme Left; the most complicated of all the Scottish radicals portrayed in the present book. He was a thinker who did not fit easily into any of the political categories of the 1920s and early 1930s. In his stimulating book *Lewis Grassic Gibbon*, Ian Campbell insists that he 'was an open Marxist though a difficult one to equate with any of the existing political parties'.[34] From Campbell's viewpoint, 'he was [also] politically a communist to the exclusion of overt nationalism'.[35]

By the late 1920s, however, Stalinist and Trotskyist communists alike either ignored his novels, biographies and serious political books like *Scottish Scene* or dismissed him as 'anarchist' - though there were a few exceptions. Ideologically, Gibbon's diffusionism estranged him from the CPGB anyway, and from the standpoint of what passed for Marxism at that time he was seen as being much closer to anarchism than to Marxism.

Although both V. Gordon Childe, the distinguished Marxist scholar, and *Plebs* magazine were much less orthodox and more critical in their Marxist views than the CPGB, they would not tolerate anarchist ideas in any shape or form. For example, in an article in the more heterodox Marxist Plebs, Childe reviewed the new book by G. Elliot Smith, Bronislaw Malinowski, H. J. Spinden and A. Goldenweiser on *Culture: The Diffusion Controversy*. Explaining the irreconcilable relationship between anarchism and Marxism, he concluded that: 'Elliot Smith's school stand in fact nearer to Kropotkin and Tolstoy than to Marx and Leinin'.[36] Equally hostile to diffusionism as inherently anti-Marxist and anti-Leninist, the ultra-orthodox Stalinist 'theoretical' magazine, *Labour Monthly*, edited by R. Palme Dutt, did not review a single one of Gibbon's books.

Although *Labour Monthly* did review novels, Dutt's particularly arid and doctrinaire Stalinism was exceptionally hostile to Scottish nationalism. Reviewing a whole range of English socialist novels, Dutt did not make room for any of Gibbon's books. In the only Barke novel ever reviewed by *Labour Monthly* (in 1936), Aitken Ferguson expressed the CPGB's suspicion of all novels when he said:

> It is not often *that Labour Monthly* reviews novels, but then, it is not often that such a book as *Major Operation* is published. The evolution of Barke is interesting to watch. From his first book, *The World His Pillow*, sarcastically dubbed by the Press as 'A Highland Marxist comes to town', Barke has been finding his way towards Marxism-Leninism, and *Major Operation* shows the strides he has made in this direction.[37]

The key factor in winning the approval of the CPGB was Barke's Marxism-Leninism. By contrast, though it has not been *noticed* by the literary critics, Gibbon was authentically against 'the "vanguard" [communist] Party of a new type.'

In his novel *Stained Radiance* (1930), he was already groping his way to a socialist-humanist critique of the Stalinists' Party of a new type. It was highlighted in the passage in *Stained Radiance* where James Storman said:

His purpose was to produce money for the Anarcho-Communist Party. Pursuing this aim during the last two years, he had cajoled trade union leaders, wheedled Socialist authors, begged from Moscow, borrowed from the French Communist Party, and blackmailed business firms in Manchester. To the same end he would have sold the bones in a London cemetery.[38]

Although Stalinist scholars - and those legions of other scholars innocent of the actual history of Stalinist moral corruption - could not have acknowledged the nature of Gibbon's moral critique of the role and behaviour of 'the Party of a new type' without calling their own authenticity into question amongst working people, Gibbon repeatedly hinted at what was going on.

To grasp what Gibbon was getting at, the indispensable task of the historian of socialism is to reconstruct the complicated history of world socialism after the Bolshevik revolution. While Bolshevism, Trotskyism and anarchism did not share the same ethical values or socialist-humanist goals with Stalin or Stalinism after the 1921 Kronstadt revolt, they have usually been portrayed as belonging, in E. P. Thompson's phrase, 'to a common [international] socialist family.' But, although they did not, much of the ideological confusion in the ranks of militant working people was engendered by this tacit assumption. And Gibbon's unusual insights were intutiive - those of a great artist.

But the Trotskyists and large sections of the Independent Labour Party shared an almost semi-Stalinist conception of the role of 'the vanguard Party' in the struggle for socialism. It was because of this (more than any other single factor) that the Trotskyists found it very difficult to distance themselves from Stalinist organisations. Resisting any temptation to become a 'socialist' conformist or a comfortably off 'artist in uniform', as Max Eastman put it, Gibbon was always a democratic socialist with strong anarchist traits. Identifying in his writings and life with the historical communist movement of Marx and Engels (as distinct from the Stalinists' 'Marxism-Leninism'), he was always hostile towards Stalinism. At the heart of his vision of real socialist internationalism was the moral maxim that Immanuel Kant expressed in his *Perpetual Peace*: 'Every man is to be *respected* as an *absolute end in himself*; and it is a crime against the dignity that belongs to him as human being, to use him as a mere means for some external purpose.'[39]

By contrast, in creating 'the Party of a new type' in which the world Stalinist movement retrospectively rubbished the lives and works of John Maclean, Daniel De Leon, Rosa Luxemburg, Karl Liebknecht, and many others, Stalinist scholars, historians and novelists falsified Marxism itself. Unlike Barke, Gibbon understood this better than most of their Scottish radical contemporaries. Like Ignazio Silone and Victor Serge, he saw through the moral corruption in the Stalinist-controlled labour movements. In the third of the novels in the trilogy *A Scots Quair* he was really mocking and ridiculing Stalinist orthodoxy when he discussed the CPGB's idea of 'the vanguard party's' role and falsification of classical Marxism in trying to exploit working folk as 'history's instruments'.

To understand fully the reactionary role of Stalinism in distorting Marx's declaration that 'the emancipation of the working class' had to be 'the task of the working class themselves, the American [Stalinist] writer Joseph Freeman provided an excellent sidelight when he wrote:

> The unequal development of individuals has raised a Stalin, Djerdjinsky, Chicherin or Bukharin to that leadership which every social group requires whenever such men show a greater capacity than the average for understanding and manipulating the mechanics of history.[40]

Besides, in his insistence in *Grey Granite* that Jim Trease, the CPGB's organiser 'would betray the young idealist Ewan Travendale if it suited the Party's purposes,' Gibbon was describing the reality of what was happening in Scottish cities by the late 1920s.

By then, Gibbon was reading a wide range of anti-Stalinist literature, including Ignazio Sione's novel *Fontamara*. Unknown to Gibbon, however, was Silone's novel *The Seed Beneath the Snow*, not published in English until 1943. Portraying the Stalinists' same cynical exploitation of peasants and workers in the 1930s as 'history's instruments' that Gibbon had criticised in *Grey Granite*, Silone focused on the moral decay of the Italian Communist Party when the following dialogue occurred between two of his characters:

To tell the truth, they did not hold much with friendship in the Party; there was something suspicious about it, as if it might engender the formation of cliques and gangs. For this reason I should even rightly admit that friendship, in the true and human meaning of the word, was regarded and despised as a remant of bourgeois individualism... After a long silence Simone got up to make ready his bed and murmured: I didn't know how widespread was the decay.[41]

Hugh MacDiarmid wrote rather vaguely that: 'Towards the end of his life he [Gibbon] became better equiped to call himself a communist, albeit with ineradicable Trotskyist leanings.' Certainly, at a time when Trotsky's name was anathema in CPGB circles, Mitchell/Gibbon published a profile of 'Grieve-Scotsman' in which he described Grieve's attack on the writer Dr J. M. Bulloch:

Then, wiping the blood from the blade, he came back, glanced at the verse, saw a flicker of life in it, extinguished it, and departed - probably to teach revolutionary tactics to Trotsky or confer with the leaders of the Pan-African Congress.'

Written at a time when Stalin had just sacrificed the colonial struggles of the Blacks against Western imperialism to foster a 'Popular Front' with 'the great democracies' against fascism and George Padmore had been expelled from the communist Third International for 'petty-bourgeois nationalism', Gibbon was in turn criticised very persistenly by De Leonists like Frank Maitland.[42]

Maitland's particular attitude to Gibbon and *A Scots Quair* was interesting for a number of reasons. This prominent member of a dissident De Leonist group in Edinburgh in the early 1930s, Maitland helped to form the British Revolutionary Socialist Party (RSP) in the mid-1930s before affiliating to Trotsky's Fourth International in 1938.

In a strange article in the February 1934 issue of *Plebs*, Maitland was almost unique among left-wing writers anywhere in the 1930s in criticising Walter Scott from a socialist perspective. Responding to an artilce in a previous issue of *Plebs* by the Stalinist T. A. Jackson, Maitland offered a perceptive and unusual critique:

Of all that was published about Walter Scott during the centenary and before I have read no more interesting article than that of T. A. Jackson's. Yet I feel bound to deny the importance which he gives to Scott, and certainly to the idea that the *proletariat* can get any good out of reading him, apart from a strictly historical exercise.

Maitland's critique of Scott was intelligent and original. However, in anticipating the praise that he would bestow on Sir James Barrie at the expense of Gibbon in another article in the April 1935 issue of *The Adelphi*, he argued that: 'If the *proletariat* wants history, take up a history book rather than Scott; if he [*sic!*] wants character, take up Dickens; if he wants Scotland, take up Galt, or *Johnny Gibb of Gushetneuk*, or the recent *Sunset Song* by Gibbon, or Barrie's *Margaret Ogilvy*.'[43] But there were very few books on Scottish history from a socialist viewpoint, anyway; and Maitland's recommendation of one of Barrie's Kailyard novels was either very puzzling or a literary trick employed to make his polemical points seem more plausible than they were.

The Scottish Left's Authoritarianism and Kailyard Myths

Meanwhile, Gibbon had alienated sectarians like Maitland by describing himself in the pages of the Scottish nationalist magazine *The Free Man* as 'an anarchist'. Expressing his continuing hatred for fascism and totalitarianism - a concept Maitland was incapable of understanding in the 1920s and early 1930s - Gibbon said: 'I am a Scotsman, an artist, and - an integral part of my being - an anarchist. My art is implicit anarchy.' Estranging himself still further from the Stalinists, the pseudo-Stalinists and the unconscious Stalinists - or 'the authoritarians of the "Left"' like Maitland - Gibbon concluded:

> News of battle! If this is the new Nationalism, it is likely to win converts to its wastes from the ranks of those who, like myself, have seen in its stead the vision of Cosmoplis, the City of God; who would find a return to the harbourage of such hazy conceits as repulsive as a racial return to cannibalism.[44]

Nor was the 'Left's' attitude to him softened by his generous definition of 'who or what' was a Scot or his attack on right-wing nationalism and 'the fascist State.'

In that very condescending article on Lewis Grassic Gibbon in the influential London magazine *The Adelphi* in April 1935, Maitland anticipated the nature of the Stalinists' later attacks on Gibbon's novels. Praising *Sunset Song* in order to dismiss the allegedly un-Marxist second and third novels of the trilogy *Cloud Howe* and *Grey Granite* and Gibbon as a serious socialist, he warmed to his sectarian themes. He should therefore be quoted at some length. Emphasising that he liked *Sunset Song*, Maitland wrote:

> He wrote faithfully about the Scottish folk. *Sunset Song* is a true picture. It reaches a height in the description of Ewan Tavendale's corruption, a description that brings home the filth of war like a stab - as a piece of anti-war writing for the romantic it is to be recommended. But when Gibbon left the village and proceeded to a more stirring centre, with social and political events crowding into his canvas, he was not so succcessful. Indeed, he quite failed to satisfy in regard to the social problem. Although he considered himself a socialist, really he was not. There is no doubt that his sentiments lay with working folk, but he did not understand socialism in them. Socialism was dragged into his books because, believing himself to be a socialist, he felt bound to propagate in its favour. But socialism did not fill his whole life, the socialist philosophy did not occupy his whole mind. And, his socialism being unreal, young Ewan is also unreal. No, though Gibbon viewed himself as a socialist writer, even a revolutionary writer, he was too much of an anarchist to be that. He was a rebel, not a revolutionary. He was an individual in revolt, not understanding the historical background to his own rebellion, and he could not speak for the people who inhabit his books.

While he was rightly critical of 'coarse creatures', he did not understand why their actions were misguided. He did not understand the inner movements of the class struggle, therefore his 'characters and their surroundings are unrelated. His picture of social unrest and of the turning of young Ewan to communism is perfunctory... It seems to me that *Sunset Song* was known to him, but the social unrest in Seggat and the communist action of Ewan he had only read about.'[45]

Coming as this did from the pen of a Marxist, who praised Barrie's *classless* novels to the high heavens, Maitland was revealing his own simplistic and doctrinaire consciousness of the world around him.

Reflecting a Marxism that was much closer to Stalin than the class struggle socialism from below of Marx, De Leon or even Trotsky, Maitland could not escape the muddle-headedness of most of the 'Left' of that period. As he moved closer to the Left Opposition that would become the Fourth International in 1938, without knowing anything about John Carstairs Matheson's articles on Scottish history in the 1900s Maitland would also insist that the Highland Clearances had been historically unavoidable or 'inevitable.'

In a careful analysis of Kailyard myths minus Kailyard literature or James Barrie, Maitland subsequently insisted that socialist books on Scottish history did not exist. In one powerful passage of polemic, he said: 'The glories of Scottish history to which the Nationalists point are the glories of capitalist robbery and cruelty, written for working-class consumption in the school history books. Robert the Bruce, Black Agnes of Dunbar, Mary Queen of Scots, General Gordon, Dr Laws of Livingstonia - a whole host of historical figures badly need debunking (the Protestant pioneers not among the least).' Scottish nationalism was presented as a conscious ruling-class conspiracy to keep Scottish working-class men and women from participating in the continuing world revolution from which they were excluded by their Kailyard 'education.' In a colourful paragraph fashioned for the purpose of closing the debate on 'What is Scottish Nationalism?', Maitland concluded:

> Nationalism, we repeat, belongs to the capitalist class, which used it in order to free itself from feudal restrictions, and now, when nationalism restricts the development of inter- national socialism and must inevitably give way to the international Socialist Republic, the capitalist system uses

nationalism in order to confuse and divide the world's workers.[46]

The Trotskyists, who ought to have embraced Gibbon's novels as expressions of socialism from below, were too embattled and - in Maitland's specific case - too sectarian and utilitarian in their approach to ideas to do so. Besides, as Gibbon struggled towards the end of his life to understand the history of the Covenanters, Maitland exposed the inability of the advocates of 'internationalism as a sort of international jingoism' to grapple with the reality of Scottish radical cultural history.

Adopting a more sympathetic attitude towards Scottish nationalism during the last few years of his life, Gibbon used A Scots Quair to express the most radical and revolutionary nineteenth-century ideas of the anarchists and the classical Marxists at a moment when Stalinism was trying to eradicate these ideas from human consciousness. Certainly, no one familiar with the history of nineteenth- and early twentieth-century socialism could remain unaware of Gibbon's defence of the classical Marxist interpretation of history against the counterfeit Stalinist one that dominated most labour movements throughout the 1930s.

By an irony of history, when Gibbon was working on his novels the CPGB and other Stalinist organisations throughout the world were pursuing their ultra-sectarian policy of 'Class against Class.' So the CPGB were far from happy with his portrayal of working-class struggles and attitudes towards the historical process itself. When the theoretical journal of the CPGB subsequently published Ian Milner's article 'An Estimation of Lewis Grassic Gibbon's A Scots Quair' (1954), Milner argued that:

> Like Ewan, Gibbon himself was conscious of coming to the workers' revolutionary movement as an intellectual, from outside. He felt the need for some kind of sacrificial dedication on his part to the revolutionary cause as an earnest of whole-souled participation, particularly if one wished to become a communist. Ewan's development would seem to represent fairly closely his own feelings though, unlike Ewan, he apparently did not join the Communist Party.[47]

The reason Gibbon did not join the CPGB was that he was an anti-Stalinist libertarian socialist.

Ignoring the real nature of Stalinist organisations, Milner dismmised Gibbon's portrayal of the two communists Ewan and Jim Trease as 'a certain romanticised fatalism characteristic of the intellectual spectator which accords ill with the affirmation of complete class identity at the end'. Summing up, he said:

> And again, in nodding agreement to his thought that Trease would betray him, or Mrs. Trease, to the police if it suited his Party's purpose, Ewan concludes: 'Neither friends nor scruples nor honour not hope for the folk who took the workers' road; just life that sent tiredness leaping from the brain...' It is as if Ewan was obsesssed with putting himself to a self-imposed test as a would-be revolutionary. But does the test here take such a form in real life or is it rather the projection of Ewan's intellectualised and at times inhuman conception of the workers' struggle for socialism?[48]

The answer to Milner's rhetorical question is that Gibbon's social picture of the moral corruption of the CPGB was very similar to Silone's depiction of the underground Communist Party of Italy under Mussolini's fascism in the 1930s. To underline this point, I can still remember with horror encountering 'communists' like Trease in the Scottish town of Falkirk in the late 1940s.

When the Party's international policy of 'Class against Class' was succeeded by the 'Popular Front' just before Gibbon's death, the dissident socialist novelist's interpretation of Scottish working-class history was still unacceptable to the CPGB. The Party of the 'Popular Front' did not like Gibbon's description [in *Sunset Song*] of the behaviour of the crofters, who, in bashing in 'the windows' of Kinraddie Castle owned by the Jacobin laird, 'thought equality should begin at home' rather than in revolutionary France.[49] Moreover, Gibbon's exceptional grasp of international socialist history was seen in his comment in *Grey Granite* that 'he [Trease] had been out with Connolly at Easter in Dublin, an *awfully mismanaged* Rising that.'[50]

Gibbon's Attitude Towards the Martyrdom of Labour and Culture

Beginning with his active participation in the Soviet founded in the Scottish city of Aberdeen from 1917 onwards, Gibbon would always support the libertarian ideas of the Bolshevik revolution. The evidence for this is in his novels, including the first ones. He was estranged from Stalinism, especially during the early 1930s when it took courageous perception for any artist to admit to such estrangement. Moreover, when he pitted himself against the dominant Stalinist culture of even the independent Left in the 1930s, by adopting a critical attitude toward such questions as the martyrdom of Labour and culture, his novels were destined to be neglected by most of the Left.

To appreciate Gibbon's literary genius in portraying the martyrdom of Labour throughout most of human history, it needs to be emphasised that even most anarchists gave critical support to the Bolshevist revolution during the decades of the 1920s and 1930s. It was not until 1980 that Royden Harrison felt confident enough to say:

> That Marxism as method can be made to deliver conclusions about Marxism as ideology - where ideology is conceived in the strictly Marxist sense of 'Necessarily false consciousness' - is, so far as I am aware, an original proposal. I do not believe that it is to be found in Preobrazhensky, or Trotsky, Carr or Deutscher, Gerschenkron or Marcuse, Wittfogel or Nove - despite the fact that all of them may be more or less helpful in suggesting the need for it.

But Harrison's most telling point was about what Moshe Lewin told him about his experiences in Russia in the late 1930s: 'When I worked in the Urals, workers knew who they were and that it was the nachalstvo, the bosses, who had the power and the privileges'.[51]

Moreover, Harrison also said: 'Moshe Levine has described to me how, in the 1930s, [Russian] workers who were chained to their benches nevertheless were persuaded that they were contributing to a world-historical event big with eventual liberation'.[52] In the Western world many important anarchists (with the exception of Emma Goldman and Alexander Berkman in America), though critical of Bolshevism, adopted a similar outlook. Though by the late 1920s, members of the CPGB in the Socialist Sunday School movement in the Fife coalfields struck out the following verse of Jim Connells's untitled song where it said:

> We hail the living heroes, too
> who now in anguish pine;
> who wait for death in a German fort,
> Or deep in Russian mine.[53]

Some dissident Marxists and anarchists in Fife were using those words as a critique of Stalinist Russia.

By the 1930s, when the Stalinists, in the words of Eric J. Hobsbawm 'banished traditional workers' internationalism to the wings', and created an 'anti-fascist nationalism' as ' a new kind of internationalism', Gibbon adhered to - and wrote about - the older socialist internationalism'. [54] In *A Scots Quair*, the major character Ewan Tavendale expressed Gibbon's own traditional sense of international socialist solidarity when he allowed his main character to speak to himself in the cell of a Scottish jail:

> He moved a little the arm he'd thought broken, it wasn't, only clotted with bruises, the dryness had left his throat, he lay still with a strange mist boiling, blinding his eyes, not Ewan Tavendale at all any more but lost and be-bloodied in a hundred broken and tortured bodies all over the world, in Scotland, in England, in the torture-dens of the Nazis in Germany, in the torment-pits of the Polish Ukraine, a livid, twisted thing in the prisons where they tortured the Naking Communists, a Negro boy in an Alabama cell while they thrust the razors into his flesh, castrating with a lingering cruelty and care. He was one with them all, a long wail of sobbing mouths and wrung flesh, tortured and tormented by the world's Masters while those Masters lied about Progress through Peace, Democracy, Justice, the Heritage of Culture.[55]

Setting him apart from most writers and artists on the Left at that time, Gibbon's attachment to diffusionist theories of the historical process

235

allowed him to focus on the ancient martyrdom of Labour when Stalinists were trying to eradicate this central idea of classical socialism.

In his chapter on 'The So-Called Primitive Accumulation' in volume one of *Capital*, Karl Marx stressed that: 'The legend of theological original sin tells us certainly how man came to be condemned to eat his bread in the sweat of his brow; but the history of *economic original sin* reveals to us that there are people to whom this is by no means essential.' At the end of the same long paragraph, he says: 'As a matter of fact, the methods of primitive accumulation are anything but idyllic.' But in summing up this long historical process of creating an army of landless labourers for the new factories and mines in Britain, Marx added the comment that:

> And the history of this, their expropriation, is written in the annals of mankind in letters of blood and fire.[56]

When a similar, though much more rapid and brutal, process was occurring in Russia with tragic consequences for the history of twentieth-century world socialism, Gibbon intuitively understood what was happening. Though he made few explicit criticisms of Stalinism, his novels were full of moral criticisms of the Stalinists' excuses for the martyrdom of Labour and totalitarian attitudes to culture. Locating himself in the culture of traditional humanistic socialism, Antonio Labrioa in 1912 argued:

> Labor, which is the prerequisite of all progress, has pressed the sufferings, the privations, the travail, and the ills of the multitude into the service of the comfort of the few. History is like an inferno. It might be presented as a somber drama, entitled *The Tragedy of Labor*.[57]

Inheriting and identifying with this older socialist culture - a culture implicitly antagonistic to forced Stalinist industrialisation and corruption of socialist moral values - Gibbon's novels were unique in the 1930s.

Against the grain of Stalinist and the other institutions of the international Labour movement influenced by Stalinism, Gibbon depicted the unbroken continuity of the martyrdom of Labour by describing in *Grey Granite* Tavendale's visit to 'the Museum Galleries':

Passed in a minute, that flaring savage sickness,
and you got to your feet and went on again: but
the same everywhere, as though suddenly
unblinded, picture on picture - pictures of the poor
folk since history began, bedevilled and murdered,
trodden underfoot, trodden down in the bree, a
human slime, hungered, unfed, with their
darkened brains, their silly revenges, their infantile
hopes - the men who build Munster's City of God
and were hanged and burned in scores by the
Church, the Spartacists, the Blacks of Toussaint
L'Ouverture, Parker's sailors who were hanged at
the Nore, the Broo men man-handled in Royal
Mile.[58]

Breaking through the developing totalitarian Stalinist vision of history, socialism and culture, Gibbon's depiction of the classical socialist view of 'the primitive accumulation of capital' and its art and culture was remarkable.

Gibbon's Challenge to Totalitarianism

Most certainly influenced by diffusionist theories of historical development, Gibbon would have agreed with the view of Peter Kropotkin, the Russian anarchist, that:

When a Greek sculptor chiselled his marble he
endeavoured to express the spirit and heart of the
city. All its passions, all its traditions of glory, were
to live again in the work. But today the united city
has ceased to exist; there is no more communion
of ideas. The town is a chance agglomeration of
people who do not know one another, who have
no common interest, save that of enriching
themselves at the expense of one another.[59]

But the roots of the latent new totalitarian 'socialist' approach to culture began to bud during the First World War.

Expressing her anger from inside her Berlin prison cell, where she had been jailed for her anti-war agitation, Rosa Luxemburg got her

The Junius Pamphlet smuggled out to the world outside. When she denounced the international bourgeoisie's hypocrisy about the destruction of 'cultural treasures' in 1914, she expressed the traditional socialist idea about culture:

> Another such war, and the hope of socialism will be buried under the ruins of imperialistic barbarism. That is more than the ruthless destruction of Liege and of the Rheims Cathedral. That is a blow, not against capitalist civilisation of the past, but against socialist civilisation of the future, a deadly blow against the force that carries the future of mankind in its womb, than alone can rescue the precious treasures of the past over into a better state of society.[60]

However, in introducing the new 'totalitarian' approach to world culture that would be fostered by the powerful Stalinist '"socialist" sixth of the world', Romain Rolland (1916) challenged Luxemburg's traditional socialist-humanism by arguing:

> Among the many crimes of this infamous war which are all odious to us, why have we chosen for protest the crimes against things and not against men, the destruction of works and not of lives? Many are surprised by this, and have even reproached us for it - as if we have not as much pity as they for the bodies and hearts of the thousands of victims who are crucified! Yet over the armies which fall, there flies the vision of their love, and of *la Patrie* to which they sacrifice themselves - over these lives which are passing away passes the holy Ark of the art and thought of centuries, borne on their shoulders. The bearers can change. May the Ark be saved! To the elite of the world falls the task of guarding it. And since the common treasure is threatened, may they rise to protect it?[61]

When such ideas became common currency in the international working-class movement in the late 1920s and early 1930s, Gibbon rejected them in his novels by portraying the counter-attitudes of the anarchistic socialists more sympathetically than was then usual on the Left.

Like his contemporary Walter Benjamin (1892-1940), the German art historian, who also tried to synthesise classical Marxist with anarchist ideas about art and culture, Gibbon tried to persuade the international working class to identify with those whom Benjamin called 'their enslaved ancestors' and not their 'liberated grandchildren'.[62]

Sharing the attitude to fascism of the Benjamin who wrote 'only that historian will have the gift of fanning the spark of hope in the past who is firmly convinced that not even the dead will be safe from the enemy if he wins', Gibbon expressed similar political attitudes towards fascism in his novels.[63] Expressing the traditional socialist attitude towards culture, Benjamin wrote:

> According to traditional practice, the spoils are carried along in the procession. They are called cultural treasures, and a historical materialist views them with cautious detachment. For without exception the cultural treasures he surveys have an origin which he cannot contemplate without horror. They owe their existence not only to the efforts of the great minds and talents who have created them, but also to the anonymous toil of their contemporaries. There is no document of civilisation which is not at the same time a document of barbarism.[64]

Out of the cauldron of bitter theoretical disputes between the wars about the role of culture from a socialist standpoint, Walter Benjamin's closeness to the anarchists in France and Germany inhibited him from accepting the dominant Stalinist attitudes in the labour movement. It was significant that Benjamin's comments were published in his article entitled 'Theses on the Philosophy of History'; and the reader will already have noticed Gibbon's traditional Scottish radical preoccupation with 'metaphysics' at a time when the Stalinists were shouting about the need for more action and less thought.

Not very much of this concrete socialist history was known to J. F. Horrabin, Frank Maitland, Christopher Murray Grieve, the Scottish poet, or Gibbon's other 'socialist' critics; and it was relatively easy for Hugh MacDiarmid to get away with dismissing Gibbon as an emotional and un-scientific socialist. In his essay on 'Glasgow' in the book entitled *Scottish Scene* - a book written in collaboration with MacDiarmid - Gibbon confronted Stalinist attitudes to art and culture head-on. In an admittedly purple passage he wrote:

> There is nothing in culture or art that is worth the life and elementary happiness of one of those thousands who rot in the Glasgow slums. There is nothing in science or religion. If it came (as it may come) to some fantastic choice between a free and independent Scotland, a centre of culture, a bright flame of artistic and scientific achievement, and providing elementary decencies of food and shelter to the submerged proletariat of Glasgow and Scotland, I at least would have no doubt as to which side of the battle I would range myself. For the cleansing of that horror, if cleanse it they could, I would welcome the English in suzerainty over Scotland till the end of time.

At a moment in 1935 when MacDiarmid was popular in the CPGB and completing his manuscript on 'Red Scotland', he referred to the passage quoted above and remarked: 'So would I, only I know it is not to be got in those ways.'[65]

In 1944 MacDiarmid wrote an essay on 'Lewis Grassic Gibbon'; it was published in a book of essays in London in 1946. Opposing the socialist-humanism of Marx, Engels, Labriola and Luxemburg as a self-confessed Stalinist 'Marxist', he reflected the prefigurative Stalinist attitudes of Rolland when he said:

> This, alas, is just hooey - 'sound and fury signifying nothing.' A purple passage of emotional humanism - the very antithesis of the way in which these evils can ever be overcome. As I have said, in one of my poems, I on the other hand would sacrifice a million people any day for one immortal

lyric. I am a scientific socialist: I have no use whatever for emotional humanism.[66]

To decode the meaning of MacDiarmid's so-called 'scientific socialism', it will be enough to say that he was a inconsistent Stalinist.[67] Furthermore, in his poetry written in the 1930s, he repeatedly defended the totalitarian crimes in Stalinist Russia.[68]

Throughout his great trilogy *A Scots Quair*, the intensity of Gibbon's compassion for the oppressed and commitment to the democratic struggle for socialism from below comes through in remarks like 'the bars of the whooming *furnace* of History.' And, discouraged as he was by the retreats forced upon the genuine Left, Gibbon shared with Victor Serge an exceptional sensitivity to the continuity of the common people's struggles.

As late as 1939 Serge, though equally pessimistic about the outcome of the socialists' struggles, refused to abandon hope of the better world to come and used the traditional image of 'the seed beneath the snow'. But in his last novel *Les Annees sans pardon*, written in Mexico in 1946, though not published in Paris until 1971, he spoke about 'funeral masks [which] keep under the earth.' But then he added the comment that there were so many 'that nothing is ever lost'.[69]

But the philistine 'authoritarians of the "Left"' have never missed an opportunity to attack Gibbon; and in the spirit of Stalin's question about how many battalions the Pope had, Tom Nairn restricted himself to making negative and dismissive remarks about the man in Welwyn Garden City without pausing to acknowledge his cultural achievements. Linking the names of the novelists George Douglas Brown and Gibbon as typical examples of Scottish radicals' utter failures from 1707 onwards, Nairn offered his own very *worldly* cynicism by insisting that 'It is almost as difficult for a Scots intellectual to get out of the Kailyard as to live without an alias.' [70]

Nairn's judgment was political rather than cultural or historiographical. But in 1937, Marion Nelson, a Scot who was teaching in Queen's University, Kingston, Ontario, contributed a piece to the Canadian communists' magazine the *New Fronter*. She said: 'Of all Scots writers save Burns, whom in some respects he resembles, Lewis Grassic Gibbon has drawn closest to the folk "universality" of the ballads. That is, he reflects not the Scottish "Kailyard" but the problems of the Scottish people today.'

Yet, despite Nelson's sensitive understanding of imaginative literature, she was writing as an ideological policewoman. So she stressed that 'Gibbon lacked familiar knowledge of the class-conscious workers whom he set out to portray.' When she went to the heart of her criticism of *A Scots Quair*, she said:

> His heart, as it were, was with them [the workers], but he had never plumbed their minds as he did the minds of his petty-bourgeois and peasants. This fault, which would undoubtedly have been corrected had he lived, led him to a romantic view of the communists' role; a view which is still widesprerad among intellectuals who are sympathetic to Marxism but have few contacts with worker-Marxists.

Claiming him as one of their own, Nelson nevertheless highlighted the universal Party line about Gibbon by accepting him as 'a revolutionary writer' whose 'treatment of decaying capitalism [was] more accurate than his picture of its gravediggers.'[71] In all of the Stalinist dismissals of Gibbon as a writer who did not *understand* 'the workers', no one took the trouble to recommend socialist novelists who did.

Barke's Early Novels and Radical Cultural History

During the 'Class against Class' phase of international communist history, in a series of three articles in the *Communist Review* in 1932-33 Scottish nationalism was dismissed as a reactionary force. At a time when Barke was expressing quite romantic ideas about the relationship between Glasgow and the Scottish Highlands, the Scots who represented the CPGB put things into a proper theoretical perspective.

All three contributors to the discussion in the *Communist Review* supported the Party's opposition to Home Rule for Scotland. In the opening article R. MacLennan denied that there was 'a national problem in Scotland'. The Highlanders' Gaelic language was dismissively equated with 'the decadent jazz culture' of the Blacks in America. Though Barke was not mentioned by name, those socialists who, like him, wanted assistance for the Gaelic language were accused of attempting to 'resurrect the dead in order to bolster up the decaying capitalist system'. In another contribution Helen Crawfurd accused Lord

Beverbrook and 'certain sections of the capitalist class' of trying to get the youth of Scotland to support Home Rule to get them 'away from the class struggle.' All three contributors asserted that only the petty-bourgeois elements supported the Scottish national movement. [72]

Barke was always a fascinating figure: a man whose motivation for (a) identifying with what he perceived to be traditional radicalism and (b) writing his first three novels was obscured rather than illuminated in his autobiography. There was something almost 'mysterious' about the motivation behind his theoretically confused 'socialism' before he joined the CPGB.

In a sympathetic account of his home on Tulliallan estate between 1907 and 1918, the obituary writer in *The Times* said:

> The war of 1914-18 meant the end of the estate - and of Barke's beloved forest - after its owner had died, and at the age of 11 he found himself helping to value the timber chosen for his extraordinary knowledge of trees. Trees and birds formed the boy's strongest links with Nature and these, with the end of the estate, were broken, for the family moved to Glasgow. He trained as an engineer and while still working in that profession wrote his first novel, *The World His Pillow.*[73]

Ignoring his politics altogether, the obituary writer in the newspaper of the Brits' Establishment mentioned none of his first five novels except *The World His Pillow.*

Anyone reading his novels in the 1930s would have been astonished to learn that Barke had spent his formative years on an estate less than fifty miles from Glasgow. In those novels he was struggling to understand industrial Glasgow, its politics, and social problems and their place in the much bigger world outside Scotland. Although he did not display too much knowlege of Scottish nationalism in his novels, he was saying things about the Highlands and Highlanders that went against the grain of Scottish socialist attitudes, whether inherited or contemporary. Indeed, *The World His Pillow* (1933), *The Wild Macraes* (1934) and *The End of the High Bridge* (1935) were surprisingly preoccupied with the 'dialectic' of the relationship in personal and historical consciousness between the Highlands and Lowland Scotland.

In his review of *The World His Pillow,* Gibbon was intrigued by Barke's interest in the links between Glasgow and the Scottish Highlands. Although *The Wild Macraes* was the least impressive of the first three novels, in asserting that he would like to 'see the claymore unsheathed' and 'the black knife sticking between the ribs of a Sassenach', Captain Stewart, one of Barke's characters, was challenging the dominant socialist orthodoxy about the future of socialist internationalism.[74]

At the heart of Barke's conception of Scottish radical cultural history was his unorthodox socialist attitutde to the Jacobite rebellion of 1745. Sketching different Lowland attitudes towards the Highlands one of the characters muses:

> The old Highland stock had not been able to combat against the invasion any more. Not since '45. The world moved. Races like individuals passed away.[75]

Clearly, however, by the early 1930s 'the Highlands' had become a metaphor in Barke's mind for the Tulliallan estate.

From the standpoint of Scottish radical cultural history, the most interesting character in this novel was Mary MacKinnon. An intellectual and a schoolteacher who had been trained in Glasgow, she was a Fabian socialist elitist, who, in applying 'a class analysis' to the Highlands, allowed Barke to express his own idea of Celtic communism. As he put it:

> She had a beautiful vision for the future of her native Highlands. The glens filled again with the people, the Gaelic culture revived. Cut away from the South altogether. Sinn Fein: we ourselves. Scotland was two nations: North and South: Highland and Lowland. The Lowlands had probably been destroyed by industrialism. Too late now for a revival of Doric; and ploughing with a pair of horses was already an anarchronism. But not too late in the Highlands for a revival of the Gaelic and the old essential tradition: the clan system communalised in the light of the age.[76]

Certainly, such ideas were at odds with the attitudes of Scottish socialist culture, though Barke was not so un-Marxist as the CPGB had assumed.

Unknown to most socialists everywhere in the 1930s and 1940s, during the last decade of his life Karl Marx had simply changed his mind about the role of 'primitive peoples' in the world. In his pioneering article on 'Karl Marx and The Iroquois', Franklin Rosemont emphasised Marx's 'radical new focus on the primal peoples of the world'.[77] In Scotland, America and elsewhere, the Left's thought-world was preoccupied with industrialism's *progressive* role in the world.

Jacobitism, the Highlands and the national question were major themes in the radical cultural history of Scotland from the eighteenth century. And, despite the ever recurring and often sharp breaks in the Scots consciousness of their own history, those questions, including the land question, came up again and again. When he published his three novels - *The World His Pillow, The Wild Macraes,* and *The End of the High Bridge* - Barke was living in Glasgow where he had resided since 1918.

The first two novels were, as Gibbon suggested, full of literary promise of better novels to come. But in their own right *The World His Pillow* and *The End of the High Bridge* were well above the average novels of the 1930s. Struggling to understand different socialist doctrines, including Fabianism - he was, like Gibbon, consistently contemptuous of Labourism and in *The End of the High Bridge* some of the themes of his best novel, *The Land of the Leal* (1939), were already foreshadowed.

When Barke identified in *The End of the High Bridge* with a mythical Highlands, he was really writing about Tulliallan yet again. John MacLeod, the main character, was clearly autobiographical:

> Something finer than all the grand engineering shops in Glasgow: priceless beyond rubies compared with the dirty whores in the pictures Ronny MacLeod smirked over. Tonight he was seeing that. It would be fine to see what things were like in the South.[78]

But the preoccupation with the Rebellion of 1745 was never far from Barke's mind, and as the narrator he said things that he would repudiate when he joined the CPGB.

Barke was already anticipating the themes of such books as Alex Haley's *Roots* (1967) and Dee Brown's *Bury My Heart at Wounded Knee*

(1968), and he was, as a socialist thinker, in advance of his time. In talking to himself on the high bridge, John MacLeod said:

> Defeated and dispersed in the noon-day of their power, his forefathers had crept back to their glens and straths only to be further preyed upon and despoiled. They turned to the beliefs of an ancient and similar people who had once travailed through not dissimilar vicissitudes. The medicine men of Jehovah, those of the clan of Knox and Calvin, rose powerful among them thundering their *small* thunder. They exhorted the people to burn their bagpipes and smash their fiddles and to destroy the music of their golden age.[79]

Yet, despite his sensitivity to major events in the history of the Scots radical culture, Barke's early novels were ignored by the Left in Scotland.

Before 1936 there was nothing at all sectarian or doctrinaire about Barke. Friends from early 1933 until Gibbon's death, Barke and Gibbon exchanged several letters. In 1933 and again in 1934 Gibbon and wife spent several days in Barke's home in Glasgow. In one of about a dozen letters to Barke, Gibbon said: 'So you've met the Douglasite-Nationalist-Communist-Anarchist Grieve. What a boy!' On 6 February 1934 writing yet another letter to the man he regarded as the greatest Gaelic scholar he knew, he said: 'You have quite a Lawrentian quality in dealing with the human flesh.' [80]

The Tillicountry-based *Plebs* magazine did not review any of the five novels that Barke published between 1933 and 1939. The influential Scottish socialist newspaper *Forward* did not review one of those novels; and *Plebs, Forward* and *Labour Monthly* did not publish an obituary notice on his death. Moreover, although *Labour Monthly* noticed none of Barke's novels except *Major Operation*, the approval of the CPGB in Scotland was sufficient to put him on the map. Out of this seal of approval, he began to contribute to *Left Review*. So did Gibbon, Edwin and Willa Muir.

The Stalinists had always hated Gibbon/Mitchell. Thus as early as July Marion Nelson wrote to ask Barke for really hostile information about Gibbon. Hating and dismissing his honest portrait of the CPGB without getting any encouragement from Barke before she wrote her review of *A Scots Quair*, she asked:

How much of his life was spent in Scotland? How close was he to the country, apart from being a Scot? I have heard it said [in Canada] that he wrote of Scotland as from a distance. And in view of his rather priggish picture of a communist in *Grey Granite*, how much did he really know about communists?[81]

But Barke was no more a Stalinist in relation to the question of 'the vanguard Party' than Gibbon had been. Writing to Gibbon on 12 November 1934, Barke, who was not yet in the CPGB, said:

> Only one thing do I regret - that Tavendale couldn't (and of course he couldn't) experience deep love for the working class. Lenin had the degree of affection I had in mind. Spartacus, Wallace [*sic!*], Dimitrov, etc., etc. A Communist Party leader especially needs it to carry him through - understanding of historical necessity alone rarely does.[82]

As a sentimental member of the ILP, Barke was idealistic and naive. But once he had joined the CPGB after Gibbon's death, the Stalinists continued to criticise the ideological 'faults' in Gibbon's novels at the same time as they deliberately overlooked similar faults in Barke's novels of the later 1930s. Furthermore, in *Major Operation*, Barke's portrayal of the CPGB, though the party was not referred to by name, also suggested that the Glaswegian proletariat was seen by MacKelvie, the novel's hero, as 'history's instruments'. Blurring the moral problems of building the so-called 'vanguard' Party that Gibbon at least tried to confront, Barke said:

> MacKelvie liked his mates. They were raw but they were genuine - when you got to know them. They weren't angels of course. Razor-slashers, wife-beaters, incestmongers, adulterers, blackmailers, gangsters... But a man, morally rotten, didn't work long with MacKelvie.[83]

Moreover, the CPGB and their brethren in other countries did not like Gibbon's attitudes toward sex. In his article 'An Estimation of A Scots Quair', Ian Milner, a New Zealander, wrote:

> Throughout the work one can sense Gibbon's contempt for the actual prurience of a middle-class sex morality based largely on repression. But in the last volume it sometimes takes on a strident emphasis out of prorportion to its significance in the narrative.

Not only was this not true; but, when Scottish radicals like Edwin Muir criticised Barke for his preoccupation with bawdy behaviour in the Burns novels, the CPGB defended him. Adherence to the Party line was always much more important than specific points of 'Marxist-Leninist' theory.

But, although he was emotionally and intellectually on the extreme Left, Gibbon was much closer to Silone than to the admirable Serge in seeing through what he described as 'Bolshevik blab'. Though Silone reviewed Serge's novel *Midnight in the Century* after referring to him as 'a great writer!', Jean P. Samson wrote about Silone's review as follows:

> Taking his inspiration from Gide and wishing, he thought, to stigmatise in this way the doctrinaire spirit of Trotskyism, he had called it *The Mass in Latin*. Because, he explained, in this book one only saw people who, though they might be oppositionists, continued, even persecuted, even expelled, to belong from the depth of their being to the Party... He [Silone], still absorbed then in the effort to free himself from the remains of the Leninist orthodoxy, could not but be hyersensitive to what, in Serge's thought in the Thirties, must necessarily seem to our Italian friend an extension of obedience all the more obsessive as his own viewpoint had not entirely freed itself from it.[84]

Steeped in the Scots *carnaptious* radical culture, sympathetic to Lenin and Trotsky and a practitioner of the real 'democratic intellect', Gibbon believed in socialists' *avant-garde* role in the struggle for socialism from below without ever accepting any Stalinist ideas.[85]

Twice the Scottish newspaper *Forward* acknowledged Gibbon's talent as an outstanding novelist without understanding the nature of his specific socialist politics.[86] But in his sincere tribute to his friend Gibbon in the *Left Review*, Barke toted the Party line by criticising Gibbon's attitude to Scottish nationalism. Arguing somewhat perversely that Gibbon's real internationalism resided in his alienation from Scotland, Barke wrote: 'He was much more at home in London than he would have been in Glasgow, Edinburgh or Aberdeen.'

To drive home the CPGB's attitude to the Scottish national question, he added the comment that: 'For Scottish nationalism is largely inspired by the superior race-theory of the Gael and the current demagogy of Major Douglas'.[87] Barke ought to have re-read what Gibbon wrote in his article on 'The Writers' International' in *Left Review* in February 1935:

> I hate capitalism; all my books are implicit or explicit propaganda. But because I am a revolutionist I see no reason for gainsaying my own critical judgement.

Attacking the Stalinists' 'bad Marxian patter and the application of the single adjective "bourgeois" to such displays of spiteful exhibitionism as warrant the attentions of a psycho-analyst', he refuted the idea that a 'decadent' capitalism was about to collapse. Summing up this point, he said:

> It is not a decayed and decrepit dinosaur who is the opponent of the revolutionary writer, but a very healthy and vigorous dragon indeed - so healthy that he can still afford to laugh at the revolutionist.[88]

Barke and Gibbon As Critics of Labourism and Stalinism

Radicalised by mass unemployment, poverty, racist tension between the Orange Order and the Irish in Glasgow and, above all, the rise of European fascism, Barke agonised over the role of the Left in a world apparently gone 'mad'. He had been in the Independent Labour Party (ILP) from the mid-1920s until 1936. However, on 6 August 1932, he recorded his private thoughts in his diary: 'I am quite prepared to believe

Karl Marx's interpretations; but I am not prepared to take William Gallacher's interpretation of Karl Marx.' Admitting to what was his life-long tendency to hero-worship, he confessed to a strong disenchantment with Jimmy Maxton. As he put it:

> As I began to hear all this from Jimmy's own lips I confess I began to lose some of my hero-worship for Maxton. And he told me that if I joined the Communist Party I would 'require to tell my employers that they were a lot of dirty capitalists and then leave.' I was staggered.

By this time he had been, according to a publishers' blurb 'the manager of one of the largest shipbuilding firms in Glasgow'.[89]

A left-wing activist in the Patrick branch of the ILP, he was writing long and mostly unpublished theoretical articles on Marxism and art. He had obtained rare books and pamphlets on the history, language, customs, bagpipes and literature of Gaelic civilisation in the Highlands. Writing to ask him for advice, Gibbon told him that 'you are the only expert on the Gaelic Highlands that I know.' And in a long unpublished 76-page typescript entitled 'The Formation', written in 1933, Barke said: 'The clan system as an aspect of primitive communism developed a very high artistic culture.'[90]

Although he was struggling to understand socialist theory, he had been on the Left since the mid-1920s. When he sent a copy of his first novel to Theodore Dreiser in 1933, he said: 'My concluding word is that you may become as great a power in that direction (the overthrow of world capitalism and the establishment of the workers' dictatorship) as you have so magnificently been in the world of letters.'[91] Like the radicals in this book, Barke did not inherit a viable Scottish national historiography. However, before he joined the CPGB in 1936 he was much more sympathetic to Gaelic civilisation in the Highlands. Since this sympathy coloured his first three novels, his readers could not have guessed that he was a very Lowland Scot. In one of his unpublished theoretical articles written in 1933, he wrote:

> When the young Pretender and his Highland forces were defeated at Culloden Moor in 1746, there followed a ruthless military occupation of the

Highlands. The clan system was broken up and all forms of Gaelic culture were suppressed.[92]

Supporting the *possibility* of a revival of the economy of the Highlands and Gaelic culture, he was challenging the dominant radical culture in Scotland including that of the CPGB.

Even before Barke was later influenced by Christopher Caudwell's influential book *Studies in a Dying Culture* (1938), he contributed two articles to *Left Review*, organ of the CPGB, in 1936. In his article on 'The Scottish National Question' he implicitly repudiated what he had written about the Scottish Highlands in his first three novels as well as in unpublished articles on Gaelic culture. An expert on Scotland's Celtic fringe and Gaelic culture, whose erudition was recognised by Gibbon, he had read and made notes from thirty books by among others Magnus Maclean, John Mackenzie, Donald MacKinnon, John Stuart Blackie, John Grant and W. L. Manson. But he did not know how to evaluate 'Bonnie Prince Charlie' in Scottish history in a Brit Marxist magazine that had no sympathy for either the Stuarts, Jacobitism, or Celtic communism.

By 1936 the 'Popular Front' policy had replaced that of 'Class against Class', and presenting the Brits' Party line, Barke said:

> It was capitalism that enclosed the common lands of England. It was the self-same capitalism that destroyed the Highlands as the land of the Gael, broke the Lowland peasantry, and drove them into the factories and mines.... And today, before our very eyes, it is capitalism that is destroying, and destroying beyond all possibility of resurrection, the last traces of An Gaidhealtachd.

However as a very Scottish radical, who was steeped in the history of Gaeldom, Barke refused either to praise or blame 'Bonnie Prince Charlie.' And he had no intention of rubbishing the Gaels' way of life before 1745. At the same time as he showered praise on his hero William Wallace, he employed a masterly formula to defend pre-1745 Gaeldom without identifying with Prince Charles Edward Stuart. As he put it:

> If we jump from the field of Bannockburn to the Moor of Culloden, we find that large sections of

251

the Highland clans went forth in '15 and '45 not on any fantastic romantic-chivalrous and madly quixotic defence of the claims of the Pretenders. They took to arms to defend the very basis of their predominantly Celtic politico-economy. (They lost, and that basis was ruthlessly shattered.) [93]

After he joined the CPGB, and contributed to *Left Review*, he became and remained an ideological policeman of the CPGB in Scotland until the outbreak of the Second World War. Unlike the Left's mostly open attacks on Gibbon during his lifetime, most of the anti-communist Left's denunciation of Barke was oral rather than written. Ignoring Barke's work before the war, the Left in Scotland after 1945 would engage in a characteristically *sleekit* denigration of his work, though this was equally destructive and wounding.

Sharing a rare and equally strong committment to socialism, Barke would probably not have joined the CPGB if his friend Gibbon had lived longer. In an unpublished typescript article entitled 'Retrospect 1935', Barke, a compulsive writer, wrote:

> But as I watched his coffin enter the cremation chamber, I was filled with a disturbing envy. Never again could he be made to suffer or feel pain. For his life, like the life of all those who swim against the stream, who cannot ape and conform to the prevailing fads and fancies, was a hard, if magnificent, struggle.[94]

However, by 1936 Barke, in writing to R. Palme Dutt, was desperate to be taken seriously as a Marxist thinker. In an unpublished and really very heretical review of William Gallacher's book *Revolt on the Clyde*, he struggled to embrace the CPGB's concept of 'the vanguard Party'. As he put it: 'The main lesson to be drawn from the book is that however courageous and militant the workers, they are almost certainly doomed to failure without an equally courageous, trained and level-headed leadership - and an organisation built around this leadership.'[95]

When he spoke for the Scottish nationalists on 'Wallace Day', 1939, Barke began to distance himself from the CPGB. But in keeping with his emotional attachment to the Stalinists' 'Popular Front', he again somersaulted on the Scottish national question. Although the *Daily*

Worker had published enthusiastic reviews by J. R. Campbell and William Gallacher of *Major Operation* and *The Land of the Leal*, the CPGB ignored his autobiography *The Green Hills Far Away* (1940). Challenging the CPGB's interpretation of Scottish history in this outspoken autobiography, he said:

> In a paroxysm of furious indignation I gave him [an American visitor] a short but burning sketch of Scotland's history. I explained why Sutherlandshire was a howling wilderness in terms of the Highland Clearances, extirpation and mass murders. I painted the history of Butcher Cumberland.[96]

In a quite perceptive notice in *The Times* in March 1958, an anonymous obituarist ignored all of Barke's early novels except for a brief reference to *The World His Pillow*. Focusing on the Burns novels, the writer commented:

> They were, perhaps, more successful with the public than with the critics, some of whom found Barke inclined to make the most of the legend of the Untutored Ploughboy. The novels were based on much loving research - perhaps too much! - for at times Burns himself was almost submerged beneath the mass of detail that his research produced.[97]

Just as the left-wing critics generally damned Gibbon and more or less ignored Barke in the early 1930s, so they lambasted the latter in their often semi-drunken pub 'criticism' in the 1940s and 1950s. In the philistine Scottish society of the 1950s, Barke's novels on Burns were dismissed on the Left - despite De Lancey Ferguson's favourable but private comments to the contrary - because he was making money from them. Barke's made a lot of money from the novels on Burns, and the Left, including his own former comrades in the CPGB, did not like it. But in making considered and similar literary criticisms of Howard Fast, the American communist novelist, whose political formation also took place in the 1930s, Alan Wald also focused on the literary promise unfulfilled.

What Wald said about Fast could have applied to Barke: 'His early works in particular display strengths of craft and creativity that, under other circumstances, might have enabled him to develop into a novelist of greater distinction'. But with Barke's as with Fast's case those circumstances were located in the history of the perverted socialist internationalism of the twentieth century after 1917.

Insisting that the Left in Scotland in particular was always philistine - in the twentieth century - in relation to socialists' aesthetic activity, Hugh MacDiarmid was undoubtedly right, despite his own elitist way of expressing his argument. Making similar points about Barke's novels on Burns in his fascinating article 'Pictures of the Homeland: The Legacy of Howard Fast', Wald asked:

> Shouldn't we be grateful for the existence of a writer like Fast who brings relatively enlightened values to a mass-market audience that might otherwise be reading Harold Robbins and Rosemary Rogers? There are significant problems with this line of argument, but I think it is the most effective way we have at present of responding to the elitism of a single standard [i.e., the middle-brow and highbrow culture of 'high modernism'] for evaluuating diverse cultural phenomena.

In any case, Barke, like Fast, whose communism was formed during the Stalinists' 'Popular Front' period, in the novels on Burns 'saluted', as Wald's put it, 'little people instead of workers and waved the flag of idealised patriotism instead of socialist internationalism.' But he also created something of a sort of socialist Kailyard novel.[98]

On the other hand, the CPGB and - through men like Jack Mitchell - the international communist movement, continued until the collapse of 'communism' in Russia and Eastern Europe in 1989 to promote Barke at the expense of Gibbon. Between 1946 and 1954, Collins published Barke's five novels on the national bard, Robert Burns (1759-1796) - *The Wind that Shakes the Barley, The Song in the Green Thorn Tree, The Wonder of all the Gay World, The Crest of the Broken Wave, The Well of the Silent Harp* novels - described in somewhat Kailyard language by W. R. Aitken as 'The Immortal Memory'.

Describing Barke's last novel *Bonnie Jean* as a postscript to 'The Immortal Memory', Aitken was not perhaps aware how far his hero had travelled from his radical quest of the interwar years. Nevertheless Barke's novels were best-sellers; and he was again marginalised by a puritanical Left. Savaged by the critics, Barke increasingly distanced himself from his fellow socialists.

The Scottish writer Eddie Boyd remembered him working in the Unity Theatre, Glasgow, in the 1940s as 'a very lonely and sad man' who loved using 'big' and 'obscure' words. Certainly, he was at the top of his creative peak when he published *The Land of the Leal* in 1939; and, alienated by the attacks on his Burns novels from the critics and the Left generally, he dropped out of the CPGB without making any public statement. Although Professor De Lancey Ferguson told Sydney Goodsir Smith that he thought *The Song in the Green Thorn Tree* was 'magnificent', no other *writer* except Gibbon bothered to bestow much praise on him throughout his life as a Scottish radical writer.[99]

During the Second World War Barke had put on such plays in Unity Theatre, Glasgow as *The Night of the Big Blitz* and *When The Boys Come Home*. But, although he seems to have kept his political opinions to himself after that war, he had become increasingly pessimistic about the future of an authentic socialism. He did not participate in the CPGB's affairs after 1945, though they continued to claim him as one of theirs. As the Scottish equivalent of the American novelist Howard Fast, Barke had created a sort of left-wing socialist Kailyard literature - a literature for which there is still a demand.

In 1950 he replied to a letter from Geoffrey Wagner at the University of Rochester, in America, requesting information about Gibbon. In a note in his own handwriting at the bottom of Wagner's letter, he said: 'Glad to be of any help to you about Leslie Mitchell who was my dearest literary friend and comrade.' However, in his direct reply to Wagner, he acknowledged that he had written about Gibbon in *Left Review* and hoped to write 'a cultural biography' of him. Then he said:

> Your Edinburgh friends have probably confused
> me with someone else. In so far as the *Daily Worker*
> and *Our Time* are concerned, I would not touch
> them with a barge pole.[100]

Then in 1956 he upset the CPGB by supporting the workers' revolution in Hungary. He died two years later.

A.S. Neill (1883-1973) and R. F. Mackenzie (1910-1987): *The Search for the 'Democratic Intellect'*

'On that day democracy was born' - Edinburgh, round about 1560. 'The Scottish education system is the finest in the world' - even if the rest of the world no longer thinks so, even though our schools depend on corporal punishment to an extend surpassed perhaps only in Ireland.

Father Anthony Ross
(1971)

Fears are sometimes expressed that the working classes are getting too highly educated. Educated? No! but foolishly crammed with (for some of them) indigestible food, through the injudicious action of parents or teachers, with the result that a feeble half-starved professional man is the the miserable product of what might, with appropriate training, have been a self-respecting artisan.

John Kerr (1903)

Scottish Democracy and 'Democratic' Education: An Introduction

When I went to the University of Stirling in the summer of 1968, Dr. Anand Chitnis came into the staff room in high dudgeon. Returning from a seminar at the University of Edinburgh, where he had given 'a paper' on the eighteenth-century Scottish Enlightenment and the 'democratic intellect', he was most upset because a fellow historian had asked him how he could square the 'democratic intellect' with the well-known serfdom of the Scottish coalminers until their emancipation in 1799.

It was a very good question; and Chitnis's response - at least in private - was that the question had been unfair. Such questions, though unanswered, will simply not go away. But just as the two inherited Scottish radical traditions, stretching back to James Thomson Callender and Alexander Rodger and James MacFarlan, were personified in the twentieth century by James Ramsay MacDonald and John Maclean, so the real nature of the 'democratic intellect' would subsequently bother and bewilder radicals like A. S. Neill and R. F. Mackenzie.

At the heart of the enquiries into the actual *history* of Scottish education conducted by Neill and Mackenzie was this question: how far had pupils and students ever been encouraged to think for themselves? Since this book is about the hidden history of Scottish radical culture and ruling-class 'education', I wish to stress that in the late twentieth century the question an obscure historian asked Dr. Chitnis about the compatibility of a 'democratic intellect' with some workers' actual serfdom remains exceptionally important - as well as unanswered.

Moreover, although educationalists like Neill and Mackenzie did not accept the so-called historical existence of a Scottish 'democratic intellect', 'democratic' education in Scotland has been equated by the majority of thinkers, including some nominal radicals, with 'upward social mobility' or, in plain English, 'getting on' in the (capitalist) world. But the role of encouraging critical thinking in Scottish educational history has been ignored, except by the radical minority like Neill and Mackenzie. For example, in an interview in the *Edinburgh Review* in 1988, while boasting about the 'advanced' Scottish educational system, Stuart Hood responded to the question 'Did none of your teachers *make [sic!]* you think', by saying: 'No, not really'.[1] Really?

It was not until 1961 that George Elder Davie published his influential book *The Democratic Intellect*. At the heart of his concept of the so-called 'democratic intellect' was the assumption of an exceptionally advanced Scottish educational system in the eighteenth century before it was afterwards eroded by the process of the Anglicisation. This process of myth-making had been reinforced in 1950 when the American historian L. J. Saunders published his book described by Eric J. Hobsbawm as 'the ill-named *Scottish Democracy, 1815-1840'*.[2] Moreover, in devoting large parts of their lives to the search for an Anglo-Scottish 'democratic intellect', A. S. Neill (1883-1973) and R. F. Mackenzie (1910-1987) upset many people.

Since Davie's discovery of the powerful eighteenth-century Anglo-Scottish ruling-class bequest of a uniquely Scottish 'democratic intellect' has been defended by the most unlikely Scots, no one has noticed that the title of Davie's book did not match his argument. Ignoring the character of 'education', or more accurately social oppression, in both primary and secondary schools and universities in the eighteenth and nineteenth centuries, Davie was primarily concerned with the mediating role of the intellectuals in eighteenth- and early nineteenth-century Scottish universities. In his pamphlet on *The Social Significance of the Scottish Philosophy of Common Sense*, Davie ignored brutality and the 'shaming' of 'the cutty-stool' and the general heresy-hunting of the 'Holy Willies' satirised by the national bard Robert Burns. Explaining what the *democracy* of the 'democratic intellect' consisted of in a society where radicalism and trade unionism were suppressed, Davie argued that 'a science-based society can maintain the intellectual standards necessary to material progress only by bridging the gap between the expert few and the lay majority'. Thus making it possible, in his view, for 'each party to keep the other up to scratch by mutal criticism, in much the same way as, under their religious system, the minister's theological supervision of the congregation was checked and balanced by the congregation's common sense scrutiny of the minister'. Elsewhere Davie argued that 'the function of the [ruling-class] '"democratic intellect"' was to use education to 'counteract atomisation by building a sort of intellectual bridge between all classes'.[3] By making a considerable impact on modern historiography through his earlier articles, Davie influenced historians like James Kellas.[4]

However, in so far as a 'democratic' Scottish educational system existed in the nineteenth and early twentieth centuries, it had nothing in common with the really democratic vision of the radical Scots portrayed in this book. In his Ph.D thesis on The Liberal Party in Scotland, 1868-1895 (1966), Kellas expressed the dominant Presbyterian view when he wrote:

> Scottish democracy was the ideological basis of the Liberal Party in Scotland, but it could not apply to the Irish. Roman Catholic, uneducated, and not too concerned with the dignities of man *(sic!)* in

258

the face of a struggle for survival, the Irish working class (and there were not many in any other class) seemed a *threat* to the *Scottish way of life*.[5]

Recognising the social reality of late-nineteenth-century Scotland, Kellas emphasised that the restricted 'democracy' and 'education' in Scotland had always been for the Calivinist elect rather than the irreligious Scots or the Irish.

When, in his autobiography *Memories: Gay and Grave* (1903) he complained about the Scottish working class getting too much 'education', John Kerr, trained at Cambridge University, had just retired as an Inspector of Education for Scottish schools. Though dissecting and combing his autobiography from beginning to end, the historian can find no evidence of a 'democratic intellect' in Kerr's nineteenth-century Scotland. While the Anglo-Scottish myth of the 'democratic intellect' was always at the core of ruling-class awareness from the eighteenth century, working-class resentment at inequality and injustice saw through the still powerful Kailyard propaganda.

Scottish education was characterised by very extreme authoritarian attitudes, middle-class elitism towards working people, and an arid 'intellectualism' that refused to acknowledge any of the distinctive features of Scottish culture, literature or radicalism and still less the distinctiveness of Gaeldom. And yet when Professor Roy H. Campbell was appointed as *the* Professor of Scottish history at the University of Stirling in the early 1970s, he *instructed* me to recommend Kerr's book to the students in our shared class on Scottish history between 1707 and the present.[6]

But, although I refused to recommend Kerr's book in the classes that I taught, I did quote it in my pioneering article on 'Belt, Book and Blackboard: The Roots of Authoritarianism in Scottish Education'.[7] Published in *Scottish International* in April 1973 and exposing the myth about the Scottish Enlightenment's invention of a 'democratic intellect' and the continuity of brutal corporal punishment in State schools, this article brought my ideas to the attention of A. S. Neill and Father Anthony Ross, and deepened my friendship with R. F. Mackenzie.[8]

Writing to me on 24 June 1972 from his Summerhill school in Leiston, Suffolk, Neill said:

> Your history of Scots education sounds genuine and true. Snag is that a historian sees what he

wants to see. My old Prof in Edinburgh Sir Richard Lodge would have written a different version. The bugger is that Scotland still seems to be retrograde with its discipline and tawse and its fatuous M.A. degrees. Make a book of your article, adding your remedies for the insane system. Then you may get the sack.[9]

Next day I told my colleagues in the staff-room about Neill's letter, and I was told that, in time, 'it will be worth money'. Brendan Behan wrote that the 'middle class put years on him'; but he did not know the philistine Scottish middle class or their real attitudes towards education.

At this time, too, R. D. Laing was influencing men like Mackenzie and Father Anthony Ross. The publication in 1960 of Laing's influential book, *The Divided Self*, popularised the notion that madness was the outcome of a repressive society.[10] But, although it came out of a very distinct Scottish milieu, it did not encourage the romanticism of James Hogg's *Confessions of a Justified Sinner*. Besides, Laing's world view was openly anti-capitalist.

Later on, in May 1971, Ross published in *Scottish International* his article on 'Resurrection: A Diagnosis of Contemporary Scottish Culture and Society'. When he criticised the educational system with biting, incisive skill, Ross recommended the creation of a real 'democratic intellect' before adding:

> Such a system might ensure a kind of discussion at staff and pupil levels which is rarely possible now. It might even lead to a broadening of school libraries, which at present so often represent the narrowness of outlook expressed in the spontaneous statement of a Scottish educationalist: 'Oh! But I wouldn't dream of reading any of your books...' It might even affect the highly placed member of the Scottish Education Department who publicly declared that he preferred old myths to more truthful historical analysis.[11]

But the critique of Scottish education Ross developed at all levels was sometimes more devastating that he ever realised. Nevertheless it was Mackenzie, a radical practitioner of real democratic and radical education in State schools, who, in experiencing on his strong shoulders the Alps-like weight of the past, discovered how unenlightened and undemocratic the Anglo-Scottish ruling class really was in action.

Of all the powerful myths about Scottish history, the strongest insists that the eighteenth-century Anglo-Scottish ruling class created a 'democratic intellect' *unique* to Scotland. When he coined the phrase the 'democratic intellect' on the eighteenth-century Scottish intelligentsia and their significant contribution to human knowledge, including important ruling-class figures like Lord Kames, George Elder Davie was fostering the illusions about the Scottish democracy that Ross objected to and exposed as muddled-headed. Thus, in his interview in *Scottish International* entitled 'Storms in our Time', Ross said:

> It is still the case, as George Elder Davie once remarked, talking about Dundee High School during his time in the fifth year, that thinking is discouraged. I mean the basic attitude in most Scottish schools seems to be that 'you are here to learn what you ought to know'.[12]

A major paradox of Scottish cultural radicalism in the 1990s is that both sections of the Scottish nationalist Left, a few 'Marxists', and a few of the anarchist Left personified by the influential novelist James Kelman, have insisted on the existence of a lost eighteenth-century Scottish 'democratic intellect'. In the pages of the *Glasgow Herald*, defending Davie's history of the so-called 'democratic intellect', Kelman of all people ought to have had a better understanding of Scottish education's inherent authoritarianism from at least the Industrial Revolution onwards.

But, although Davie's two books *The Democratic Intellect* (1964) and *The Decline of the Democratic Intellect* (1989) perpetuated a myth of a democratic educational system at the level of school and Scottish university, this myth is simply not true. These myths have also been reinvented by Andrew L. Walker's very nationalistic book *The Revival of the Democratic Intellect* (1995); he has created a whole host of new myths at a time when Scottish historians ought to be debunking myths and rediscovering our real radical educational history as it developed under the inspiration of Neill and Mackenzie.[13]

Suffering from the absence of a Scottish national historiography chronicling the educational activities of their radical predecessors, Neill and Mackenzie did not know anything about those radical teachers in the 1880s and 1890s - men like Archibald McLaren, R. F. Muirhead, James Mavor, or Alexander Dickenson. As pioneering socialists in the major Scottish cities, they had campaigned for the abolition of corporal punishment and democracy in the State schools. Then, in the early twentieth century, William M. Haddow, John Carstairs Matheson, James Maxton, John Maclean and many other members of the Scottish Socialist Teachers' Society fought for the democratisation of the State schools and universities. By the late 1920s Stalinism was trying to eradicate all knowledge of the real democratic heritage of Scottish radicalism and socialism. As radical educators of the working class, Neill and Mackenzie were not unique, though during the various and often dramatic moments of their isolation from mainstream Labourism it often seemed that they were.

The Radicals' Critique: The Biographies of Neill and Mackenzie

Neill was born in 1883 and Mackenzie in 1910; and both learned that, far from being about democracy or humanism, Scottish education was about authoritarian thought-control and 'good' behaviour. Moreover, during the early lives of both men, when Scottish education was allegedly the envy of the world and provided 'the lad of pairts' from a humble background with opportunities to 'make it' to the top of a hierarchical capitalist society, intellectual accomplishments were about social status, money and power rather than about enlightenment or democracy.

Far from the admittedly pernicious process of anglicisation being responsible for the appalling nature of Scottish education in the twentieth century, a philistine and authoritarian Presbyterian ruling class had tried to stifle creativity and self-development from the Reformation onwards. Furthermore, from the Industrial Revolution, they had succeeded in persuading some working-class Scots that 'education' was about 'upward social mobility'. By the beginning of the twentieth century, the function of education was restricted to personal advancement. Thus Flora Garry, who was born in the North of Scotland in 1900, and became a student at King's College in the University of Aberdeen in the 1920s, wrote:

My folks had a croft in Glenardle. Learning's the
thing they would say.
To help you up in the wardle [world].[14]

Moreover, in an extraordinary private letter sent to Christopher
Murray Grieve (Hugh MacDiarmid) in June 1937, George Elder Davie,
future author of *The Democratic Intellect*, wrote:

> I've been ordered by the doctor to take three
> months of complete rest, and have been permitted
> to finish my philosophy degree only on condition
> of leaving Edinburgh, and studying in Germany. I
> have also been told that I can count on academic
> promotion in my career *only* if I cut loose from
> politics and cease to give you aid. Thus ends in
> temporary defeat and surrender a very worrying
> conflict. But I am submitting only because I myself
> must have a rest, a change and peace to study and
> because the oposition forces (especially [the Edwin
> and Willa] Muir-Communist alliance) are far too
> numerous and in point of influence powerful to
> dish with my present resources. On the advice of
> my professors, I think my mother is to write to
> you telling you to withhold your 'corrupting
> influences' etc.[15]

At a time when the Communist Party of Great Britain (CPGB) were
trying to recruit Edwin and Willa Muir to their ranks, Davie had drafted
a letter on the Scottish question on MacDiarmid's behalf.[16] However,
the most fascinating aspect of Davie's letter to Grieve is the near-
totalitarian attempt at censorship, if not thought-control, by some
professors at the University of Edinburgh. It was an old witch-hunting
tradition at the University of Edinburgh - a tradition responsible for
victimising the philosopher Dugald Stewart at the time of the so-called
'democratic intellect'.

As Neill might have discovered after the First World War and
Mackenzie might have rediscovered after the Second if a decent Scottish
historiography had existed, the only late- nineteenth- and early-
twentieth century Scots who believed in and exhibited a 'democratic
intellect' were John Carstairs Matheson, John Maclean, Jimmy Maxton

263

and the members of the Scottish Socialist Teachers' Society.[17] Unknown to Neill, who was born on 17 October 1883 in Forfar, his pioneering predecessors in the Scottish Socialist Teachers' Society saw the need for a comprehensive and all-round education as the means of emancipating the common people and particularly the working class from capitalism. However, as Neill wrote in his autobiography *Neill! Neill! Orange Peel*:

> Forfar Academy was the stepping stone to a university education. To my father, advancement in life meant advancement in learning.[18]

Like Gibbon, Barke and Mackenzie, Neill's background was a rural one. Though of coalmining stock, Neill's father, who was a schoolteacher, was a practitioner of bourgeois sexual morals. While 'fornication' was, according to Neill, common between ploughmen and servant lassies and 'getting in the family way seemed just as common', he described his boyhood experience of sex:

> For any sexual offence in school, my father always gave a savage punishment. I remember his giving Jock Ross six with the cane, on his hand held down on the desk, for pretending to drop his slate pencil while taking the occasion to put his hand up a girl's petticoats.

Sketching his own sexual education, Neill wrote:

> Masturbation must have been known to me all the same, for I was chided one day by my father for making the dog Boulot jump on my arm. I also have a vague memory of Neilie and me being in a locked room, and Uncle Neill demanding entrance. When we let him in, he looked at us in a leering way and said: 'Aha, showing birdies!' We were most indignant, a circumstance that to any self-respecting psychoanalyist would have denoted our guilt.[19]

But, although Neill traced the origins of his later interest in sexual repression back to his rural upbringing in Forfarshire, it owed much to the advanced Austrian socialist educational system he encountered in Vienna in the 1920s.

Though Neill was a talented writer, he was not a deep or consistent thinker. Developing an early interest in psychology as a source of human beings' emancipation from oppressive social surroundings, he did not identify the strong and inherited authoritarianism in Scottish society as the main source of his own development as a progressive educationalist.

There were, moreover, contradictions in the dialectical interplay between his thought and his practice. In the dedication to his first book *A Dominie's Log* (1915), Neill wrote:

> As a boy I attended a village school where the bairns chattered and were happy. I trace my love of freedom to my free life there, and I dedicate this book to my former dominie, my father.

However, in his autobiography *'Neill!, 'Neilll!, Orange Peel'*, he said: 'I see now that Father did not like any children; he had no contact with them'.[20] Moreover, as Mackenzie emphasised, Neill and Sir James Barrie experienced 'common, bleak upbringings in which there was little love or laughter'.[21]

Unlike Neill, Mackenzie did not produce an autobiography. But the latter's books and lectures were always full of autobiographical references. Those reactionaries who search for the origins of individuals' radicalism in unhappy childhoods will however be disappointed by the biographical comments made by Neill and Mackenzie.

When he was a boy, Neill's father did not like him. By contrast, Mackenzie's father encouraged his latent radicalism from an early age. When he told me in a conversation (in 1973) that his father was always more affectionate and physically demonstrative than his mother, with whom he got on well, he attributed this fact to his father's origins as a Gael and his mother's origins as a Lowlander.

Separated by a whole generation from Neill's own experiences at the University of Edinburgh at an early age, Mackenzie was nevertheless influenced by internationalist radical influences in rural Aberdeenshire. Mackenzie was the son of an unusual radical father - a rural stationmaster who was originally employed by the L.M.S. railway company as a porter - and his development as a radical was gradually shaped by his cumulative disillusionment with the nature of higher education in secondary schools and universities. But he was in no doubt about his father's role in shaping his *basic* radical and socialist values. In a private letter to me dated 3 April 1986, he said:

> I had a religious upbringing to which I owe much. It was part of our upbringing that minorities were treated with respect, even with reverence. Indian pedlars, Breton onion-sellers, Jewish merchants were treated by my father with the same human dignity as any other visitors. This attitude may have derived basically from the Christian doctrine of calling nothing common or unclean. The general attitude of the community was to make fun of what was unusual. Many years later the Italian novel *Christ Stopped at Eboli* (meaning that Christianity never penetrated farther inland into Italy than the coastal strip terminating at Eboli) was a revelation for me and suggested that central Aberdeenshire also had been less interpenetrated by Christianity that the General Assembly of the Kirk would have liked us to think. The general community, unaffected by Christian teaching, made fun of Jews and "Ingin Johnnies", stammerers, homosexuals, Holy Wullies, agnostics, left-wing politicians and everybody else who threatened the norm. I find it difficult today to decide if my father's humanity, his reverence for life, sprang from human goodness or the fact that he took the Christian teachings more seriously than our neighbours did. But the extra respect which we were brought up to show to the Jews was scriptural.[22]

However, when Neill's first book *A Dominie's Log* was published in 1915, five years after Mackenzie was born, Scotland was a more *unknown country* than the letter that Mackenzie sent me in 1986 might suggest.[23]

When radicals or nonconformists attempt at a mature age to explain the origins of their dissent or nonconformity, they have always faced a difficult one. In his longest, most thoughtful book *A Search for Scotland,*

Mackenzie came back to his often-told tale of his encounter with a railway clerk:

> 'Aye, aye', said the railway clerk to me one evening as I stepped on to the platform after listening to a day's lectures at King's College in Aberdeen, 'and what was the [pause] PROFESSOR saying today?' Since then I've never been able to hear the word 'professor' without hearing the faint hiss of air escaping from a punctured balloon.'[24]

Towards the end of this book - really the 1980s equivalent of Edwin Muir's *Scottish Journey* (1935) - he wrote about his father's indirect, and belated, influence in shaping his later radicalism. As he put it:

> Two Scots personified the initial [democratic socialist] vision and the modified version. The difference between the two Highlanders, John Maclean and Ramsay MacDonald, goes deep into our psychological make-up... I encountered this unbearable quality in our home in Aberdeenshire. I felt uncomfortable when my father disagreed with the friendliest of neighbours, maintaining what I felt to me an uncomfortable integrity. He had a vision of inner truth to which he was totally loyal, even if its expression hurt a friend's feelings. I, however, longed for accord, protection, friendship, reassurance. It was part of a north-east upbringing. We were brought up to be 'respectable', doing the right things, not being uncouth in any way.[25]

The two different Scottish-International traditions of radicalism had been visible from the days of James Thomson Callender.

But, although Mackenzie enjoyed a much better relationship with his father than Neill did with his, it was the former who developed the most radical critique of the State educational system in much less favourable circrcumstances. When he contributed a long essay to the programme of the Wildcat theatre company's play entitled *Jotters* (with an ironical and double-edged meaning), Mackenzie said:

One of the myths that I grew up with was that the Scottish Education Department and its masters in Whitehall wanted just that, a generation of confident youth asking questions about everything. My own experience of the Department was that that was the last thing they wanted. They wanted docile pupils. 'He or she never gave any trouble in class,' that was regarded as a great compliment to a pupil, a testimonial guaranteeing a favourable response to a job application. The maintenance of apartheid. 'Education for servitude', as Huddleston described black education in South Africa.[26]

Anti-Democratic Education, Scottish Radicalism and Neill

In his first book, *A Dominie's Log*, Neill's naivety in assuming that he could teach as he pleased in an authoritarian State school was expressed with crystal clarity. Notwithstanding his unsophisicated simplicity, he said:

> The word 'Republican' came up today in a lesson, and I asked what it meant. Four girls told me that their fathers were Republicans, but they had no idea of the meaning of the word. One lassie thought that it meant 'a man who is always quarelling with the Tories'... a fairly penetrating defintion. I explained the meaning of the word, and said that a Republican in this country was wasting his time and energy. I pointed to America with its Oil Kings, Steel Kings, Meat Kings, and called it a country worse than Russia.[27]

However, whatever his limitations as a radical thinker, he was in the Scottish-Internationalist radical tradition when he also raised the question of racism in South Africa.[28]

At that stage of his evolution as a Scottish radical critic of established society, he wanted a new Education Guild to be 'directly responsible to the State, which will remain the supreme authority'. For all his anticapitalism, socialism was to come from the top down and not from the bottom up. Yet this did not inhibit him from criticising teachers who 'never write or talk forcibly' - teachers who could be compared to the Labour Members of Parliament, who desired to be 'respectable at any price'. [29]

Throughout his long life Neill persistently referred to George Douglas Brown's novel *The House with the Green Shutters* as a revelation of the nature of social life in Scotland. If Tulliallan became a metaphor for the Scottish Highlands in James Barke's early radical novels, *The House with the Green Shutters* was Neill's metaphor for the Calvinist authoritarianism that he detested. But during the early part of his career as a thinker, he was preoccupied with socialist ideas. So in *A Dominie Dismissed* (1917), he wrote about his Headmaster:

> I used to be stumped by the anti-socialist cry: socialism will destroy enterprise!... If enterprise has made modern capitalism and industrialism, by all means let it be destroyed. MacDonald will crow over what he considers my failure to be consistent, but, it will never once strike him that my frank self-analysis is a thing that he will never practise himself. [30]

Though such radical views were incompatible with teaching in any State school in Britain and self-analysis alien to the dominant culture in Scotland at that time, Neill's teaching career could only end in him getting his 'jotters' or dismissal.

In *A Dominie Dismissed* Neill's later and even more radical ideas on education were foreshadowed when he said:

> If we make our schools decent places the poor profiteers will be in the soup, won't they? Our present schools do no harm; the discipline of the classroom prepares a bright lad for the discipline of the wagery shop, and, of course, a girl accustomed to the atmosphere of a city school won't object to the ventilation obtaining in the factory. [31]

It was already obvious that this critical, radical teacher would make his mark.

When he published *A Domine in Doubt* in 1921, Neill was under the influence of the Bolshevik revolution and 'Red Vienna'.[32] Yet he was more interested in psychology than in Marxism. Sketching out what were to become his lifelong concerns, he wrote: 'Discpline thwarts the boy at every turn, and our adult authority is fatally injuring the boy's character. Our task is to provide the child with opportunity to wield his power. We suppress it and the lad shows his power in destructive instead of constructive activities.'[33]

He was still pro-Scottish; and he said that: 'I presume that the typical joke about Scots' meanness appeals to the Englishman, because Englishmen are mean themselves'.[34] But, although his connections with Scots and Scotland after the First World War were at best tenuous, Neill could not escape the authoritarian and radical traditions of the Athens of the North. It was always his reference point: the core of what his Scottish-International radicalism was about.

Nevertheless in 1921 he founded his International School in Hellerau, near Dresden and, with Lilan Neustter whom he married in 1927, kept it going until 1924. He undertook pyschoanalysis in Vienna under Wilheim Stekel between 1921 and 1924, and helped to introduce such advanced ideas to a few relatively privileged Scots. Edwin Muir was another radical Scot who developed into a mature critic of Scotland after undergoing pyschoanalysis.

When Neill published *A Dominie Abroad* in 1923 his ideas were already known to a small group of radical Scots like James Barke, Muir and Lewis Grassic Gibbon. Unlike most of the other Scottish radicals discussed in this book, Neill seldom said much about the workers' appalling social conditions and life-styles, whether in Scotland, England, Germany, Austria or wherever. And yet social conditions in Scotland in the 1920s (including death-rates, the consumption of alcohol, ill-health, crime rates, the number of people imprisoned, life expectancy, poor housing and poor wages) were not simply worse than those in England: they were among the worst in Western Europe. The best social picture of Scottish workers' lives was presented by the English journalist William Bolitho in his book *Cancer of Empire* (1924).[35]

In all of the books written by Neill the references to social conditions were cursory and oblique. In *A Dominie Abroad*, for example, he said:

Berlin is crowded with beggars and stall-holders. I am told that street vendors were unknown before the war. To me it seems that you can buy anything and everything on the street now.

Ignoring the extreme destitution engenderd by the Allies' post-war policy and, at least in part, the appalling poverty responsible for helping to bring the Nazis to power later on, he engaged in stereotyping when he wrote: 'What babies the Germans are!'[36]

The crucial point about Neill's life as a Scottish radical is that there was no space for him in Scotland after the First World War. He was forced to leave 'home' in 1924, and in the book *All the Best: Letters from Summerhill*, its editor Jonathan Croall wrote:

> For the next fifty years, first at Lyme and then at Leiston in Suffolk, Neill strove to prove that children could cope with freedom. Under the ir.fluence of Lane, Freud and the New Psychology, he based his early work with problem children, and effected some remarkable 'cures'. In the belief that 'childhood should be playhood', he refused to make lessons compulsory, insisting that children learn best when motivation comes from within.[37]

But, although he continued to contribute articles to such Scottish socialist newspapers as *Forward*, Neill's physical distance from Scotland prevented him from having a major influence on his country of origin. Nevertheless his subsequent impact on radical Scots, though slow and cumulative, was considerable; and his best pupil, R. F. Mackenzie, was always closer to the chalk-face of Scottish working-class life.

When he published a new version of his book *Scotland and Nationalism* in 1994, Christopher Harvie the tame and licensed Fabian 'radical', ignored the exiled Dominie's impact on post-1945 Scotland through Mackenzie and others. At the same time as he pretended that Mackenzie had not existed, Harvie wrote thus in his sole reference to Neill:

> Despite A. S. Neill, Scottish education was always teacher-centred, but this orthodoxy was challenged by new methods of primary instruction

developed mainly in the south, and applied to
Scotland after 1965.[38]

Even after he joined the Scottish National Party in 1988, Harvie's
impressionist journalism lacked the insight of a real radical cultural
historian like Willy Maley.

Historically speaking, Scottish radicalism was always characterised
by those who, almost irrespective of their personal circumstances,
preferred analysing the human condition more than the struggle to
confront appalling social conditions. Neill reflected the specific tradition
of interpretive 'metaphysics'. Furthermore, Neill's book *A Dominie
Abroad* was permeated from beginning to end with radical 'metaphysics'
rather than with a concrete programme seeking to transcend the existing
international capitalist social order. Yet none of this detracted from the
importance of his contribution to educational theory; for the process
of interpreting the world is a basic pre-condition for changing it.

By the 1920s Neill was an enthusiastic anti-fascist and supporter of
what he mistook for 'communism' in Russia. The emergence of
Stalinism did not change his attitude for some time. From the
perspective of the late twentieth century the democratic Left during
'the devil's decade' of the 1930s, including Neill, was often muddled
and confused. Thus, in an article in *the New Leader*, a writer said:

> One accepts, therefore, with thankfulness and
> relief, those novels which are neither a way of
> escape or of oblivion: novels which are a protest
> and a warning, an incitement and an indictment.
> Among recent books in this class, first place must
> be given to *Journey to the End of the Night* by Louis-
> Ferdinand Celine.[39]

Tragically the contributors to the *Socialist Leader* were not aware of the
Frenchman's fascist sympathies.

In the world of the 1930s, depicted by the anti-totalitarian democratic
Left as 'crazy', Neill was a voice of sanity and common humanity. But
the article that he contributed to the *New Leader* in 1933 was less than
convincing. Engaging his left-wing critics head-on, he said:

> One or two of my communist friends accuse me
> of running a bourgeois school, but I always say to

272

them: 'Queer, then, that the Russians who come to Arcos send me their kids'... We have families of titled folk, children of army and navy officers, rich and poor children, but I have never once seen any sign of class feeling: a son of a die-hard colonel will chum up with the son of a communist.

But it simply was not true that there were 'poor children' at his progressive experimental school; and the school could only survive, anyway, because, as he said, 'I am all for a war cry of No Propaganda of Any Kind'. In the 1930s in particular 'propaganda' was a matter of interpretation.[40] Moroever, Neill's advertisement for himself about 'How I Run A Free School' was compatible with Independent Labour Party authors' books like Maxton's on what I would do *If I Were Dictator*.

Yet, despite his consistent predilection for socialism from above rather than below, Neill did not want to be a dictator, educational or otherwise; and he believed in the need for children's freedom. Nevertheless it did not occur to him that the children of the Russian officials in London were the well-off children of the members of a highly privileged bureaucracy. Sensitivity to actual social conditions in society was never his strong point.

In what was in many ways his best, most searching, and most analytical book *Is Scotland Educated?* (1936), he indicated the radicalisation of his own ideas about education in State schools. In one passage collaborated by an orthodox Scottish educationalist C. W. Thomson, he said:

Our schools are conditioned and regulated by the State. The State is a capitalist, imperialist State, apparently ruled by a sham democracy, but in reality ruled by the minority, who hold the power and the wealth. The schools must not therefore teach anything that might be subversive of this State. Like the daily press, the school history books must not say a single thing that matters, and, like the press, the history books seek always to further the propaganda that the ruling class wants to disseminate.[41]

Analysing the very core of Anglo-Scottish culture in the 1930s, he looked at the way English cultural imperialism in Scotland was mediated by the 'native' [Anglo-Scottish] ruling class. He puts the democratic Left's argument with exceptional sharpness:

> And a good suburbanite will always seek the standards of the West End. To be Englified is the ambition of all Scottish West Ends, and our speech *bewrayeth* us. I speak not as one superior to linguistic weakness. I speak English with a Scots accent... To speak dialect is to betray your belonging to the lower orders, that is the orders who do most of the work in life.[42]

Then, in a searching socialist analysis of Scottish society, he depicted 'our' universities:

> Our Scots universities are conservative of the Right (Tory) or of the Left (Liberal). Psychologically there is no difference between a Tory and a Liberal: both support capitalism and the Old Men of life. Our professional classes, university trained, show much less originality than our Clydeside workers show.

But, as befitted someone raised in a Calivinist milieu, he went on to make the perceptive comment that:

> In Scotland you retain your social position after death, and in the cemeteries the rich refuse to lie beside the poor. It may be so in other lands, but I never noticed class distinctions in a German or Swedish cemetery.[43]

Reinforcing what Edwin Muir wrote about social conditions in his book *Scottish Journey* (1936), Neill sided with MacDiarmid on the national question. As he put it:

> In political matters Scotland is nowhere. It accepts English rule with due servility, and, when London pulls the strings, the docile Scots forms fours and marches to fight for the all-powerful Imperialist Capitalism.

Echoing Grassic Gibbon's observation about Scottish slums in Glasgow and Dundee being much worse than their English counterparts, he suggested rather surprisingly that 'possibly slums strike one forcibly in Scotland because of the innate feeling of equality among men that the Scots have'.[44]

At that time, when Neill displayed an unusual interest in concrete social conditions in workers' communities, Gibbon and the English historian Allen Hutt had raised general awareness about Scottish slums. After detailing the almost unimaginable social conditions in industrial Scotland, Hutt said:

> Capitalist society inflicts on the workers of Glasgow the barbarous living conditions that have now been sufficiently exposed; and in this way it bears the criminal responsibility for the brutal fact that Glasgow has traditionally had an infant mortality rate far greater than any other city.[45]

The tradition of struggle encouraged and developed by John Maclean was still a catalyst for opposition to capitalism. In reponse to a British Socialist Party 'Demonstration for Russia' a correspondent in Glasgow had as early as 1920 reported in *The Call* that:

> The Scots are a slow people, but when they do move, well - they do. Besides, as you must know, the English revolution will be a Scotch Revolution. And that's that.[46]

With the death of Maclean in 1923, the Scottish labour movement was, though increasingly de-radicalised, still more militant than its English counterpart. By the 1930s the Scottish national question was, however, pushed into the background by those 'internationalists' who turned 'internationalism into a form of international jingoism'. Nevertheless writers like Neill and Muir helped to defend the radical Scots sense of nationality in the spirit and name of Rosa Luxemburg.

Neill did not, of course, develop in a vacuum: he was the product of the radical educational milieu created by John Maclean and such pioneering women teachers of the Scottish Socialist Teachers' Society as Helen Currie, Mary Shennan, Madge Nelson and Mary Guthrie. Before the 1960s Scottish radical writers like Neill and James Barke were dependent on the London publishing houses; and, if anyone went against the dominant culture of 'A Very English Socialism', it was near-impossible to support oneself as an independent writer or teacher.

The Scottish Socialist Teachers' Society was formed in 1908 and its critique of State education opened up the space for Neill in the 1920s. By contrast, English socialist teachers did not form a Teachers' Labour League until 1925. (Incidentally, it was much less critical of capitalism than its Scottish counterpart had been). This did not, however, inhibit T. C. Smout in his book *A Century of the Scottish People, 1830-1950* - the work of an academic who, as one of my students said, 'could not count' - from portraying Scots history down to 1950 as a history of undiluted compliance and docility.[47]

When he developed his own critique of State schools inside the Independent Labour Party in the late 1920s and 1930s, there is no evidence that James Barke was influenced by Neill's books on education. Even so, he gave lectures, wrote mostly unpublished articles and agitated for a fundamental transformation of State schools, including the abolition of corporal punishment. Under the continuing influence of John Maclean's hostility to the Anglo-Scottish ruling-class 'democratic intellect', Barke was reflecting Scottish radical attitudes notwithstanding the possibility that he had been belted at Tulliallan.

In their radical ideas towards State schooling, Scottish socialists were in advance of their time. Certainly, Barke put great emphasis on the need for libertarian or progressive education. Furthermore, in his first novel *The World His Pillow* (1933), he devoted several pages of his first chapter, entitled 'The Highland Laddie', to two brutal teachers - a man and a woman - and belting. He focused on exposing the hypocrisy surrounding Bible teaching in particular; and he lauded to the high heavens the decency of the ordinary people on 'Balcreggan estate'. At the same time as he was saying similar things to what Neill was saying in his books, Barke wrote:

> Discipline was one of the important things at Glenaraig Public School. His [MacLaren's] favourite maxim was: 'Bring up a child in the way it should go, and when it is old it will not depart from it.' MacLaren had his moments when he afforded himself the luxury of being lenient. They were few, it is true; but nevertheless they were sufficiently numerous to give unobserving people

a wrong impression regarding his views on crime and punishment.[48]

In the 1930s Neill's head and heart remained in the Scotland with which he had had 'a bitter-sweet' relationship. And in Scotland up to the period between the two wars, the Falkirk-born novelist James Drawbell dissected the heritage of the land of the 'democratic intellect':

> Education has always played an important part in Scottish life. It is a faith instilled into one, as potent as the country's religion. The two merge beautifully together into a single credo: salvation and reward through trial and error.

Yet in his same autobiographical volume, *Scotland: Bitter-Sweet*, he could also write without any sense of apparent contradiction that:

> You conformed in this homeland of mine, or you stagnated. Or you became one of the forty thousand men and women each year who emigrated from it.[49]

By 1944, when Neill published his book *Hearts Not Heads In The School*, he was much more pessimistic about a new democratic education developing in the State schools after the war against fascism than was the then optimistic Mackenzie. As Neill put it:

> Today, in the autumn of 1944, education is almost front-page news... We are all handicapped by our ignorance of what tomorrow is going to be. If we are to return to our previous system of a capitalist society with an East and a West End that meet only on the street, education will continue to be a divided affair, with schools for the poor and schools for the rich, and any planning will be a compromise formation with Class as a humiliating factor. If our ruling classes, faced with the possibility of a Socialist Britain, go Fascist, and if a class war results, then education planning will be held up for a generation.[50]

277

However, the tendency that manifested itself in his earliest books, to expect socialism from a strong State, was seen yet again.

Nevertheless he was in advance of many of his radical contemporaries in finally seeing through Russian 'communism'. In this same book, published in 1944, he wrote:

> And so many of us who looked to Russia to lead the way in politics and education must sigh, and decide to plough our lonely furrows. We have many things to learn from the Soviet Union, but we have nothing to learn from it in education and a new orientation to creative, spiritual life.[51]

But, although Neill's books were not easily accessible in public libararies in many parts of Scotland in the 1930s and 1940s, they were often to be found on the open shelves in England. Certainly, I and my fellow young socialists in Stirlingshire did not learn anything about Neill until I became a student at Newbattle Abbey College, Dalkeith, in 1952. But in a private conversation a radical who became a distinguished English writer and historian told me of Neill's impact on his life in the 1940s. Though this socialist writer wishes to remain anonymous, I persuaded him to write a few notes on this early influence in his life. As he put it:

> Now, as to Neill, I 've thought about it, and the best thing is to tell the plain truth. When I was 12 my extremely authoritarian father, a Merchant Navy officer who had a heavy hand with his belt and whom I feared and hated, warned me that, if I masturbated, I would lose "the equivalent of a pint of blood" each time I did so. This did not make much physiological sense to me, but I was still very much in awe of my father. At 13, I was admitted to the 'adult' library; my father was by now out in Iraq dredging the Shatt al Arab, and was to remain there for some five years; thanks to freedom from his censorship I was able for the first time to read freely. I devoured A. S. Neill: first the Domine books, then *That Dreadful School* and some of the others (*Problem Child* and *Problem Parent*, I think).

By my fifteenth birthday, in February 1942, Neill's thought had had a profoundly liberating effect on me.

Here was a kindly, wise, life-loving writer who hated the infliction of pain on children, and who exposed what he called the "masturbation Verbot" as pernicious nonsense. Here, in fact, was a surrogate father, very different from the tyrant whom fate had bestowed upon me. And whatever hostile critics say about Summerhill, and whatever nonsense Neill swallowed from Reich, I still have a deep affection for him, and gratitude towards him for switching a light on inside my head, and for showing me the way out of the stifling mental prison in which I'd been brought up.

And that was the point: the importance of Neill in bringing many men and women from middle-class backgrounds into prominence within the left-wing of the workers' movement.

When Wilhelm Reich published his pioneering book on *The Mass Psychology of Fascism* (1933), it was inevitable that he would influence Neill. As an exiled socialist in America, Reich became eccentric and odd as he clashed with the American authorities. As a result of the development of his strange ideas about capitalism and mental health, in 1954 the Food and Drug Administration of the U.S.A ordered the 'banning and *burning* of all of Reich's books'.[52]

However, when Neill contributed to a book by several writers on Wilheim Reich in 1957, he expressed rather absurd opinions about the Reich affair. And he wrote to the exiled Austrian: 'If Dulles and Ike and Macmillan and Krushchev are all sane then you are mad, and I am all for madness'. Then he added:

> Many a time I have heard Reich say that our asylums are full of people who cannot live in a mad world outside. My own lay opinion is that he was so far in advance of all of us that his personality could not stand the strain of his intense insight into the world's neurosis... I cannot think Reich became crazy. He may have shown himself capable of illusion. We all have more or less paranoidal

fantasies. To believe that an American Federal Court was instigated from Moscow is no more odd than believing that communism is kind and loving.[53]

By the 1950s Neill was disillusioned with all politics. In his book *The Free Child* (1953) he had already written:

'In the years following the October Revolution Russian education was free; children could choose to learn or play; they had self-government in their schools... Today we see our hopes shattered.'[54] But Neill continued to teach and write; and Summerhill school was at the centre of all his projects. Howwever, during the 1960s and 1970s he remained a marginal figure in the world of education: a figure out of touch with his native Scotland except through correspondence.

In Max Rafferty's book *Summerhill: For and Against* (1973), a right-wing American educationalist asserted that 'It [Summerhill] degrades true learning to the status of an organised orgy'. Paul Goodman, a Trotskyist turned anarchist, was also very critical of Neill's project. Even so, he did admit that:

'Neill reacted against the trend to 1984 as Orwell came to call it, against obedience, authoritarian rules, organisational role-playing instead of being, the destruction wrought by competition and grade-getting.'[55]

But, as Neill faded into the background, Mackenzie came into prominence. Influenced by his non-authoritarian Christian father - a man who took egalitarianism very seriously indeed - Mackenzie was self-confident and sure of himself from an early age. Unlike Neill, Mackenzie was not enchanted in the 1930s by either Marxism or the Bolshevik revoution, though as he experienced the deepening corruption of Parliamentary Labourism in the early 1950s he became increasingly interested in the factors responsible for the degeneration of the October Revolution of 1917.

R. F. Mackenzie:A Radical's Early Odyssey

Though R. F. Mackenzie was not so prolific a writer of books as A. S. Neill, he was more of a 'doer' or activist. Much closer to the chalk-face of the real tradition of Scottish radical culture from the eighteenth century, he was interested in political action and activity as much as in metaphysics. Under the influence of Neill's ideas, he taught in 'experimental' schools in Switzerland and England in the early 1930s. He once told me that Grassic Gibbon's *A Scots Quair* had helped to 'stiffen' his hatred of fascism.[56] He contributed talks, ideas and inspiration informally to the labour movement in the north of Scotland from his teenage years, and his latent radicalism was developed during 'the devil's decade' of the 1930s.

Mackenzie went to the local school at Turriff before going on to Robert Gordon's College, where he became Dux or 'head pupil'.. He graduated Master of Arts from the University of Aberdeen in 1931. After trying his hand at journalism and casual teaching in England, his short spell in Nazi Germany was not accidental: in love with books and learning, though also in search of experience, he already knew that the answers to life's puzzles could not be found in books alone.

When Mackenzie and Hunter Diack published their youthful book *Road Fortune: An account of a cycling journey through Europe* in 1935, no one could have predicted that Mackenzie would become one of the great socialist-humanist radicals of this century. And yet the hints of the latent radicalism - a radicalism simultaneously Scottish and international - were evident in his first book.

When he wrote to me in April 1986 about his religious upbringing, he went on to say:

> I was teaching in Germany during the Hitler pogroms and on Kristall Nacht (the Night of the Broken Glass) in November 1938 I returned late from work to find my room, in the house of a Jewish family, smashed. For two or three weeks thereafter I slept in the house (my passport under my pillow) while my Jewish host and his wife, fearful of being taken away in the darkness to a concentration camp, slept in a friend's house.
>
> An Aberdonian friend and I made an excursion into Holland to transport Dutch Jews' valuables

that would help these German Jews when finally they got their exit permits from Hitlerite Germany. My concern for the German Jews was not religious. Political, rather, and literary. Heine had been 'a soldier in the Liberation War of Humanity''' and I was proud to be a private soldier in the same war. Einstein was a spokesman for humanity. Several Jews, in widely different spheres, spoke in words that vibrated to the core of my being, echoing my upbringing. Wesker wrote a play about Jerusalem, too. It was a natural idiom for us to use.[57]

Radicalised by his personal experience of fascism in Nazi Germany, he saw himself as an old-fashioned Scottish-International radical rather than a Marxist.

Joining the the Royal Air Force in 1939 and serving with Bomber Command as a navigator throughout the Second World War, Mackenzie became increasingly critical of the degeneration of the Bolshevik revolution and the 'patriotism' of the Communist Party of Great Britain. As a result of the RAF's wartime political education classes, he became convinced of the need for international solidarity after the war and the importance for emancipation of mass education.

The horrors of the Second War World played a major role in turning Mackenzie into an anti-militarist. In his essay introducing the left-wing play *Jotters*, he said:

Scotland conceals ugly reality from its young or hurries them past it with vague generalisations. I want to give you two examples. It was an incident in my early days in the RAF that exposed for me the ugly reality of war. One fine day in 1941 we were doing bayonet drill, sticking the bayonet into straw-filled sacks, pulling the bayonet out and advancing against the next row of sacks. The corporal explained that it would be much more difficult to extract a bayonet from an enemy belly. That was because of the suction. You have to kick the bayonetted belly hard with your left foot and at the same time pull with all your might. That piece of realism had been missing from the dictated answers we memorised to pass Higher History.

During that war he read the writings of the American progressive educationalist John Dewey; and he agreed with the Dewey who wrote during an earlier world war, in 1916, that: 'Thinking which is not connected with incerease of efficiency in action, and with learning about ourselves and the world in which we live has something the matter with it'.[58]

Certainly, Mackenzie's father had been the catalyst behind the belated radicalism that made him, like Grassic Gibbon, 'the speak of the place'. Since he spent much of the Second World War in South Africa and developed an impressive knowledge of the Boers and their history and culture, he became a practitioner of the radical Scots own 'democratic intellect'. In his book *A Search For Scotland*, he argued that (1) that war radicalised millions of people everywhere and (2) gave rise to illusions about the Labour Party's potential for introducing real change. As he explained:

> The 1939-45 war brought a clarifying of ideas, and an expansion of knowledge. After initial disadvantage, the postman understood the Theory of Flight as well as the university graduate, and the clerk asked basic, concrete questions about a cold front that made the Met. officer scratch his head. The war presented to us the contrasting experiences that made us look again at our own, stirring us into new awareness. Soldiers' minds were fertilised with ideas that had their origin in the ends of the earth. [59]

Anticipating the coming struggles of the Black workers in South Africa, he nevertheless placed much of his hope in the Labour Party during the two decades after the end of the war.

Mackenzie got married in Galashiels in 1946. He left Galashiels in 1952 when he was appointed as the Principal Teacher of English at Templehall Secondary School in Kirkcaldy. But, although he remained there until 1957, when he was appointed as Headmaster of Braehead Secondary School in Buckhaven, he was already a controversial figure. A small number of radical teachers were on the staff of Templehall at that time - for example, Ronnie Wood and Jack Stewart - and they openly identified with left-wing socialist agitations including the Campaign for Nuclear Disarmament and the abolition of capital punishment. Yet, despite Mackenzie's unilateral abolition of the corporal punishment and advocacy of School Councils run by the pupils, an apparently radical Labour administration appointed him to the Headmaster's post at Buckhaven.[60]

The Links Between Neill and Mackenzie

Antonio Labriola insisted that ideas did not 'drop from the sky'. In 1968 Mackenzie told me that he had been influenced by Neill's book *Is Scotland Educated?* But, although Neill asserted in that book that he preferred 'communism to capitalism', Mackenzie was more interested in his ideas on education. Unlike Neill, Mackenzie developed what he later described as 'illusions' about the Labour Party as a radical social and political force. As a thinker who gobbled books in the 1930s, Mackenzie's radical ideas owed much to the stubborn radicalism of his Gaelic ancestors, and particularly his father.

Even in the 1960s and very early 1970s Mackenzie still believed in the importance of a high standard of literacy for his working-class pupils. By contrast, Neill wrote to me in 1972 to say:

> Not sure if a high standard of literacy has much value. Guy like [Malcolm] Muggeridge is highly literate but has he anything to say? How many in Scotland were literate last century? The genius George Douglas Brown, the inferior sentimental Barrie, the good poet Edwin Muir. But I have long been out of touch with Scottish literature.

Furthermore, he insisted that:

> Bob Mackenzie was not trying to follow me or anyone else; braver than I for he fought inside the Establishment. I hear he is off work ill. A good lad is Bob.[61]

Initially trusted by the Labour administration in Fife, Mackenzie soon attracted their hostility by attempting to put progressive educational ideas into practice, including the abolition of corporal punishment. It was during the years at Braehead, however, that his books *A Question of Living* (1963), *Escape from the Classroom* (1965) and *The Sins of the Children* (1967) were published. Attacking the British Labour Party's defence of educational apartheid and class privilege, he made powerful enemies. Yet, despite the fact that the 1960s was an enlightened, liberal and radical decade seemingly 'dominated' by strong trade unions, Mackenzie was dismissed from his post in 1968.

In his books *A Question of Living* and *Escape from the Classroom*, he depicted his personal experiences as Headmaster of the junior secondary school in Buckhaven he called 'Coal Town' school. At a radical moment in Scottish history, when the 7.84 theatre company was focusing on the historical rather than the contemporary oppression of working people, and portraying them as cardboard-like figures, Mackenzie was almost unique in his identification of the Labour Party's role in helping to oppress workers' children.

During the comparative full employment of the 1960s, in the junior secondary 'Coal Town' school Mackenzie could not escape from his pupils' massive social and psychological problems. So he decided to expose these problems before Scottish society. As he developed new educational techniques by taking increasing numbers of his pupils into the countryside to learn about nature, he antagonised the orthodox Labour adminstration.

In 1963 and 1965 he used his books *A Question of Living* and *Escape from the Classroom* to portray his pupils' often awful lives, and he exposed the British Labour Party's shallow radicalism at a time when many of us had illusions about the Party's efficacy as an instrument of social change. But he was always his own man, and not a man for all seasons.

Plunging deeper into the social causes of workers' oppression and exploitation than was common on the Left at that time, he wrote thus:

> It will take a long time for the Labour Party to realise that a traditionally-educated child will become a conformist. You cannot change the political system unless your change the educational system.[62]

By getting closer to the working folk in 'Coal Town', he tried to interpret the world from his pupils' standpoint and challenged traditional teaching methods:

Together with too little attention to the significance of individual words goes too little attention to the machniery of fitting words together... Speech, being a living thing, just will not fall neatly into the pattern drawn up for it by the grammarians. Some teachers say that you use a full stop to show a pause in speech, but people run sentences together as Lewis Grassic Gibbon does in *Sunset Song*, which better reflects what he calls the "speak" of the people.[63]

Moreover, in *A Question of Living*, he defended such a prosaic thing as higher wages for steel workers and teachers. But the radical Headmaster refused to be uncritical of his fellow teachers, and he reported that:

I have heard a woman teacher, normally kind and intelligent, refer to her class of girls of slightly under-average intelligence as "just dross". She was not angrily expressing an emotion about a class which had been giving trouble. She was, she imagined, expressing a scientific fact, based on a psychological measure of their intelligence.[64]

He also argued that: 'If your treasure is a child and that child is in a junior secondary school, your heart will be in a junior secondary school. But few, if any, Cabinet Ministers in this country (whether Conservative or socialist) have children who attend a junior secondary school'.[65]

But, although he attracted the support of many Scottish progressives like Gavin Maxwell and James Kennoway at the same time as he moved in a nationalist direction, he refused to identify with such bourgeois nationalist groups as the Saltire Society. Criticising the books published by that Society, he wrote:

The pupils and I alike found them dull, their idiom and outlook alien to Coal Town. We did not recognise ourselves or anybody we knew in these pages. This was a Scottish idiom and vocabulary and background no longer true of industrial Fife.[66]

Refusing to be a respectable conformist, Mackenzie left an important legacy to posterity.

More important than his irriating radicalism, from an Anglo-Scottish educational Establishment viewpoint, was his defence of those working-class pupils who refused to have corporal punishment inflicted upon them. In a striking passage in *The Sins of the Children*, he said:

> Next day another, white with anger and frustration, came to report that, during the showing of a film, this boy had been whistling. He had refused to take the belt for this. I spoke to the boy, after the teacher had returned to his class. He admitted frankly (as indeed on all occasions on which I had spoken to him) that he had been whistling. He said he hadn't whistled deliberately. (Like a girl who years earlier had been asked why she swore at a teacher; she said 'it had just come out.')

And therefore he did not see why he should be punished. Unfortunately, the 'authorities' in education thought otherwise.

But predicting the further alienation, estrangement and rebellion of the working-class pupils in Scottish - and English - junior secondary schools, he wrote: 'It is anybody's guess how long the politeness and forbearance will last. Five years? Perhaps ten? But the raising of the school leaving age in 1970 is likely to accelerate the pace, and in that session great extra pressures will be put on the schools, pressures that we may not be able to contain.'[67]

Analysing the dimension of social class in secondary school education everywhere, Mackenzie also glanced at American education inside the citadel of Western capitalism. Exposing the hypocrisy of all ruling classes, including the Russian one, he said:

> The Americans gave other reasons for the failure of working-class children in the education race. They are more difficult to keep quiet and therefore teachers spend more time just trying to keep them quiet than in teaching them.[68]

Since he believed that the rich potential creativity of his working-class pupils was being suppressed and stifled by an oppressive educational system, he openly identified with his rebellious pupils.

'A Labour Man' turns into a Radical Educationalist

By 1968 Mackenzie was challenging head-on the whole traditional conformist and authoritarian ethos of Scottish education. As Headmaster of the 'Coal Town' school in Buckhaven, he was [in 1968] forced to allow recruiting officers from the British army to address his pupils. When I was at Braehead for a couple of months in 1968, he upset many teachers on his staff by inviting American speakers from the Students for a Democratic Society to counter ruling-class propaganda by speaking to staff and pupils on the brutality and horrors of the Vietnam war. To get rid of an irrepressible critic, the Labour County Council closed the school down.

Athough he had enjoyed his spell of teaching in the Borders, it was Fife that made the biggest impact on his ideas about education and radicalism. Towards the end of his life, when he was struggling against cancer, he wrote:

> I was a schoolteacher in Fife for sixteen years and tried to communicate to pupils (the sons and daughters of miners, factory workers, linnoleum workers, motor mechanics, shopkeepers) an awareness of this parcel of earth on which they had found themselves. In the summer term the school chaplain, the Rev. Robin Mitchell, who was the BBC's bird-man, took the pupils on country walks through Keil's Den and over to Pitscottie.
>
> The pupils, freed from the classroom pressures, became different people, relaxed, smiling, reacting sensuously to the natural world. Sometimes in their exuberance they hardly noticed Mitchell, but it was he who had noiselessly pulled back this gauzy curtain and let them into a new world.[69]

When he discovered that the Labour members of the Education Committee in Fife were the most passionate defenders of traditional discipline, including corporal punishment, he felt compelled to appeal to the wider labour movement and socialist groups to campaign for the abolition of corporal punishment. What he could not stomach was the new role of the Labour Party bosses in initiating anti-democratic behaviour. At the end of his life he recalled what 'a Labour miner' and Provost (or Mayor) of Buckhaven and Methil told him:

> In the old days of the Tories we would be standing about talking, waiting for the county council meeting to begin, and the Earl of Elgin would say, "Well, gentlemen, maybe we should make a start. But now we have a Labour convenor, and an official comes smartly into the room and orders us, "Be upstanding for the County Convenor." We stand up beside our seats round the table and the County Convenor strides in and says, "Be seated, gentlemen," and we all sit down and the meeting begins.

When he told those stories at countless meetings, members of the CPGB would agree with him until he insisted: 'It happened that way in Russia, too'.[70]

In 1946 Mackenzie had been appointed as a teacher of English at Galashields Secondary School in the Borders. As a trade unionist and socialist activist, who was basically interested in democratic and humanist education, he was already known in socialist circles. When I first met him in a small tea-shop in Lochgelly in 1962, he was reading Raya Dunayevskaya's *Marxism and Freedom* (1958). He immediately told me that he was becoming increasingly disillusioned with the Labour Party's pro-capitalist educational policies, and that he had been encouraged by Dunayevskaya's conception of complete freedom for all human beings, including those in Russia and Africa.

Out shopping with my wife in Kirkcaldy in 1968, we met Janet Leslie, a former Principal of Fod Nursing College, Dunfermline, where my wife had been a student nurse. On learning that I was doing some temporary teaching at Braehead Junior Secondary School, where Mackenzie was the controversial radical Headmaster or 'Red', she told me that she had taught alongside him at Galashiels. Asked if he had been 'a character' even then, she replied: 'Characters and radicals are born, not made'. In those years, as she recalled, he was a humane and optimistic teacher - a man particularly devoted to all his pupils and to democratic teaching.

However, in 1968 prominent Scottish, English and European intellectuals and influential segments of the Scottish labour movement rallied behind Mackenzie's vision of democratic education in the State schools. Although he did not lack his working-class critics in Fifeshire, many Fifers supported Mackenzie. And even popular newspaper like the *Daily Record* were forced to provide Mackenzie's supporters with space to express their views.

In 1968 the Labour administration in Aberdeen appointed Mackenzie as Headmaster of Summerhill Academy. Despite sustained opposition to his appointment from the most right-wing and reactionary elements in Scottish society, he remained until 1974 at Summerhill Academy, named in honour of A. S. Neill's school in England.

In his book *The Unbowed Head: Events at Summerhill Academy, 1968-74* (1974), with a foreword by Harry Reid, Mackenzie defended his stewardship during the turbulent years when he tried to introduce democratic educational principles. The Labour administrators in Aberdeen, though allegedly more advanced than their counterparts in Fife, could not tolerate the intervention of a real practitioner of the 'democratic intellect'. It was an old story.

When he published in the *Glasgow Herald* on 10 December 1987 a tribute to the greatest radical educationalist since the days of John Maclean, Harry Reid described the events at Summerhill. As he put it:

> Before he was suspended (as it turned out, sacked; he never taught again) on 1 April, 1974, R. F. Mackenzie was allowed to speak to Aberdeen Education Committee. He gave a supremely eloquent address. It was a public meeting, and many people who witnessed it thought it was the most moving speech they had ever heard. He spoke of children with wounds in their souls. He could have cured these wounds, but he was not allowed to because he had been given a divided staff. He was not on trial, he said; it was the comprehensive school that was on trial.

Refusing to conceal his utter disenchantment with the existing social order in the West as well as East, he tried to turn his disruptive pupils' creativity into a positive force for fundamental social change.

When I interviewed Harry Reid, Deputy Editor of *The Herald*, on 29 June 1995, he told me that Bob Middleton and Andrew Walls had spoken up in defence of Mackenzie. Then he continued:

> They both made very strong speeches, but nothing to compare with the actual climactic speech that Mackenzie made. And it was really magnificent. I mean, people often speak about Martin Luther King's great speech in 1968, you know the famous King speech was the first great speech of the television age, captured on television. I wish there had been television cameras in there. We all have our views on television, in some ways it is a pernicious influence; but I wish that speech had been recorded for posterity, the way he delivered it.[71]

As former educational correspondent of *The Scotsman* newspaper, Reid was better informed about Mackenzie's purpose than most of his counterparts in the Scottish press. When he summed up the achievements of the Summerhill Headmaster, Reid said:

> He had a felicitous and lucid prose style, a testimony to his own traditional education at Robert Gordon's College. But he came to regard his own formal education as worthless, just as he came to regard examinations as a tyrannical anti-educational device for oppression, and just as he came to regard disruptive pupils as the salt of the earth.[72]

Unlike most Scottish - or indeed other - Headmasters, Mackenzie deepened the divisions among his own teachers by supporting the abolition of the belt and the founding of a School Council in which pupils could voice their own opinions. Far from this being acceptable in the so-called land of the 'democratic intellect', it upset the Calvinist

291

(and Catholic) defenders of the *status quo*. Nevertheless, in *The Unbowed Head*, he argued that:

> In spite of the difficulties and discouragements, I was heartened by the signs of enquiry and original thinking and independence that emerged and gave us ground for believing that if only teachers could overcome their fear of 'pupil power', the Council would be successful.[73]

But, although his publishers Collins refused to publish *The Unbowed Head* because there was no longer any evidence of 'the humane feelings' in his earlier books, Gordon Brown (now Labour Shadow Chancelllor in Parliament and a real shadow of his former radical self) persuaded the Edinburgh University Students' Publication Board to publish it. Refusing to be silenced or gagged, Mackenzie gave occasional university lectures at the same time as he addressed small left-wing groups. Although he remained critical of the Scottish National Party, he increasingly identified with the Scots struggle for national independence from 'Great Britain'. In the last chapter of this book, entitled 'A Cultural Revolution', he said:

> The people of Scotland are coming of age, asking questions about how to use the heritage on which they are entering. Our purpose as teachers is to educate the young so that when they grow up they will be adequately equipped with the understanding to take over their heritage. Like Zimbabwe, Scotland is an emergent Nation.[74]

During the next few years he worked on a long manuscript entitled *Curriculum for a Cultural Revolution;* and it was finished by 1979. Collins refused to publish it, though just after his death in 1987 they published his huge book *A Search for Scotland*. In response to my tribute to him in the *Times Higher Educational Supplement*, the Open University expressed interest in the unpublished manuscript before offering some pretext about the times not being right for such a book. It remains unpublished.

Unlike Neill, whose disillusionment with the process of democratic struggle was quite negative by the time of his death, Mackenzie did not lose the simplicity of his heritage of Scottish-International radical culture. But there were brief moments when he, too, felt despair. In the letter he sent to me dated 3 April 1986, he said apropos the Israel in which he placed so much hope after 1948:

> Who would have believed that an oppressed minority, having suffered unspeakable cruelty in the German Holocaust, would have jumped with such alacrity into the role of oppressors? The warlike Israeli government, right wing and left wing alike, burning, torturing, clearing out minority populalations, fraternising with Reagan and American Capital, have forced humanity to reconsider their basic assumptions about the essential goodness of human nature. Few things in our incalculable twentieth century have so shaken me as the relapse of the righteous Jewish dispensation into barbarity. Nothing is clear any more. Everything is possible. Were we wrong to have rejected the Scottish Kirk's assertion of original sin?[75]

But in his innermost heart of radical hearts, he did not believe in original sin.

Indeed, his secularism hardened, though he continued to use religious metaphors with great effect when he argued the case for democratic socialism from below. When he wrote to me on 25 November 1983, he said:

> Two days ago our son Alasdair was married to a Singaporeen lassie. It amazed me (although it shouldn't) that when she talks of her parents (of Chinese origin) in Singapore, they are exactly like country people we know in staunch Aberdeenshire villages - the same interests, habits, outlook. It is amazing the extent to which my upbringing in a capitalist society has concealed from me our common humanity. The only difference between her and any other Aberdeen lassie is that she has a calmer attitude to life (perhaps because of her Buddhist upbringing) than others in Aberdeen. It

was the first time we'd attended a Registry Office wedding. It was quiet and dignified. Then we went to a hotel. The waiter looked around and fixed on me and said 'would you say grace?' There was a hush and I realised there was no way out. I thought of Burns's Selkirk grace, but I was not sure if I remebered it properly. So I said, 'For what we are about to receive...' and then realised (as Bunyan might have said) a capitalist God straddling the path, and for once in my life I thought quietly and sidestepped him and continued, 'for what we are about to receive, may we be truly thankful. Amen.[76]

As a man he had his faults; but who has not? Yet he was never pretentious, false or superficial.

I remember being in the chair at a Marx centenary meeting in Falkirk in early 1983 when Mackenzie expressed regret that he had not read more of Marx's writings in his earlier years. But, as a powerful voice of simplicity and dignified radicalism, he spoke for the most oppressed segments of our society and for all of the outspoken radicals and dissidents depicted in this book.

With his strong empathy for the coalminers and their children, he had defended them in an article in *The Scotsman* newpaper in November 1963.[77] Then, during the British coalminers' strike of 1984-85, he defended the strike in the correspondence columns of that same newspaper, spoke at meetings in support of the miners in Aberdeen, and helped to collect money for them. It was little wonder that the Anglo-Scottish Establishment hated everything he stood for.

Acknowledging his debt to A. S. Neill in letters and newspaper articles over many years, it was in his 1987 essay on *Jotters* that Mackenzie identified with the national and the class struggle and summed up the beliefs of successive generations of Scottish-International radicals:

We are coming up to a major crisis in human history, a head-on clash between two irreconcilable views of human personality. There is the Odyssey view which has shaped Western society and is propagated in most classrooms in Scotland, a view in which most of us are seen as a mute, inglorious rabble, second-class citizens. The other view insists on the worth of every human being, his or her right to the dignity of full membership of the human race. I tried to describe it as recognition of the worth and infinite potential of every human being. It's an ancient idea that survives in our minds in spite of aristocrats' and capitalist control over our thoughts. Three thousand years ago in Jerusalem a temple singer expressed it in the speech pattern of his time, and more simply than I've done. 'Ye are gods; and all of you are children of the Most High'. He said, 'All of you, YE ARE GODS; AND ALL OF YOU ARE CHILDREN OF THE MOST HIGH.'

Neill wrote much more than Mackenzie; and it a testimony to their seriousness during an era of television and news-bites that both still play a role in shaping how posterity evaluates the radical tradition. However, despite the worldwide counter-revolution that began in the 1980s, Neill's ideas have gained greater attention than Mackenzie. Though quite comfortably off himself, Mackenzie was more sensitive to workers' poverty and specific material oppression than was his mentor Neill. In concluding this chapter, I would like to quote from my tribute to Mackenzie in *The Times Educational Supplement*:

He was a unique figure in the educational world... He was a good man committed to the good society. If he sometinmes offended the doctrinare Left as much as the horrified doctrinaire Right, he was a dreamer and a visionary who rejected the competitive and hierarchical principles of the 'business culture'. He will not easily be replaced, though his example of critical criticism will continued to inspire all those who believe in the spirit of free enquiry and practice.[78]

Chapter Eight

The New World Order and The Experience of Defeat: A Born-Again Radicalism

The Scottish literary tradition is quite clear. You speak out for the people all the time. Whoever or whatever happens to coincide with the people's tradition, you back them up and you don't split hairs. That's how you keep with the thing. Solidarity without compromise.

Thurso Berwick

We want a socialist world not because we have the conceit that men would therefore be happy...but because we feel the moral imperative in life itself to raise the human condition, even if this should ultimately mean no more than man's suffering has been lifted to a higher level.

Norman Mailer

The 1970s saw the crystallisation of an idea that had been forming in Scotland for some time, namely that socialism could profitably be harnessed to a developing Scottish political identity The Scottish socialist historian James D. Young produced a number of challenging essays on Red Clydesider John Maclean, and his *The Rousing of the Scottish Working Class* (1979) ably illustrated the links between Scottish radicalism and the struggle for independence.

Willy Maley (Cultural Devolution, 1994).

Scotland and The Worldwide Counter-Revolution.

The ruling classes' international counter-revolution began in Scotland in 1979 with the election of Margaret Thatcher as the Prime Minister of Great Britain. She was known ironically in Scotland as 'Queen' Thatcher, and set the new counter-revolutionary agenda for her American and Russian counterparts. Elected to the American presidency in 1980, Ronald Reagan was soon able to assist Thatcher to guide the collapsing 'communist' economies of Russia and Eastern Europe towards 'democratic capitalism'. By 1991 Boris Yeltsin, who had just been elected as the President of 'the Russian Republic', was more than enthusiastic about co-operating with Thatcher and George Bush in trying to establish the inherent 'democracy' of the free play of market forces.[1] This international counter-revolution consisted in privatisation, de-regulation, mass unemployment, the creation of dirt-cheap wages and assaults on trade unions. As an inextricable part of this process, Scotland did not escape 'the winds of change.'

Yet, despite a succession of British Labour and Tory governments after 1945, the Scottish demand for self-government has become increasingly assertive. Far from following the international drift to the Right in politics, the Scots as a whole have, by increasingly rediscovering their distinctive radical past, become more radical without yet resorting to the rioting that took place in English cities in 1981.

Moreover, in 1979 a majority of 'the very bastards of creation' - and particularly the working class - voted in a Referendum organised by the British government in response to the election of 11 Scottish Nationalist members of Parliament in 1979. The Scots insistent demands for an autonomous Scottish Parliament in Edinburgh could no longer be ignored. In four successive British general elections - in 1979, 1983, 1987 and 1992 - the majority of Scots rejected Thatcherite Toryism at the polls.

After 1979 in particular the Tory government did not - and does not - have a mandate to govern Scotland; and the Labour Party holds the majority of the Parliamentary seats for Scottish constituencies. Committed to devolution - or a Scottish Parliament for purely Scottish affairs - the Labour Party in Scotland has always been afraid to challenge the *status quo*. So it is crucial that socialists in Britain and elsewhere should support the Scots democratic struggle for self-government. However, in rediscovering their own radical cultural history, an increasingly number of Scots are sympathetic to radical socialist policies.

The prospects for putting democratic socialism from below back on the agenda are better than at any time since the First World War. Moreover, despite the return of the primitive capitalism of the years before 1939, the continuing and unprecedented cultural resurgence in Scotland, the voices of humanist democratic socialism or radicalism, are strong, articulate and attractive. At the very least, there is a strong possibility that Scotland could become 'a Tory-free zone' at the next British general election.

Yet, despite the Left's partial victories - for example, in sit-ins and resistance to factory and hospital closures - in the Athens of the North since 1979, there have been defeats, too. Inevitably, with the Brits' partial eradication of post-1945 welfare and health provisions, together with the advent of serious unemployment and the deregulation of higher education in favour of the well-off and privileged, Thatcherism has had some impact.

Defending the post-1945 social settlement in Britain as a whole, the Scottish journalist Joyce McMillan sums it up exceptionally well when she says:

> This new right is about the destruction and discrediting of all those bulwarks of political power, from public education systems to employment legislation, which are capable of protecting the poor, offering them dignity, civilising their lives.

By glancing back to the world she grew up in before deregulation and privatisation, she argues that:

> What I feel - what I know is that the State surrounded me, in my early life, set me free - to an extent that previous members of my family could not have imagined. I was free from the terror of disease that dominated poor people's lives in the age before proper sanitation, clean public water supplies, and the National Health Service.[2]

But the Scots have always been dour; and Scotland has been 'a wrong-resenting country' since 1707.

Scotland: Unknown Country, 1970-79

A product of the late 1960s, the Scottish cultural, literary and political magazine *Scottish International* was at the height of its influence in the mid-1970s, just before it became the victim of right-wing witch-hunters through letters published in *The Scotsman* newpaper. Together with the *New Edinburgh Review*, *Scottish International* made a big impact on the evolving radical thought of the time. As well as encouraging and fostering articles on Scotland and Scottish working-class history, they introduced the socialist humanism and subtle and inherently anti-authoritarian Marxism of the Italian thinker Antonio Gramsci. Gramsci's Marxism was introduced to a new generation of Scots by the tireless Scottish radical Hamish Henderson. And he was helped and encouraged by the warm, compassionate and heretical Father Anthony Ross.

Ross had worked with Hugh MacDiarmid in Edinburgh in the 1930s to keep alive the Scottish working class's threatened sense of its distinctive national and class awareness. By the 1970s he was emerging as an important social reformer; and he was very popular with students and homeless young people. Sympathetic to 'liberation theology', he, Mackenzie and *Scottish International* were detested by all sections of the Establishment, including the hierarchy of the Catholic Church.

Agitating and writing for social change and democratic radical socialism from below, Ross, Mackenzie and many others, who were not directly involved in Parliamentary politics, abandoned *aliases*. This reflected modern capitalism's deep and serious crises and modern Scots growing confidence. In one of his finest interviews in *Scottish International*, entitled 'Storms in our Time' (1970), Ross made unusually sharp criticisms of the existing social order. Distancing himself from the SNP, though not from the struggle for Scottish independence, he said:

> In my student days [in the 1930s] I was active in reviving the SNP in the university, but saw the SNP then as something that would be a radical movement. And the SNP now seems to me to be very much a middle-class bourgeois thing.[3]

In a powerful article in the same magazine, entitled 'Resurrection: A Diagnosis of Contemporary Scottish Culture and Society' (1970), Ross said:

> 'There is no strong image of Scotland to inspire a struggle with the economic and social problems which oppress people here today. There are still powerful elements to frustrate any radical analysis and programme which might be produced.'

But the Catholic priest, who taught Marxism, believed in socialist spirituality. Besides, in his thought-world of 'a new and holy mystery', he anticipated RESURRECTION not just in Scotland but in the world at large.[4] In the 1970s, too, Ross and Mackenzie lectured to my students at the University of Stirling, and I was afterwards informed that 'my "Bolshie" students' were always challenging the authorities at the Teachers' Training Colleges.

When I was appointed to the staff of the Department of History at the University of Stirling in 1970, Scotland was a much more outgoing, very optimistic, self-critical and internationalist country than the Scottish nation I had grown up in. All the same most Scottish universities were - and are - authoritarian and hierarchical, with no room for really radical thinkers like the real Scottish internationalists A.S.Neill, R.F.Mackenzie, R. D. Laing or Father Anthony Ross. On the surface at least, Scotland's newest and most innovative University was democratic; and before the Queen's visit to Stirling in 1973, Tom Cottrell, the Principal, was committed to educational experiment.

The formation of the John Maclean Society in 1968 - the year when R. F. Mackenzie was dismissed by a Labour administration for trying to introduce democratic education into a State school - highlighted the new mood of optimism on the Left in the Athens of the North. In 1972 the talented and neglected Mary Brooksbank published a collection of her poetry, *Sidlaw Breezes;* and in 1973 she published her autobiography, *No Sae Lang Syne: A Tale of This City.* She had always been in trouble with the Communist Party of Great Britain in 1930s for refusing to denounce Leon Trotsky; and she was only one of many unaffiliated Republican socialists who reappeared in the 1970s.[5] She upset the Anglo-Scottish academics with her song 'Love and Freedom', where she wrote:

No longer from industry's sons
Does Labour seek improvement,
The Cambridge and the Oxford Don
Have pinched the Labour Movement.

In Scotland as a whole, the history of radicalism and radical culture
was researched and explored with unprecedented depth, energy and
commitment. The trade unions and labour movement were stronger,
more assertive and more interested in labour history as well as cultural
activities. The years between 1970 and the election of Margaret Thatcher
as the *Brits'* (as distinct from the Scots) Prime Minister in 1979 were
characterised by radical workers' confidence, students' and workers'
sit-ins, factory occupations against redundancy and other threats to
working-class rights. Then, during the three general elections in 1974
and 1979, the Scottish National Party (SNP) succeeded first in electing
4 and then 11 members of Parliament.

In a powerful and perceptive essay, 'Cultural Devolution?
Representing Scotland in the 1970s', Willy Maley argued that:

> The collapse of Upper Clyde Shipbuilders in 1971
> and the general decline of heavy industry, read
> alongside the rising fortunes of the SNP, might
> lend credence to the view that the patriot was
> displacing the proletariat, rather than giving the
> Scottish workers a way of expressing their
> discontent in a different language from that of
> Labourism. But the miners' strikes of 1972 and
> 1974, and a strong communist presence in the
> Scottish National Union of Mineworkers (NUM),
> gave notice that the 1970s were going to be a
> battleground as far as industrial relations were
> concerned.[6]

In his wide-ranging essay, in which he was more critical of what he
described as 'Scottish socialist nationalism' than I would be, he
defended traditional Marxist internationalism at the same time as he
lambasted visionless *Labourism*.

Acknowledging that radical Scots like the perceptive Andrew Noble
and other dissidents had some sort of presence in the Scottish
universities, Maley focused on the nick or the jail. After criticising the

romantic Kailyard social pictures of a Scottish past that never existed, he said:

> Paradoxically, it was in a Scottish prison that arguably one of the most significant developments in terms of cultural politics took place, the opening of an institution which offers a compelling sidelight on the Scotland of the 1970s

Sketching the development of the Special Unit at Barlinnie prison, where one of my maternal uncles was a warden in the 1930s, and the transformation of Jimmy Boyle into a talented artist, he went on to say that 'Boyle's working-class autobiography, like Bill Douglas's *Trilogy*, demolished the myth of lost childhood innocence that had haunted Scottish culture, and brought home the bitter reality of social division by using individual portraits to epitomise the suffering of a class.' [7] But the important thing about Maley's essay is that he stresses the importance of workers' struggle for their rights as *a civilising* force.

Through the work of the Scottish 7.84 theatre company - and particularly John McGrath's *The Game's a Bogey* focusing on John Maclean, the internationally famous Clydeside socialist - radical and working-class history was popoularised. (No one in those years would have dreamt that rumours would circulate in the early 1990s that McGrath had been writing speeches for Neil Kinnock). But, in the 1970s, Dave Anderson, Hector MacMillan and Peter MacDougall used their plays to reinvent radical Scotland and, despite Thatcher's displeasure, turn it to the far Left.

Moreover Bill Forsyth and Bill Douglas made films about the Scotland of the common folk: honest, analytical and unashamed. In 1975 William McIlvanney established himself as an important Scottish novelist: *Docherty*, his novel about working-class life, made a big impact on Scottish consciousness. When he summed up the general developments in Scottish culture in the 1970s - and despite his quite justified suspicion of the most progressive nationalism - Maley said:

> Socialism allied to an inclusive Scottish nationalism offered a possible antidote to sectarianism and to xenophobic tendencies. The socialist nationalism embodied by John McGrath in the 1970s inspired the popular theatre of the 1980s; and in the 1990s

it engendered Artists for Independence, an organisation of Scottish writers and artists dedicated to a separate Scotland.[8]

In an editorial in the very the first issue of the quarterly magazine *Calgacus*, the editor, the tireless Lowland Scot Ray Burnett, wrote: '*Calgacus* is guilty of that most henious sin in the catalogues of the British Left - we admit that Scotland exists.' It carried articles on Scottish, including Gaelic culture and poetry - including my own piece on John Murdoch - and Sorley Maclean's poetry. Thoroughly internationalist and cultural, it was committed to the project of helping to create a socialist Scotland. But, although only three issues were published as a result of the big booksellers' reluctance to distribute it, *Calgacus* made an impact on a new generation of radical Scots and laid the foundations for the new Scottish Labour Party (SLP).[9]

In politics the advent of the breakaway SLP under the inspiration of Jim Sillars was an important development. Unnoticed by Henry M. Drucker, American author of *Breakaway: The Scottish Labour Labour Party* (SLP), such well-know radical Scots as R. F. Mackenzie, Father Anthony Ross and Kay Carmichael were on the verge of joining it. In private conversations both Mackenzie and Ross told me, in 1978, that they had been alienated by the authoritarian behaviour of Sillars. Certainly, Sillars did not improve his standing among radicals when he expelled the present author from the SLP for simply defending the democratic rights of the far-Left.

Attacking British *Labour's* support for European capitalism, Western imperialism and the Vietnam war, and arguing for a socialist Scotland, Sillars became a real and popular 'working-class hero'. More than any other single factor, his project came unstuck as a result of his inherited Labourist authoritarianism. In my opinion the failure of the SLP was not at all predestined; and with wiser leadership it could have produced a counterpoint to the middle-class nationalism of the SNP.

Appealing to the passionate socialist sympathies of many Scots, Sillars expressed the political as well as the cultural resurgence in the Scotland of the 1970s. When he analysed the openness of the SLP in 1976 before its disintegration, Drucker wrote:

So far from appearing cynical, this obviously incomplete series of slogans attracted a small number of *the most* intelligent political *thinkers* in

Scotland. Its very incompleteness suggested the possibility of joining and working towards a more comprehensive, more 'class-conscious' ideology. Tom Nairn, Bob Tait, and Jim Young, all prominent members of the Party, joined partly for this reason.p[10]

Other major Scottish radical books were published in the 1970s, including *The Unbowed Head* by R. F. Mackenzie (1975), *The Socialist Poems of Hugh MacDairmid*, edited by T. S. Law and Thurso Berwick (1978), and *The Rousing of the Scottish Working Class* (1979) by James D. Young.[11] Though the latter book upset some academic historians by openly siding with 'the people' against 'the system', as one reviewer put it, *The Rousing of the Scottish Working Class* was a best-seller.

When Hugh MacDiarmid, the complex Scottish poet, radical and opponent of the Anglo-Scottish ruling class, died in 1978, the Scottish people were more disaffected from the existing social order than ever before. At his graveside in September 1978, Seumas MacNeil, of the Glasgow College of Piping, played the 'Lament for the Children'.[12] Thanks to his hard work in resurrecting the culture and history of the Scottish working class, MacDiarmid would not be forgotten. And there is still a chance that Scotland will again make a significant contribution to the struggle for socialist internationalism.

The Decade of the 1980s: Scotland Remains Radical

At the very end of 1979 the quarterly magazine *Cencrastus* appeared; and it has survived until the present. Inspired to a large extent by the visionary Marxist Morris Blythman (Thurso Berwick) and Raymond Ross, the very first issue foreshadowed a promise it has largely fulfilled over sixteen years. Although it has expressed its strong Scottish nationalist commitment to promoting the work of Hugh MacDiarmid, *Cencrastus* is a unique voice of the thirty-seven varieties of Scottish radicalism. There is no equivalent to it in England, though the latter country has much greater resources.

In 1980 Professor G. W. S. Barrow opened the new decade by publishing his inaugural lecture as the champion of Scottish history at the University of Edinburgh, in a pamphlet entitled *The Extinction of Scotland*. Light-years away from my own attitude to and vision of a new socialist Scotland as part of a really radical and egalitarian New

World Order, he revealed himself as much more radical than most of his fellow Scottish historians. Analysing the historical roots of the Scottish cringe and the obsequiousness after 1707 of writers like James Boswell, Barrow ridicules the 'argument' for the incorporating Union with England. As he puts it:

> The argument seems to boil down to the proposition that suicide is preferable to murder. It ignores as irrelevant the plea that remaining alive might be preferable to both.

Reporting on the attitudes of the Anglo-Scottish ruling class just before the Referendum of 1979, Barrow said:

> A distinguished scientist solemnly assured me that 'we are a very poor country and always have been'. The head of a well-known girls' school declared 'We have never been good at governing ourselves and managing our own affairs'. An eminent philosopher of advanced age asked me: 'What is going to happen to my pension?' These statements I judged to be the quintessential voice of the Scots bourgeoisie.[13]

(By then, it was becoming increasingly obvious that post-1945 ruling-class propaganda of 'jobs for life' - or, among University teachers, 'security of tenure' with guaranteed pensions - consisted of the illusion of security, anyway). But, despite the beginnings of the Thatcherite counter-revolution of the New Right, the Scottish working class and an increasing section of a radicalised middle class were not so easily cowed, intimidated or turned into obsequious automatons.

Unlike England, Scotland emerged a radical country: a country rediscovering itself yet again during the decade of the 1980s. Summing up the decade of the 1980s, Willy Maley wrote:

> In the 1980s, a number of Scottish publishing ventures flourished, from the larger presses such as Mainstream, Cannongate and Polygon to smaller enterprises like Dog and Bone and Clydeside Press. Scotland had its literary journals

too, to promote a cultural identity with nationhood, with *Cencrastus, Chapman* and the *Edinburgh Review* proving to be particularly influential.

In 1985 James D. Young published his book *Women and Popular Struggles: A History of Scottish and English Working Class Women, 1500-1984* (1985). Attracting much more favourable attention from such English newspapers as *The Guardian* than it did in *The Scotsman* or in Scotland - except for the *Journal of Scottish Labour History* - it made an important impact.[14] Then in 1987 Young published his volume of autobiography *Making Trouble: Autobiographical Explorations and Socialism, in* which he discussed his working-class upbringing in Grangemouth in the 1930s. This book also contained a well-researched, though also impressionistic chapter on 'Contemporary Scotland: Unknown Country' and it was almost universally acclaimed as a contribution to literature.[15]

At the level of unnecessary suffering and misery for an increasing number of Scots, the decade of the 1980s was morally rotten through and through. But, although I am not a Leninist, I agree with the pre-1917 V. I. Lenin who said that 'A slave who is conscious of his slavery is only half a slave.' Besides, despite the very real hardships caused by unemployment, naked poverty, atrocious housing conditions, homelessness and the attacks and undermining of the Welfare State, most Scots are aware of the radical possibilities offered by the prospect of regaining our national independence: independence from British imperialism and multinational corporations. While I am very aware of the Scottish Left's *Experience of Defeat* at turning-points in our history, particularly in the late eighteenth century and between the two world wars, I am focusing on the undeniable fact that towards the end of the twentieth century the majority of Scots remain unvanquished.

In an important article in the *Times Higher Educational Supplement* in 1989, MacDonald Daly and Colin Troup, two post-graduate students at the University of Oxford, contributed a searching analysis of contemporary Scotland. In one paragraph, they argued that:

> In material terms, the cultural surrender to England undoubtedly improved the daily lot of the Scottish people, as James D. Young acknowledges in the opening chapter of his *The Rousing of the Scottish Working Class* (Croom Helm, 1979). But, as Young

also demonstrates, there was a profound continuity between the authoritarianism of the Scottish philosophers' coup and the social ills - 'women's oppression, cultural dependency, inarticulacy and our internationally high levels of crime, ill-health and alcholism - which would bedevil the lives of Scottish working people in subsequent centuries.[16]

However, alongside the priceless gains and cultural rediscovery of Scotland's hidden radical past, an alien Toryism and multinational capitalism inflicted serious defeats on the Scots. Now incompatible with the newly evolving capitalist New World Order, institutions like Newbattle Abbey College - a full-time adult education college - was got rid of despite mass protests and demonstrations.[17]

The major humanist novels *Lanark* by Alasdair Gray and *The Big Man* by William McIlvanney, and the paintings of radical and socialist Glasgow by Ken Currie, were on Scotland's new cultural map. At the same time, highly qualified Scottish students were increasingly kept out of the universities in Scotland to make way for incomers who could not get into British universities elsewhere. In a time of sloth and reaction, the Anglo-Scottish ruling class did not want an educated or politically conscious 'labour force'.[18]

It was in radical Glasgow that the struggle between the new right-wing capitalism and the radical Left was most unendingly prolonged and bitter. The year 1987 saw the official opening of Ken Currie's paintings of the Glasgow History Cycle.[19] When James D. Young made the opening speech inaugurating Ken Currie's magnificant mural history of radical and working-class struggle in Glasgow beteen 1778 and 1978 in the People's Palace, the reactionaries were simply furious. As Young said in his opening speech before six hundred people:

> Although the result of the general election in June 1987, means that the Scots are now standing at a crossroads-crisis marked 'National re-birth' at the hands of the multinational corporations or 'national rebirth' under the inspiration of our centuries-old radical tradition and outward-internationalism, Ken Currie's mural history of

working-class Glasgow is another major sign of our growing confidence and self-confidence.[20]

Glasgow's Radical Heritage and the City of Culture

The year 1990 was an extraordinary year in the history of the Scots cumulative radical culture. At an international conference of the Left in Glasgow in January 1990, Noam Chomsky, together with Kelman and many others, tried to put liberterian socialism back on the map. Now the focus of international attention by writers, intellectuals, artists and thinkers on the Left, the traditional authoritarian 'socialism' of yesteryear was being sidelined and marginalised. But the Anglo-Scottish Establishment did not like the unprecedented and growing influence of Scottish-International radical ideas.

With Glasgow now the City of [European] culture, Thatcherite Tories, with the assistance of the loyal Labour Party, attempted to create a new yuppie 'enterprise' culture in the centre of Glasgow. The Left in general and the People's Palace in particular were ideological road-blocks in the path of the new capitalism; and the attempts to get rid of Ken Currie's paintings of radical Glasgow succeeded in victimising Elspeth King, who had built up the Palace as a museum of Glaswegian life. In a superb article in *Art Work* in June/July 1990, David Kemp wrote:

> But Elspeth is in their [the radicals] great tradition. Her crime has been to fight for her people and her values with an obsessive zeal. There are those, we know, who see that as an atavistic,pre-Thatcherite behaviour, particularly when there's real money to be made in the City of Culture - just as long as the 'culture' bit isn't taken too seriously. The battle-lines could not be be more clearly drawn.[21]

Thanks to the Thatcherite Labour Party in Glasgow, radical Scotland lost that battle. Yet the Scottish radicals remain bloody but unbowed and retain the self-confidence and resources to express the Scots ancient attitude of 'The Truth aagainst the World'.

In 1990, too, the book *Scotland at the Crossroads: A Socialist Answer* carried two superb articles on 'Stands Scotland Where it Did?' by William MacIlvanney and 'When the Finger Points at the Moon' by Ray Burnett. Defending Scotland's historical radical culture, McIlvanney dissected the nature of modern capitalism from a socialist-humanist standpoint. And Burnett provided a sharp analysis of the role of the Anglo-British State in Scotland and the Thatcherites reinvention of Britification in the Athens of the North.[22]

At a conference organised in the Traverse Theatre, Edinburgh in August 1990, Hector McMillan, James Kelman and James D. Young addressed the audience on the theme of 'The Suppression of Scottish History'. Summarising a conference that had been rather ironically financed by the English newspaper *The Independent*, Robbie Dinwoodie said:

> It [his upbringing] brought home to McMillan how lucky he had been. 'A folk memory kept it [the sense of class-conscious Scottish history] alive. I got it at the family fireside and my father before me;'. As he put it in conclusion: 'We're falling over backwards trying not to be Scots. Above all let's make this debate a daily one.[23]

But in his wide-ranging article in the *Glasgow Herald* on Salman Rushdie's novel *The Satanic Verses*, Kelman revealed the real nature of the Scottish 'democratic intellect' - a democratic intellect that has always developed independently of the nominally 'Scottish' universities. Introducing to a Scottish readership Third World writers and historians like Sadaat Hasan Manto and Bipan Chanda, he attacked the 'marginalisation of indigenous cultures.' There are, of course, contradictions in Kelman's arguments about history and politics: a champion of the unenlightened and undemocratic eighteenth-century 'democratic intellect', he is unaccountably hostile to the struggle for Scottish independence.[24] Yet he has made incisive criticisms of late-twentieth-century world capitalism.

Before the advent of Glasgow's role as the City of [European] culture in 1990, there had been a build up of tension between the forces of the new Right and the Left. Another marked feature of the Scotland of 1988-90 was the pamphleteering war between the extreme Thatcherite Right and the intransigent Left. It was perhaps only in Scotland that two major [Scottish] novelists - Allan Massie and James Kelman - could issue pamplets debating literature, politics and the human condition.

The titles of their pamphlets were significant, provocative and confrontational - *The Novelist's View of the Market Economy* by Allan

Massie (1988) and *Fighting for Survival: The Steel Industry In Scotland* (1990). From beginning to end, Massie's pamphlet was coloured by a strong *moral* schizophrenia about both the Scottish identity and the inherent perniciousness of industrial capitalism. In his concluding paragraph, he said:

> This is why the relationship between the market economy and the novel can never be other than uneasy. The first is utilitarian; the second poses the questions 'What is happiness? What is the right conduct? What is the end of life?' It is aware that the creation of wealth involves destruction of something else.[25]

Yet, despite Massie's allegedly 'superior' higher education by comparison with Kelman's, the fact that the 'arguments' in his pamphlet are riddled with inconsistencies is inseparable from the real world breaking into his consciousness from time to time. Hence his silly comment about the 'utterly mysterious nature of money.' Furthermore, when he says that in 'writing a novel I would be on the side of the steel workers', the Scottish radical wonders if there is not somewhere inside the ultra-right-wing writer a potentially decent man struggling to get out. But, although he is a more complex man than the vulgar Marxist would ever admit, he is clearly insensitive to the 'human suffering and despair' around him.

Refusing to separate his literature from political stances, Kelman is a better novelist than Massie. In the foreword to his pamphlet designed to help in the fight to save the Ravenscraig steel plant, he wrote:

> If you write a poem or a story through the eyes of a man or woman whose daily use of language includes certain words which are conventionally regarded as 'taboo' then there is never any likelihood of your story or poem being used by the media. As recently as last year, when my novel *A Disaffection* was published, an Arts Page member of the editorial team at *The Scotsman* was not allowed to publish extracts from it.

With no illusions about the harshness of the Scottish steel workers' way of life, Kelman insisted on the inseparability of life and literature.

With a good writer's sharp analtyical tools, Kelman, while criticising the SNP, wrote from the perspective of a cumulative Scottish radicalism when he said:

> One aspect of my argument is the need to examine 'Thatcherism'. The term is misleading; it distorts the issue and the Left should scrap its use immediately. The Prime Minister is simply a cog in a much larger machine. The world of Capital is more sophisticated than the use of the term implies... The history of high politics in the 50s, 60s and 70s is one of collusion, of covert operations, and not only in Ulster. One of the most interesting features in U.K. politics is not the part played by folk on the Right, but those on the so-called Left, especially those linked to 'the core organisation' in these anti-communist (anti-socialist) manoeuvres in the British labour movement - the Trades Union Congress.

As a painter and novelist attracting attention and praise from the London media and literary Establishment, Alasdair Gray produced a *major* 64-page pamphlet during the 1992 general election entitled *Independence: Why Scots Should Rule Scotland*. Utilising the newer radical history - a history critical of the Anglo-Scottish ruling class's eighteenth-century defintion of 'Scotland' - he wrote thus: 'Even David Hume and Thomas Carlyle - Lowland Scots of very different tempers - wrote histories in which Scotland appears like a Northern slum whose voters sometimes have to be pacified but which produces some queerly talented people.'

Steeped in the whole history of radical Scotland, Gray did not see Scotland through the lens of the Kailyard. Identifying with the struggle for democracy, independence and humanistic socialism, he confronted Kailyard images of Scotland as a classless, conflict-free nation when he described a meeting in 1985 with the Scottish poet Norman MacCaig: 'Since MacCaig was from Edinburgh and his accent struck my ear as upper-class I had though MacCaig would be against the miners - I give that as an example of the stupid prejudice which develops in a split-apart land'.[26]

But, although a majority of Scots voted for political parties committed to the setting up of a Scottish Parliament in Edinburgh, the Tories - Tories who ignored the Referendum vote in 1979 - were revealing themselves in Orwellian 'double-speak' as 'democratic' dictators. One consequence of this was that *The Scotsman* newspaper reported that '[Donald] Dewar calls for referendum: Labour policy switch as 4,000 rally for home rule'.[27]

However, the best post-election essay was published in *Scotland on Sunday* by William McIlvanney, entitled 'He is dead who will not fight' on 19 April 1992. Opening his stirring article expressing the confusion of an unvanquished Scottish people, he said:

> Scotland's will seems to live on. On 9 April, 1992, something died in this place, but it was not Scotland's stubborn, if confused, sense of its distinctiveness. Nor was it the Scottish people's determination to govern themselves.

Attempting to rally the forces for change and recalling the more traditional socialism of Gibbon and Barke, he said:

> It will be a long haul and the outcome cannot be certain. But at least the fight is on, the fight for a Scottish Parliament outside the cynical machinations of Westminster. It is, I believe, the fight most worth fighting in Scottish politics today. I hope you join in. Pick your side. There is not much room for [national] neutrality here.[28]

Then, in March and May 1993, Freddy Anderson, author of the fine satirical novel *Oiney Hoy*, helped to organise a photographic exhibitions of the hidden history of the Irish in Scotland and the Belfast/Glasgow connection. Focusing on the links between Scottish and Irish working-class history, this pioneering exhibition helped to challenge racism, social injustice and corruption. An Irish-Scotsman rather than a Scottish-Irishman, he is well known for his defence of all working people without reference to caste, colour or creed.[29]

Conclusion

The ten years between 1985 and 1995 have in fact constituted a thoroughly rotten decade: much worse than 'the devil's decade' of the 1930s. As happened during the distinctive periods of the great French revolution of the late eighteenth century and the Russian revolution of the early twentieth-century, late twentieth century Scottish culture and radicalism have been circumscribed by major technological changes and almost immeasurable social unheaval. Unlike what happened during those two world-shattering revolutions, the new worldwide Revolution personified by Boris Yelsin, Ronald Reagan, Bush, and Margaret Thatcher has actually been a counter-revolution against all progressive, democratic and radical ideas.[30]

In Scotland (as in the rest of the increasingly dis-United Kingdom), the defeat of the British miners' strike in 1985 was a harbinger of much worse things to come. By then, however, the Scots were beginning to express a strong *national* consciousness of their cultural distinctiveness; and novelists and poets like William McIlvanney, Freddy Anderson, Farquhar McLay, James Kelman and Tom Leonard were writing about and speaking for the most deprived segments of the Scottish working class.

Inside Scotland's unprecedented radical cultural renaissance and resurgence, the Left can no longer be denied an influential voice. Emancipated from the leftist Party dogmas of the past, radical Scottish artists, writers, intellectuals and historians have become innovative and experimental. Thus, in an interview with Ajay Close in *Scotland on Sunday* in May 1992, Ken Currie admits that he now needs the insights of Freud, Erich Fromm and surrealism as well as Antonio Gramsci to grapple with his understanding of Scotland in the modern world. As he told Close:

> The main theme of my work at the moment is an examination of human destructiveness: where it comes from, why are we fundamentally aggressive? I am constantly looking at myself and other people in contemporary Glasgow to find out where the killing urge comes from. The apotheosis of it is Auschwitz, but I am trying to find out what it is in day-to-day life.[31]

Scotland has always been preoccupied with metaphysics over profits and polemics over the 'politics' of the so-called 'great and good'. But, although the Scottish newspapers have played up the dislikes between Kelman and Currie - and indeed the alleged tensions between the cities of Glasgow and Edinburgh - the continuing rediscovery of radical Scotland's hidden historical culture has helped to unify the Scots against the New World Order.

Although Kelman's genius resides in his refusal to ape in his short stories and novels the literary traditions or forms of such earlier Scottish radicals such as Lewis Grassic Gibbon and James Barke, he is much closer to the poorest of the Scottish working class than they ever were. Moreover, by gaining the Booker prize for his latest novel *How Late It Was, How Late* (1993), Kelman forced the British literary Establishment to focus on the distinctiveness of Scottish radical culture. Even before then his literary achievements were on such a scale that he could not be ignored as a radical critic of the established social order. Thus in 1995 Ian Bell could write in the London-based *Observer* about most Scots sense of disaffection from what Lenin called '*their* House of Commons and their British Museum'. Furthermore, Bell concluded his article *in The Observer* by saying:

> For the moment, our self-involved neighbour knows little and cares less. This does not sound like a recipe for a strong and prosperous Union, but it might explain why, increasingly, Scots are ceasing to understand what it means to be British.[32]

At the heart of the Scottish radical cultural tradition, the autodidactic Kelman describes himself as a libertarian socialist or anarchist. Identifying with what he knows of the Scottish libertarian past and the ideas of authentic internationalists like Noam Chomsky, he too has suffered from the absence of a Scottish national historiography and consciousness of the cultural past since 1707. But in his novels he has probed into and portrayed the lives, culture and way of life of the most deprived segments of the Glaswegian working class.

Like John Maclean, the famous Clydeside socialist, and R. F. Mackenzie, Kelman is estranged from the dominant Parliamentary *Labourist* tradition of seeking *amelioration* for the intolerable social conditions of large segments of the unemployed, the deprived, the sick and the old through general elections every four or five years. Moreover

314

he employs his authority as novelist, writer and activist to give existing Scottish cultural radicalism a stronger internationalist slant; and he is tireless in introducing to a Scottish reradership writers from oppressed national and cultural minorities.

But some Scottish literary critics - those who empathise with the very polite, genteel literary traditions of English Parliamentarianism's constitutional politics as distinct from the much ruder and more impolite Scottish radical tradition - are apparently very disturbed by Kelman's *carnaptiousness*. In criticising his novels, and particularly *How Late It Was, How Late*, his Scottish critics have really been complaining more about his radical politics and cultural dissidence than about his contribution to 'literature'.

At a time of de-radicalisation, depoliticisation, right-wing triumphalism and 'defeat' for the Left everywhere, Kelman has upset those of his *genteel* critics who want the amelioration of appalling and insufferable social conditions and oppression through a humane Parliamentary mechanism. But, although William McIlvanney is closer to the radical political and literary tradition of Callender, Rodger, MacFarlan, Murdoch, Robertson, Barke and Gibbon than is Kelman, a long and hidden Kelmanite literary tradition exists in 'Hawkie's writings on nineteenth-century Glasgow and ought to be researched and portrayed.

Commenting on the resounding victory of the left-wing Republican SNP candidate Roseanna Cunningham during the Parliamentary by-election in Perth and Kinross in the summer of 1995, Ian Bell dismissed the Brits' Labour Party by arguing that:

> A Party programme conservative in both letter and spirit? The prospect of a Labour government that will harness the mighty groundswell of anti-Tory feeling simply to enact policies stolen from the Tories? A choice that is, increasingly, no choice at all?[33]

But such is the the extent of right-wing Tory 'triumphalism' in Scotland that Allan Massie can write about the same by-election quite complacently under the title of 'Salvation lies in becoming a Scottish Gaulist party'.[34]

Yet late-twentieth-century Scotland exists within a much bigger world in which there has been a communications revolution. So the

315

international counter-revolution personified by Yeltsin, Reagan, Thatcher and Major is motivated by their collective project of lowering consciousness in general and democratic consciousness in particular, as a pre-condition for creating a very hierarchical society. To achieve their anti-democratic counter-revolution inside Scotland, they have tried to extirpate the whole cultural tradition of Scottish-International radicalism.

Of course, in so far as they approve of the (peaceful) amelioration of existing conditions, most middle-class Scots (as distinct from the powerful right-wing Anglo-Scottish minority like Allan Massie) are radical and leftist. During a time of sloth and reaction, however, the world's ruling classes are aware that radical cultural traditions and literary culture are a barrier in the way of further achieving their right-wing counter-revolutionary project. But because a nakedly undemocratic and alien Thatcherism has simply served to bring an older radical consciousness to the surface, Kelman's most impressive critics have come from the genteel 'Left'.

In a review of Kelman's *How Late It Was, How Late*, entitled 'Edge of Anger', Douglas Dunn wrote:

> Far more worrying altogether is the extent to which a book like this might be seen as representative of the country as a whole. Much new writing seems incapable of telling the whole story. Too often, its emphases are on squalor, poverty, despair, crime, psychological and physical hardships, one anguish after another. True, life in Scotland is not all hunky-dory, and for more people than it should be it is lousy. That fiction should depict that side of social reality, and in its own idioms, cannot be questioned. But a consequence of good writing should be raising the level of consciousness, not its depression. A lot of new Scottish fiction seems to issue from political defeat more than understandable frustration. Although inadvertently, it comes close to celebrating, or exploiting, conditions of life which are otherwise objects of rage.

(Dunn's staggering complacency about the appalling unemployment, ill-health, poverty and dirt-cheap wages of many Scots is a sad reflection of his own middle-class 'gentility'. The same is true of Chaim Bermant's conscienceless 'gentility'). Ignoring Kelman's role as a novelist and political activist in raising working folk's consciousness of their indefensible oppression, Dunn stands in the same spiritual shoes as those genteel critics who were dismissive of the work of Gibbon, Barke, Neill and Mackenzie.

In an interesting article in *The Herald*, entitled 'How genteel it was, how genteel', Chaim Bermant reinforces Dunn's criticism of Kelman's portrayal of Glasgow and working-class Scotland. As Bermant argues:

> During a recent visit to Glasgow, I read two Glasgow novels. The first *Swing Hammer Swing* won the Whitbread; the other *How Late It was, How Late*, the Booker. Both are grim, but the first one brought out the stoicism, geniality, and native wit of the Glaswegian, while the second only conveyed squalor. The first is a great book, the second only sensational. It has originality and power but it does not amount to a novel, and certainly not to a great novel, and I suspect it won the Booker partly because the literary world needs a Lower Depths to confirm its vision of a depraved humanity which, by common consent, is to be found in Glasgow.[35]

But, ultra-complacent as Dunn's *social picture* of present-day Glasgow is, he is 'bested' by Bermant.

A social product of the ever so 'genteel' Glasgow, where he spent his formative years in the 1940s and 1950s, Bermant is a modern Kailyarder in the tradition of John Galt and Sir James Barrie. (What's all this nonsense about Kelman's class struggle? The Glaswegians are genial and happy!). In a self-portrait of himself as 'a son of the manse', whose father was 'rabbi of one of the four local synagogues', Bermant is very unhappy with Kelman's depiction of Glasgow. It really upsets him and makes him feel very uncomfortable, though Kelman is writing about decent working-class victims of the new process of modernisation and incipient totalitarianism. Celebrating the *new* Glasgow of Thatcherite capitalism, Bermant cites as evidence of cultural health the two new universities, the new art gallery and the Burrell Collection rather than

317

Kelman's novels.[36] (Incidentally, the leftist novels and writings of Alastdair Gray and Tom Leonard seem to be unknown to him). Besides, the Burrell Collection was an example of British imperialist loot and the slavery of Black peoples in the Empire: Glasgow's 'cultural treasures' bore the marks of, in Walter Benjamin's phrase, 'the anonymous toil of their contemporaries' as well as of 'the great minds and talents'.[37]

Clearly, then, critics of Kelman's novels like Dunn and Bermant are making rather *sleekit* political criticisms of his radical approach to life and literature; and at the heart of their defence of a Glasgow gone beyond recall is their social vision of traditional Kailyard gentility in a modern guise. In a giveaway phrase, Bermant contrasts the good human qualities of the Glaswegian people with Kelman's dour depiction of them, before concluding that 'Friendliness, geniality, and warmth, however, are not the stuff of prize-winning novels'. And in making a very political judgment, he asserts that, despite bad housing, high unemployment and a large number of settlers from outside Scotland, Glasgow was the only major city in Britain to escape the riots during the summer of 1981.

Attributing the absence of riots in Glasgow in the summer of 1981 to 'the friendliness, geniality, and warmth of its people', it is really Bermant and - in a quite different way - Dunn who are trying to lower the Scots high consciousness of the ugly reality surrounding them in the mid-1990s.

And yet we live in an ugly world of racism, militarism, injustice and massive social inequality; and Scottish radicals have a role to play in struggling for the better world to come. Against all the odds, and against conventional wisdom, an authentic socialist internationalism could lead humankind to a new paradise on earth. It is within our grasp; but, although no one can predict the outcome of the struggles that will be engendered by the policies of the New Right in the future, the Scots and other working folk throughout the world remain undefeated.

But world socialism - or indeed the survival of the planet - are not at all inevitable. And I find it difficult to disagree with the conclusion of Eric J. Hobsbawm's book *The Age of Extremes* that:

> If humanity is to have a recognisable future, it cannot be by prolonging the past or the present. If we try to build the third millennium on that basis, we shall fail. And the price of that failure, that is to say, the alternative to a changed society, is *darkness*.

Notes and References

Chapter One: Scottish Nationalism and Plebeian Radicalism, 1707-1832

1 P. Berresford Ellis and Seumas Mac A' Ghobhainn, *The Scottish Insurrection of 1820* (London, 1970), pp.36-50.
2 The obligatory references to Jacobitism in the book *Scottish Capitalism*, (London, 1980), edited by Tony Dickson, (1970), are superficial and sometimes inaccurate.
3 Quoted in Morrison Davidson, *Leaves from The Book of Scots* (Glasgow, 1914), p.4-5.
4 Quoted in ibid., p.46.
5 Ibid., p.43.
6 'Another distinction he achieved during his brief Parliamentary career was that of being the first member of Parliament suspended from the House of Commons for using the word "damn"'. Hugh MacDiarmid, *R. B. Cunninghame Graham* (Glasgow, 1952), p.27.
7 S. B. Chrimes, *English Constitutional History* (Oxford, 1949), p.151.
8 Royden Harrison, 'A Very English Socialism', *Socialismo Storio*, No.3, 1991, p. 635.
9 J. Bowles Daly, *Radical Pioneers of the Eighteenth Century* (London, 1886), p.21.
10 W. E. H. Lecky, (London, 1892), Vol.2., p.333. A History of England in the Eighteenth Century
11 Ibid., p.326.
12 E, P. Thompson, *The Making of the English Working Class* (Penguin, 1968), p.14.
13 G.. D. H. Cole and Raymond Postgate, *The Common People, 1746-1946* (London, 1949), p.98.
14 Ernest Campbell Mossner, *The Life of David Hume* (Oxford, 1980), p.370.
15 Daly, Radical Pioneers of the Eighteenth Century, p.34.
16 Mossner, The Life of David Hume, p.421.
17 Raphael Samuel, 'British Marxist Historians', *New Left Review*, No.120, April 1980, p.41.
18 Gwyn A. Williams, *Artisans and Sans-Culottes* (London, 1968), p.11.
19 J. Steven Watson, *The Reign of George III, 1760-1815* (Oxford, 1960), p.133.
20 Quoted in Morrison Davidson, *Africa for the Africaners* (London, 1902), p.6.
22 *The Conversations of Dr. Johnson. Extracted from the Life of James Boswell* (London, 1949), edited Raymond Postgate, p103.
23 Ibid., p.175.
24 *Boswell's London Journal*, edited F. A. Pottle (london, 1950), pp.71-2.
25 H. J. Hanham, *Scottish Nationalism* (London, 1969), p.34
26 James D. Young, *The Rousing of the Scottish Working Class* (London, 1979), pp.11-36
27 Quoted in John W. Oliver, 'Ferguson and 'Ruddiman's Magazine', in *Robert Ferguson, 1750-74*, edited Sydney Goodsir Smith (Edinburgh, 1952), p.91.
28 Sidney Goodsir Smith, 'Introductory: Robert Ferguson, his Life, his Death and his Work', ibid., p.43.
29 Oliver, 'Ferguson and 'Ruddiman's Magazine', p.94, ibid.
30 Ibid., p.96.
31 Smith, 'Introductory', Ibid., p.42.
32 James D. Young, *Socialism Since 1889: A Biographical History* (New York, 1988), p.24.
32 Lecky, A History of England in the Eighteenth Century, Vol.1., p.339
33 T.C. Smouth, *A History of the Scottish People, 1560-1830* (London, 1969), p.223.
34 *Book of Adjournal*, JC 13/18, Scottish Record Office, Edinburgh.
35 See my critique of T. C. Smout entitled 'The Making of the Scottish

Working Class', Bulletin of the Society for the Study of Labour History, No.28., 1974, pp.6-8.

36 SO 54/5, Public Record Office, London and *Scots Magazine*, April 1778, p.219.

37 Caledonian Mercury, 9 October 1779.

38 Christopher Harvey, *Scotland and Nationalism* (London, 1994), p.149.

38 J. A. Oughton to Weymouth, 1779, S.P.54/57. Public Record Office, London.

39 Young, The Rousing of the Scottish Working Class, op. cit.,42-4.

40 *First or Old Statistical Account* (Edinburgh, 1792), Vol.9., p.190.

41 *Annual Register for 1788* (London, 1789), p.209.

42 *Deformities of Dr. Samuel Johnson. Selected from his Works*. Introduction by G. J. Kolb and J. E. Congleton (Los Angeles, 1971), p.i and *A Critical Review of the Works of Dr. Samuel Johnson* (Edinburgh, 1783), p.3

43 Introduction by Kolb and Congleton, p.iii.

44 Ibid.

45 Hamish Henderson, 'It Was In You That It A' Began', in *The People's Past*, edited by Edward J. Cowan (Edinburgh, 1980), pp.17-31.

46 Henry Jephson, *The Platform: Its Rise and Progress* (London, 1892), Vol. 1., p.l and p.20.

47 Young, The Rousing of the Scottish Working Class, p.41.

48 Robert Palmer, The Age of the Democratic Revolution (Princeton, 1959), Vol.2., p.472

49 A. L. Morton, 'French Revolutionaries and English Democrats', *Labour Monthly*, No. 9., 1939.

50 Gordon Donaldson and Robert S. Morpeth, *A Dictionary of Scottish History* (Edinburgh, 1977), p.86.

51 Francis Hart Russell, The Disaster of Darien (London, N.D.), p.172.

52 'Second Report of the Committee of Secrecy', *Parliamentary History of England*, Vol. XXXI, 1794-95, p.746.

53 Ibid., p.850.

54 George Penny, *Traditions of Perth* (Perth, 1830), pp-66-68.

55 Peter Mackenzie, *The Trial of Thomas Muir, Esq., Advocate* (Glasgow, 1836), p.42.

56 Ibid., pp.43-47.

57 Address from the Four Belfast Societies of United Irishmen to the Scottish Friends of the People, in *Belfast Politics*, 1794), pp.103-4.

58 R. R. Madden, *Literary Remains of the United Irishmen of 1789 and Selections from other popular lyrics of their Times* (Dublin, 1887), p.167.

59 T. B. and T. J. Howell, *A Complete Selection of State Trials, Vol.XXII*, Col.224.

60 Smout, A History of the Scottish People, 1560-1830, p.445.

61 W. D. Lyell, *The Real Weir of Herminston* (Glasgow, 1903), p.8

62 Francis Watt, *Terrors of the Law* (London, MDCCCCII), p.11.

63 Daly, Radical Pioneers of the Eighteenth Century, p.201.

64 'Even in 1819-21 when the Government and the prosecuting societies carried almost every case...', it still was not not possible to speak of "totalitarian" of "Asiatic" depostism'. E. P. Thompson, The Making of the English Working Class, p.795. The Scots on the other hand were the victims of a"totalitarian" despotism unacknowledged by English radicals and later English and Anglo-Scottish historians.

65 George W. T. Omond, *The Lord Advocates of Scotland* (London, 1914), Vol. 2., p.202.

66 Ibid., pp.198-199.

67 George Gilfillan, *The Life and Poetry of Robert Burns* (Glasgow, 1898), p.54.

68 Eric J. Hobsbawm, *The Age of Revolution, 1789-1848* (New York, 1962), p.103.

69 Ibid.

70 *Annual Register for 1817* (London, 1818), p.206.

71 Williams, Artisans and Sans-Culottes, p.97

72 *Annual Register for 1799* (London, 1800), p.172.

73 *Glasgow Mercury*, 28 January 1799.

74 *Caledonian Mercury*, 13 January 1798.

75 Thomas Johnson, *The History of the Working Classes in Scotland* (Glasgow,1922), p.231.

76 *Scots Magazine*, April 1797, p.704.

77 W.E. F. Skene, *Celtic Scotland* (Glasgow, 1888), p. Vol.2.,134.

78 Peter Kropotkin, *Mutal Aid* (London, 1912), p.236.

79 W. W. Straka, 'Reform in Scotland and the Working Class', *Scottish Tradition*, Vol.2., No.2, 1972, p.41.

80 Young, The Rousing of the Scottish Working Class, Chapter One.

81 Linda Colley, Forging The Nation, 1707-1837(London, 1994), p.12.

82 Hobsbawm, The Age of Revolution, p.254

83 Franz Mehring, Absolutism and Revolution in Germany, 1525-1848 (London, 1975), pp.160-61.

84 *Memorials and Correspondence of Charles James Fox,* ewdited Lord John Russell (London, 1854), Vol. 3., p.264. Emphasis in the orginal.

85 Mackenzie, The Trial of Thomas Muir, p.53.

86 Jurgen Kuczynski, *The Rise of the Working Class* (London, 1967), p.120.

87 Smout, A History of the Scottish People, 1560-1830, p.223.

88 R. De Bruce Trotter, *Galloway Gossip or the Southern Abbanich 80 Years Ago* (Dumfries, 1901), p.lo3.

89 David D. McElroy, A Century of Scottish Clubs,1700-1800, Ph. D. thesis, University of Edinburgh, pp.148-155.

90 James D. Young, Women and Popular Struggles. *A History of Scottish and English Working-Class Women, 1500-1984* (Edinburgh, 1985), pp.64-70.

91 Sean Damer, *Glasgow: Going for a Song* (London, 1990), p.43.

92 Jurgen Kuczynski, A Short History of Labour Conditions Under Capitalism (London, 1942), p.53.

93 Young, The Rousing of the Scottish Working Class, pp.56-59

94 Ken Logue, 'Eighteenth-Century Popular Protest', in The People's Past, edited by Edward J. Cowan, p.86.

95 Ibid., p.89.

96 As a typical Scottish-Unionist Whig, Henry Cockburn's writing are permeated with a radicalism of the mouth. See, for example, Henry Cockburn, *Journal* (Edinnburgh, 1874), Vol.2.,p.105.

97 Peter Mackenzie, *Reminiscences of Glasgow and the West of Scotland* (Glasgow, 1890), p.l08.

98 *Scots Magazine*, July 1816, p.633.

99 *Edinburgh Evening Courant*, 30 June 1814 and Charles W. Thomson, *The Scottish Lion* (Glasgow, 1920), p.44.

100 Young, The Rousing of the Scottish Working Class, p.59.

101 William Aiton, *A History of the Encounter at Drumclog* (Hamilton, 1821), pp. 970-99.

102 It is because Karl Marx praised Scott so much that English Marxist historians are particularly uncomfortable with any criticism of the great falsifier of Scottish history.

103 Aiton, A History of the Rencounter at Drumclog, introductory chapter.

104 Young, The Rousing of the Scottish Working Class, p.58.

105 Provost of Dunfermline to the Lord Advocate, 9 December 1816, HO. 102, Vol.XXVI, P.R.O., London.

106 *Edinburgh Review*, Vol. XXXIV, 1820, p.149.

107 *Edinburgh Annual Register for 1820* (Edinburgh, 1823), p.20.

108 P. Berresford Ellis and Seumas Mac A' Ghobhainn, *The Scottish Resurerction of 1820* (London, 1970),p.267.

109 Young, The Rousing of the Scottish Working Class, pp.49-52.

110 John Stevenson, *A True Narrative of the Radical Rising* (Glasgow, 1835), pp.13-18.

111 *The Scotsman,* 16 April 1820.

112 *Edinburgh Weekly Journal*, ll April 1820.

113 Stevenson, A True Narrative of the Radical Rising, p.15.

114 Major General Bradford to Sidmouth, 31 December 1819, RH 2/4 Vol.128. P.R.O., London.

115 Thomas Carlyle, *Reminiscences* (London, 1881), Vol.2., p.212.

116 Marion Lockhead, John Gibson Lochhart (London, 1954), p.72.

117 Ibid., p.170.

118 John Stevenson, A True Narrative of the Radical Rising, p.8.

119 Peter Mackenzie, *The Trial of James Wilson* (Glasgow, 1832), p.37.

120 George W. T. Omond, *Lord Advocates of Scotland* (Edinburgh, 1914), Vol.1.,p.233.

121 Janet Hamilton, *Poems, Sketches and Essays* (Glasgow, 1885), p.412.

122 Andrew Noble, 'MacChismo in Retrospect', *Bulletin of Scottish Politics*, No.2., 1981, p.79.

123 For a muddled view of this process, seeTom Nairn, *The Break-Up of Britain* (London, 1977), p.150

124 Henry Cockburn, *The Life of Lord Jeffrey* (Edinburgh, 1852), Vol. 1., p.272.

125 John Galt, *The Literary Life* (Edinburgh, 1834), Vol. 2., p.196.

126 James Leslie Mitchell (Lewis Grassic Gibbon), *Niger: The Life of Mungo Park* (London, 1934), p.13.

127 In the eighteenth and early nineteenth centuries, the English Left in particular denounced and made persistent sarcastic remarks about 'the Irish Paddies' and 'the Scots Sawnies'.

128 Cockburn, The Life of Lord Jeffrey, Vol. 1., p.260.

129 Peter Mackenzie, *Reminiscences of Glasgow and the West of Scotland*, Vol. 1., p.155.

130 John Galt, *Ringan Gilhaize or The Covenanters* (Edinburgh, 1984), p.324.

131 Peter Berresford Ellis and Seumas Mac A' Ghobhainn, *The Scottish Insurrection of 1820* (London, 1989), pp.9-12.

132 Quoted in W. L. Mathieson, *Church and Reform in Scotland* (Glasgow, 1916), p.168.

133 *Edinburgh Annual Register for 1822* (Edinburgh, 1824), p.237.

134 Robert Mudie, *A Historical Account of His Majesty's Visit to Scotland* (Edinburgh, 1822), p.90 and p.311.

135 Peter Berresford Ellis and Seumas Mac A' Ghobhainn, *The Scottish Insurrection of 1820*, (1989 edition) p.13.

136 John Stevenson also criticised William Aiton's interpretation of what had happened in 1820.

137 John Galt, *The Gathering of the West* (Edinburgh, 1823), p.48.

138 Marion Lochhead, John Gibson Lockhart, p.109.

139 *Glasgow Chronicle*, 7 April 1821.

140 *Caledonian Mercury*, 9 April 1825 and 23 April 1825.

141 RH 24/155, Scottish Record Office.

142 Young, The Rousing of the Scottish Working Class, p.80.

143 Cockburn, Journal, Vol., 1., p.25.

144 Ibid., Vol. 1., p.35.

145 Ibid.

146 William Chambers, *The Book of Scots* (Edinburgh, 1830), p.326.

Chapter Two: James Thomson Callender (1758-1803): A Scottish Internationalist

1 There is a note in the margin of one of the copies of *The Political Progress of Britain* in the handwriting of Worthington C. Ford saying that James Thomson Callender had been born in Glasgow. The Library of Congress, Washington, D.C.

2 Anon., *The Political Progress of Britain or an Impartial Account of the Principal Abuses in the Government of the Country from the Revolution of 1688* (Edinburgh, 1792). National Library of Scotland, Edinburgh.

3 Thomas Jefferson and James Thomson Callender, 1798-1802, edited by Worthington C. Ford (Historical Printing Club, Brooklyn, N.Y., 1897), p.3.

4 Letter to the author from Jo Currie, the librarian of the University of Edinburgh archives and special collections, 3 April 1990.

5 T. C. Smout, *A History of the Scottish People, 1560-1830* (London, 1969), p.483.

6 Letter to the author from Jo Currie, University of Edinburgh, 3 April 1990.

7   William Cobbett, *A Bone to Gnaw For the Democrats or Observations on A Pamphlet Entitled 'The Political Progress of Britain'* (London, 1797), p.52.and p.83.
Ibid., p.2 and J. F C. *Harrison, Robert Owen and the Owenities in Britain and America (London, 1969), p.10.*

9   Perry Anderson, *Arguments Within English Marxism* (London, 1980), pp.176-207.

11 John Merrgington, 'Town and Country in the Transition to Capitalism', *New Left Review*, No.93., 1975, p.71.

12 Eric J. Hobsbawm, 'Capitalism and Agriculture: The Scottish Reformers of the Eighteenth Century', *Annales*, Summer 1978, p.58. I wish to thank my friend and colleague Alister Blyth in the French Department at the University of Stirling, for translating this long article into English.

13 pp.57-58.

14 A. James Gregor, A Survey of Marxism (New York, 1965),, p.145 and p.148.

15 Adam Smith, *Lectures on Justice, Police, Revenue and Arms*, edited Edwin Cannan (Oxford, 1896), p.15.

16 Adam Smith, *The Wealth of Nations*, edited R. H. Campbell and A. S. Skinner (Oxford, 1976), Vol.2., Book V., Chapter i., part II, p.710.

17 Lewis S. Feuer, *Marx and the Intellectuals* (New York, 1969), p.202.

18 Thomas Hamilton, *Cyril Thornton* (Edinburgh, 1827), Vol., 1, p.183.

19 Andrew MacGeorge, *Glasgow* (London, 1888), pp.221-22.

20 Kenneth Logue, *Popular Disturbances in Scotland* (Edinburgh, 1979),p.217.

21 Lord Dundonald, *Description of the Estate of Culross* (Edinburgh, 1793), p.73.

22 Thomas Johnson, *The History of the Working Classes in Scotland* (Glasgow, 1922), p.232 and p.231.

23 John H. Gray, Autobiography of a Scotch Gentleman (Privately printed, 1865), p.216.

24 Dugald Stewart, *Collected Works*, edited William Hamilton (Edinburgh, 186)) Vol.X, p.87.

25 Lewis Coser and Irving Howe, 'Authoritarians of the Left', *Voices of Dissent*, edited Irving Howe (New York, 1958), p.95.

26 James D. Young, The Rousing of the Scottish Working Class (London, 1979), pp.49-52.

27 John Robison, *Proofs of a ConspiracyAgainst All the Religions and Governments of Europe* (London, 1792), passim.

28 Young, The Rousing of the Scottish Working Class, pp.51-52.

29 D. H. Horn, *A Short History of the University of Edinburgh* (Edinburgh, 1967), p.40.

30 Notes on the situation at the University of Edinburgh, *Edinburgh Annual Register* (Edinburgh, 1821), p.146.

31 Stewart, *Collected Works*, Vol.X.,p.87. Also Veitch's Memoir, ibid., Vol. 10, p.1.,

32 In discussing the phenomena of Alias MacAlias, the Caledonian Antiszygy and Dr. Jekyll and Mr. Hyde, no one has looked for the material origins (as distinct from the legendary psychological roots) of this exceptionally well-discussed development in the eighteenth century.

33 George Pratt Insh, Unpublished Manuscript Biography of Thomas Muir of Huntershill, p.41. Copy in the author's possession.Stewart, Collected Works, Vol., X., p.86.

34 E. P. Thompson, 'The Peculiarities of the English' in *The Poverty of Theory* (London, 1978), p.59.

35 Roy Pascal, 'Property and Society: The Scottish Historical School of the Eighteenth Century', *Modern Quarterly*, Vol.L, No.2., 1938, passim and Ron Meek, 'The Scottish Contribution to Marxist Sociology', *Democracy and the* British Labour Movement, edited John Saville (London, 1954), pp.54-99.

36 *Leters of Crito on the Causes, Objects and Consequences of the Present War* (Edinburgh, 1796), p.6. Crito was Millar's pen name. By the late eighteenth century the tradition of Alias MacAlias was well established.

37 David Hume, *The Philosophical Works*, edited T. H. Green and H. Grose (Berlin, 1964), Vol. 2., p.109.

38 It is a great pity that English historians like E. P. Thompson and Royden Harrison had not actually read more of the writings of David Hume, Dugald Stewart and John Millar.

39 Michael Ignatieff, 'John Millar and Individualism', Wealth and Virtue, edited Istvan Hont and Michaael Ignatieff (Cambidge, 1983), pp.324.

40 *Letters of Crito [i.e. John Millar] on the Causes, Objects and Consequences of* the Present War, p.6.

41 Ibid., p.50 and p.26.

42 Peter Kropotkin, *Fields, Factories and Workshops* (London, 1912), p.206 and pp.158-61. and Peter Kropotkin, *Ethics Origins and Development* (New York, 1924), p.235.

43 George Lichtheim, The Origins of Socialism (London, 1969), p.4.

44 Nobert Waszek, 'The Division of Labour: From the Scottish Enlightenment to Hegel', *The Owl of Minerva*, Vol. 15., No.l., 1983, p.56.

45 Ignatieff, 'John Millar and Individualism', p.325.

46 Ibid., p.326.

47 Worthington Ford, *Thomas Jefferson and James Thomson Callender, 1798-1802* (Brooklyn, New York, 1897), p.34.

48 *James Boswell's Life of Johnson*, edited J. Brady (New York, 1968), p.297.

50 Anon., *The Deformities of Dr. Samuel Johnson* (Edinburgh, 1782), pp.84-87.

51 Anon., *A Critical Review of the Works of Dr. Samuel Johnson* (Edinburgh, 1783), p.32. and pp.l-2.

52 *The Deformities of Dr. Samuel Johnson* with Introduction by G. J. Kolb and J. E. Congleton (Los Angeles, 1971), p.i.

53 RH2/4/68, fos 27-7, Scottish Record Office SRO), Edinburgh.

54 James Thomson Callender to Andrew Stewart, 5 December 1789, Ms 8261, SRO.

55 Ibid., Ms., fos, 72, SRO.

56 Gwyn A. Williams, *Artisans and Sans-Culottes* (London, 1968), p.97.

57 Andrew Hook, *Scotland and America, 1750-1835* (Glasgow, 1975), p.239.

58 RH2/4/68, fosa 26-7.

59 RH2/4/68, SRC.

60 RH2/4/68, fos, 27-28.

61 JC7/47, SRO.

62 JC3/46, SRO.

63 A. and E. G. Porritt, The Unreformed House of Commons (Cambridge, 1903), Vol., 2, pp.4-5.

64 Ibid., p.6.

65 Thomas Jefferson and James Thomson Callender,, 1798-1802, p.39.

66 A.and E. G. Porritt, The Unreformed House of Commons, Vol., 2, pp.4-5.

67 Anon., *The Political Progress of Britain* (Edinburgh, 1792), p.43.

68 Ibid., pp1-2.

69 Ibid., p.7.

70 Ibid., p.9.

71 Ibid., p.16.

72 Ibid., p.1

73 Ibid., p.3.

74 Ibid., p.7

75 *Oxford Companion to English Literature*, edited Sir Paul Harvey (Oxford,1958), p.171.

76 W. E. Woodward, *Tom Paine: America's Godfather* (New York, 1945), p.310.

77 Moncure D. Conway, The Life of Thomas Paine (London, 1909), p.33.

78 Ibid., p.95.

79 Ibid., p.34, p.lll and p.293

80 When I was doing research for this chapter, it became increasingly obvious to me that Cobbett had planted hostile information about Callender in a whole range of American newspapers in the 1790s.

81 It is the third English edition that is the British Library, London.

82 G. Spater, *The Poor Man's Friend* (Cambridge, 1982), Vol.1, p.55.

83 Ibid., p.54.

84 M. E. Clark, *Cobbett in America* (Oxford, 1939), p.27.
85 Quoted in ibid., p.52
86 William Cobbett, *A Bone to Gnaw From the Democrats and Observations on A Pamphlet Entitled 'The Political Progress of Britain'* (London, 1975), p.51.
87 Ibid., p.23.
88 Ibid., p.40
89 Woodward, Tom Paine: America's Godfather, p.310.
90 Worthington C. Ford, Thomas Jefferson and James Thomson Callender,1798-1802, p.7.
91 Williams, Artisans and Sans-Culottes, p.97.
92 *The Autobiography of Archibald Rowan*, edited William H. Drummond (Dublin, 1972), p.290.

93 Worthington C. Ford, Thomas Jefferson and James Thomson Callender, 1798-1802, p.1 and p.4.
94 Ibid., pp.5-6.
95 Worthington C. Ford, Thomas Jefferson and James Thomson Callender, 1798-1802, p.5.
96 *Political Censor*, April 1797. Library of Congress, Washington, D.C.
97 Worthington C. Ford, *Thomas Jefferson and James Thomson Callender, 1798-1802*, p.11.
98 John Spencer Bassett, *The American Nation*, Vol.2., (New York, 1940), p.264.
99 Ibid., p.209 and p.282
100 Williams, Artisans and Sans-Culottes, p.103.
101 William Cobbett, A Bone to Gnaw, p.63.
102 *Philadelphia Gazette*, November 1797. Library of Congress.
103 William Cobbett, A Bone to Gnaw, Part II, p.45.
104 *Philadelphia Gazette*, September 1798. Library of Congress.
105 Worthington C. Ford, Thomas Jefferson and James Thomson Callender, p.1.
106 Bassett, The American Nation, Vol.2., p.209.

107 *Dictionary of American History*, edited James Truslow Adams (London, 1940), Vol..1, 1949.
108 Merrill D. Peterson, *Thomas Jefferson: A Biography* (New York, 1970), p.635.
109 Worthington C. Ford, Thomas Jefferson and James Thomson Callender, 1798-1802, p.19.
110 Peterson, Thomas Jefferson: A Biography, Vol.2., p.637.
111 This was a point made again and again by his enemies during the last two years of his life.
112 RH2/4/68, fos 26-7, SRO.
113 Worthington C. Ford, Thomas Jefferson and James Thomson Callender, 1798-1802, p.36.
114 Peterson, Thomas Jefferson: A Biography, p.637.
115 Conway, The Life of Thomas Paine, p.33.
116 *The Gentleman's Magazine*, September 1803.
117 Dumas Malone, *Thomas Jefferson: A Biography* (Boston, 1970), Vol.4.,p.212 and p.211.
118 James D. Young, 'Culture and Imperialism: The Importance of Hugh MacDiarmid', *Cencrastus*, Summer, No.52 1995.

Chapter Three: Alexander Rodger (1784-1846) and James MacFarlan (1832-1862): The Voices of a Subdued People

1 Peter Fryer, 'Their Feet lf Clay: the un-Marxist Side of Marx and Engles', forthcoming.
2 David Hume, *The History of England* (London, 1778), Vol. V., p.357.
3 Richard Ned Lebon, *White Britain and Black Ireland* (Philadelphia, 1976), passim.
4 Eric J. Hobsbawm, *Nations and Nationalism since 1870* (Cambridge, 1990), p. 41.
5 George Eyre-Todd, *The Glasgow Poets: Their Lives and Poems* (Glasgow, 1906), p.171.

6   Alexander Rodger, *Poems and Songs: Humorous and Satirical* (Glasgow, 1838), p.17.

7   Tom Leonard, Radical Renfrew: Poetry from the French Revolution to the First *World War* (Edinburgh, 1990), p. 8.

8   Ibid., p. 10.

9   Biographical notes by John M'Kechnie and Charles Rattray to *Stray Leaves*, edited by Alexander Rodger (Glasgow, 1842), p. vii.

10 Alexander Somerville, *The Autobiography of a Working Man* (London, 1951), pp. 16-18.

11 Thomas Johnson, The History of the Working Classes in Scotland (Glasgow, 1922), p. 237.

12 James D. Young 'A Very English Socialism and the Celtic Fringe; *History Workshop*, No. 35, 1993.

13 Annual Register for 1817 (London, 1818), p. 40.

14 *Scots Magazine*, 1820, p. 179 and p. 282

15 *The Gorgon*, 26 September 1818.

16 Ibid., 17 April, 1819

17 Richard Carlisle, *A New Year's Message to the Reformers of Great Britain* (London, 1820), pp. 3-5.

18 Henry Cockburn, *Memorials of His Time* (Edinburgh, MCMX), p. 80.

19 E. P. Thompson, The Making of the English Working Class, (London, 1965), p. 80.

20 Dave Leslie, 'A Page of Glasgow History: Alexander Rodger (1784-1846)', in *Essays in Honour of William Gallacher* (Berlin, 1966), pp. 131-140.

21 Ibid.,

22 Henry G. Graham, Scottish Men of Letters in the Eighteenth Century (London, 1901), p. 208.

23 Henry Cockburn, *Life of Lord Jeffrey* (Edinburgh, 1852), Vol. 1., p. 46.

24 John Galt, *The Literary Life* (Edinburgh, 1834), Vol. 2., p. 196 and ibid., Vol. 1., p. 235.

25 'English has made no encroachment on me, yet, though I speak more Scotch than English...I cannot even get my own children to do more than pick up a *queer* word of him here and there.' Henry Cokburn, *Journal* (Edinburgh, 1874) Vol. 2., p. 87.

26 Alexander Rodger, Poems and Songs: Humorous and Satirical (Paisley, 1897), edited with an Introduction by Robert Ford, p. xvii.

27 *Scotch Poetry: Consisting of Songs, Odes, Anthems and Epigrams* by Alexander Rodger (London 1821). An Operative Weaver of Glasgow. Printed and published by R. Carlisle, Fleet Street.

28 Rodger, Poems and Songs, p. 151.

29 He, too, contributed to the coalescence of the Scottish-Unionist cultural forces of the Dr. Jekyl and Mr. Hyde syndrome with Kailyardism in imaginative literature.

30 Henry Cockburn, Journal, Vol. 2., p. 105.

31 No English radical writer or poet had protested against Rodger's imprisonment in 1820.

32 *The Letters of Sir Walter Scott, 1819-1821*, edited D. Cook and w. M. Parker (London, 1934), Vol. X., p. 20.

33 Thomas Carlyle, 'The Signs of the Times', in *Critical and Miscellaneous Essays* (London, 1889) Vol. 2., p. 82.

34 Ibid., p. 84

35 'The Late James MacFarlan: Proposed Fund for His Family', *The Glasgow* Sentinel, 22 November, 1862.

36 In *The Book of Eminent Scotsmen* (Edinburgh, MDCCCLXXXI), Joseph Irving ignored Alexander Rodger. At the same time as he condescended to recognise James MacFarlan as 'a minor poet', he stood in the Kailyard tradition by not mentioning his Irish father or Irish wife. In the fat volume of *Scottish Biography* (Glasgow, 1938) touching on the lives of the so-called 'great and good', Rodger and MacFarlan were again ignored.

37 *Radical Renfrew* (Edinburgh, 1990), edited by Tom Leonard, p. xxii.

38 What E. P. Thompson called 'The enormous condenscension of posterity' towards radical working people was always much stronger in Scotland than in England.

39 James D. Young, 'James Thomson Callender, 1758-1803', Cencrastus, No. 47., 1994, pp. 19-22.
40 James Kelso Hunter, *Life Studies of Character* (Greenock, 1870), passim.
41 Tom Nairn, *The Break-Up of Britain* (London, 1977), p. 157.
42 'It appears in retrospect as a characteristic expression of the "Red", outward-bound strain in intelligentsia, as opposed to the "Black", stay-at-hone one closer to nationalism. I am indebted to Christopher Harvie for this distinction.' Nairn, The Break-Up of Britian, p. 168. To 'prove' that all Scottish intellectuals, poets and writers who stayed in Scotland after 1707 were 'Black' (as distinct) from 'Red', Harvie and Nairn have had to inhibit the rediscovery of Callender, Rodger, MacFarlan, Alexander Robertson, John Murdoch, John Maclean and others.
43 Hunter, *Life Studies of Character* (Greenock, 1970), p. 127.
44 E. P. Thompson, 'The Peculiarities of the English', in *The Poverty of Theory* (London, 1978), pp. 35-91.
45 Andrew Noble, 'MacChismo in Retrospect', Bulletin of Scottish Politics, No. 2., 1981, p. 79.
46 Letter from Royden Harrison to the author, 30 August, 1984.
47 Ibid., p. xx.
48 Quoted in Eric Williams, Capitalism and Slavery (London, 1964), p. 60 and p. 64.
49 Stuart Cosgrave, 'Hurricane Whips Up Our Murkey Past', *Observer Scotland*, 13 April, 1990.
50 D. MacLeod Malloch, *The Book of Glasgow Anecdotes* (Glasgow, 1912), p. 179 and John O. Mitchell, *Old Glasgow Essays* (Glasgow, 1905), p. 142.
51 But, although the literary work of Rodger and MacFarlan was suppressed, they forced their way through the 'Black' Anglo-Scottish bourgeoisie's barrier of silence.
52 See the anonymous comment on Alexander Rodger in *The Modern Scottish Minstrel; Or The Songs of Scotland of the Past Half Century,* (Edinburgh, 1856), Vol. III., p. 71 and 'The Late James MacFarlan', *The Glasgow Sentinel*, 122 November, 1862.
53 See below.
54 John Younger, *Autobiography* (Kelso, 1881), p. xxii.
55 *Chartist Circular*, 13 February, 1841.
56 William Chambers, *The Book of Scots* (Edinburgh, 1830), p. 231.
57 Anonymous (Jack Wade), *The Black Book or Corruption Unmasked* (London, 1835), p. 380.
58 T. C. Smout, *A History of the Scottish People, 1560-1830* (London, 1969), p. 506.
59 *British Trade Unionism, 1750-1850: The Formative Years*, edited by John Rule (London 1988), p. 17.
60 Stray Leaves, p. x.
61 Alexander Rodger, *Poems and Songs: Humourous and Satirical* (Glasgow, 1838), p. 355 and p. 295.
62 James Kilpatrick, *Literary Landmarks of Glasgow* (Glasgow, 1893), pp. 207-214.
63 Peter Mackenzie, *Old Reminiscences* (Glasgow, 1935), pp. 136-140.
64 *The Weavers' Journal*, 1 August 1836.
65 J. Morrison Davidson, The Annals of Toil (London, N.D.)
66 *Chartist Circular*, 30 May, 1840.
67 *Caledonian Mercury*, 19 August, 1842.
68 AD14/44/81, AD 14 42/354 and AD2/14. Scottish Record Office. James Myles, Rambles in Forfarshire (Edinburgh, 1850), p. 79 and the Norther Star, 22 February, 1845.
69 *Chartist Circular*, 28 August, 1841.
70 'Death of Alexander Rodger', *The Scotch Reformers' Gazette*, 3 October, 1946.
71 Julius Braunthal, History of the International, 1864-1914 (London, 1966), p. 168.
72 Royden Harrison, 'Afterword' to Samuel Smiles, *Self-Help* (London, 1968), p. 263.
73 W. H. Marwick, *A Short History of Labour in Scotland* (Edinburgh, 1967), p. 22.

74 Hamish Whyte, 'The Miseries of Hope: James MacFarlan (1832-1862)', in *A Glasgow Collection*, edited by Kevin Carra and Hamish Whyte (Glasgow, 1990). For the evidence of the Scots' hatred of the Irish immigrants and their offspring, see James D. Young, 'The Irish Immigrants' Contribution to Scottish Socialism' 1880-1926', Saothar, No.13, 1988.

75 Joseph Irving, *Dictornary of Eminent Scotsmen* (Edinburgh, MDCCCLXXXI), p. 301.

76 'The Late James MacFarlan: Proposed Fund For His Family', *Glasgow Sentinel*, 22 November, 1862.

77 *The Glasgow Poets: Their Lives and Poems*, edited by George Eyre-Todd, (Glasgow, 1896) p. 379.

78 George Eyre-Todd, The Glasgow Poets: Their Lives and Poems, p. 379.

79 A. A., 'Sketch of the Author's Life', *Lyrics of Life* (London, 1856), p. vi.

80 Ibid., p. vii.

81 George Eyre-Todd, The Glasgow Poets: Their Lives and Poems, p. 379.

82 The Poetical Works of James MacFarlan with a Memoir by Colin Rae-Brown (Glasgow, 1882), p. vi.

83 *The Glasgow Sentinel*, 22 November, 1862.

84 From the few unpublished manuscript pages of Alexander Rogers' Autobiography, in the *Glasgow Scrap Book*, Vol. 19., p. 178. Mitchell Library, Glasgow.

85 Quoted in George Eyre-Todd, The Glasgow Poets: Their Lives and Poems, p. 377.

86 James MacFarlan, *The Poetical Works with a Memoir* by Colin Rae-Brown (Glasgow, 1862), p. ix.

87 William Hodgson, 'James MacFarlan, Pedlar and Peot', *Fifeshire Journal*, November 1862.

88 James MacFarlan, *The Poetical Works with a Memoir* by Colin Rae-Brown (Glasgow, 1862), p. ix.

89 Ibid., p. 9. Emphasis added.

90 Ibid., p. 11.

91 'The Late James MacFarlan', *Glasgow Gazette*, 22 November, 1862.

92 James D. Young, 'Racialism and the British Labour Movement', *New Edinburgh* Review, Winter, 1974.

93 James D. Young, 'The American Civil War and the Growth of Scottish Republicanism', *Labor History*, Vol. 15, No. 1., 1974, pp. 98-108.

Chapter Four: Alexander Robertson (1825-1893) and John Murdoch (1818-1903): Highland Land and Labour Agitators and the Wider World.

1 For my essay on 'Alexander Robertson: The Clans and the Kailyard, see the *New Edinburgh Review Anthology*, edited James Campbell (Edinburgh, 1982), pp.71-79. and James D. Young, 'John Murdoch: A Scottish Land and Labour Pioneer', *Bulletin of the Society for the Study of Labour History*, No.19., 1969, pp.22-26.

2 'During his later years he visited America', where he met and exchanged ideas with American radicals and Labour agitators. *The Scotsman*, 31 October 1893.

3 Ignoring Robertson altogether, W. H. Marwick referred very briefly to John Murdoch as 'a former excise officer, [who] edited *The Highlander*, an Inverness weekly (1873-81), and wrote The Crofters' Revolt (1886). W. H. Marwick, *A Short History of Labour in Scotland* (Edinburgh,1967), p.73. Unfortunately, no copy of *The Crofters' Revolt* has survived.

4 For biographical information on Robertson and Murdoch, see James D. Young, 'The Kailyard Myths of Scottish History', *New Edinburgh Review*, Winter 1978,pp.40-49.

5 'Dundonachie', *The Scotsman*, 31 October 1893, 'Death of Dundonachie', *Perthshire Constitutional*, 1 November 1893; 'The Last of Dundonachie', *Dundee Advertiser*, 2

November 1893; and 'Dundonachie', *People's Journal*, 4 November 1893.

6 *Glasgow Herald*, 4 November 1893.

7 James D. Young, Working Class and Radical Movements in Scotland and the Revolt from Liberalism, 1866-1900, Ph. D. thesis, University of Stirling, 1974, passim.

8 *North British Daily Mail*, 1 May 1870.

9 'Death of Dundonachie', *North British Daily Mail*, 31 October 1893.

10 Henry Dryerre, *Blairgowrie, Stormont and Strathmore Worthies* (Blairgowrie, 1903), p.270.

11 Ibid., pp..271-273.

12 The folowing information was obtained from Volume One of Murdoch's handwritten Autobiography. The pages were not numbered properly, and he was almost blind when he struggled to complete his multi-volume record of an adventurous and dissenting life.

13 T. C. Smout, *A Century of the Scottish People* (London, 1986), pp.1-318

14 Autobiography, Volume One.

15 *Glasgow Weekly Mail*, 4 November 1893.

16 Ibid.

17 See the anonymous pamphlet *The Dream of the Mountain Seer*, attributed to David Todd, Perth Pamphlets (LO. 40 LB ROB), Perth Public Library.

18 Autobiography, Vol.One.

19 Ibid.

20 Ibid., Vol Two.

21 Ibid.

22 James Hunter, For the People's Cause (Edinburgh, 1986), p.22.

23 James D. Young, *The Rousing of the Scottish Working Class* (London, 1979), p.143

24 John Murdoch to an unknown correpondent, 12 March 1878, pasted into his Autobiography, Vol.3. Mitchell Library, Glasgow.25

25 W. H. Marwick, A Short History of Labour in Scotland, p.73.

26 R. Alister, *Extermination of the Scottish Peasantry* (Edinburgh, 1853), p.1 and p.9

27 R. Alister, *Barriers to the National Prosperity of Scotland* (Edinburgh, 1856), p.265 and p.165.

28 Ibid., p.167, p.292 and p.291.

29 Ibid., p.262 and p.265.

30 Ibid., p.259.

31 Ibid., p.167 and p.1o7.

32 *The Spectator*, 8 March 1985.

33 Dryerre, Blairgowrie, Stormont and Strathmore Worthies, p.271.

34 Alexander Robertson, *The Deer Forests* (London, 1967), pp.5-6.

35 James D. Young, 'Alexander Robertson or Dundonachie', *Cencrastus*, No.51., 1995, pp.19-21.

36 There is a copy of this book in the National Library of Scotland, though none of his pamphlets seem to have survived..

37 Alexander Robertson, *The Philosophy of the Unconditioned* (London, 1866), p.29

38 For evidence of similar debates in Glasgow in the 1830s and 1840s, see John Kelso Hunter, Life Studies of Character (London, 1870).

39 Dryeere, Blairgowrie, Stormont and Strathmore Worthies, p.277.

40 'How Highlanders Abolish Tolls: The Revolt of a Clan', *Glasgow Sentinel*, 18 July 1868.

41 Ibid.

42 Dryeere, Blairgowrie, Stormont and Strathmore Worthies, p.280.

43 David Robertson, *A Brief Account of the Clan Donnachiadh* (Glasgow, 1894) p.49.

44 *Minute Book of the High Court of Edinburgh*, 14 March 1870. JC8/71, Scottish Record Office, Edinburgh.

45 Precognitions JC8/71.

46 *Minutes of the Labour Representation Committee*, 19 May 1874. Library of the London School of Economs and Political Science.

47 Hunter, For the People's Cause, p.38.

48 *Glasgow Weekly Mail*, 7 February 1903.

49 E. P. Lawrence, *Henry George in the British Isles* (East Lancing, 1957), p.17.

50 Ibid., p.8.

51 James D. Young, 'Changing Images of American Democracy and the British Labour Movement',1866-

1900', *International Review of Social History*, Vol. XVIII, Part I, 1973.

52 James Leatham, The Gateway, Mid-May, 1919, p.18.

53 Archives of the Socialist League, International Institute of Social History, Amsterdam, Folder F.62.

54 See James Leatham's letter pasted into the front page of *The Gateway*, Vol, VI, National Library of Scotland and Andreas Scheu Papers, International Institure of Social History, Folder s.91/B.

55 Archibald MacLaren to R. F. Muirhead, 16 November 1887. MacLaren-Muirhaed Correspondence, Ballie's Institute, Glasgow.

56 See the Minto Papers, Box. 175, National Library of Scotland.

57 *Minutes of the Scottish Liberal Association*, 22 Octrober and 22 November 1889.

58 *Hamilton Advertiser*, 20 September 1884.

59 The Papers of William Small, National Library of Scotland, Mss. Acc.3359; Dunfermline Journal, 27 September; and Joseph Wall, *Andrew Carnegie* (New York, 1970), pp.447-448.

60 *Glasgow Observer*, ll September and 15 October 1887.

61 Andrew Carnegie on 'Socialism, Labour and Home Labour', an interview reprinted from *the Northern Daily News*, Aberdeen, 23, 24, 26 and 29 September 1892.

62 Dryeere, Blairgowrie, Stormont and Strathmore Worthies, p.283.

63 'Dundonachie', *Hanged For the Game Laws* (Leith, 1884), p.1.

64 Bob Selkirk, Bob Selkirk told me the story of the coalminers hanged for the game laws' before I eventually found a copy of Robertson's pamphlet about the two coalminers who were hanged in 1884.

65 Robertson. Our Deer Forests, p.4.

66 Letter from Bob Selkirk to the author, 25 December 1973.

67 See Charles Cameron's Letters to the Lord Advocate, revealing his role as a spy. Box of Lord Advocate's Papers, Scottish Record Office.

68 The few items in the Perth Public Library have been perserved quite carefully, though my attempts to persuade librarians of Robertson's importance as a major historical figure have fallen on deaf ears. And at the Clan Robertson Library in Perthshire, the people in charge are not very interested in 'Dundonachie' the radical Scot.

69 Perth Pamphlets, Vol.13, Sandeman Public Library, Perth.

70 *The Scotsman*, 31 March 1891.

71 James Crabb Watt, John Inglis: Lord-Justice General of Scotland: A Memoir (Edinburgh, 1903), p.317.

72 Dryeere, Blairgowrie, Stormont and Strathmore Worthies, p.283.

73 'Death of "Dundonachie", Dundee Advertiser, *Perthshire Constitutional*, 1 November 1893 and 'The Last of "Dundonachie", *Dundee Advertiser*, 2 November 1893.

74 Hugh MacDiarmid, *The Company I've Kept* (London, 1966), p.127.

75 David Lowe, *Souveneirs of Scottish Labour* (Glasgow, 1919), p.18

76 William *Stewart, J. Keir Hardie: A Biography* (London, 1921), p.43.

77 James D. Young, 'Alexander Robertson or "Dundonachie"', *Cencrastus*, No.51 1995

78 *North British Mail*, 31 March 1893.

79 *Glasgow Weekly Mail*, 3 April 1893..

Chapter Five: Keir Hardie (1856-1915) and John Maclean (1879-1923): Scottish Nationalists and Socialist Internationalists

1 William Stewart, *J. Keir Hardie: A Biography* (London, 1921), p.374.

2   Raymond Challinor, *A Radical Lawyer in Victorian England* (London, 1990), pp.1-302.

3   James D. Young, 'The Rise of Scottish Socialism', in *The Red Paper on Scotland*, edited by Gordon Brown (Edinburgh, 1977), pp. 812-288.

4   John Maclean, *In the Rapids of Revolution: Essays: Articles and Letters, 1902-23*, edited with an introductory essay by Nan Milton (London, 1978), pp.42-43 and p.207.

5   Royden Harrison, 'A Very English Socialism: The Fabians, 1884-1914', in *Socialismo Storio* No.3. 1991, p.635 and G. D. H. Cole, *British Working-Class Politics, 1832-1914* (London, 1941), p.182

6   Kenneth O. Morgan, *Keir Hardie: Radical and Socialist* (London, 1975), p.284 and p.45.

7   Tom Nairn, *The Break-Up of Britain* (London, 1977), p.125 and Christopher Harvie, *Scotland and Nationalism: Scottish Society and Politics, 1707-1977* (London, 1977),

8   Eric J. Hobsbawm, 'Reflections on the Break-Up of Britain', *New Left Review*, No.105, 1977.

9   Eric J. Hobsbawm, *Industry and Empire* (London, 1968), pp.264-265.

10 William Stewart, *J. Keir Hardie: A Biography* (London, 1921), p.1

11 Fred Reid, *The Making of a Socialist* (LOndson, 1978), p.20

12 Ibid., p.40.

13 James D. Young, 'Changing Images of American Democracy and the Scottish Labour Movement, 1866—1900', *International Review of Social History*, Vol.XVIII, Part I, 1973 and James D. Young, 'The Rise of Scottish Socialism'.

14 James Cameron, 'William J. Nairn: In Memorium', *Justice*, 11 January 1902.

15 J. Bruce Glasier, *William Morris and the Early Days of the Socialist Movement* (London, 1921), pp.25-33.

16 Cole, British Working-Class Politics, 1832-1914, p.l00

17 Fred Reid, *The Early Life and Political Development of James Keir Hardie, 1856-*

18 James Keir Hardie, *Review of Reviews*, A Biography, p.38

19 William Stewart, J. Keir Hardie: A Biography, p.38

20 George Lichtheim, *A Short History of Socialism* (London, 1970), p.182

21 Socialist League Archives, K.2219/3, International Institute of Social History, Amsterdam.

22 Ibid., K.1298/1

23 Ibid., K.11543/3

24 K. D. Buckley, Trade Unionism in Aberdeen, 1878-1900 (Edinburgh, 1955), p.95.

25 Fiery Cross, 25 June 1892.

26 T. A. Jackson, *Solo Trumpet* (London, 1954), p.164 and Frank Budgen, *Myselves When Young* (London, 1970), p.83

27 David Lowe, *Souvenirs of Scottish Labour* (Glasgow, 1919), p.21.

28 A. F. Tschiffely, *Don Roberto. Being an Account of the Life and Work of R. B. Cunninghame Gramham* (London, 1937), p.83

29 Stewart, J. Keir Hardie: A Biography, p.40.

30 H. M. Hyndman, *Further Reminiscnces* (London, 1912), p.242.

31 James D. Young, 'The Rise of Scottish Socialism', in *The Red Paper on Scotland*, edited Gordon Brown (Edinburgh, 1977), p.287.

32 *Falkirk Herald*, 2 May 1896 and for more detail James D. Young, *Working-Class and Radical Movements in Scotland and the Revolt from Liberalism, 1866-1900*, Ph.D. thesis, University of Stirling, 1974, passim.

33 Hobsbawm, Industry and Empire, p.267.

34 Jim Connell, Brothers At Last (Glasgow, 1896), p.8.

35 James D.Young, 'John Leslie, 1856-1921: A Scottish Irishman As Internationalist', *Saothar*, No.18, 1993, pp.55-61.

36 *Justice*, 10 August 1901.

37 Reid, Keir Hardie: The Making of a Socialist, p.151.

1892, Ph.D. thesis, Oxford, 1969, p.199.

38 James D. Young, 'Marxism and the Scottish National Question', *Journal of* Contemporary History, April 1983, pp.141-163

39 Guy Aldred, *John Maclean: The Man, His Work, and His Worth* (Glasgow, 1932), p.4

40 Nan Milton, *John Maclean* (London, 1973), p.15.

41 Tom Bell, *John Maclean: A Figher for Freedom* (Glasgow, 1944),pp.2-3.

42 Tom Anderson, John Maclean, M.A. (Glasgow, 1944), p3.

43 John Broom, *John Maclean* (Edinburgh, 1973), p.17.

44 Aldred, John Maclean, p.6.

45 James D. Young, *John Maclean: Educator of the Working Class* (Glasgow, 1988), pp.1-36.

46 John Macelan to the Clerk of the Govan School Board, 21 May 1915, John Maclean Papers, National Library of Scotland, Edinburgh.

47 Daniel De Leon, 'The American *Flag'*, The Weekly People, 4 July, 1914.

48 James D. Young, *John Maclean: Clydeside Socialist* (Glasgow, 1992), pp. 160-164.

49 John Carstairs Matheson, 'A Reversion: The Folly of National Sentiment', *The* Socialist, May 1910.

50 James D. Young, 'John Maclean's Place in Scottish History', *Bulletin of the Society of the Study of Labour History*, No. 39, 1979, pp. 84-87.

51 Gael (John Maclean), *Justice*, 23 August, 1913.

52 Gael (John Maclean), 'Scottish Notes', ibid., 27 July, 1912.

53 J. W. Keith, 'Bydand', *The Vanguard*, July 1913.

54 Gael (John Maclean), 'Scottish Notes, ibid., 9 December 1911 and ibid., 24 August, 1912.

55 Eden and Cedar Paul, *Creative Revolution* (London, 1921), p. 58.

56 John Saville, 'Prospects for Socialism in the 1970s', *The Scottish Register*, edited by Ralph Miliband (London, 1970), p. 206.

57 T. C. Smout, *A Century of the Scottish People, 1830-1950* (London, 1986), pp. 258-259.

58 Keith Webb, *The Growth of Nationalism in Scotland*, (Glasgow, 1977), p. 40.

59 Eddie and Win Roux, *Rebel Pity* (London, 197), p. 7.

60 William Stewart, *J. Keir Hardie: A Biography*, p. 365.

61 Victor Kiernan, 'After Empire', New Edinburgh Review, No. 37, 1977.

62 The American Labor Year Book (New York, 1916), p. 190.

63 James D. Young, 'John Maclean, Socialism and the Easter Rising', *Saothar*, No. 16, 1991, pp. 23-24.

64 *New York Call*, 2 March 1915 and 1 April 1916.

65 Ibid., 18 December 1816 and 'The Strike on the Clyde', *International Socialist Review*, June 1916.

66 'Glasgow Catholic Socialist Society Notes', *Irish Worker*, 10 March 1917.

67 Ibid., 17 March 1917.

68 *Forward*, 12 February 1918.

69 James D. MacDougall, 'The Scottish Coalminer', *The Nineteenth Century and After*, December 1927.

70 *Forward*, 6 April and 22 June 1922.

71 Ibid., 16 November 1918.

72 Harry Hanham, *Scottish Nationalism* (London, 1969), pp. 9-11.

73 William Diack, The Future of the Scottish Labour Party', *The Scottish Review*, Summer, 1919, p. 390.

74 'Jim Larkin Says Irish Working Class Will Resist *Draft'*, *New York Call*, 18 April 1918.

75 'Glasgow's Declaration', *Voice of Labour*, 4 May 1918.

76 Desmond Ryan, *James Connolly: His Life and Work*, (Dublin, 1924), p. 257.

77 P. Coats, 'Irish Aspirations and the British Labour Movement', *Voice of Labour*, 29 December 1917.

78 Crystal Eastman, 'The Workers of the Clyde', *The Liberator*, October 1919.

79 August Hamon, *Le Mouvement Ourvrier en Grande-Bretagne*, (Paris, 1919) pp. 23-35

80 Eden adn Cedar Paul, 'A French Comrade's View of the British Labour Movement', *The Worker*, 1 November 1919.

81 The Scottish Review, Summer 1919.

82 William Diack, 'Scottish and Irish Labour Colleges', ibid., Winter 1919.

83 James D. Young, 'Bolshevik Myths and Scottish and English Workers' Movement', *Socilaismo Storia*, No. 3, 1991, pp. 133-157 and James D. Young, 'John Maclean', *Biographical Dictionary of Marxism*, edited R. A. Gorman (Westport, Connecticut, 1986), pp. 204-207.

84 Harry Hanham, Scottish Nationalism, p. 138.

85 James D. Young, 'The Irish Immigrants' Contribution to Scottish Socialism, 1880-1926', *Saothar*, No. 13, 1988, p. 96.

86 Ibid., p. 97.

87 'Republican Demonstration in Glasgow', *Voice of Labour*, 4 May, 1918.

88 'John Maclean in Dublin', ibid., 23 August 1919 and Sylvia Pankhurst, 'Labor and Sinn Fein', *Socialist Review* (New York), April 1920.

89 William Bolitho, *The Cancer of Empire*, (London, 1924), p. 16.

90 *The Voice of Labour*, 23 August 1919.

91 John Maclean, 'A Scottish Communist Party', The Vanguard, December 1920.

92 John Maclean, In the Rapids of Revolution, edited Nan Milton (London, 1978), p. 217.

93 Patriot, 'The Centenary of Scottish Independence', *Liberty*, 2 October 1920.

94 Ibid.

95 Erskine of Marr, 'Bannockburn and its Lessons', ibid., June 1920.

96 John Maclean, *In the Rapids of Revolution*, p. 232 and John Broom, John Maclean, p. 139.

97 *Scottish Home Rule Association News-Sheet*, January 1921.

98 *Annual Report of the Scottish Trades Union Congress*, 1921, p. 64.

99 John Ball, 'Industrial Notes', *The Communist*, 30 April 1921.

100 John S. Clarke, 'A Dessertation on the Cant of Nationalism', *The Worker*, 21 January 1922.

101 *Scottish Home Rule Association News-Sheet*, November 1923.

102 *Ibid., May 1924.*

103 C. M. Grieve, *Albyn or Scotland and the Future*, (London, 1927), p. 7.

104 John Maclean, 'Campbell Library and Municipalism', *Pollockshaws News*, 2 July 1905.

105 James D. Young, *John Maclean: Clydeside Socialist*, passim and James D. Young, *Socialism Since 1889: A Biographical History*, (London, 1988), pp. 145-147.

106 'One Big Union's Lone Fight for Seamen', *The Voice of Labour*, 21 April 1923.

107 John Maclean, *In The Rapids of Revolution*, p. 237.

108 Ralph Fox, *The Colonial Policy of British Imperialism*, (London, 1933), p. 115.

109 *New Leader*, 10 June 1927.

110 David A. Vaughan, *Negro Victory: The Life Story of Dr. Harold Moody* (London, 1950), p. 47.

111 Sorley Maclean, 'Poetry, Passion and Political Consciousness', *Scottish International*, May 1970, p. 14.

Chapter Six: Scotland, Marxism, and Internationalism: Lewis Grassic Gibbon (1901-1935) and James Barke (1905-1958)

1 Lewis Grassic Gibbon and Hugh MacDiarmid, *Scottish Scene* (London, 1934), pp. 293-294.

2 Ian S. Munro, *Leslie Mitchell: Lewis Grassic Gibbon* (Edinburgh, 1966), pp. 14-25.

3 The factual details in the obituary in *The Times* (21 February, 1935) are sometimes inaccurate.

4 Peter Whitfield, *Grassic Gibbon and His World* (Aberdeen, 1994) p.138.

5 Ian S. Munro, *Leslie Mitchell: Lewis Grassic Gibbon* (Edinburgh, 1966), p. 42.

6 James Barke, *The Green Hills Far Away* (London, 1940), p. 35.

7 Ibid., p. 53.

8 Ibid., p. 29.

9 Ibid., p. 280.

10   Sidney Goodsir Smith, 'James Barke', *Saltire Review*, Vol. 5, No. 15, 1958.

11   James Barke, *The Green Hills Far Away* (London, 1940), p. 268.

12   'From them [his parents] I got the history of Galloway.' Ibid., p. 54.

13   Munro

14   Lewis Grassic Gibbon, 'Scots Novels of the Half Year', *The Free Man*, 24 June, 1933.

15   Lewis Grassic Gibbon, 'Mr. Barke and Others', *The Free Man*, 24 February, 1934.

16   James Leslie Mitchell to George MacDonald, 20 January 1924. MS 26109, National Library of Scotland (NLS).

17   James Leslie Mitchell to Neil Gunn, 2 November, 1934. D. 2901/17, NLS.

18   Quoted in James D. Young, 'Totalitarianism, Democracy and the British Labour Movement begore 1917', *Survey*, Vol. 20, No. 1, 1974, p. 133.

19   Quoted in Bertram D. Wolfe, *Marxism: 100 Years in the Life of a Doctrine* (London, 1967), p. 158.

20   Quoted in Max Shachtman, The Bureaucratic Revolution (New York, 1962), p. 212.

21   Antonio Labriola, *Essays on the Materialist Conception of History* (Chicago, 1908), p. 139.

22   Isaac Deutcher, *The Prophet Armed: Trotsky, 1921-1929* (Oxford, 1959), p. 139.

23   Jasmes Leslie Mitchell, *The Thirteenth Disciple* (London, 1931), p.64.

24   Ibid., p.100.

25   Ibid., p.83 and p.85.

26   J. F. Horrabin, 'Books, Bias and Broadcasting', *Plebs*, December 1933.

27   G.M., 'The Dark Corridor'. ibid., May 1931.

28   I am grateful to John Manson for giving me a sight of his unpublished article on 'Lewis Grassic Gibbon's Glasgow'.

29   Guy Aldred, 'Wanted - A Workers' Scottish Republic', *The Free Man*, 15 October 1932.

30   *The Commune*, March 1929.

31   'Towards Trotskyism', *The Council*, June 1932.

32   'Trotsky's History' and 'Trotskyism', Ibid., November and February 1932.

33   James Leslie Mitchell to Mr. and Mrs. Alexander Gray, MS 26109, National Library of Scotland.

34   Ian Campbell, *Lewis Grassic Gibbon* (Edinburgh, 1985), p.10.

35   Ibid, p.49.

37   See above notes.

38   Aitken Ferguson, 'A Marchers' Novel', *Labour Monthly*, October 1936.

39   Lewis Grassic Gibbon, *Stained Radiance* (London, 1930), p.54.

40   Quoted in Julius *Braunthal, In Search of the Millennium* (London, 1945), p.96.

41   Joseph Freeman, *An American Testament* (London, 1938), p.204.

42   Ignazio Silone, *The Seed Beneath the Snow* (London, 1943), pp.251-253.

43   James Leslie Mitchell, 'Grieve-Scotsman', *The Free Man*, 9 September 1933

44   Frank Maitland, 'History - Which Made Scott Necessary', *Plebs*, February 1934.

45   Lewis Grassic Gibbon, 'News of Battle: Queries for Mr. Whyte', *The Free Man*, 17 March 1934.

46   Frank Maitland, 'Lewis Grassic Gibbon', *The Adelphi*, Vol.10, No.1., April 1935.

47   Frank Maitland, 'What Is Scottish Nationalism?', *British Revolutionary Socialist*, October 1937.

48   Ian Milner, 'An Estimation of Lewis Grassic Gibbon's *A Scots Quair*', *Marxist Quarterly*, Vol.1., No.4., 1954.

49   Ibid., p.216.

50   Gibbon, A Scots Quair, p.17.

51   Ibid., p.481.

52   Quoted in James D. Young, *Socialism Since 1889: A Biographical History* (London and New York), p.121 and p.140.

53   Ibid., p.481.

54   James D. Young, 'The ghost who haunts Tony Blair', *Irish Post*, 29 April 1995.

55 Eric J. Hobsbawmn, *Nations and Nationalisn Since 1870* (Cambridge, 1990), pp.146-148.

56 Gibbon, A Scots Quair, p.451.

57 Karl Marx, *Capital* (London, 1946), pp.736-738.

58 Antonio Labriola, *Socialism and Philosophy* (Chicago, 1912), p.109.

59 Gibbon, A Scots Quair, p.407.

60 Peter Kropotkin, *The Conquest of Bread* (London, 19134), p.149.

61 Rosa Luxemburg, *The Junius Pamphlet* (London, N.D., probably 1966), p.134.

62 Romain Rolland, *Above the Battle* (London, 1916), p.87

63 Walter Benjamin, Illuminations, edited Hannah Arendt (London, 1970), p.262.

64 Ibid., p.257.

65 Ibid., p.258.

66 I owe this information to my friend the Scottish poet John Manson.

67 Hugh MacDiarmid, 'Lewis Grassic Gibbon', in *Little Reviews Anthology* 1946, edited by Denys Val Baker (London, 1946), p.211.

68 James D. Young, *The Rousing of the Scottish Working Class* (London, 1979), pp.213-220.

69 James D. Young, 'Hugh MacDiarmid', 30 October 1993, *Glasgow Herald*.

70 I owe this information to John Manson.

71 Tom Nairn, *The Break-Up of Britain* (London, 1977), p.162.

72 Marion Nelson, 'The Kailyard Comes to Life - Lewis Grassic Gibbon', *New Fronter*, January 1937.

73 R. MacLellan, 'The National Question and Scotland'; Helen Crawfurd, ''The Scoittish National Movement'; and Oliver Bell, 'The Scottish National Question, *Communist Review*, October 1932 and February and April 1933.

74 'Mr. James Barke: Burns's Life As Fiction', *The Times*, 21 March 1958.

75 James Barke, The Wild Macraes (London, 1934), p.47.

76 Ibid., p.129

77 Ibid., pp.85-89.

78 Franklin Rosemont, 'Karl Marx and the Iroquois', *Arsenal: Surrealist Subversion* (Chicago, N. D., probably 1992).

79 James Barke, *The End of the High Bridge* (London, 1935), p.42.

79 Ibid., p.192.

80 James Leslie Mitchell to James Barke, 24 January 1934 and 6 February 1934, in the James Barke Papers, Box.4, Mitchell Library, Glasgow. I am the first scholar to have consulted those papers, and they are a real treasure-trove of material on Scottish literature, history and politics.

81 Marion Nelson [Duthie] to Edgell Rickwood, 25 July 1936. Ibid., Box 2.

82 James W. Barke to James Leslie Mitchell, 12 November 1934. Ibid Box.4.

83 Manfred Malzahn, 'The Industrial Novel', in *The History of Scottish Literature*, edited Cairns Craig (Edinburgh, 1987), p.235.

84 Jean P. Samson, *Temoins* [Zurich], February 1959.

85 James D. Young, 'Three Scottish Writers', *World News and Views*, November 1953.

86 'Sunday Reading' and 'The End of A Scots Quair', *Forward*, 8 july 1933 and 17 April 1934.

87 James Barke, 'Lewis Grassic Gibbon', *Left Review*, February 1936.

88 Lewis Grassic Gibbon, 'Writers' International', ibid., February 1935.

89 James Barke Papers, Box.5, and blurb by Collins, the publishers, in Box.1.

90 Ibid., Box.2.

91 James Barke to Theodore Dreisser, undated letter, ibid., Box 4.

92 James Barke, 'Notes on Gaelic Culture', ibid., Box 4.

93 James Barke, 'The Scottish National Question', *Left Review*, October l936.

94 James Barke, unpublished typescript entitled 'Retrospect', in James Barke Papers, Box.2.

95 Unpublished review of William Gallacher's autobiography *Revolt on the Clyde*, ibid., Box.2.

96 James, *The Green Hills* Far Away (London, 1940), p.19.

97 James Barke, 'Burns's Life As Fiction', *The Times*, 21 March 1958.

98 Alan Wald, 'Pictures of the Homeland: The Legacy of Howard Fast', *Radical America*, Vol.17., No.1., 1983.

99 Sidney Goodsir Smith, 'James Barke', *Saltire Review*, Vol.5., No.15., 1958.

100 James Barke to Geoffrey Wagner, undated letter, Box. 1., James Barke Papers, Box.4.

Chapter Seven: A. S. Neill (1883-1973) and R. F. Mackenzie (1910-1987): Internationalism and The Search for 'Democratic Intellect'

1 *Edinburgh Review*, April, 1988, p.176.

2 Eric J. Hobsbawm, *Industry and Empire* (London, 1968), p.319.

3 George E. Davie, *The Social Significance of the Scottish Philosophy of Common Sense* (Dundee, 1973), pp.7-8

4 James G. Kellas, The Development of the Liberal Party in Scotland, 1868-1895, Ph.D thesis, University of London, 1966, p.26.

5 John Kerr, *Memories: Gay and Grave* (London, N.D., probably 1903), p.1-379.

6 James D. Young, 'Belt, Book and Blackboard: The Roots of Authoritarianism in Scottish Education', *Scottish International*, April 1973.

7 Anthony Ross, 'Resurrection: A Diagnosis of Cotemporary Scottish Culture and Society', *Scottish International*, May 1971.

8 A. S. Neill to the author, 24 June 1972. Acc. 10465, National Library of Scotland.

9 R. D. Laing, The Divided Self (London, 1960).

10 'Storms in our Time': An Interview with Anthony Ross, ibid., May 1970.

11 Ibid.

12 Andrew L. Walker, *The Revival of the Democratic Intellect* (Edinburgh, 1995).

13 James D. Young, John Maclean: Educator of the Working Class (Glasgow, l988), p.12-33.

14 I owe this reference to my friend John Manson.

15 George Elder Davie to C. M. Grieve, 15 June l937, Hugh MacDiarmid Collection, University of Edinburgh. I thank John Manson for drawing this letter to my attention.

16 I owe this information to John Manson.

17 James D. Young, *John Maclean: Educator of the Working Class* (Glasgow, 1988), pp.19-25.

18 A. S. Neill, *Neill! Neill! Orange Peel* (New York, 1972), p.34.

19 Ibid., pp.81-82.

20 Neill, Neill! Neill! Orange Peel, p.31.

21 R. F. Mackenzie, A Search for Scotland (London, 1989), p.88.

22 A. S. Neill to the author 3 April 1986.

23 See 'Contemporary Scotland: Unknown Country' in *MakingTrouble: Autobiographical Explorations and Socialism* (Glasgow, 1987).

24 Mackenzie, A Search for Scotland, p.49.

25 Ibid., p.259.

26 R. F. Mackenzie, *Jotters*, l987.

27 A. S. Neill, A Dominie's Log (London, 1915), p.95.

28 Ibid., p.163.

29 Ibid., p.125.

30 A. S. Neill, *A Dominie Dismissed* (London, 1917), p.60.

31 Ibid., p229.

32 A. S. Neill, A Domine in Doubt (London, 1921), p.181.

33 Ibid., p.187.

34 William Bolithio, *The Cancer of Empire* (London, 1924).

35 James D. Young, *Socialism Since 1889: A Biographical History* (New York, 1988), p.24.

36 A. S. Neill, *A Dominie Abroad* (London, 1923), p57-.59.

37 *All the Best: Letters from Summerhill*, edited Jonathan Croall (London, 1983), p.x.

38 J. E., 'Books Which Reflect This Crazy World', New Leader, 28 December 1934

39 Christopher Harvey, Scotland and Nationalism (London, 1994).

40 A. S. Neill, 'How I Run A Free School', ibid., 1 September.

41 A. S. Neill, Is Scotland Educated? (London, 1936).

42 Ibid., pp.27-28.

43 Ibid., p.33 and p.42.

44 Ibid., p.17 and p.37.

45 Allan Hutt, Crisis on Clydeside (Glasgow, 1934), p.25.

46 Red Feather, 'B. S. P. Demonstration for Russia', The Call, 5 February 1920.

47 T. C. Smout, A Century of the Scottish People, 1830-1950 (London, 1986), p.275 and James D. Young, John Maclean: Educator of the Working Class (Glasgow, 1988), pp.1-36.

48 James Barke, The World His Pillow (London, 1933, p.21.

49 James Drawbell, Scotland: Bitter-Sweet (London, 1972), p.22 and p.10.

50 A. S. Neill, Hearts Not Heads In The School (London, 1944), p.71.

51 Ibid., p.134.

52 James D. Young, 'An idealist behind the lines: A tribute to R. F. Mackenzie', Times Higher Educational Supplement, 15 January 1988.

53 A. S. Neill. Paul and Jean Ritter, Myron Sharaf and Nick Waal, Wilhelm Reich (Nottingham, 1957), p.51.

54 A. S. Neill, The Free Child (London, 1953), p.119.

55 Summerhill: For and Against, edited Max Rafferty (London, 1973), p.24.

56 R. F. Mackenzie to the author 3 April 1986.

57 John Dewey, Democracy and Education (New York, 1916), p.153.

58 Mackenzie, A Search for Scotland, p.245.

59 Interviews with Ronnie Wood and Jack Stuart on 10 Jully 1968.

60 A. S. Neill, The Free Child (London, 1953), p.119.

61 Summerhill: For and Against, edited by Max Rafferty (London, 1973), p.24

62 R. F. Mackenzie, A Question of Living (London, 1963), p.118.

63 Ibid., p.177.

64 Ibid.

65 R. F. Mackenzie, Escape from the Classroom (London, 1965), p.58 and p.64.

66 R. F. Mackenzie, In Search of Scotland (London, 1980), p.189.

67 Ibid., p.96.

68 Ibid., p.61.

69 A. S. Neill to the author, 19 June 1972. National Library of Scotland.

70 Harry Reid, 'Foreword' to R. F. Mackenzie: The Unbowed Head (Edinburgh, 1974).

71 Interview with Harry Reid at The Herald office, Glasgow, 29 June 1995.

72 R. F. Mackenzie, The Sins of the Children (London, 1967), pp.25-27and A. S. Neill to the author, 19 June 1972. National Library of Scotland.

73 Harry Reid, 'An educationalist who wouldn't compromise', Glasgow Herald, 10 December, 1987.

74 R. F. Mackenzie, The Unbowed Head (Edinburgh, 1974), p.69.

75 Ibid, p.115.

76 R. F. Mackenzie to the autor, 3 April 1986.

77 R. F. Mackenzie to the author, 25 November 1986

78 The Times Higher Educational Supplement, 15 January 1988.

Chapter Eight: The New World Order. The Experience of Defeat

1 Eric J. Hobsbawm, Age of Extremes: The Short Twentieth Century, 1914-1991 (London, 1994), p.495.

2 Joyce McMillan, 'We must protect the state support that set a generation free', Scotland on Sunday, 28 May 1995.

3 Anthony Ross, 'Storms in our Time', Scottish International, May 1970.

4 Anthony Ross, 'Resurrection', ibid, May 1971.

5 Mary Brooksbank, Sidlaw Breezes (Dundee, N.D., probably 1972) pp.1-

65 and *No Nae Lang Syne* (Dundee, N.D., probably 1973), pp.1-59.

6 Willy Maley, 'Cultural Devolution? Representing Scotland in the 1970s', in *The Arts in the 1970s: Cultural Closure?*, edited Bart Moore-Gilbert (London, 1994), p.81.

7 Ibid., p.94.

8 Ibid., 91.

9 *Calgacus*, No.1., No.2 and No.3, 1976 and 1976.

10 H. M. Drucker, *Breakaway: The Scottish Labour Party* (Edinburgh, 1978), p.60.

11 See R. F. Mackenzie's review of 'The Rousing of the Scottish Working Class' in *Big Print*, February 1980.

12 Neal Ascherson, 'GravesideLament for Hugh MacDiar-mid', *Scotsman*, 14 September 1978.

13 G. W. S. Barrow, *The Extinction of Scotland* (Edinburgh, 1980).

14 James D. Young, *Making Trouble* (Glasgow, 1987), passim.

15 James D. Young, *Women and Popular Struggles* (Edinburgh, 1985).

16 MacDonald Daly and Colin Troop, 'Oxford no' come back again', *Times Higher Education Supplement*, 6 *January 1989*.

17 Ian S. Wood and Mary Ross, 'Newbattle Abbey's real offence', The Scotsman, 15 December 1987.

18 'Rob Brown examines the evidence of anglicisation: A harsh lesson for Scots students', ibid., 28 December 1987.

19 *The People's Palace History Paintings* (Glasgow, 1990), pp.1-39.

20 James D. Young, 'Culture and Socialism: Working-Class Struggle, 1778-1978'. in *Workers' City: The Real Glasgow Stands Up*, edited Farquhar McLay (Glasgow, 1988), p.139.

21 David Kemp, 'How Elspeth lost in Palace coup', *Art Work*, No.44, June/July 1990.

22 *Scotland at the Crossroads* (Glasgow, 1990),edited by James D. Young pp.1-112.

23 Robbie Dinwoodie, 'In the dock over the suppression of Scottish History', *Glasgow Herald*, 18 August 1990.

24 James Kelman, 'English Literature and the Small Coterie', *Glasgow Herald*, 14 April 1990 and James Kelman, 'Unfair Criticism', ibid., 24 January 1990.

25 Allan Massie, *The Novelist's View of the Market Economy* (Edinburgh, 1988), p.18.

26 Alasdair Gray, *Independence: Why Scots Should Rule Scotland* (Ediburgh, 1992), p.43 and p.57.

27 *The Scotsman*, 13 April 1992.

28 William McIlvanney, 'He is dead who will not fight', *Scotland on Sunday*, 19 April 1992.

29 James D. Young, 'Speaking louder than words' and 'Exposing Glasgow's hidden history', *Irish Post*, 20 March 1993 and 22 May 1993.

30 For an assessment and review of Yeltsin's autobiography *Against the Grain*, see James D. Young, 'Rebel as moralist', *Glasgow Herald*, 17 March 1990.

31 Ajay Close, 'The Boy Done Well', *Scotland on Sunday*, 24 May 1992.

32 Ian Bell, 'Patriotism turned putrid', *The Observer*, 19 February 1995.

33 Ian Bell, 'Wheel falls off Blair's wagon', *The Observer*, 28 May 1995.

34 Allan Massie, 'Salvation lies in becoming a Scottish Galulist party', Independent *on Sunday*, 28 May 1995.

35 Douglas Dunn, 'Edge of Anger', *The Herald*, 26 March 1994.

36 Chaim Bermant, 'How genteel it was, how genteel', ibid., 27 May 1995.

37 Walter Benjamin, *Illuminations* (Glasgow, 1977), p.258.

Index